AMERICAN POLITICAL THOUGHT

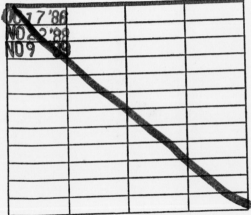

AMERICAN POLITICAL THOUGHT
Readings

Edited by

LARRY I. PETERMAN
University of California, Davis
and
LOUIS F. WESCHLER
University of Southern California

APPLETON–CENTURY–CROFTS
Educational Division
New York   MEREDITH CORPORATION

CONTENTS

AMERICAN
POLITICAL
THOUGHT

1
INTRODUCTION
Fundamental Principles

It is fitting that a collection of readings in American political thought begin with the editors' submitting to temptation. We note this because one of the principal themes in almost all of what follows is how the American people do or should respond to the dual temptations of their politics: equality and liberty. We take the liberty of beginning this introduction with Pericles' salute to Athenian democracy, the funeral oration. It is useful, for it exemplifies what is central to the investigation of the American, as well as Athenian, democratic experience. In both cases, not only is the general nature of democratic problems at issue, but also and importantly the particular nature of the regime in question.

The Athens to which Pericles directs his words is an imperial democracy. It is already at war and in the process of stretching its boundaries far beyond the city walls. The funeral speech is an established ceremony in honor of those who fall first in the city's wars. The very circumstances of the speech, therefore, indicate that it is directed at the martial potential of Athens, that Athens exists in a hostile world, and that external foes are, at least for the moment, her greatest fear. Thus Pericles does not engage in philosophic speculations upon the inherent difficulties and fragility of democracy. His concerns are for the manner in which Athens conducts herself toward her neighbors and what is demanded of her sons and daughters to keep the city strong.[1]

Overt similarities between contemporary America and fourth-century Athens are not difficult to perceive. America is a nation with global involvements and since World War II has seen her sons fighting in numerous conflicts.

Indeed many of Pericles' words to the Athenian citizenry would not be foreign to American ears.

Our form of government does not enter into rivalry with the institutions of others. We do not copy our neighbors, but are an example to them. It is

[1] Thucydides, *The Peloponnesian War*, trans. B. Jowett (New York: Bantam Books, 1960), p. 114.

true that we are called a democracy, for the administration is in the hands
of the many and not of the few. But while the law secures equal justice
to all alike in their private disputes, the claim of excellence is also
recognized; and when a citizen is in any way distinguished, he is preferred
to the public service, not as a matter of privilege, but as the reward of
merit. Neither is poverty a bar, but a man may benefit his country
whatever be the obscurity of his condition.[2]

A democratic citizenry had to be reminded that it fought for a worthy
cause. Thus Pericles sought to strengthen Athenian resolve by extolling
what her citizens would fight to defend and preserve. The martial spirit
and tone of the funeral oration, then, presupposed respect for Athens
among those who listened to the speech. It is no different in America. If
Americans were not predisposed toward their own nation, they would not
so readily listen to and accept the martial rhetoric of their leaders. Yet
despite the similarities between contemporary America and Athens in the
fourth century B.C., there is an important difference between the funeral
oration and the great statements of American political thought.

    Americans, like Pericles' listeners, are familiar with being asked to
fight for their country and the things for which it stands. But while
Pericles' rhetoric and the context of his speech are familiar, his
unproblematic assumption of the nature of the Athenian regime is not
typical of American experience. The funeral oration suggests that
one must be cognizant of events to understand American political thought
in its fullness. But it does not indicate a consistent feature of American
political experience—a constant and self-aware concern about the internal
tensions that beset American democracy. In America, consideration
of expanding the scope of democracy is coupled with a concern for the
stability of the political order itself. Like Pericles, we devote our attention
to the problems of the time. In doing so, however, we understand that
the fragility of the democratic regime has been a central concern
throughout our history. A proper understanding of current conflicts,
practical and philosophical, rests on an awareness of the theoretical
struggle that has colored all of American experience: the struggle
between liberty and equality.

    Thus to understand the period of the American founding means to
understand the special circumstances of the founding generation, i.e., the
interplay of events with the principles of liberty and equality. The
problems the founders faced were markedly different from those that
faced Pericles. Pericles was leading Athens into war when he spoke; those
who formulated the American Constitution, and fought for it, did so
in a time of peace, if not of calm. To a degree impossible in the funeral
oration they were able to direct themselves to the difficulties inherent

[2] *Ibid.*, p. 116.

in democratic theory in the abstract. But that they were able, because of their circumstances, to be more speculative than Pericles does not mean they could be purely speculative. America's founding generation is notable for the manner in which it sought to meld the fundamentals of democratic theory with established American practice. In the very first number of the *Federalist*, for example, "Publius" identifies one of the great issues which underlay the discussions of the framers and then makes clear that the issue would be decided in the context of the particular political situation in America.

It has been frequently remarked that it seems to have been reserved to the people of this country, by their conduct and example, to decide the important question, whether societies of men are really capable or not of establishing good government from reflection and choice, or whether they are forever destined to depend for their political constitutions on accident and force.[3]

The answer to this great question depends, he goes on to say, on satisfactorily deciding what relationship would exist between the states which already existed and the central government envisaged by the framers. It is the struggle over this question which jeopardizes both the Constitution and the proposition that good governments can be established through reflection and choice. It had already begun.

We already hear it whispered in the private circles of those who oppose the new Constitution, that the thirteen States are of too great extent for any general system, and that we must of necessity resort to separate confederacies of distinct portions of the whole; . . . nothing can be more evident to those who are able to take an enlarged view of the subject than the alternative of an adoption of the new Constitution or a dismemberment of the Union.[4]

The American political experience is the result of a generalized theory of government (which we choose to call democratic) as it comes into contact with the perquisites of American practice. To study the American political experience demands an awareness, it follows, of what constitutes democratic theory and how the unique elements of American practice bear on that theory. We are constantly confronted with the problem of deciding what is or seems changeless in American political life and what is or seems fluid. At the first level, the American regime is the outcome of a self-aware attempt to resolve certain "important questions" in a way that would command American politics indefinitely. Hence there are

[3] *The Federalist Papers* (New York: New American Library, 1961), p. 33.
[4] *Ibid.*, pp. 36–37.

certain ideas delineated at the founding which are so fundamental to the regime that continual concern with them is a constant in American life.

The proposition which compels all subsequent American political thought is stated most explicitly in the Declaration of Independence.

We hold these truths to be self-evident, that all men are created equal, that
they are endowed by their Creator with certain unalienable Rights,
that among these are Life, Liberty, and the pursuit of Happiness. That to
secure these rights, Governments are instituted among Men, deriving
their just powers from the consent of the governed.

Appeals to American political principle, regardless of the practical problems that give rise to them, are most readily understood from the perspective of the Declaration's propositions. In the United States, no claims are more legitimate than those which spring from the equality of men or their unalienable rights. It follows that those who argue for a particular policy or philosophy in the American context justify their arguments in respect to these propositions. Thus the Constitution itself— which Lincoln called the "picture of silver" enclosing the "apple of gold" of the Declaration[5]—had to be defended as true to these principles before it would be accepted. In turn, the opponents of ratification sought to convince those who had the responsibility for ratifying that the new document was positively a threat to the rights set forth under the Declaration. In particular they argued that the Constitution was a direct threat to liberty. Patrick Henry, who led the fight against ratification in Virginia, put the argument quite succinctly.

This proposal of altering the government is of a most alarming nature.
Make the best of the new government, say it is composed by anything but
inspiration—you ought to be extremely cautious, watchful, jealous of
your liberty; for instead of securing your rights you may lose them forever.
If a wrong step be now made, the republic may be lost forever. If this
new government will not come up to the expectation of the people, and
they should be disappointed, their liberty will be lost, and tyranny
must and will arise.[6]

The Constitution was just the first issue that would be fought out along these lines. As will become evident in these readings, the themes of the Declaration remain the most useful framework through which to consider American political thought.

[5] Roy Basler, ed., *The Collected Works of Abraham Lincoln* (New Brunswick, N.J.: Rutgers University Press, 1953), Vol. IV, p. 169. The phrase is taken from Proverbs 25:11, "A word fitly spoken is like apples of gold in pictures of silver."
[6] Hugh Blair Grigsby, ed., *The History of the Virginia Federal Convention of 1788* (Richmond, Va.: The Virginia Historical Society, 1890), p. 81.

That these themes color all American political experience must not be taken to mean that they and their effects are perfectly clear and free of ambiguity. The Declaration depends on the principle of self-evidence, but American history offers abundant proof that what is self-evident for one may not be so for all. Indeed, the question of what the self-evident truths of the Declaration connote is a primary impetus to American political debate and political thought. Thus, the themes of the Declaration not only inform American experience, they—because of their ambiguity and unspecified character—become a spur to discussion and dispute. There is, we would suggest, a parallel between the way Americans view the Declaration and the Constitution and the way religious scholars view scripture. In both cases the fundamental law serves both as the foundation for what comes later and as the source of the compulsion to investigate the fundamentals themselves. The Declaration and Constitution, America's scripture, are the source of the American faith and the constant urge to investigate and interpret that faith.

Moreover, inasmuch as the Declaration expresses the principles upon which the nation was founded, all subsequent American political thought is, in some degree at least, a reaction to it. The format of this book is developed in accordance with this fact. The chapters which follow attempt to illustrate how American political thought—indeed, American political life—reflects and deals with the principles and tensions incorporated in the Declaration of Independence. Each set of readings is arranged in a loose historical sequence and, more importantly, coalesces around an issue which we shall introduce with short statements at the beginning of each chapter. The primary work of analysis will be left to the student. We shall attempt only to clarify how the readings relate to the major theme of this volume, the tension between liberty and equality which runs through the entire American political experience.

The first half of this book examines the manner in which the propositions which govern American life were given the political form which Lincoln hoped would be at the heart of an American political religion.[7] The remainder is in large part directed at the subsequent testing and proving of these propositions. The tests take many forms. For example, and in keeping with Lincoln's concept of a political religion, it is characteristic of America that political differences find their way into the courts, where they are settled according to the tenets of the fundamental faith. Such resolution often requires that the courts interpret the faith in the light of changing times. But, it is our contention that the fundamentals of the faith are constant, and that the tests of American history bear this out. The Civil War is typical of what we mean. There

[7] Basler, *op. cit.*, Vol. I, p. 112.

the traditional conflict resolution of the courts failed and the political
faith was tested by arms rather than words. For good reason this test has
been called the "most characteristic phenomenon"[8] in American history
for at no other moment has the tension and conflict inherent in the
American faith been more explicitly exposed. It was the ultimate test of
whether a nation dedicated to the proposition of human equality could
abide the existence of chattel slavery defended in the name of individual
property rights. Thus it bears out the problems that spring from a
political foundation resting on the principles of equality and
individual rights.

The focus on the problems exposed in the war changes in ensuing
years. New interpretations of the political implications of equality and
liberty are forthcoming. The war led to enormous growth in the national
government and new perspectives on what governmental protection of
rights does and does not mean. The nationalization of American politics
is carried forward in the name of liberty toward the end of wealth.
The movement of black Americans toward full equality declines in
the face of national concern for political and economic expansion. The
Bloody Shirt might be waved, but late nineteenth-century America
was more interested in conquering a continent and industrializing her
economy. Thus a rush toward wealth, justified in the name of liberty as
the war had been justified in the name of equality, pushes aside the
problems of America's colored peoples for the moment. Capitalism and
anticapitalist revolt replace slavery and political equality as immediate
political issues, but their battles are fought in the name of the same
principles. The combatants may change, but the quarrels are part of the
constant fabric of American life. The courts produce an aristocracy of
entrepreneurs in order to protect "the right of the individual to liberty of
person and freedom of contract."[9]

Although capitalism might win in the courts and become the
orthodox mode for economic, social, and political thought, it was not
unopposed nor did it entirely conquer its critics. Fueled largely by the
discontent of laborers and farmers, of immigrants brutalized in sweatshops
and pauperized on farms, of those all but disenfranchised by the politics of
corruption, a radical strain of American thought arose to challenge the
prevailing ideas—which had come to be known as Liberalism. The revolt
of the Populists and Progressives represents a return to what was thought

[8] We follow Harry Jaffa's interpretation here. "While it is true, happily, that we have
not had more than one Civil War, I believe that the Civil War, even if an exception in
one sense, is also the most characteristic phenomenon in American politics, if by
characteristic we mean that which reveals the innermost character of that politics."
Harry V. Jaffa, "The Nature and Origin of the American Party System," in Robert
Goldwin, ed., *Political Parties, U.S.A.* (Chicago: Rand McNally, 1964), p. 64.
[9] *Lochner* v. *New York*, 198 US 45 (1905).

to be the democracy of Jefferson and Paine. William Jennings Bryan
made it clear to the assembled delegates at the Democratic National
Convention in 1896 that he stood with Jefferson and that this meant
understanding what had to be done if America were to remain
true to her heritage.

> They tell us that this platform was made to catch votes. We reply to them
> that changing conditions make new issues; that the principles upon
> which Democracy rests are as everlasting as the hills, but they must be
> applied to new conditions as they arise. . . . I stand with Jefferson rather
> than with them.[10]

It was upon such principles that the Populists and Progressives
enunciated practical programs aimed at political reform, reform which
would limit the abuses and corruption of city and state political machines
and protect the people at large from the encroachments of organized
wealth. Spread prosperity throughout the land, Bryan told the assembled
Democrats, for "if you make the masses prosperous, their prosperity will
find its way up through every class which rests upon them." [11]
Trickle-down economic theories in a nation of independent and
politically equal men could not be allowed. Gradations in wealth might
be allowed, but they did not sanction economic slavery. The immediate
concern of the delegates was bimetallism, but the fundamental issue
was the liberty promised in the Declaration.

> It is the issue of 1776 over again. Our ancestors, when but three million in
> number, had the courage to declare their political independence of every
> other nation; shall we, their descendents, when we have grown to seventy
> millions, declare that we are less independent than our forefathers? [12]

In the name of independence and political equality, then, radical
reformers provided entrance into the middle class for large numbers
of Americans. By the time of Wilson's election to the Presidency, white
America was well on its way to "making it." The classical poor of the
city—Eastern European immigrants—had risen to positions of political
power. Poor farmers, soon to suffer in the depression that followed
World War I, had won some battles with the railroads and the urban
political machines. But the nonwhite population was not so fortunate.
Populism and Progressivism, at the turn of the century and after,
were not directed at alleviating the lot of black, red, and yellow peoples.
Indeed, racism was built into their appeals. Thus at the same time
that the white middle class was burgeoning and beginning to prosper as

[10] Henry S. Commager, ed., *Documents of American History* (New York:
Appleton-Century-Crofts, 1948), pp. 175–176.
[11] *Ibid.*, p. 177.
[12] *Ibid.*

never before, American Indians were being literally incarcerated; Orientals were being restrained within the boundaries of small urban ghettos, marked by extreme poverty; Spanish-Americans and Mexican-Americans were living in rural poverty; and the American Negro was finding freedom more frustrating than slavery.[13] The liberal creed of equal opportunity and liberty under the law had yet to be extended to America's nonwhite population. The march of 50,000 robed and hooded Klansmen before the White House in the summer of 1925 was a sign of what some of the costs of Populism and Progressivism had been. White America, indeed, was prospering, but the extension of effective liberty and equality to nonwhites had been stalled, even denied, as a consequence. The call to the principles of the Declaration does not necessarily culminate in the extension of those principles to all men, or even to most. Sometimes testing the fundamental faith does not have altogether salutary results.

Yet, whatever the consequences, the testing goes on. During a period of economic crisis so cataclysmic that we identify it simply as "THE Depression," the national government took unprecedented steps to alleviate social and economic inequities. Franklin Delano Roosevelt offered the nation a New Deal. But as unprecedented and new as it was, FDR's administration fit within the traditional framework of American political life.

It is said that when Saint Paul visited Athens he found there an altar to an "Unknown God." Such an inscription would never be found on any altar erected in the name of political religion in America. The New Deal was no exception. It offered the most strenuous government activity in behalf of the principle of equality that the nation had ever known. The emphasis on governmental activity was novel but its end was not. An invigorated national government sought support to enlarge the scope of the egalitarian principles. Social welfare was now to be an intrinsic part of assuring the American faith. The Democratic Party Platform of 1936 is indicative.

Democratic leadership . . . has returned the people themselves to the place of authority, and has revived in them new faith and restored the hope which they had almost lost. . . . WE HOLD THIS TRUTH TO BE SELF-EVIDENT— that government in a modern civilization has certain inescapable obligations to its citizens, among which are:

　　1. Protection of the family and the home.

　　2. Establishment of a democracy of opportunity for all the people.

　　3. Aid to those overtaken by disaster.[14]

[13] C. Vann Woodward, *The Strange Career of Jim Crow* (New York: Oxford University Press, 1960).
[14] Commager, *op. cit.*, pp. 538–539.

And when the Republicans responded, they too relied on the trusted principles. If the Democrats were out to expand the meaning of equality, the Republicans were equally insistent that liberty not be lost in the attempt. Their 1936 platform is as instructive as that of the Democrats.

America is in peril. The welfare of American men and women and the future of our youth are at stake. We dedicate ourselves to the preservation of their political liberty, their individual opportunity and their character as free citizens, which today for the first time are threatened by Government itself.[15]

Once more the tension between liberty and equality set the tone for American political discourse.

The process continues. In the name of new ideas and hopes, the old faith is tested, probed, proven, and sometimes shaken. The political movements of our own day, whether conscious of it or not, take their places in a long tradition of protest and activism. They may call frighteningly for the destruction of the political regime as presently constituted—frightening because it may happen— but they call for it in the name of the most American of principles. Our last chapters deal in part with the new radicals and indicate that they too are interested in questions concerning the scope of equality and liberty. It is not by chance that contemporary discord and unrest sound and feel familiar. They fit in a consistent tradition of American political thought and practice.

We began this introduction by submitting to temptation. We must end it by noting the dangers which may arise in the wake of such democratic submission. The American political experience, we argue, is characterized by continual testing, probing, and realigning of the fundamental principles of the nation: equality and liberty. The health and preservation of America demand that this tradition not be abrogated. Without the constant interplay and tension between the principles, it is not unlikely that tyranny would arise in the name of either. The constant danger of American politics is the possible triumph of a single principle. There could be no such triumph save at the cost of the other principle. To win liberty at the cost of equality or equality at the cost of liberty is no victory at all.

Thus, America's political health is predicated on the existence of continual elements of conflict and difference. Our democratic faith is unique in that it does not call for unquestioning obedience or acceptance. Rather, it demands constant investigation and affirmation. The source of the regime's strength, therefore, is also a source of its fragility. The regime may be, and often is, strained to the limits by the testing. It is a

[5] *Ibid.*, p. 534.

measure of the seriousness of this problem that what was earlier called the most characteristic event in American history—the Civil War—was also the bloodiest. There is no guarantee that the strains which result from testing our principles may not cause a rupture. This is as true today as during the Civil War. For Lincoln, the question of whether a nation dedicated to the Declaration of Independence could be preserved was undecided.

Four score and seven years ago our fathers brought forth upon this continent, a new nation, conceived in Liberty, and dedicated to the proposition that all men are created equal. Now we are engaged in a great civil war, *testing* whether that nation, or any nation, so conceived, and so dedicated, *can long endure.*[16]

It still remains so.

[16] Basler, *op. cit.*, Vol. VII, pp. 18–19. (Emphasis added.)

2

THE FOUNDING

The principles of the American Revolution may be said to have been as various as the 13 states that went through it, and in some sense as diversified as the individuals who acted in it. In some few principles, or perhaps in one single principle, they all united.

JOHN ADAMS to MERCY WARREN, 1807

In a pronouncement which set the standard for political inquiry for centuries and still echoes today, Aristotle said that the beginning of the study of the principles of things is more than half of the whole.[1] Such a criterion is especially valuable when inquiring into American political thought for it warns against insufficiently considering the earliest expression of American political principle, the Declaration of Independence. Too often there is a tendency to take for granted the document which explicitly offers the principles according to which Americans assume "among the powers of the Earth, the separate and equal Station to which the Laws of Nature and of Nature's God entitle them." Inasmuch as the Declaration is the place in which American political thought, as something distinctly American, begins to emerge, it is the first thing that we, as students of American political thought, must attend to. D. W. Brogan does well to remind us that "We the People of the United States" did not exist prior to 1776, and Henry Commager in recalling that Jefferson intended the Declaration "to be an expression of the American mind, and to give to that expression the proper tone and spirit called for by the occasion," helps to impress upon us that the Declaration was a conscious break with the things which had formerly controlled colonial life.[2] This is not to say that the Declaration occurs in a vacuum or is unconnected to strains of European and, indeed, classical political thought. Notions of natural rights and consensual government were extant and popular long before 1776, but the American expression of these

[1] *Nicomachean Ethics* 1098b 6.
[2] D. W. Brogan, *Politics in America* (Garden City, N.Y.: Doubleday, 1960), p. 3; Daniel Boorstin, ed., *An American Primer* (New York: New American Library, 1968), p. 85.

ideas in its founding document was distinctive and colors all subsequent American political life. The Declaration of Independence is the single most important political document of American history.

The basic propositions of the Declaration—the equality of men, their unalienable rights, the securing of these rights by instituting governments which rest upon consent, that governments destructive of such rights may, in turn, by right be overthrown—are familiar enough that we need not investigate their origins and development here. However, it must be remembered that the statement of the propositions in the Declaration does not mean that they are entirely compatible. If they were, the task of the Constitutional Convention in Philadelphia in 1787 would probably have been unnecessary. The questions presented to the men gathered in Philadelphia are considered in the next chapter but we must note at this juncture that the questions were not answered precisely in the Declaration. The Declaration depends on the principle of self-evidence for its support. It offers no proof that men are created equal nor does it specify the exact nature of the rights with which men are endowed. To define equality and liberty precisely takes us beyond the words of the Declaration itself. Indeed, the very success of the American "experiment" —as the *Federalist* put it— can be said to rest on the ambiguity of the terms as they exist in the founding document. We are said to be equal but not said to be the same; thus we are left to try to decide what it means to be equal within the meaning of the Declaration. We are said to have individual rights to life, liberty, and the pursuit of happiness but we are not told how far these rights extend in relation to the rights of others; thus we are left to try to decide where liberty becomes license. We are told government rests upon the consent of the governed but that any government destructive of the rights of men may be overthrown; thus we are left to decide to what extent consensual governments may be destructive of individual rights without inviting revolution. In short, the Declaration presents the general bearings of American political life but leaves it to subsequent American experience to work out precisely how these bearings are applied. There are no simple definitions of what equality and liberty and consent of the governed mean in American life. What we have are examples of them in action and thought and attempts to ameliorate the possible effects of clashes between them. In the chapters which follow we shall examine some of these examples and, we hope, begin to show what equality and liberty, especially, have come to mean in America. There is no more important issue in American life, for, as John Stuart Mill said so succinctly: "Where all are equal, all must be alike free or alike slaves." [3]

[3] Review of *Democracy in America*, included in Alexis de Tocqueville, *Democracy in America* (New York: Schocken Books, 1961), Vol. I, p. xiv.

We begin the process of examination with the Declaration of Independence and the Virginia and Massachusetts Bills of Rights. The Virginia Bill of Rights is the most famous and influential of the bills of rights included in the earliest state constitutions and illustrates the early American understanding of the character of the "unalienable rights" of the Declaration and how they were to be protected from the incursions of government. The Massachusetts Bill of Rights covers much the same ground but is notable for its explicit recognition of the compact theory of American government—implied in the Declaration's recognition of the consent of the governed—and its suggestions about how the force of equality and liberty is manifested in American governing.

THE DECLARATION OF INDEPENDENCE (4 JULY 1776)

THE UNANIMOUS DECLARATION OF THE THIRTEEN UNITED STATES OF AMERICA

When in the course of human events, it becomes necessary for one people to dissolve the political bands which have connected them with another, and to assume among the powers of the earth the separate and equal station to which the Laws of Nature and of Nature's God entitle them, a decent respect to the opinions of mankind requires that they should declare the causes which impel them to the separation.

We hold these truths to be self-evident, that all men are created equal, that they are endowed by their Creator with certain unalienable rights, that among these are life, liberty, and the pursuit of happiness. That to secure these rights, governments are instituted among men, deriving their just powers from the consent of the governed. That whenever any form of government becomes destructive of these ends, it is the right of the people to alter or to abolish it, and to institute new government, laying its foundation on such principles and organizing its powers in such form, as to them shall seem most likely to effect their safety and happiness. Prudence, indeed, will dictate that governments long established should not be changed for light and transient causes; and accordingly all experience hath shown, that mankind are more disposed to suffer, while evils are sufferable, than to right themselves by abolishing the forms to which they are accustomed. But when a long train of abuses and usurpations, pursuing invariably the same object evinces a design to reduce them under absolute despotism, it is their right, it is their duty, to throw off such government, and to provide new guards for their future security. Such has been the patient sufferance of these Colonies; and such is now the necessity which constrains them to alter their former systems of government. The history of the present King of Great Britain is a history of repeated injuries and usurpations, all having in direct object the establishment of an absolute tyranny over these States. To prove this, let facts be submitted to a candid world.

He has refused his assent to laws, the most wholesome and necessary for the public good.

He has forbidden his Governors to pass laws of immediate and pressing importance, unless suspended in their operation till his assent should be obtained; and when so suspended, he has utterly neglected to attend to them.

He has refused to pass other laws for the accommodation of large districts of people, unless those people would relinquish the right of representation in the legislature, a right inestimable to them and formidable to tyrants only.

He has called together legislative bodies at places unusual, uncomfortable, and distant from the depository of their public records, for the sole purpose of fatiguing them into compliance with his measures.

He has dissolved representative houses repeatedly, for opposing with manly firmness his invasions on the rights of the people.

He has refused for a long time, after such dissolutions, to cause others to be elected; whereby the legislative powers, incapable of annihilation, have returned to the people at large for their exercise; the State remaining in the meantime exposed to all the dangers of invasion from without and convulsions within.

He has endeavoured to prevent the population of these States; for that purpose obstructing the laws for naturalization of foreigners; refusing to pass others to encourage their migration hither, and raising the conditions of new appropriations of lands.

He has obstructed the administration of justice, by refusing his assent to laws for establishing judiciary powers.

He has made judges dependent on his will alone, for the tenure of their offices, and the amount and payment of their salaries.

He has erected a multitude of new offices, and sent hither swarms of officers to harass our people, and eat out their substance.

He has kept among us, in times of peace, standing armies without the consent of our legislatures.

He has affected to render the military independent of and superior to the civil power.

He has combined with others to subject us to a jurisdiction foreign to our constitution, and unacknowledged by our laws; giving his assent to their acts of pretended legislation:

For quartering large bodies of armed troops among us:

For protecting them, by a mock trial, from punishment for any murders which they should commit on the inhabitants of these States:

For cutting off our trade with all parts of the world:

For imposing taxes on us without our consent:

For depriving us in many cases of the benefits of trial by jury:

For transporting us beyond seas to be tried for pretended offences:

For abolishing the free system of English laws in a neighbouring

Province, establishing therein an arbitrary government, and enlarging its boundaries so as to render it at once an example and fit instrument for introducing the same absolute rule into these Colonies:

For taking away our Charters, abolishing our most valuable laws, and altering fundamentally the forms of our governments:

For suspending our own Legislatures, and declaring themselves invested with power to legislate for us in all cases whatsoever.

He has abdicated government here, by declaring us out of his protection and waging war against us.

He has plundered our seas, ravaged our coasts, burnt our towns, and destroyed the lives of our people.

He is at this time transporting large armies of foreign mercenaries to compleat the works of death, desolation, and tyranny, already begun with circumstances of cruelty and perfidy scarcely paralleled in the most barbarous ages, and totally unworthy of the head of a civilized nation.

He has constrained our fellow citizens taken captive on the high seas to bear arms against their country, to become the executioners of their friends and brethren, or to fall themselves by their hands.

He has excited domestic insurrections amongst us, and has endeavoured to bring on the inhabitants of our frontiers the merciless Indian savages, whose known rule of warfare is an undistinguished destruction of all ages, sexes, and conditions.

In every stage of these oppressions we have petitioned for redress in the most humble terms: our repeated petitions have been answered only by repeated injury. A prince whose character is thus marked by every act which may define a tyrant, is unfit to be the ruler of a free people.

Nor have we been wanting in attention to our Brittish brethren. We have warned them from time to time of attempts by their Legislature to extend an unwarrantable jurisdiction over us. We have reminded them of the circumstances of our emigration and settlement here. We have appealed to their native justice and magnanimity, and we have conjured them by the ties of our common kindred to disavow these usurpations, which would inevitably interrupt our connections and correspondence. They too have been deaf to the voice of justice and of consanguinity. We must, therefore, acquiesce in the necessity, which denounces our separation, and hold them, as we hold the rest of mankind, enemies in war, in peace friends.

We, therefore, the Representatives of the United States of America, in General Congress assembled, appealing to the Supreme Judge of the world for the rectitude of our intentions, do, in the name, and by authority of the good people of these Colonies, solemnly publish and declare, That these United Colonies are, and of right ought to be Free and Independent States; that they are absolved from all allegiance to the British Crown, and that all political connection between them and the State of Great Britain is and ought to be totally dissolved; and that as Free and Independent States they have full power to levy war, conclude peace, contract alliances, establish commerce, and to do all other acts and things which independent States may of right do. And for the support of this declaration, with a firm reliance on the protection of Divine Providence, we mutually pledge to each other our lives, our fortunes and our sacred honor.

THE VIRGINIA
BILL OF RIGHTS (1776)

At a General Convention of Delegates and Representatives, from the several counties and corporations of Virginia, held at the Capitol in the City of Williamsburg on Monday the 6th May 1776.

A Declaration of Rights made by the representatives of the good people of Virginia, assembled in full and free Convention; which rights do pertain to them and their posterity, as the basis and foundation of government.

1. That all men are by nature equally free and independent, and have certain inherent rights, of which, when they enter into a state of society, they cannot by any compact deprive or divest their posterity; namely, the enjoyment of life and liberty, with the means of acquiring and possessing property, and pursuing and obtaining happiness and safety.

2. That all power is vested in, and consequently derived from, the people; that magistrates are their trustees and servants, and at all times amenable to them.

3. That government is, or ought to be instituted for the common benefit, protection, and security of the people, nation, or community; of all the various modes and forms of government, that is best which is capable of producing the greatest degree of happiness and safety, and is most effectually secured against the danger of maladministration; and that when any government shall be found inadequate or contrary to these purposes, a majority of the community hath an indubitable, unalienable and indefeasible right to reform, alter or abolish it, in such manner as shall be judged most conducive to the public weal.

4. That no man, or set of men, are entitled to exclusive or separate emoluments or privileges from the community, but in consideration of publick services; which, not being descendible, neither ought the offices of magistrate, legislator or judge to be hereditary.

5. That the legislative and executive powers of the state should be separate and distinct from the judiciary; and that the members of the two first may be restrained from oppression, by feeling and participating

the burthens of the people, they should, at fixed periods, be reduced to a private station, return into that body from which they were originally taken, and the vacancies be supplied by frequent, certain, and regular elections, in which all, or any part of the former members to be again eligible or ineligible, as the laws shall direct.

6. That elections of members to serve as representatives of the people in assembly, ought to be free; and that all men having sufficient evidence of permanent common interest with, and attachment to the community, have the right of suffrage, and cannot be taxed or deprived of their property for publick uses, without their own consent, or that of their representatives so elected, nor bound by any law to which they have not, in like manner, assented for the public good.

7. That all power of suspending laws, or the execution of laws, by any authority without consent of the representatives of the people, is injurious to their rights, and ought not to be exercised.

8. That in all capital or criminal prosecutions a man hath a right to demand the cause and nature of his accusation, to be confronted with the accusers and witnesses, to call for evidence in his favour, and to a speedy trial by an impartial jury of his vicinage, without whose unanimous consent he cannot be found guilty; nor can he be compelled to give evidence against himself; that no man be deprived of his liberty, except by the law of the land or the judgment of his peers.

9. That excessive bail ought not to be required, nor excessive fines imposed, nor cruel and unusual punishments inflicted.

10. That general warrants, whereby an officer or messenger may be commanded to search suspected places without evidence of a fact committed, or to seize any person or persons not named, or whose offence is not particularly described and supported by evidence, are grievous and oppressive, and ought not to be granted.

11. That in controversies respecting property, and in suits between man and man, the ancient trial by jury is preferable to any other, and ought to be held sacred.

12. That the freedom of the press is one of the great bulwarks of liberty, and can never be restrained but by despotick governments.

13. That a well-regulated militia, composed of the body of the people trained to arms, is the proper, natural and safe defence of a free state; that standing armies in time of peace should be avoided as dangerous to liberty; and that in all cases the military should be under strict subordination to, and governed by, the civil power.

14. That the people have a right to uniform government; and, therefore, that no government separate from, or independent of the government of Virginia, ought to be erected or established within the limits thereof.

15. That no free government, or the blessings of liberty, can be preserved to any people, but by a firm adherence to justice, moderation, temperance, frugality and virtue, and by frequent recurrence to fundamental principles.

16. That religion, or the duty which we owe to our Creator, and the manner of discharging it, can be directed only by reason and conviction, not by force or violence; and therefore all men are equally entitled to the free exercise of religion, according to the dictates of conscience; and that it is the mutual duty of all to practise Christian forbearance, love, and charity towards each other.

THE MASSACHUSETTS
BILL OF RIGHTS (1780)

A DECLARATION OF THE RIGHTS OF THE INHABITANTS OF THE COMMONWEALTH OF MASSACHUSETTS

ARTICLE I. All men are born free and equal, and have certain natural, essential, and unalienable rights; among which may be reckoned the right of enjoying and defending their lives and liberties; that of acquiring, possessing, and protecting property; in fine, that of seeking and obtaining their safety and happiness.

II. It is the right as well as the duty of all men in society, publicly, and at stated seasons, to worship the SUPREME BEING, the great Creator and Preserver of the universe. And no subject shall be hurt, molested, or restrained, in his person, liberty, or estate, for worshipping GOD in the manner and season most agreeable to the dictates of his own conscience; or for his religious profession of sentiments; provided he doth not disturb the public peace, or obstruct others in their religious worship.

III. [a] [As the happiness of a people, and the good order and preservation of civil government, essentially depend upon piety, religion, and morality; and as these cannot be generally diffused through a community but by the institution of the public worship of GOD, and of public instructions in piety, religion, and morality: Therefore, to promote their happiness, and to secure the good order and preservation of their government, the people of this commonwealth have a right to invest their legislature with power to authorize and require, and the legislature shall, from time to time, authorize and require, the several towns, parishes, precincts, and other bodies politic, or religious societies, to make suitable provision, at their own expense, for the institution of the public worship of GOD, and for the support and maintenance of public Protestant teachers of piety, religion, and morality, in all cases where such provision shall not be made voluntarily.

And the people of this commonwealth have also a right to, and do, invest their legislature with authority to enjoin upon all the subjects an attendance upon the instructions of the public teachers aforesaid, at stated times and seasons, if there be any on whose instructions they can conscientiously and conveniently attend.

Provided, notwithstanding, that the several towns, parishes, precincts, and other bodies politic, or religious societies, shall, at all times, have the exclusive right of electing their public teachers, and of contracting with them for their support and maintenance.

And all moneys paid by the subject to the support of public worship, and of the public teachers aforesaid, shall, if he require it, be uniformly applied to the support of the public teacher or teachers of his own religious sect or denomination, provided there be any on whose instructions he attends; otherwise it may be paid towards the support of the teacher or teachers of the parish or precinct in which the said moneys are raised.

And every denomination of Christians, demeaning themselves peaceably, and as good subjects of the commonwealth, shall be equally under the protection of the law: and no subordination of any one sect or denomination to another shall ever be established by law.]

IV. The people of this commonwealth have the sole and exclusive right of governing themselves, as a free, sovereign, and independent state; and do, and forever hereafter shall, exercise and enjoy every power, jurisdiction, and right, which is not, or may not hereafter be, by them expressly delegated to the United States of America, in Congress assembled.

V. All power residing originally in the people, and being derived from them, the several magistrates and officers of government, vested with authority, whether legislative, executive, or judicial, are their substitutes and agents, and are at all times accountable to them.

VI. No man, nor corporation, or association of men, have any other title to obtain advantages, or particular and exclusive privileges, distinct from those of the community, than what arises from the consideration of services rendered to the public; and this title being in nature neither hereditary, nor transmissible to children, or descendants, or relations by blood, the idea of a man born a magistrate, law-giver, or judge, is absurd and unnatural.

VII. Government is instituted for the common good; for the protection, safety, prosperity, and happiness of the people; and not for the profit, honor, or private interest of any one man, family, or class of men: Therefore the people alone have an incontestible unalienable, and indefeasible right to institute government; and to reform, alter, or totally change the same, when their protection, safety, prosperity, and happiness require it.

VIII. In order to prevent those who are vested with authority from becoming oppressors, the people have a right, at such periods and in such manner as they shall establish by their frame of government, to cause their public officers to return to private life; and to fill up vacant places by certain and regular elections and appointments.

IX. All elections ought to be free; and all the inhabitants of this commonwealth, having such qualifications as they shall establish by their frame of government, have an equal right to elect officers, and to be elected, for public employments.

X. Each individual of the society has a right to be protected by it in the enjoyment of his life, liberty, and property, according to standing laws. He is obliged, consequently, to contribute his share to the expense of this protection; to give his personal service, or an equivalent, when necessary: but no part of the property of any individual can, with justice, be taken from him, or applied to public uses, without his own consent, or that of the representative body of the people. In fine, the people of this commonwealth are not controllable by any other laws than those to which their constitutional representative body have given their consent. And whenever the public exigencies require that the property of any individual should be appropriated to public uses, he shall receive a reasonable compensation therefor.

XI. Every subject of the commonwealth ought to find a certain remedy, by having recourse to the laws, for all injuries or wrongs which he may receive in his person, property, or character. He ought to obtain right and justice freely, and without being obliged to purchase it; completely, and without any denial; promptly, and without delay; conformably to the laws.

3

AN AMERICAN CONSTITUTION

The expression of that principle [Liberty to all] in our Declaration of Independence, was most happy, and fortunate. . . . The assertion of that principle, at that time, was the word, "fitly spoken" which has proved an "apple of gold" to us. The Union, and the Constitution, are the picture of silver, subsequently framed around it. The picture was made, not to conceal, or destroy the apple, but to adorn, and preserve it. The picture was made for the apple—not the apple for the picture.

ABRAHAM LINCOLN, 1861

That it is easier to make a revolution than to construct a government is so commonplace an idea it is often regarded as a cliché. Yet, a truth is no less true for being a cliché—and the American political experience is no exception. It was much easier for the men who made the revolution to propound and defend revolutionary principles than it was for the framers to put such principles to work in a functioning government. Thomas Jefferson wrote the bulk of the Declaration of Independence in two weeks; it took more than forty men the greater portion of a hot Philadelphia summer to write the Constitution. And almost two additional years went by before the various state conventions ratified the document. In short, American experience demonstrates that it is easier to expound principles than to put them into practice.

Recognition of the difficulty of translating principle into practice is essential for an understanding of what was involved in the framing and ratification of the Constitution, the subject matter of this chapter. It was left for the Constitutional framers to effectuate the principles of the Declaration, which were not necessarily concordant with one another. They had to decide, for example, how to fashion a government based upon "consent of the governed" without allowing individual liberties and "unalienable rights" to be submerged by overwhelming majorities. Somehow, they had to formulate a system in which the presupposition of equality did not lead to a denial of the differences—in avocation, in taste, in wealth, in any number of things—which they understood as the accompaniment to liberty. To put it simply, the problem that underlay the debates in Philadelphia and at the state conventions was how to translate the principles of the Revolution and the Declaration into a workable government without damaging irreparably the principles themselves.

In studying the Constitutional period, there are two especial points to remember. First, the principles enunciated in the Declaration of Independence were the working framework for the Constitutional debates. Whatever differences existed among the delegates to the national and state conventions, the men were by and large agreed that the Constitution would have to be faithful to the revolutionary principles.[1] Second, the struggles at the conventions were caused as much by the inherent tensions in these principles themselves as they were by the conflicting interests of the delegates. To be sure, both proponents and opponents of the several Constitutional plans were concerned about how their particular states, not to mention interests, would fare in the new government. However, before such issues could be decided, it had to be determined whether a large government based upon popular consent and promising individuals the right to "life, liberty, and the pursuit of happiness" was feasible. Where all are considered equal, a government unresponsive to the people who live under it is, by definition, despotic. Yet popular consent, the delegates believed, might become popular tyranny or might raise tyrants to power. In short, could there be egalitarian government relatively free from the danger of destruction of individual rights and liberties?

One must not take this to mean that the debates in the conventions were concerned only with great theoretical questions. That is not the case. The delegates were men of particular, and not infrequently peculiar, interests. The greater portion of their time was taken up by arguments over issues such as the basis and method of taxation, protections for property, assuring that small states would not be overwhelmed by their larger and wealthier neighbors, and methods of representation. However, these questions could be settled peaceably only because of prior assumptions about the type of government necessary in the American context. The governmental framework, the delegates agreed, was

[1] This interpretation of the proceedings at the Philadelphia Convention is not shared by all students of the period. Cf. Charles A. Beard, *An Economic Interpretation of the Constitution* (New York: Macmillan, 1954); Robert Brown, *Charles Beard and the Constitution* (Princeton: Princeton University Press, 1956); Forest McDonald, *We The People: The Economic Origins of the Constitution* (Chicago: University of Chicago Press, 1958); Richard Hofstadter, *The American Political Tradition* (New York: Vintage Books, 1956); John P. Roche, "The Founding Fathers: A Reform Caucus in Action," *American Political Science Review*, LV (December 1961), pp. 799–816; Martin Diamond, "Democracy and the *Federalist:* A Reconsideration of the Framers' Intent," *American Political Science Review*, LIII (March 1959), pp. 52–68.

already suggested by what they accepted as basic American political principles. Melancthon Smith, a member of the New York State Convention, noted that the delegates might argue over taxation, methods of election, representation, and similar issues, but

> these differences are on matters of small importance, and of such a nature as the persons who hold different opinions will not be tenacious of. Perfect uniformity of sentiment on so great a political subject is not to be expected. Every sensible man is impressed with this idea, and is therefore prepared to make concessions and accommodate on matters of small importance. It is sufficient that we agree in the great leading principles, which relate to the preservation of public liberty and private security. And on these I will venture to affirm we are as well agreed, as any people ever were on a question of this nature. I dare pronounce that were the principal advocates for the proposed plan to write comments upon it, they would differ more in the sense they would give the constitution, than those who oppose it do, in the amendments they would wish.[2]

Smith's point was well taken. Because the delegates were generally in agreement about the principles underlying the Constitution, they could afford to compromise on lesser but more immediate issues. Compromise assumes that the parties at odds have more to gain than lose by the compromise, and concessions on particular points depend on some sort of mutual acceptance of goals. Such acceptance, the *Federalist* suggested, made possible the accomplishment at Philadelphia.

> The real wonder is that so many difficulties should have been surmounted with a unanimity almost as unprecedented as it must have been unexpected; ... the convention must have enjoyed, in a very singular degree, an exemption from the pestilential influence of party animosities—the disease most incident to deliberative proceedings. The second conclusion is that all the deputations composing the convention were either satisfactorily accommodated by the final act, or were induced to accede to it by a deep conviction of the necessity of sacrificing private opinions and partial interests to the public good, and by a despair of seeing this necessity diminished by delays or new experiments.[3]

Agreement upon underlying principles does not, however, mean that such principles are easily translated into action. This is especially so when the principles are not entirely compatible. Thus, the framers might agree upon the ideas central to American life, while disagreeing about how to provide for them. To erect a libertarian regime prone to aristocratic or even monarchic rule was no more acceptable than an

[2] Paul Leicester Ford, ed., *Pamphlets on the Constitution of the United States* (Brooklyn, N.Y.: n.n., 1888), p. 104.
[3] *Federalist* No. 37, in *The Federalist Papers* (New York: New American Library, 1937).

egalitarian regime which denied liberty. Proponents and opponents of the
Constitution recognized the tension inherent in the relationship between
the egalitarian and libertarian idea, at least insofar as they saw how
difficult it would be to develop a government based upon general consent
yet safeguarding personal liberty. Hence they discarded the idea of
trying to institute the most egalitarian of governments, a pure democracy.
Such a regime placed personal rights and liberties in an insecure position.
Proponents and opponents of the Constitution, in common, agreed
on that.

Such democracies have ever been spectacles of turbulence and contention;
have ever been found incompatible with personal security or the rights
of property; and have in general been as short in their lives as they have
been violent in their deaths. Theoretic politicians, who have patronized
this species of government, have erroneously supposed that by reducing
mankind to a perfect equality in their political rights, they would at the
same time be perfectly equalized and assimilated in their possessions,
their opinions, and their passions.[4]

Instead of pure democracy, supporters of the Constitution—the Federalists
—urged a republican form of government as the answer to the
"inconveniences of democracy consistent with the democratic form of
government."[5] On this point, the battle between the Federalists and
their opposition—the Antifederalists—was joined. Antifederalists charged
that the Federalist plan was not in keeping with American political
belief. In a country as large as America, they argued, a republic would
render equality absurd:

The idea of an uncompounded republic, on an average one thousand miles
in length, and eight hundred in breadth, and containing six millions of
white inhabitants all reduced to the same standard of morals, of habits, and
of laws, is in itself an absurdity, and contrary to the whole experience
of mankind.[6]

Human individuality—indivorceable from the belief in liberty—they
continued, made such a regime unworkable:

It is natural, says Montesquieu, "to a republic to have only a small territory,
otherwise it cannot long subsist; . . . in large republics, the public good
is sacrificed to a thousand views."[7]

[4] *Federalist* No. 10, *op. cit.*
[5] Max Farrand, ed., *Records of the Federal Convention* (New Haven: Yale University
Press, 1966), p. 135.
[6] "Agrippa XII," in Paul Leicester Ford, ed., *Essays on the Constitution of the United
States* (Brooklyn, N.Y.: n.n., 1892), p. 91.
[7] Morton Borden, ed., *The Antifederalist Papers* (Lansing, Mich.: Michigan State
University Press, 1965), p. 37.

Finally, they asked how equality could be preserved in a large republic where genuine consent of the governed would be problematic at best.

Where there is but one representative to 30,000 or 40,000 inhabitants, . . .
he can only mix and be acquainted with a few respectable characters
among his constituents. Even double the general representation, and then
there must be a very great distance between the representatives and the
people in general represented.[8]

According to the Antifederalists, then, the Constitution did not provide a means whereby equality and liberty could coexist workably.

The Federalist defense of the Constitution was dictated by these charges. They had to prove, in the words of the *Federalist*, that:

In the extent and proper structure of the Union, therefore, we behold a
republican remedy for the diseases most incident to republican government.[9]

They argued that the new plan did not place American principles in contradictory or inconsistent positions, but, rather, that the very size of the large republic would provide safeguards for personal liberties and minority rights by making it difficult for overwhelming majorities to coalesce. Ambiguities and tensions in American principles might continue, but the Constitution provided latitude for them to be worked out and dissipated. Because this argument carried the day, future conflicts concerning American political principles would occur in the context of a new Constitutional system.

The selections which follow are examples of the arguments over the Constitution. The Federalist position is represented by portions of the *Federalist*; the Antifederalist by the public letters of Governor Clinton of New York ("Cato"), Richard Henry Lee of Virginia ("The Federal Farmer"), and portions of Patrick Henry's attack on the Constitution at the Virginia Ratifying Convention. A historical postscript is added in William Manning's *The Key of Libberty*, a continuation of the Constitutional debates some twenty years after their formal conclusion. In Manning's book, we see that the formulation of a Constitution did not entirely settle the questions about American political philosophy which had bedeviled the framers. Those questions remain and provide the themes for subsequent chapters of this volume.

[8] *Ibid.*, p. 161
[9] *Federalist* No. 10, *op. cit.*

THE FEDERALIST

THE FEDERALIST NO. 1 (HAMILTON)

To the People of the State of New York:

After an unequivocal experience of the inefficiency of the subsisting federal government, you are called upon to deliberate on a new Constitution for the United States of America. The subject speaks its own importance; comprehending in its consequences nothing less than the existence of the UNION, the safety and welfare of the parts of which it is composed, the fate of an empire in many respects the most interesting in the world. It has been frequently remarked that it seems to have been reserved to the people of this country, by their conduct and example, to decide the important question, whether societies of men are really capable or not of establishing good government from reflection and choice, or whether they are forever destined to depend for their political constitutions on accident and force. If there be any truth in the remark, the crisis at which we are arrived may with propriety be regarded as the era in which that decision is to be made; and a wrong election of the part we shall act may, in this view, deserve to be considered as the general misfortune of mankind.

This idea will add the inducements of philanthropy to those of patriotism, to heighten the solicitude which all considerate and good men must feel for the event. Happy will it be if our choice should be directed by a judicious estimate of our true interests, unperplexed and unbiased by considerations not connected with the public good. But this is a thing more ardently to be wished than seriously to be expected. The plan offered to our deliberations affects too many particular interests, innovates upon too many local institutions, not to involve in its discussion a variety of objects foreign to its merits, and of views, passions and prejudices little favorable to the discovery of truth.

Among the most formidable of the obstacles which the new Constitution will have to encounter may readily be distinguished the obvious interest of a certain class of men in every State to resist all changes which may hazard a diminution of the power, emolument, and consequence of the offices they hold under the State establishments; and the perverted ambition of another class of men, who will either hope to aggrandize themselves by the confusions of their country, or will flatter themselves with fairer prospects of elevation from the subdivision of the empire into several partial confederacies than from its union under one government.

It is not, however, my design to dwell upon observations of this nature. I am well aware that it would be disingenuous to resolve indiscriminately the opposition of any set of men (merely because their situations might subject them to suspicion) into interested or ambitious views. Candor will oblige us to admit that even such men may be actuated by upright intentions; and it cannot be doubted that much of the opposition which has made its appearance, or may hereafter make its appearance, will spring from sources, blameless at least, if not respectable—the honest errors of minds led astray by preconceived jealousies and fears. So numerous indeed and so powerful are the causes which serve to give a false bias to the judgment, that we, upon many occasions, see wise and good men on the wrong as well as on the right side of questions of the first magnitude to society. This circumstance, if duly attended to, would furnish a lesson of moderation to those who are ever so much persuaded of their being in the right in any controversy. And a further reason for caution, in this respect, might be drawn from the reflection that we are not always sure that those who advocate the truth are influenced by purer principles than their antagonists. Ambition, avarice, personal animosity, party opposition, and many other motives not more laudable than these, are apt to operate as well upon those who support as those who oppose the right side of a question. Were there not even inducements to moderation, nothing could be more ill-judged than that intolerant spirit which has, at all times, characterized political parties. For in politics, as in religion, it is equally absurd to aim at making proselytes by fire and sword. Heresies in either can rarely be cured by persecution.

And yet, however just these sentiments will be allowed to be, we have already sufficient indications that it will happen in this as in all former cases of great national discussion. A torrent of angry and malignant passions will be let loose. To judge from the conduct of the opposite parties, we shall be led to conclude that they will mutually hope to evince the justness of their opinions, and to increase the number of their converts by the loudness of their declamations and the bitterness of their invectives. An enlightened zeal for the energy and efficiency of government will be stigmatized as the offspring of a temper fond of despotic power and hostile to the principles of liberty. An over-scrupulous jealousy of danger to the rights of the people, which is more commonly the fault of the head than of the heart, will be represented as mere pretence and artifice, the stale bait for popularity at the expense of the public good. It will be forgotten, on the one hand, that jealousy is the usual concomitant of love, and that the noble enthusiasm of liberty is apt to be infected with a spirit of narrow and illiberal distrust. On the other hand, it will be equally forgotten that the vigor of government is essential to the security of liberty; that, in the contemplation of a sound and well-informed judgment, their interest can never be separated; and that a dangerous ambition more often lurks behind the specious mask of zeal for the rights of the people than under the forbidding appearance of zeal for the firmness and efficiency of government. History will teach us that the former has been found a much more certain road to the introduction of despotism than the latter, and that of those men who have overturned the liberties of republics, the greatest number have begun their career by paying an obsequious court to the people; commencing demagogues, and ending tyrants.

In the course of the preceding observations, I have had an eye, my fellow-citizens, to putting you upon your guard against all attempts, from whatever quarter, to influence your decision in a matter of the utmost moment to your welfare, by any impressions other than those which may result from the evidence of truth. You will, no doubt, at the same time, have collected from the general scope of them, that they proceed from a source not unfriendly to the new Constitution. Yes, my countrymen, I own to you that, after having given it an attentive consideration, I am clearly of opinion it is your interest to adopt it. I am convinced that this is the safest course for your liberty, your dignity, and your happiness. I affect not reserves which I do not feel. I will not amuse you with an appearance of deliberation when I have decided. I frankly acknowledge to you my convictions, and I will freely lay before you the reasons on which they are founded. The consciousness of good intentions disdains ambiguity. I shall not, however, multiply professions on this head. My motives must remain in the depository of my own breast. My arguments will be open to all, and may be judged of by all. They shall at least be offered in a spirit which will not disgrace the cause of truth.

I propose, in a series of papers, to discuss the following interesting particulars:—*The utility of the Union to your political prosperity—The insufficiency of the present Confederation to preserve that Union—The necessity of a government at least equally energetic with the one proposed, to the attainment of this object—The conformity of the proposed Constitution to the true principles of republican government—Its analogy to your own State constitution—and lastly, The additional security which its adoption will afford to the preservation of that species of government, to liberty, and to property.*

In the progress of this discussion I shall endeavor to give a satisfactory answer to all the objections which shall have made their appearance, that may seem to have any claim to your attention.

It may perhaps be thought superfluous to offer arguments to prove the utility of the UNION, a point, no doubt, deeply engraved on the hearts of the great body of the people in every State, and one, which it may be imagined, has no adversaries. But the fact is, that we already hear it whispered in the private circles of those who oppose the new Constitution, that the thirteen States are of too great extent for any general system, and that we must of necessity resort to separate confederacies of distinct portions of the whole. This doctrine will, in all probability, be gradually propagated, till it has votaries enough to countenance an open avowal of it. For nothing can be more evident, to those who are able to take an enlarged view of the subject, than the alternative of an adoption of the new Constitution or a dismemberment of the Union. It will therefore be of use to begin by examining the advantages of that Union, the certain evils, and the probable dangers, to which every State will be exposed from its dissolution. This shall accordingly constitute the subject of my next address.

PUBLIUS

THE FEDERALIST NO. 10 (MADISON)

To the People of the State of New York:

Among the numerous advantages promised by a well-constructed Union, none deserves to be more accurately developed than its tendency to break and control the violence of faction. The friend of popular governments never finds himself so much alarmed for their character and fate, as when he contemplates their propensity to this dangerous vice. He will not fail, therefore, to set a due value on any plan which, without violating the principles to which he is attached, provides a proper cure for it. The instability, injustice, and confusion introduced into the public councils, have, in truth, been the mortal diseases under which popular governments have everywhere perished; as they continue to be the favorite and fruitful topics from which the adversaries to liberty derive their most specious declamations. The valuable improvements made by the American consti- tutions on the popular models, both ancient and modern, cannot certainly be too much admired; but it would be an unwarrantable partiality, to contend that they have as effectually obviated the danger on this side, as was wished and expected. Complaints are everywhere heard from our most considerate and virtuous citizens, equally the friends of public and private faith, and of public and personal liberty, that our governments are too unstable, that the public good is disregarded in the conflicts of rival parties, and that measures are too often decided, not according to the rules of justice and the rights of the minor party, but by the superior force of an interested and overbearing majority. However anxiously we may wish that these complaints had no foundation, the evidence of known facts will not permit us to deny that they are in some degree true. It will be found, indeed, on a candid review of our situation, that some of the distresses under which we labor have been erroneously charged on the operation of our governments; but it will be found, at the same time, that other causes will not alone account for many of our heaviest misfortunes; and, particularly, for that prevailing and increasing distrust of public engagements, and alarm for private rights, which are echoed from one end of the continent to the other. These must be chiefly, if not wholly, effects of the unsteadiness and injustice with which a factious spirit has tainted our public administrations.

By a faction, I understand a number of citizens, whether amounting to a majority or minority of the whole, who are united and actuated by some common impulse of passion, or of interest, adverse to the rights of other citizens, or to the permanent and aggregate interests of the community.

There are two methods of curing the mischiefs of faction: the one, by removing its causes; the other, by controlling its effects.

There are again two methods of removing the causes of faction: the one, by destroying the liberty which is essential to its existence; the other, by giving to every citizen the same opinions, the same passions, and the same interests.

It could never be more truly said than of the first remedy, that it was worse than the disease. Liberty is to faction what air is to fire, an aliment without which it instantly expires. But it could not be less folly to abolish liberty, which is essential to political life, because it nourishes faction, than it would be to wish the annihilation of air, which is essential to animal life, because it imparts to fire its destructive agency.

The second expedient is as impracticable as the first would be unwise. As long as the reason of man continues fallible, and he is at liberty to exercise it, different opinions will be formed. As long as the connection subsists between his reason and his self-love, his opinions and his passions will have a reciprocal influence on each other; and the former will be objects to which the latter will attach themselves. The diversity in the faculties of men, from which the rights of property originate, is not less an insuperable obstacle to a uniformity of interests. The protection of these faculties is the first object of government. From the protection of different and unequal faculties of acquiring property, the possession of different degrees and kinds of property immediately results; and from the influence of these on the sentiments and views of the respective proprietors, ensues a division of the society into different interests and parties.

The latent causes of faction are thus sown in the nature of man;

and we see them everywhere brought into different degrees of activity, according to the different circumstances of civil society. A zeal for different opinions concerning religion, concerning government, and many other points, as well of speculation as of practice; an attachment to different leaders ambitiously contending for pre-eminence and power; or to persons of other descriptions whose fortunes have been interesting to the human passions, have, in turn, divided mankind into parties, inflamed them with mutual animosity, and rendered them much more disposed to vex and oppress each other than to co-operate for their common good. So strong is this propensity of mankind to fall into mutual animosities, that where no substantial occasion presents itself, the most frivolous and fanciful distinctions have been sufficient to kindle their unfriendly passions and excite their most violent conflicts. But the most common and durable source of factions has been the various and unequal distribution of property. Those who hold and those who are without property have ever formed distinct interests in society. Those who are creditors, and those who are debtors, fall under a like discrimination. A landed interest, a manufacturing interest, a mercantile interest, a moneyed interest, with many lesser interests, grow up of necessity in civilized nations, and divide them into different classes, actuated by different sentiments and views. The regulation of these various and interfering interests forms the principal task of modern legislation, and involves the spirit of party and faction in the necessary and ordinary operations of the government.

No man is allowed to be a judge in his own cause, because his interest would certainly bias his judgment, and, not improbably, corrupt his integrity. With equal, nay with greater reason, a body of men are unfit to be both judges and parties at the same time; yet what are many of the most important acts of legislation, but so many judicial determinations, not indeed concerning the rights of single persons, but concerning the rights of large bodies of citizens? And what are the different classes of legislators but advocates and parties to the causes which they determine? Is a law proposed concerning private debts? It is a question to which the creditors are parties on one side and the debtors on the other. Justice ought to hold the balance between them. Yet the parties are, and must be, themselves the judges; and the most numerous party, or, in other words, the most powerful faction must be expected to prevail. Shall domestic manufactures be encouraged, and in what degree, by restrictions on foreign manufactures? are questions which would be differently decided by the landed and the manufacturing classes, and probably by neither with a sole regard to justice and the public good. The apportionment of taxes on the various descriptions of property is an act which seems to require the most exact impartiality; yet there is, perhaps, no legislative act in which greater opportunity and temptation are given to a predominant party to trample on the rules of justice. Every shilling with which they overburden the inferior number, is a shilling saved to their own pockets.

It is in vain to say that enlightened statesmen will be able to adjust these clashing interests, and render them all subservient to the public good. Enlightened statesmen will not always be at the helm. Nor, in many cases, can such an adjustment be made at all without taking into view indirect and remote considerations, which will rarely prevail over the immediate interest which one party may find in disregarding the rights of another or the good of the whole.

The inference to which we are brought is, that the *causes* of faction cannot be removed, and that relief is only to be sought in the means of controlling its *effects*.

If a faction consists of less than a majority, relief is supplied by the republican principle, which enables the majority to defeat its sinister views by regular vote. It may clog the administration, it may convulse the society; but it will be unable to execute and mask its violence under the forms of the Constitution. When a majority is included in a faction, the form of popular government, on the other hand, enables it to sacrifice to its ruling passion or interest both the public good and the rights of other citizens. To secure the public good and private rights against the danger of such a faction, and at the same time to preserve the spirit and the form of popular government, is then the great object to which our inquiries are directed. Let me add that it is the great desideratum by which this form of government can be rescued from the opprobrium under which it has so long labored, and be recommended to the esteem and adoption of mankind.

By what means is this object attainable? Evidently by one of two only. Either the existence of the same passion or interest in a majority at the same time must be prevented, or the majority, having such coexistent passion or interest, must be rendered, by their number and local situation, unable to concert and carry into effect schemes of oppression. If the impulse and the opportunity be suffered to coincide, we well know that neither moral nor religious motives can be relied on as an adequate control. They are not found to be such on the injustice and violence of individuals, and lose their efficacy in proportion to the number combined together, that is, in proportion as their efficacy becomes needful.

From this view of the subject it may be concluded that a pure democracy, by which I mean a society consisting of a small number of citizens, who assemble and administer the government in person, can admit of no cure for the mischiefs of faction. A common passion or interest will, in almost every case, be felt by a majority of the whole; a communication and concert result from the form of government itself;

and there is nothing to check the inducements to sacrifice the weaker party or an obnoxious individual. Hence it is that such democracies have ever been spectacles of turbulence and contention; have ever been found incompatible with personal security or the rights of property; and have in general been as short in their lives as they have been violent in their deaths. Theoretic politicians, who have patronized this species of government, have erroneously supposed that by reducing mankind to a perfect equality in their political rights, they would, at the same time, be perfectly equalized and assimilated in their possessions, their opinions, and their passions.

A republic, by which I mean a government in which the scheme of representation takes place, opens a different prospect, and promises the cure for which we are seeking. Let us examine the points in which it varies from pure democracy, and we shall comprehend both the nature of the cure and the efficacy which it must derive from the Union.

The two great points of difference between a democracy and a republic are: first, the delegation of the government, in the latter, to a small number of citizens elected by the rest; secondly, the greater number of citizens, and greater sphere of country, over which the latter may be extended.

The effect of the first difference is, on the one hand, to refine and enlarge the public views, by passing them through the medium of a chosen body of citizens, whose wisdom may best discern the true interest of their country, and whose patriotism and love of justice will be least likely to sacrifice it to temporary or partial considerations. Under such a regulation, it may well happen that the public voice, pronounced by the representatives of the people, will be more consonant to the public good than if pronounced by the people themselves, convened for the purpose. On the other hand, the effect may be inverted. Men of factious tempers, of local prejudices, or of sinister designs, may, by intrigue, by corruption, or by other means, first obtain the suffrages, and then betray the interests, of the people. The question resulting is, whether small or extensive republics are more favorable to the election of proper guardians of the public weal; and it is clearly decided in favor of the latter by two obvious considerations:

In the first place, it is to be remarked that, however small the republic may be, the representatives must be raised to a certain number, in order to guard against the cabals of a few; and that, however large it may be, they must be limited to a certain number, in order to guard against the confusion of a multitude. Hence, the number of representatives in the two cases not being in proportion to that of the two constituents, and being proportionally greater in the small republic, it follows that, if the proportion of fit characters be not less in the large than in the small republic, the former will present a greater option, and consequently a greater probability of a fit choice.

In the next place, as each representative will be chosen by a greater number of citizens in the large than in the small republic, it will be more difficult for unworthy candidates to practise with success the vicious arts by which elections are too often carried; and the suffrages of the people being more free, will be more likely to centre in men who possess the most attractive merit and the most diffusive and established characters.

It must be confessed that in this, as in most other cases, there is a mean, on both sides of which inconveniences will be found to lie. By enlarging too much the number of electors, you render the representative too little acquainted with all their local circumstances and lesser interests; as by reducing it too much, you render him unduly attached to these, and too little fit to comprehend and pursue great and national objects. The federal Constitution forms a happy combination in this respect; the great and aggregate interests being referred to the national, the local and particular to the State legislatures.

The other point of difference is, the greater number of citizens and extent of territory which may be brought within the compass of republican than of democratic government; and it is this circumstance principally which renders factious combinations less to be dreaded in the former than in the latter. The smaller the society, the fewer probably will be the distinct parties and interests composing it; the fewer the distinct parties and interests, the more frequently will a majority be found of the same party; and the smaller the number of individuals composing a majority, and the smaller the compass within which they are placed, the more easily will they concert and execute their plans of oppression. Extend the sphere, and you take in a greater variety of parties and interests; you make it less probable that a majority of the whole will have a common motive to invade the rights of other citizens; or if such a common motive exists, it will be more difficult for all who feel it to discover their own strength, and to act in unison with each other. Besides other impediments, it may be remarked that, where there is a consciousness of unjust or dishonorable purposes, communication is always checked by distrust in proportion to the number whose concurrence is necessary.

Hence, it clearly appears, that the same advantage which a republic has over a democracy, in controlling the effects of faction, is enjoyed by a large over a small republic,—is enjoyed by the Union over the States composing it. Does the advantage consist in the substitution of representatives whose enlightened views and virtuous sentiments render them superior to local prejudices and to schemes of injustice? It will not be denied that the representation of the Union will be most likely to possess these requisite endowments. Does it consist in the greater security afforded by a greater variety of parties, against the event of any one party being able to outnumber and oppress the rest? In an equal degree does the increased variety of parties comprised within the Union, increase this security. Does it, in fine, consist in the greater obstacles opposed to the concert and accomplishment of the secret wishes of an unjust and interested majority? Here, again, the extent of the Union gives it the most palpable advantage.

The influence of factious leaders may kindle a flame within their particular States, but will be unable to spread a general conflagration through the other States. A religious sect may degenerate into a political faction in a part of the Confederacy; but the variety of sects dispersed over the entire face of it must secure the national councils against any danger from that source. A rage for paper money, for an abolition of debts, for an equal division of property, or for any other improper or wicked project, will be less apt to pervade the whole body of the Union than a particular member of it; in the same proportion as such a malady is more likely to taint a particular county or district, than an entire State.

In the extent and proper structure of the Union, therefore, we behold a republican remedy for the diseases most incident to republican government. And according to the degree of pleasure and pride we feel in being republicans, ought to be our zeal in cherishing the spirit and supporting the character of Federalists.

PUBLIUS

THE FEDERALIST NO. 37 (MADISON)

These papers . . . solicit the attention of those only, who add to a sincere zeal for the happiness of their country, a temper favorable to a just estimate of the means of promoting it.

Persons of this character will proceed to an examination of the plan submitted by the convention, not only without a disposition to find or to magnify faults; but will see the propriety of reflecting, that a faultless plan was not to be expected. Nor will they barely make allowances for the errors which may be chargeable on the fallibility to which the convention, as a body of men, were liable; but will keep in mind, that they themselves also are but men, and ought not to assume an infallibility in rejudging the fallible opinions of others.

With equal readiness will it be perceived, that besides these inducements to candor, many allowances ought to be made for the difficulties inherent in the very nature of the undertaking referred to the convention.

The novelty of the undertaking immediately strikes us. It has been shown in the course of these papers, that the existing Confederation is founded on principles which are fallacious; that we must consequently change this first foundation, and with it the superstructure resting upon it. It has been shown, that the other confederacies which could be consulted as precedents have been vitiated by the same erroneous principles, and can therefore furnish no other light than that of beacons, which give warning of the course to be shunned, without pointing out that which ought to be pursued. The most that the convention could do in such a situation, was to avoid the errors suggested by the past experience of other countries, as well as of our own; and to provide a convenient mode of rectifying their own errors, as future experience may unfold them.

Among the difficulties encountered by the convention, a very important one must have lain in combining the requisite stability and energy in government, with the inviolable attention due to liberty and to the republican form. Without substantially accomplishing this part of their undertaking, they would have very imperfectly fulfilled the object of their appointment, or the expectation of the public; yet that it could not be easily accomplished, will be denied by no one who is unwilling to betray his ignorance of the subject. Energy in government is essential to that security against external and internal danger, and to that prompt and salutary execution of the laws which enter into the very definition of good government. Stability in government is essential to national character and to the advantages annexed to it, as well as to that repose and confidence in the minds of the people, which are among the chief blessings of civil society. An irregular and mutable legislation is not more an evil in itself than it is odious to the people; and it may be pronounced with assurance that the people of this country, enlightened as they are with regard to the nature, and interested, as the great body of them are, in the effects of good government, will never be satisfied till some remedy be applied to the vicissitudes and uncertainties which characterize the State administrations. On comparing, however, these valuable ingredients with the vital principles of liberty, we must perceive at once the difficulty of mingling them together in their due proportions. The genius of republican liberty seems to demand on one side, not only that all power should be derived from the people, but that those intrusted with it should be kept in dependence on the people, by a short duration of their appointments; and that even during this short period the trust should be placed not in a few, but a number of hands. Stability, on the contrary, requires that the hands in which power is lodged should continue for a length of time the same. A frequent change of men will result from a frequent return of elections; and a frequent change of measures from a frequent change of men: whilst energy in government requires not only a certain duration of power, but the execution of it by a single hand.

How far the convention may have succeeded in this part of their work, will better appear on a more accurate view of it. From the cursory view here taken, it must clearly appear to have been an arduous part.

Not less arduous must have been the task of marking the proper line of partition between the authority of the general and that of the State governments. Every man will be sensible of this difficulty, in proportion as he has been accustomed to contemplate and discriminate objects extensive and complicated in their nature. The faculties of the mind itself have never yet been distinguished and defined, with satisfactory precision, by all the efforts of the most acute and metaphysical philosophers. Sense, perception, judgment, desire, volition, memory, imagination, are found to be separated by such delicate shades and minute gradations that their boundaries have eluded the most subtle investigations, and remain a pregnant source of ingenious disquisition and controversy. The boundaries between the great kingdom of nature, and, still more, between the various provinces, and lesser portions, into which they are subdivided, afford another illustration of the same important truth. The most sagacious and laborious naturalists have never yet succeeded in tracing with certainty the line which separates the district of vegetable life from the neighboring region of unorganized matter, or which marks the termination of the former and the commencement of the animal empire. A still greater obscurity lies in the distinctive characters by which the objects in each of these great departments of nature have been arranged and assorted.

When we pass from the works of nature, in which all the delineations are perfectly accurate, and appear to be otherwise only from the imperfection of the eye which surveys them, to the institutions of man, in which the obscurity arises as well from the object itself as from the organ by which it is contemplated, we must perceive the necessity of moderating still further our expectations and hopes from the efforts of human sagacity. Experience has instructed us that no skill in the science of government has yet been able to discriminate and define, with sufficient certainty, its three great provinces—the legislative, executive, and judiciary; or even the privileges and powers of the different legislative branches. Questions daily occur in the course of practice, which prove the obscurity which reigns in these subjects, and which puzzle the greatest adepts in political science.

The experience of ages, with the continued and combined labors of the most enlightened legislators and jurists, has been equally unsuccessful in delineating the several objects and limits of different codes of laws and different tribunals of justice. The precise extent of the common law, and the statute law, the maritime law, the ecclesiastical law, the law of corporations, and other local laws and customs, remains still to be clearly and finally established in Great Britain, where accuracy in such subjects has been more industriously pursued than in any other part of the world. The jurisdiction of her several courts, general and local, of law, of equity, of admiralty, etc., is not less a source of frequent and intricate discussions, sufficiently denoting the indeterminate limits by which they are respectively circumscribed. All new laws, though penned with the greatest technical skill, and passed on the fullest and most mature deliberation, are considered as more or less obscure and equivocal, until their meaning be liquidated and ascertained by a series of particular discussions and adjudications. Besides the obscurity arising from the complexity of objects, and the imperfection of the human faculties, the medium through which the conceptions of men are conveyed to each other adds a fresh embarrassment. The use of words is to express ideas. Perspicuity, therefore, requires not only that the ideas should be distinctly formed, but that they should be expressed by words distinctly and exclusively appropriate to them. But no language is so copious as to supply words and phrases for every complex idea, or so correct as not to include many equivocally denoting different ideas. Hence it must happen that however accurately objects may be discriminated in themselves, and however accurately the discrimination may be considered, the definition of them may be rendered inaccurate by the inaccuracy of the terms in which it is delivered. And this unavoidable inaccuracy must be greater or less, according to the complexity and novelty of the objects defined. When the Almighty himself condescends to address mankind in their own language, his meaning, luminous as it must be, is rendered dim and doubtful by the cloudy medium through which it is communicated.

Here, then, are three sources of vague and incorrect definitions: indistinctness of the object, imperfection of the organ of conception, inadequateness of the vehicle of ideas. Any one of these must produce a certain degree of obscurity. The convention, in delineating the boundary between the federal and State jurisdictions, must have experienced the full effect of them all.

To the difficulties already mentioned may be added the interfering pretensions of the larger and smaller States. We cannot err in supposing that the former would contend for a participation in the government, fully proportioned to their superior wealth and importance; and that the latter would not be less tenacious of the equality at present enjoyed by them. We may well suppose that neither side would entirely yield to the other, and consequently that the struggle could be terminated only by compromise. It is extremely probable, also, that after the ratio of representation had been adjusted, this very compromise must have produced a fresh struggle between the same parties, to give such a turn to the organization of the government, and to the distribution of its powers, as would increase the importance of the branches, in forming which they had respectively obtained the greatest share of influence. There are features in the Constitution which warrant each of these suppositions; and as far as either of them is well founded, it shows that the convention must have been compelled to sacrifice theoretical propriety to the force of extraneous considerations.

Nor could it have been the large and small States only, which would marshal themselves in opposition to each other on various points. Other combinations, resulting from a difference of local position and policy, must have created additional difficulties. As every State may be divided into different districts, and its citizens into different classes, which give birth to contending interests and local jealousies, so the different parts of the United States are distinguished from each other by a variety of circumstances, which produce a like effect on a larger scale. And although this variety of interests, for reasons sufficiently explained in a former paper, may have a salutary influence on the administration of the govern ment when formed, yet every one must be sensible of the contrary influence, which must have been experienced in the task of forming it.

Would it be wonderful if, under the pressure of all these difficulties, the convention should have been forced into some deviations from that artificial structure and regular symmetry which an abstract view of the subject might lead an ingenious theorist to bestow on a Constitution planned in his closet or in his imagination? The real wonder is that so many difficulties should have been surmounted, and surmounted with a unanimity almost as unprecedented as it must have been unexpected. It is impossible for any man of candor to reflect on this circumstance without partaking of the astonishment. It is impossible for the man of pious reflection not to perceive in it a finger of that Almighty hand which has been so frequently and signally extended to our relief in the critical stages of the revolution.

We had occasion, in a former paper, to take notice of the repeated trials which have been unsuccessfully made in the United Netherlands for reforming the baneful and notorious vices of their constitution. The history of almost all the great councils and consultations held among mankind for reconciling their discordant opinions, assuaging their mutual jealousies, and adjusting their respective interests, is a history of factions, contentions, and disappointments, and may be classed among the most dark and degraded pictures which display the infirmities and depravities of the human character. If, in a few scattered instances, a brighter aspect is presented, they serve only as exceptions to admonish us of the general truth; and by their lustre to darken the gloom of the adverse prospect to which they are contrasted. In revolving the causes from which these exceptions result, and applying them to the particular instances before us, we are necessarily led to two important conclusions. The first is, that the convention must have enjoyed, in a very singular degree, an exemption from the pestilential influence of party animosities—the disease most incident to deliberative bodies, and most apt to contaminate their proceedings. The second conclusion is that all the deputations composing the convention were satisfactorily accommodated by the final act, or were induced to accede to it by a deep conviction of the necessity of sacrificing private opinions and partial interests to the public good, and by a despair of seeing this necessity diminished by delays or by new experiments.

PUBLIUS

THE FEDERALIST NO. 39 (MADISON)

To the People of the State of New York:

The last paper having concluded the observations which were meant to introduce a candid survey of the plan of government reported by the convention, we now proceed to the execution of that part of our undertaking.

The first question that offers itself is, whether the general form and aspect of the government be strictly republican. It is evident that no other form would be reconcilable with the genius of the people of America; with the fundamental principles of the Revolution; or with that honorable determination which animates every votary of freedom, to rest all our political experiments on the capacity of mankind for self-government. If the plan of the convention, therefore, be found to depart from the republican character, its advocates must abandon it as no longer defensible.

What, then, are the distinctive characters of the republican form? . . .

If we resort for a criterion to the different principles on which different forms of government are established, we may define a republic to be, or at least may bestow that name on, a government which derives all its powers directly or indirectly from the great body of the people, and is administered by persons holding their offices during pleasure, for a limited period, or during good behavior. It is *essential* to such a government that it be derived from the great body of the society, not from an inconsiderable proportion, or a favored class of it; otherwise a handful of tyrannical nobles, exercising their oppressions by a delegation of their powers, might aspire to the rank of republicans, and claim for their government the honorable title of republic. It is *sufficient* for such a government that the persons administering it be appointed, either directly or indirectly, by the people; and that they hold their appointments by either of the tenures just specified; otherwise every government in the United States, as well as every other popular government that has been or can be well organized or well executed, would be degraded from the republican character. According to the constitution of every State in the Union, some or other of the officers of government are appointed indirectly only by the people. According to most of them, the chief magistrate himself is so appointed. And according to one, this mode of appointment is extended to one of the coördinate branches of the legislature. According to all the constitutions, also, the tenure of the highest offices is extended to a definite period, and in many instances, both within the legislative and executive departments, to a period of years. According to the provisions of most of the constitutions, again, as well as according to the most respectable and received opinions on the subject, the members of the judiciary department are to retain their offices by the firm tenure of good behavior.

On comparing the Constitution planned by the convention with the standard here fixed, we perceive at once that it is, in the most rigid sense, conformable to it. The House of Representatives, like that of one branch at least of all the State legislatures, is elected immediately by the great body of the people. The Senate, like the present Congress, and the Senate of Maryland, derives its appointment indirectly from the people. The President is indirectly derived from the choice of the people, according to the example in most of the States. Even the judges with all other officers of the Union, will, as in the several States, be the choice, though a remote choice, of the people themselves. The duration of the appointments is equally conformable to the republican standard, and to the model of State constitutions. The House of Representatives is periodically elective, as in all the States; and for the period of two years, as in the State of South Carolina. The Senate is elective, for the period of six years; which is but one year more than the period of the Senate of Maryland, and but two more than that of the Senates of New York and Virginia. The President is to continue in office for the period of four years; as in New York and Delaware the chief magistrate is elected for three years, and in South Carolina for two years. In the other States the election is annual. In several of the States, however, no constitutional provision is made for the impeachment of the chief magistrate. And in Delaware and Virginia he is not impeachable till out of office. The President of the United States is impeachable at any time during his continuance in office. The tenure by which the judges are to hold their places, is, as it unquestionably ought to be, that of good behavior. The tenure of the ministerial offices generally, will be a subject of legal regulation, conformably to the reason of the case and the example of the State constitutions.

Could any further proof be required of the republican complexion of this system, the most decisive one might be found in its absolute prohibition of titles of nobility, both under the federal and the State governments; and in its express guaranty of the republican form to each of the latter.

"But it was not sufficient," say the adversaries of the proposed Constitution, "for the convention to adhere to the republican form. They ought, with equal care, to have preserved the *federal* form, which regards the Union as a *Confederacy* of sovereign states; instead of which, they have framed a *national* government, which regards the Union as a *consolidation* of the States." And it is asked by what authority this bold and radical innovation was undertaken? The handle which has been made of this objection requires that it should be examined with some precision.

Without inquiring into the accuracy of the distinction on which the objection is founded, it will be necessary to a just estimate of its force, first, to ascertain the real character of the government in question; secondly, to inquire how far the convention were authorized to propose such a government; and thirdly, how far the duty they owed to their country could supply any defect of regular authority.

First.—In order to ascertain the real character of the government, it may be considered in relation to the foundation on which it is to be established; to the sources from which its ordinary powers are to be drawn; to the operation of those powers; to the extent of them; and to the authority by which future changes in the government are to be introduced.

On examining the first relation, it appears, on one hand, that the Constitution is to be founded on the assent and ratification of the people of America, given by deputies elected for the special purpose; but, on the other, that this assent and ratification is to be given by the people, not as individuals composing one entire nation, but as composing the distinct and independent States to which they respectively belong. It is to be the assent and ratification of the several States, derived from the supreme authority in each State,—the authority of the people themselves. The act, therefore, establishing the Constitution, will not be a *national,* but a *federal* act.

That it will be a federal and not a national act, as these terms are understood by the objectors; the act of the people, as forming so many independent States, not as forming one aggregate nation, is obvious from this single consideration, that it is to result neither from the decision of a *majority* of the people of the Union, nor from that of a *majority* of the States. It must result from the *unanimous* assent of the several States that are parties to it, differing no otherwise from their ordinary assent than in its being expressed, not by the legislative authority, but by that of the people themselves. Were the people regarded in this transaction as forming one nation, the will of the majority of the whole people of the United

States would bind the minority, in the same manner as the majority in each State must bind the minority; and the will of the majority must be determined either by a comparison of the individual votes, or by considering the will of the majority of the States as evidence of the will of a majority of the people of the United States. Neither of these rules has been adopted. Each State, in ratifying the Constitution, is considered as a sovereign body, independent of all others, and only to be bound by its own voluntary act. In this relation, then, the new Constitution will, if established, be a *federal*, and not a *national* constitution.

The next relation is, to the sources from which the ordinary powers of government are to be derived. The House of Representatives will derive its powers from the people of America; and the people will be represented in the same proportion, and on the same principle, as they are in the legislature of a particular State. So far the government is *national*, not *federal*. The Senate, on the other hand, will derive its powers from the States, as political and coequal societies; and these will be represented on the principle of equality in the Senate, as they now are in the existing Congress. So far the government is *federal*, not *national*. The executive power will be derived from a very compound source. The immediate election of the President is to be made by the States in their political characters. The votes allotted to them are in a compound ratio, which considers them partly as distinct and coequal societies, partly as unequal members of the same society. The eventual election, again, is to be made by that branch of the legislature which consists of the national representatives; but in this particular act they are to be thrown into the form of individual delegations, from so many distinct and coequal bodies politic. From this aspect of the government, it appears to be of a mixed character, presenting at least as many *federal* as *national* features.

The difference between a federal and national government, as it relates to the *operation of the government,* is supposed to consist in this, that in the former the powers operate on the political bodies composing the Confederacy, in their political capacities; in the latter, on the individual citizens composing the nation, in their individual capacities. On trying the Constitution by this criterion, it falls under the *national,* not the *federal* character; though perhaps not so completely as has been understood. In several cases, and particularly in the trial of controversies to which States may be parties, they must be viewed and proceeded against in their collective and political capacities only. So far the national countenance of the government on this side seems to be disfigured by a few federal features. But this blemish is perhaps unavoidable in any plan; and the operation of the government on the people, in their individual capacities, in its ordinary and most essential proceedings, may, on the whole, designate it, in this relation, a *national* government.

But if the government be national with regard to the *operation* of its powers, it changes its aspect again when we contemplate it in relation to the extent of its powers. The idea of a national government involves in it, not only an authority over the individual citizens, but an indefinite supremacy over all persons and things, so far as they are objects of lawful government. Among a people consolidated into one nation, this supremacy is completely vested in the national legislature. Among communities united for particular purposes, it is vested partly in the general and partly in the municipal legislatures. In the former case, all local authorities are subordinate to the supreme; and may be controlled, directed, or abolished by it at pleasure. In the latter, the local or municipal authorities form distinct and independent portions of the supremacy, no more subject, within their respective spheres, to the general authority, than the general authority is subject to them, within its own sphere. In this relation, then, the proposed government cannot be deemed a *national* one; since its jurisdiction extends to certain enumerated objects only, and leaves to the several States a residuary and inviolable sovereignty over all other objects. It is true that in controversies relating to the boundary between the two jurisdictions, the tribunal which is ultimately to decide, is to be established under the general government. But this does not change the principle of the case. The decision is to be impartially made, according to the rules of the Constitution; and all the usual and most effectual precautions are taken to secure this impartiality. Some such tribunal is clearly essential to prevent an appeal to the sword and a dissolution of the compact; and that it ought to be established under the general rather than under the local governments, or, to speak more properly, that it could be safely established under the first alone, is a position not likely to be combated.

If we try the Constitution by its last relation to the authority by which amendments are to be made, we find it neither wholly *national* nor wholly *federal*. Were it wholly national, the supreme and ultimate authority would reside in the *majority* of the people of the Union; and this authority would be competent at all times, like that of a majority of every national society, to alter or abolish its established government. Were it wholly federal, on the other hand, the concurrence of each State in the Union would be essential to every alteration that would be binding on all. The mode provided by the plan of the convention is not founded on either of these principles. In requiring more than a majority, and particularly in computing the proportion by *States,* not by *citizens,* it departs from the *national* and advances towards the *federal* character; in rendering the concurrence of less than the whole number of States sufficient, it loses again the *federal* and partakes of the *national* character.

The proposed Constitution, therefore, is, in strictness, neither a national nor a federal Constitution, but a composition of both. In its foundation it is federal, not national; in the sources from which the ordinary powers of the government are drawn, it is partly federal and partly national; in the operation of these powers, it is national, not federal; in the extent of them, again, it is federal, not national; and, finally, in the authoritative mode of introducing amendments, it is neither wholly federal nor wholly national.

PUBLIUS

THE FEDERALIST NO. 51 (MADISON)

To the People of the State of New York:

To what expedient, then, shall we finally resort, for maintaining in practice the necessary partition of power among the several departments, as laid down in the Constitution? The only answer that can be given is, that as all these exterior provisions are found to be inadequate, the defect must be supplied, by so contriving the interior structure of the government as that its several constituent parts may, by their mutual relations, be the means of keeping each other in their proper places. Without presuming to undertake a full development of this important idea, I will hazard a few general observations, which may perhaps place it in a clearer light, and enable us to form a more correct judgment of the principles and structure of the government planned by the convention.

In order to lay a due foundation for that separate and distinct exercise of the different powers of government, which to a certain extent is admitted on all hands to be essential to the preservation of liberty, it is evident that each department should have a will of its own; and consequently should be so constituted that the members of each should have as little agency as possible in the appointment of the members of the others. Were this principle rigorously adhered to, it would require that all the appointments for the supreme executive, legislative, and judiciary magistracies should be drawn from the same fountain of authority, the people, through channels having no communication whatever with one another. Perhaps such a plan of constructing the several departments would be less difficult in practice than it may in contemplation appear. Some difficulties, however, and some additional expense would attend the execution of it. Some deviations, therefore, from the principle must be admitted. In the constitution of the judiciary department in particular, it might be inexpedient to insist rigorously on the principle: first, because peculiar qualifications being essential in the members, the primary consideration ought to be to select that mode of choice which best secures these qualifications; secondly, because the permanent tenure by which the appointments are held in that department, must soon destroy all sense of dependence on the authority conferring them.

It is equally evident, that the members of each department should be as little dependent as possible on those of the others, for the emoluments annexed to their offices. Were the executive magistrate, or the judges, not independent of the legislature in this particular, their independence in every other would be merely nominal.

But the great security against a gradual concentration of the several powers in the same department, consists in giving to those who administer each department the necessary constitutional means and personal motives to resist encroachments of the others. The provision for defence must in this, as in all other cases, be made commensurate to the danger of attack. Ambition must be made to counteract ambition. The interest of the man must be connected with the constitutional rights of the place. It may be a reflection on human nature, that such devices should be necessary to control the abuses of government. But what is government itself, but the greatest of all reflections on human nature? If men were angels, no government would be necessary. If angels were to govern men, neither external nor internal controls on government would be necessary. In framing a government which is to be administered by men over men, the great difficulty lies in this: you must first enable the government to control the governed; and in the next place oblige it to control itself. A dependence on the people is, no doubt, the primary control on the government; but experience has taught mankind the necessity of auxiliary precautions.

This policy of supplying, by opposite and rival interests, the defect of better motives, might be traced through the whole system of human affairs, private as well as public. We see it particularly displayed in all the subordinate distributions of power, where the constant aim is to divide and arrange the several offices in such a manner as that each may be a check on the other—that the private interest of every individual may be a sentinel over the public rights. These inventions of prudence cannot be less requisite in the distribution of the supreme powers of the State.

But it is not possible to give to each department an equal power of self-defence. In republican government, the legislative authority necessarily predominates. The remedy for this inconveniency is to divide the legislature into different branches; and to render them, by different modes of election and different principles of action, as little connected with each other as the nature of their common functions and their common dependence on the society will admit. It may even be necessary to guard against dangerous encroachments by still further precautions.

As the weight of the legislative authority requires that it should be thus divided, the weakness of the executive may require, on the other hand, that it should be fortified. An absolute negative on the legislature appears, at first view, to be the natural defence with which the executive magistrate should be armed. But perhaps it would be neither altogether safe nor alone sufficient. On ordinary occasions it might not be exerted with the requisite firmness, and on extraordinary occasions it might be perfidiously abused. May not this defect of an absolute negative be supplied by some qualified connection between this weaker department and the weaker branch of the stronger department, by which the latter may be led to support the constitutional rights of the former, without being too much detached from the rights of its own department?

If the principles on which these observations are founded be just, as I persuade myself they are, and they be applied as a criterion to the several State constitutions, and to the federal Constitution, it will be found that if the latter does not perfectly correspond with them, the former are infinitely less able to bear such a test.

There are, moreover, two considerations particularly applicable to the federal system of America, which place that system in a very interesting point of view.

First. In a single republic, all the power surrendered by the people is submitted to the administration of a single government; and the usurpations are guarded against by a division of the government into distinct and separate departments. In the compound republic of America, the power surrendered by the people is first divided between two distinct governments, and then the portion allotted to each subdivided among distinct and separate departments. Hence a double security arises to the rights of the people. The different governments will control each other, at the same time each will be controlled by itself.

Second. It is of great importance in a republic not only to guard the society against the oppression of its rulers, but to guard one part of the society against the injustice of the other part. Different interests necessarily exist in different classes of citizens. If a majority be united by a common interest, the rights of the minority will be insecure. There are but two methods of providing against this evil: the one by creating a will in the community independent of the majority—that is, of the society itself; the other, by comprehending in the society so many separate descriptions of citizens as will render an unjust combination of a majority of the whole very improbable, if not impracticable. The first method prevails in all governments possessing an hereditary or self-appointed authority. This, at best, is but a precarious security; because a power independent of the society may as well espouse the unjust views of the major, as the rightful interests of the minor party, and may possibly be turned against both parties. The second method will be exemplified in the federal republic of the United States. Whilst all authority in it will be derived from and dependent on the society, the society itself will be broken into so many parts, interests and classes of citizens, that the rights of individuals, or of the minority, will be in little danger from interested combinations of the majority. In a free government the security for civil rights must be the same as that for religious rights. It consists in the one case in the multiplicity of interests, and in the other in the multiplicity of sects. The degree of security in both cases will depend on the number of interests and sects; and this may be presumed to depend on the extent of country and number of people comprehended under the same government. This view of the subject must particularly recommend a proper federal system to all the sincere and considerate friends of republican government, since it shows that in exact proportion as the territory of the Union may be formed into more circumscribed Confederacies, or States, oppressive combinations of a majority will be facilitated; the best security, under the republican forms, for the rights of every class of citizens, will be diminished; and consequently the stability and independence of some member of the government, the only other security, must be proportionally increased. Justice is the end of government. It is the end of civil society. It ever has been and ever will be pursued until it be obtained, or until liberty be lost in the pursuit. In a society under the forms of which the stronger faction can readily unite and oppress the weaker, anarchy may as truly be said to reign as in a state of nature, where the weaker individual is not secured against the violence of the stronger; and as, in the latter state, even the stronger individuals are prompted, by the uncertainty of their condition, to submit to a government which may protect the weak as well as them selves; so, in the former state, will the more powerful factions or parties be gradually induced, by a like motive, to wish for a government which will protect all parties, the weaker as well as the more powerful. It can be little doubted that if the State of Rhode Island was separated from the Confederacy and left to itself, the insecurity of rights under the popular form of government within such narrow limits would be displayed by such reiterated oppressions of factious majorities that some power altogether independent of the people would soon be called for by the voice of the very factions whose misrule had proved the necessity of it. In the extended republic of the United States, and among the great variety of interests, parties, and sects which it embraces, a coalition of a majority of the whole society could seldom take place on any other principles than those of justice and the general good; whilst there being thus less danger to a minor from the will of a major party, there must be less pretext, also, to provide for the security of the former, by introducing into the government a will not dependent on the latter, or, in other words, a will independent of the society itself. It is no less certain than it is important, notwithstanding the contrary opinions which have been entertained, that the larger the society, provided it lie within a practical sphere, the more duly capable it will be of self-government. And happily for the *republican cause,* the practicable sphere may be carried to a very great extent, by a judicious modification and mixture of the *federal principle.*

PUBLIUS

The Antifederalists

"CATO" (GOVERNOR GEORGE CLINTON OF NEW YORK)

The recital, or premises on which the new form of government is erected, declares a consolidation or union of all the thirteen parts, or states, into one great whole, under the form of the United States, for all the various and important purposes therein set forth. But whoever seriously considers the immense extent of territory comprehended within the limits of the United States, together with the variety of its climates, productions, and commerce, the difference of extent, and number of inhabitants in all; the dissimilitude of interest, morals, and politics, in almost every one, will receive it as an intuitive truth, that a consolidated republican form of government therein, can never *form a perfect union, establish justice, insure domestic tranquility, promote the general welfare, and secure the blessings of liberty to you and your posterity,* for to these objects it must be directed. This unkindred legislature therefore, composed of interests opposite and dissimilar in their nature, will in its exercise, emphatically be like a house divided against itself.

The governments of Europe have taken their limits and form from adventitious circumstances, and nothing can be argued on the motive of agreement from them; but these adventitious political principles have nevertheless produced effects that have attracted the attention of philosophy, which have established axioms in the science of politics therefrom, as irrefragable as any in Euclid. It is natural, says Montesquieu, *to a republic to have only a small territory, otherwise it cannot long subsist: in a large one, there are men of large fortunes, and consequently of less moderation; there are too great deposits to trust in the hands of a single subject; an ambitious person soon becomes sensible that he may be happy, great, and glorious by oppressing his fellow citizens, and that he might raise himself to grandeur, on the ruins of his country. In large republics, the public good is sacrificed to a thousand views; in a small one, the interest of the public is easily perceived, better understood, and more within the reach of every citizen; abuses have a less extent, and of course are less protected.* He also shows you, that the duration of the republic of

"Third Letter of 'Cato,'" in *The New-York Journal* (October 25, 1787); reprinted in Morton Borden, ed., *The Antifederalist Papers* (Lansing, Mich.: Michigan State University Press, 1965), pp. 36–38.

Sparta was owing to its having continued with the same extent of territory after all its wars; and that the ambition of Athens and Lacedemon to command and direct the union, lost them their liberties, and gave them a monarchy.

From this picture, what can you promise yourselves, on the score of consolidation of the United States into one government? Impracticability in the just exercise of it, your freedom insecure, even this form of government limited in its continuance, the employments of your country disposed of to the opulent, to whose contumely you will continually be an object. You must risk much, by indispensably placing trusts of the greatest magnitude, into the hands of individuals whose ambition for power, and aggrandizement, will oppress and grind you. Where, from the vast extent of your territory, and the complication of interests, the science of government will become intricate and perplexed, and too mysterious for you to understand and observe; and by which you are to be conducted into a monarchy, either limited or despotic; the latter, Mr. Locke remarks, *is a government derived from neither nature nor compact.*

Political liberty, the great Montesquieu again observes, *consists in security, or at least in the opinion we have of security;* and this *security,* therefore, or the *opinion,* is best obtained in moderate governments, where the mildness of the laws, and the equality of the manners, beget a confidence in the people, which produces this security, or the opinion. This moderation in governments depends in a great measure on their limits, connected with their political distribution.

The extent of many of the states of the Union, is at this time almost too great for the superintendence of a republican form of government, and must one day or other revolve into more vigorous ones, or by separation be reduced into smaller and more useful, as well as moderate ones. You have already observed the feeble efforts of Massachusetts against their insurgents; with what difficulty did they quell that insurrection; and is not the province of Maine at this moment on the eve of separation from her? The reason of these things is, that for the security of the *property* of the community—in which expressive term Mr. Locke makes life, liberty, and estate, to consist—the wheels of a republic are necessarily slow in their operation. Hence, in large free republics, the evil sometimes is not only begun, but almost completed, before they are in a situation to turn the current into a contrary progression. The extremes are also too remote from the usual seat of government, and the laws, therefore, too feeble to afford protection to all its parts, and insure *domestic tranquility* without the aid of another principle. If, therefore, this state [New York], and that of North Carolina, had an army under their control, they never would have lost Vermont, and Frankland, nor the state of Massachusetts suffered an insurrection, or the dismemberment of her fairest district; but the exercise of a principle which would have prevented these things, if we may believe the experience of ages, would have ended in the destruction of their liberties.

Will this consolidated republic, if established, in its exercise beget such confidence and compliance, among the citizens of these states, as to do without the aid of a standing army? I deny that it will. The malcontents in each state, who will not be a few, nor the least important, will be exciting factions against it. The fear of a dismemberment of some of its parts, and the necessity to enforce the execution of revenue laws (a fruitful source of oppression) on the extremes and in the other districts of the government, will incidentally and necessarily require a permanent force, to be kept on foot. Will not political security, and even the opinion of it, be extinguished? Can mildness and moderation exist in a government where the primary incident in its exercise must be force? Will not violence destroy confidence, and can equality subsist where the extent, policy, and practice of it will naturally lead to make odious distinctions among citizens?

"THE FEDERAL FARMER"
(RICHARD HENRY LEE OF VIRGINIA)

The representation is insubstantial and ought to be increased. In matters where there is much room for opinion, you will not expect me to establish my positions with mathematical certainty; you must only expect my observations to be candid, and such as are well founded in the mind of the writer. I am in a field where doctors disagree; and as to genuine representation, though no feature in government can be more important, perhaps, no one has been less understood, and no one that has received so imperfect a consideration by political writers. The ephori in Sparta, and the tribunes in Rome, were but the shadow; the representation in Great Britain is unequal and insecure. In America we have done more in establishing this important branch on its true principles, than, perhaps, all the world besides. Yet even here, I conceive, that very great improvements in representation may be made. In fixing this branch, the situation of the people must be surveyed, and the number of representatives and forms of election apportioned to that situation. When we find a numerous people settled in a fertile and extensive country, possessing equality, and few or none of them oppressed with riches or wants, it ought to be the anxious care of the constitution and laws, to arrest them from national depravity, and to preserve them in their happy condition. A virtuous people make just laws,

"The Federal Farmer," in a pamphlet entitled "An Additional Number of Letters from The Federal Farmer to the Republican . . ." (1788), reprinted in Morton Borden, *op. cit.*, pp. 158–162.

and good laws tend to preserve unchanged a virtuous people. A virtuous and happy people by laws uncongenial to their characters, may easily be gradually changed into servile and depraved creatures. Where the people, of their representatives, make the laws, it is probable they will generally be fitted to the national character and circumstances, unless the representation be partial, and the imperfect substitute of the people. However the people may be electors, if the representation be so formed as to give one or more of the natural classes of men in society an undue ascendency over others, it is imperfect; the former will gradually become masters, and the latter slaves. It is the first of all among the political balances, to preserve in its proper station each of these classes. We talk of balances in the legislature and among the departments of government; we ought to carry them to the body of the people. Since I advanced the idea of balancing the several orders of men in a community, in forming a genuine representation, and seen that idea considered as chimerical, I have been sensibly struck with a sentence in the Marquis Beccaria's treatise. This sentence was quoted by Congress in 1774, and is as follows:—"In every society there is an effort continually tending to confer on one part the height of power and happiness, and to reduce the others to the extreme of weakness and misery; the intent of good laws is to oppose this effort, and to diffuse their influence universally and equally." Add to this Montesquieu's opinion, that "in a free state every man, who is supposed to be a free agent, ought to be concerned in his own government: therefore, the legislative should reside in the whole body of the people, or their representatives." It is extremely clear that these writers had in view the several orders of men in society, which we call aristocratical, democratical, mercantile, mechanic, etc., and perceived the efforts they are constantly, from interested and ambitious views, disposed to make to elevate themselves and oppress others. Each order must have a share in the business of legislation actually and efficiently. It is deceiving a people to tell them they are electors, and can choose their legislators, if they cannot, in the nature of things, choose men from among themselves, and genuinely like themselves. I wish you to take another idea along with you. We are not only to balance these natural efforts, but we are also to guard against accidental combinations; combinations founded in the connections of offices and private interests, both evils which are increased in proportion as the number of men, among which the elected must be, are decreased. To set this matter in a proper point of view, we must form some general ideas and descriptions of the different classes of men, as they may be divided by occupation and politically. The first class is the aristocratical. There are three kinds of aristocracy spoken of in this country—the first is a constitutional one, which does not exist in the United States in our common acceptation of the word. Montesquieu, it is true, observes that where part of the persons in a society, for want of property, age, or moral character, are excluded any share in the government, the others, who alone are the constitutional electors and elected, form this aristocracy. This, according to him, exists in each of the United States, where a considerable number of persons, as all convicted of crimes, under age, or not possessed of certain property, are excluded any share in the government. The second is an aristocratic faction, a junto of unprincipled men, often distinguished for their wealth or abilities, who combine together and make their object their private interests and aggrandizement. The existence of this description is merely accidental, but particularly to be guarded against. The third is the natural aristocracy; this term we use to designate a respectable order of men, the line between whom and the natural democracy is in some degree arbitrary. We may place men on one side of this line, which others may place on the other, and in all disputes between the few and the many, a considerable number are wavering and uncertain themselves on which side they are, or ought to be. In my idea of our natural aristocracy in the United States, I include about four or five thousand men; and among these I reckon those who have been placed in the offices of governors, of members of Congress, and state senators generally, in the principal officers of the army and militia, the superior judges, the most eminent professional men, etc., and men of large property. The other persons and orders in the community form the natural democracy; this includes in general, the yeomanry, the subordinate officers, civil and military, the fishermen, mechanics and traders, many of the merchants and professional men. It is easy to perceive that men of these two classes, the aristocratical and democratical, with views equally honest, have sentiments widely different, especially respecting public and private expenses, salaries, taxes, etc. Men of the first class associate more extensively, have a high sense of honor, possess abilities, ambition, and general knowledge; men of the second class are not so much used to combining great objects; they possess less ambition, and a larger share of honesty; their dependence is principally on middling and small estates, industrious pursuits, and hard labor, while that of the former is principally on the emoluments of large estates, and of the chief offices of government. Not only the efforts of these two great parties are to be balanced, but other interests and parties also, which do not always oppress each other merely for want of power, and for fear of the consequences; though they, in fact, mutually depend on each other. Yet such are their general views, that the merchants alone would never fail to make laws favorable to themselves and oppressive to the farmers. The farmers alone would act on like principles; the former would tax the land, the latter the trade. The manufacturers are often disposed to contend for monopolies; buyers make every exertion to lower prices; and sellers to raise them. Men who live by fees and salaries endeavor to raise them; and the part of the people who pay them, endeavor to lower them; the public creditors to augment the taxes, and the people at large to lessen them. Thus, in every period of society, and in all the transactions of men, we see parties verifying the observation made by the Marquis; and those classes which have not their centinels in the government, in proportion to what they have to gain or lose, must infallibly be ruined.

Efforts among parties are not merely confined to property. They contend for rank and distinctions; all their passions in turn are enlisted in political controversies. Men, elevated in society, are often disgusted with the changeableness of the democracy, and the latter are often agitated with the passions of jealousy and envy. The yeomanry possess a large share of property and strength, are nervous and firm in their opinions and habits; the mechanics of towns are ardent and changeable—honest and credulous, they are inconsiderable for numbers, weight and strength, not always sufficiently stable for supporting free governments; the fishing interest partakes partly of the strength and stability of the landed, and partly of the changeableness of the mechanic interest. As to merchants and traders, they are our agents in almost all money transactions, give activity to government, and possess a considerable share of influence in it. It has been observed by an able writer, that frugal industrious merchants are generally advocates for liberty. It is an observation, I believe, well founded, that the schools produce but few advocates for republican forms of government. Gentlemen of the law, divinity, physic, etc., probably form about a fourth part of the people; yet their political influence, perhaps, is equal to that of all the other descriptions of men. If we may judge from the appointments to Congress, the legal characters will often, in a small representation, be the majority; but the more the representatives are increased, the more of the farmers, merchants, etc., will be found to be brought into the government.

These general observations will enable you to discern what I intend by different classes, and the general scope of my ideas, when I contend for uniting and balancing their interests, feelings, opinions, and views in the legislature. We may not only so unite and balance these as to prevent a change in the government by the gradual exaltation of one part to the depression of others, but we may derive many other advantages from the combination and full representation. A small representation can never be well informed as to the circumstances of the people. The members of it must be too far removed from the people, in general, to sympathize with them, and too few to communicate with them. A representation must be extremely imperfect where the representatives are not circumstanced to make the proper communications to their constituents, and where the constituents in turn cannot, with tolerable convenience, make known their wants, circumstances, and opinions to their representatives. Where there is but one representative to 30,000 or 40,000 inhabitants, it appears to me, he can only mix and be acquainted with a few respectable characters among his constituents. Even double the general representation, and then there must be a very great distance between the representatives and the people in general represented. On the proposed plan, the state of Delaware, the city of Philadelphia, the state of Rhode Island, the province of Maine, the county of Suffolk in Massachusetts, will have one representative each. There can be but little personal knowledge, or but few communications, between him and the people at large of either of those districts. It has been observed that mixing only with the respectable men, he will get the best information and ideas from them; he will also receive impressions favorable to their purposes particularly. . . .

Could we get over all our difficulties respecting a balance of interests and party efforts, to raise some and oppress others, the want of sympathy, information and intercourse between the representatives and the people, an insuperable difficulty will still remain. I mean the constant liability of a small number of representatives to private combinations. The tyranny of the one, or the licentiousness of the multitude, are, in my mind, but small evils, compared with the factions of the few. It is a consideration well worth pursuing, how far this house of representatives will be liable to be formed into private juntos, how far influenced by expectations of appointments and offices, how far liable to be managed by the president and senate, and how far the people will have confidence in them.

THE FEDERAL FARMER

Patrick Henry

SPEECH AGAINST
THE PROPOSED CONSTITUTION

MR. HENRY. Mr. Chairman, I am much obliged to the very worthy gentleman for his encomium. I wish I was possessed with talents, or possessed of
any thing that might enable me to elucidate this great subject. I am not
free from suspicion: I am apt to entertain doubts. I rose yesterday to ask a
question which arose in my own mind. When I asked that question, I
thought the meaning of my interrogation was obvious. The fate of this
question and of America may depend on this. Have they said, We, the
states? Have they made a proposal of a compact between states? If they
had, this would be a confederation. It is otherwise most clearly a consolidated government. The question turns, sir, on that poor little thing—the
expression, We, the *people,* instead of the *states,* of America. I need not
take much pains to show that the principles of this system are extremely
pernicious, impolitic, and dangerous. Is this a monarchy, like England—a
compact between prince and people, with checks on the former to secure
the liberty of the latter? Is this a confederacy, like Holland—an association
of a number of independent states, each of which retains its individual
sovereignty? It is not a democracy, wherein the people retain all their
rights securely. Had these principles been adhered to, we should not have
been brought to this alarming transition, from a confederacy to a consolidated government. We have no detail of these great considerations, which,
in my opinion, ought to have abounded before we should recur to a
government of this kind. Here is a resolution as radical as that which
separated us from Great Britain. It is radical in this transition; our rights
and privileges are endangered, and the sovereignty of the states will be
relinquished: and cannot we plainly see that this is actually the case? The
rights of conscience, trial by jury, liberty of the press, all your immunities
and franchises, all pretensions to human rights and privileges, are rendered insecure, if not lost, by this change, so loudly talked of by some, and
inconsiderately by others. Is this tame relinquishment of rights worthy of

Jonathan Elliot, *The Debates in the Several State Conventions on the Adoption
of the Federal Constitution,* Vol. III, pp. 43–65.

freemen? Is it worthy of that manly fortitude that ought to characterize republicans? . . .

There are sufficient guards placed against sedition and licentiousness; for, when power is given to this government to suppress these, or for any other purpose, the language it assumes is clear, express, and unequivocal; but when this Constitution speaks of privileges, there is an ambiguity, sir, a fatal ambiguity—an ambiguity which is very astonishing. In the clause under consideration, there is the strangest language that I can conceive. I mean, when it says that there shall not be more representatives than one for every thirty thousand. Now, sir, how easy is it to evade this privilege! "The number shall not exceed one for every thirty thousand." This may be satisfied by one representative from each state. Let our numbers be ever so great, this immense continent may, by this artful expression, be reduced to have but thirteen representatives. I confess this construction is not natural; but the ambiguity of the expression lays a good ground for a quarrel. Why was it not clearly and unequivocally expressed, that they should be entitled to have one for every thirty thousand? This would have obviated all disputes; and was this difficult to be done? What is the inference? When population increases, and a state shall send representatives in this proportion, Congress *may* remand them, because the right of having one for every thirty thousand is not clearly expressed. This possibility of reducing the number to one for each state approximates to probability by that other expression—"but each state shall at least have one representative." Now, is it not clear that, from the first expression, the number might be reduced so much that some states should have no representatives at all, were it not for the insertion of this last expression? And as this is the only restriction upon them, we may fairly conclude that they *may* restrain the number to one from each state. Perhaps the same horrors may hang over my mind again. I shall be told I am continually afraid: but, sir, I have strong cause of apprehension. In some parts of the plan before you, the great rights of freemen are endangered; in other parts, absolutely taken away. How does your trial by jury stand? In civil cases gone—not sufficiently secured in criminal—this best privilege is gone. But we are told that we need not fear; because those in power, being our representatives, will not abuse the powers we put in their hands. I am not well versed in history, but I will submit to your recollection, whether liberty has been destroyed most often by the licentiousness of the people, or by the tyranny of rulers. I imagine, sir, you will find the balance on the side of tyranny. Happy will you be if you miss the fate of those nations, who, omitting to resist their oppressors, or negligently suffering their liberty to be wrested from them, have groaned under intolerable despotism! Most of the human race are now in this deplorable condition; and those nations who have gone in search of grandeur, power, and splendor, have also fallen a sacrifice, and been the victims of their own folly. While they acquired those visionary blessings, they lost their freedom. My great objection to this government is, that it does not leave us the means of defending our rights, or of waging war against tyrants. . . .

What, sir, is the genius of democracy? Let me read that clause of the bill of rights of Virginia which relates to this: 3d clause:—that government is, or ought to be, instituted for the common benefit, protection, and security of the people, nation, or community. Of all the various modes and forms of government, that is best, which is capable of producing the greatest degree of happiness and safety, and is most effectually secured against the danger of mal-administration; and that whenever any government shall be found inadequate, or contrary to those purposes, a majority of the community hath an indubitable, unalienable, and indefeasible right to reform, alter, or abolish it, in such manner as shall be judged most conducive to the public weal.

This, sir, is the language of democracy—that a majority of the community have a right to alter government when found to be oppressive. But how different is the genius of your new Constitution from this! How different from the sentiments of freemen, that a contemptible minority can prevent the good of the majority! If, then, gentlemen, standing on this ground, are come to that point, that they are willing to bind themselves and their posterity to be oppressed, I am amazed and inexpressibly astonished. If this be the opinion of the majority, I must submit; but to me, sir, it appears perilous and destructive. I cannot help thinking so. Perhaps it may be the result of my age. These may be feelings natural to a man of my years, when the American spirit has left him, and his mental powers, like the members of the body, are decayed. If, sir, amendments are left to the twentieth, or tenth part of the people of America, your liberty is gone forever. We have heard that there is a great deal of bribery practised in the House of Commons, in England, and that many of the members raise themselves to preferments by selling the rights of the whole of the people. But, sir, the tenth part of that body cannot continue oppressions on the rest of the people. English liberty is, in this case, on a firmer foundation than American liberty. It will be easily contrived to procure the opposition of one tenth of the people to any alteration, however judicious. The honorable gentleman who presides told us that, to prevent abuses in our government, we will assemble in Convention, recall our delegated powers, and punish our servants for abusing the trust reposed in them. O sir, we should have fine times, indeed, if, to punish tyrants, it were only sufficient to assemble the people! Your arms, wherewith you could defend yourselves, are gone; and you have no longer an aristocrati- cal, no longer a democratical spirit. Did you ever read of any revolution in a nation, brought about by the punishment of those in power, inflicted by those who had no power at all? You read of a riot act in a country which is called one of the freest in the world, where a few neighbors cannot assemble without the risk of being shot by a hired soldiery, the engines of despotism. We may see such an act in America. . . . If we admit this consolidated government, it will be because we like a great, splendid one. Some way or other we must be a great and mighty empire; we must have an army, and a navy, and a number of things. When the American spirit was in its youth, the language of America was different: liberty, sir, was then the primary object. We are descended from a people whose government was founded on liberty: our glorious forefathers of Great Britain made liberty the foundation of everything. That country is become a great, mighty, and splendid nation; not because their government is strong and energetic, but, sir, because liberty is its direct end and foundation. We drew the spirit of liberty from our British ancestors: by that spirit we have triumphed over every difficulty. But now, sir, the American spirit, assisted by the ropes and chains of consolidation, is about to convert this country into a powerful and mighty empire. If you make the citizens of this country agree to become the subjects of one great consolidated empire of America, your government will not have sufficient energy to keep them together. Such a government is incompatible with the genius of republicanism. There will be no checks, no real balances, in this government. What can avail your specious, imaginary balances, your rope-dancing, chain-rattling, ridiculous ideal checks and contrivances? But, sir, we are not feared by foreigners; we do not make nations tremble. Would this constitute happiness, or secure liberty? I trust, sir, our political hemisphere will ever direct their operations to the security of those objects.

Consider our situation, sir: go to the poor man, and ask him what he does. He will inform you that he enjoys the fruits of his labor, under his own fig-tree, with his wife and children around him, in peace and security. Go to every other member of society,—you will find the same tranquil ease and content; you will find no alarms or disturbances. Why, then, tell us of danger, to terrify us into an adoption of this new form of government? And yet who knows the dangers that this new system may produce? They are out of the sight of the common people: they cannot foresee latent consequences. I dread the operation of it on the middling and lower classes of people: it is for them I fear the adoption of this system. I fear I tire the patience of the committee; but I beg to be indulged with a few more observations. When I thus profess myself an advocate for the liberty of the people, I shall be told I am a designing man, that I am to be a great man, that I am to be a demagogue; and many similar illiberal insinuations will be thrown out: but, sir, conscious rectitude outweighs those things with me. I see great jeopardy in this new government. I see none from our present one.

William Manning

THE KEY OF LIBBERTY

To all the Republicans, Farmers, Mecanicks, and Labourers in America
your Canded attention is Requested to the Sentiments of a Labourer.

I am not a Man of Larning my selfe for I neaver had the advantage
of six months schooling in my life. I am no travelor for I neaver was 50
Miles from whare I was born in no direction, & I am no grate reader of
antiant history for I always followed hard labour for a living. But I always
thought it My duty to search into & see for my selfe in all maters that
consansed me as a member of society, & when the war began betwen
Brittan & Amarica I was in the prime of Life & highly taken up with
Liberty & a free Government. I See almost the first blood that was shed
in Concord fite & scores of men dead, dying & wounded in the Cause of
Libberty, which caused serious sencations in my mind.

But I beleived then & still believ it is a good cause which we aught to
defend to the very last, & I have bin a Constant Reader of publick Newspapers & closely attended to men & measures ever sence, through the
war, through the operation of paper money, framing Constitutions,
makeing & constructing Laws, & seeing what selfish & contracted ideayes
of interests would influence the best picked men & bodyes of men.

I have often thought it was imposable ever to seport a free Government, but firmly believing it to be the best sort & the ondly one approved
off by heaven it was my unweryed study & prayers to the almighty for
many years to find out the real cause & a remidy and I have for many
years bin satisfyed in my own mind what the causes are & what would
in a grate measure prove à reamidy provided it was carried into efect.

But I had no thoughts of publishing my sentiments on it untill the
adoption of the British trety in the manner it has bin done. But seeing
the unweryed pains & the unjustifyable masures taken by large numbers
of all ordirs of men who git a living without labour in Elections & many
other things to ingure the interests of the Labourer & deprive us of the
priviledges of a free government, I came to a resolution (although I have

From "William Manning's 'The Key of Libberty,'" edited by Samuel Eliot
Morison, first published in the *William and Mary Quarterly,* Vol. XIII, No. 2, 1956.
Reprinted by permission of Samuel Eliot Morison and the *William and Mary Quarterly.*

nither larning nor lasure for the purpose) to improve on my Constitutional Right & give you my sentiments on what the causes are & a remidy. . . .

A GENERAL DESCRIPTION OF THE CAUSES THAT RUEN REPUBLICKS

The Causes that I shall Indeavor to Make appear are a Conceived Difference of Interests Betwen those that Labour for a Living & those that git a Living without Bodily Labour.

This is no new docterin if I may judge from the many scraps of history I have Seen of antiant Republicks. The best information I ever had on this Subject & the gratest colection of historical accounts was by a writer who wrote ten long numbers in the Chronicle in December [17]85 & January 86 stileing himselfe a Free Republican.

In his 4 first numbers he recites a long & blody history about the fudes & animosityes, contentions & blood sheds that hapned in the antiant Republicks of Athens, Greesh & Roome & many other nations, betwen the few & Many, the Perthiens, & Plebians, Rich & poor, Dettor & Creditor, &cc. In his 5th No. he draws the dividing line betwen the few & the many as they apply to us in Amarica—amongue the few he reacons the marchent, phesition the lawyer & divine and all in the literary walkes of Life, the Juditial & Executive oficers & all the rich who could live with out bodily labour, so that the hole controvercy was betwen those that labour for a living & those who do not. Then tryes to prove that unless these few can have wait or influence in the Government according to their property & high stations in life it can not be free. Then goes on to shew how a government aught to be ballenced and proposes grate alterations in the Constitution of Masachusets—better to acomidate the Interests of the few—wishes to have the Senet represent the hole property of the State & the Representitives the persons ondly, & the Govenour to have as compleet a nagative on both as the King of Ingland has on the Parlement, which he thinks cant be so long as the people vote annully for Govenour & Senetors.

These Sentiments being urged in such a masterly manner just before the adoption of the federal Constitution, & have bin so closely followed by the administration eversence, (although they are directly contrary to the prinsaples of a free government & no dout written to destroy it) yet if they ware republished they would be of servis to the peopel in many things & convince the author (if he is yet alive) that his unweried resarches for his ten numbers ware not intirely lost any more than the doings of Josephs Brethering ware when they sold him into Egypt, & they would prove the truth of the reasons I give & the need of the Remidy I shall describe.

I have often Looked over those ten Nos. & Searched other historyes to satisfy my selfe as to the truth of his asertions, but am very far from thinking as he doth—that the destruction of free governments arises from the Licentiousness of the Many or their Representatives, but on the conterary shall indever to prove that their destruction always arises from the ungoverned dispositions & Combinations of the few, & the ignorance of the Many. Which I Shall attempt in the following Manner:—

1. Give a Description of Mankind & nesecaty of Government. 2ly. Give a Description of a free government & its administration. 3ly Shew how the few & Many differ in interests under its opperation. 4ly Shew how & by what meens the few destroy it. 5ly Elustrate by sundry remarkes on the opperations of these causes in our governments. . . .

To search into & know our selves is of the gratest importance, & the want of it is the cause of the gratest evils suffered in Society. If we knew what alterations might be made in our Minds & Conduct by alterations in our Edication, age, Circumstances, & Conditions in this Life, we should be vastly less sensorious on others for their conduct, & more cautious of of trusting them when their was no need of it.

Men are born & grow up in this world with a vast veriaty of capacityes, strength & abilityes both of Body & Mind, & have strongly implanted within them numerous pashons & lusts continually urging them to fraud violence & acts of injustis toards one another. He has implanted in him a sence of Right & Rong, so that if he would always follow the dictates of Contiance & consider the advantages of Society & mutual assistance he would need no other Law or Government. Yet as he is sentanced by the just decrees of heaven to hard Labour for a Living in this world, & has so strongly implanted in him a desire of Selfe Seporte, Selfe Defence, Selfe Love, Selfe Conceit, Selfe Importance, & Selfe agrandisement, that it Ingroses all his care and attention so that he can see nothing beyond Selfe—for Selfe (as once described by a Divine) is like an object plased before the eye that hinders the sight of every thing beyond.

This Selfishness may be deserned in all persons, let their conditions in life be what they will, & it opperates so pourfully as to disqualify them from judgeing impartially in their own cause, & a persons being raised to stations of high Honour & trust doth not clear him from this selfeishness. But on the conterary it is a solemn truth that the higher a Man is raised in stations of honour power and trust the greater are his temtations to do rong & gratify those selfeish prinsaples. Give a man honour & he wants more. Give him power & he wants more. Give him money & he wants more. In short he is neaver easy, but the more he has the more he wants.

The most comprehensive description of Man I ever saw was by a writer as followeth:—Viz—Man is a being made up of Selfe Love seeking his own hapiness to the misery of all around him, who would Damne a world to save him selfe from temporal or other punishment, & he who denyes this to be his real carrictor is ignorant of him selfe, or else is more than a man.

Many persons ware they to hear such a description of themselves would cry out as Haziel did, 'what, is thy Servent a Dog' &cc. But if they should once git into the circumstances he was in, & have the power & temtations he had, they would prove themselves to be just such a Doge as he did. Haman is annother striking evidence of the depravity & pride of the human hart, for though he could boste of the highest preferments in the gratest kingdom on Earth, the poor Divel exclamed 'all this avails me nothing so long as Mordica refuses to bow the knee.'

From this disposition of Man or the depravity of the human hart, arises not ondly the advantage but the absolute nesecaty of Sivil government—without it Mankind would be continually at war on their own spetia, stealing roving fighting with & killing one another. This all Nations on Earth have bin convinced off, and have established it in some form or other, & their soul aime in doing it is their safty & hapyness. But for want of wisdom or some plan to curb the ambition & govern those to hoom they gave power, they have often bin brought to suffer as Much under their governments as they would without any—and it still remains uncartain wheather any such plan can be found out or not. . . .

A free Government is a government of laws made by the free consent of a majority of the hole people, But as it is Impossable for a hole Nation to meet to gether & deliberate, So all their laws Must be made judged & executed by men chosen & appointed for that purpose. And the Duty of all those men are to act & do in makeing judging & executing those laws just as all the people would, provided they ware all together & equilly knew what was for their interest. If any of said officers or any who are chosen to elect or appoint any person into office doth any thing conterary to the true interests of the majority of the peopel, he violates his trust and aught to be punnished for it. . . .

In the swet of thy face shall thou git thy bread untill thou return to the ground, is the erivarsable sentance of Heaven on Man for his rebellion. To be sentanced to hard Labour dureing life is very unplesent to humane Nature. Their is a grate avartion to it purceivable in all men—yet it is absolutly nesecary that a large majority of the world should labour, or we could not subsist. For Labour is the soul parrant of all property—the land yealdeth nothing without it, & their is no food, clothing, shelter, vessel, or any nesecary of life but what costs Labour & is generally esteemed valuable according to the Labour it costs. Therefore no person can posess property without labouring, unless he git it by force or craft, fraud or fortun out of the earnings of others.

But from the grate veriety of capacietyes strength & abilityes of men, their always was, & always will be, a very unequel distribution of property in the world. Many are so rich that they can live without Labour. Also the marchent, phisition, lawyer & divine, the philosipher and school master, the Juditial & Executive Officers, & many others who could honestly git a living without bodily labours. As all these professions require a considerable expence of time & property to qualify themselves therefor, & as no person after this qualifying himselfe & making a pick on a profession by which he meens to live, can desire to have it dishonourable or unproductive, so all these professions naturally unite in their skems to make their callings as honourable & lucrative as possable. Also as ease & rest from Labour are reaconed amongue the gratest pleasures of Life, pursued by all with the greatest avidity & when attained at once creates a sense of superiority & as pride & ostentation are natural to the humain harte, these ordirs of men generally asotiate together and look down with two much contempt on those that labour.

On the other hand the Labourer being contious that it is Labour that seports the hole, & that the more there is that live without Labour & the higher they live or the grater their salleryes & fees are, so much the harder he must work, or the shorter he must live, this makes the Labourer watch the other with a jelous eye & often has reason to complain of real impositions. . . .

On the federal Constitution

The Federal Constitution by a fair construction is a good one prinsapaly, but I have no dout but that the Convention who made it intended to destroy our free governments by it, or they neaver would have spent 4 Months in making such an inexpliset thing. As one said at the time of its adoption, it is made like a Fiddle, with but few Strings, but so that the ruling Majority could play any tune upon it they pleased. The tretymaking power which has caused to much rout was as well garded as any part of it, but as it has bin exercised, destroys the hole foundation & end the peopel had in makeing of it. For the soul end the peopel had in vue was to establish a government for national purposes ondly, reserving local consarns to the State governments, & in ordir that it mite be Representitive, declared that they would not be represented with less than one from every thirty or forty thousand inhabitants, in said government.

The letter of the Constitution as it respects the trety stands thus. In part ıt Sect ıt it saith—All Lejeslative powers herein granted shall be vested in a Congress of the United States, which shall consist of a Senet & a house of Representitives, & it declares that all powers & soverantyes not expresly given to Congress, is reserved to the State Governments, & all the express powers given to Congress are enumerated in part ıt Sect

8th without the least excepttion for any legeslative athority aniwheir else. In part 2d Sect 2d their is a solitary claws that Saith the president shall have power by & with the advice & consent of the Senit to make tretyes—but dont say what kind of tretyes—and their are saveral sorts of them. Their are tretyes of peace with foron nations, & with rebels & insurgents, that need no law to carry them into execution. These he may make with advice &cc but not without, for this clause must be considered as a restriction rather than an inlargement of his power. For the true & ondly meening of the letter of the Constitution & of the peopel that excepted of it, was that all tretyes & dealings with forron nations should be done by the supreem authority of the Nation, which is the Legeslative power, & negotiated through the president, in the same manner as the president corrasponds with foron Ministers through his sicratary.

Much has bin said about treatys being the Supreem Law of the Land, which if admited would finely inlarge the power of the Juditial & innable them by constructions to destroy all our laws. But I cant se a word of it in the Constitution. In part 6th their is a clause that plainly declares that the Federal Constitution, the federal laws, & all treetys shall be supreem to the state laws & constitutions, but nothing determining which of the three is supreem, excepting that it appears reasonable to take them as they stand, viz:—it the Constitution. 2dly, the Laws. 3dly, tretys.

By such an explanation the Judge is bound by his oath not to give judgment against either of them in favour of a treaty. If he doth he pergures himselfe. I would not be understoot that I think tretyes are less binding than laws when they are constitutially made, for it is the duty of the federal Legeslature to see that the Constitution, tretyes and laws do not clash with each other, & as their objects of legeslation are few they are to blame if their is any clash. Consiquently the bisness of the Juditial & Executive powers must be clear & plane.

This is a fair construction of the letter of the Constitution & the sence & meening of the peopel when they excepted it. As to the mening of the Convention that formed it, it has nothing to do in the question, & it was an insult on the peopel to keep their debates secret at that time, & a grater one to site us to them now for an explanation, as Worshington did to the house of Representitives. The peopel excepted of it as it is, & no other way. So that the plane truth is that the British trety was unconstitutionly & treasonably made & those that made it aught to have bin impeached & brought to tryal immediately, before—ah here is the rub. The house of Representitives can impeach by a bare majority, but the Senet must try all impeachments, & two thirds of them agreed before they can punnish, so that in this case one halfe the trators must agree to condemn themselves before any of them can be condemned. Blush

Amaricans, blush at your bosted Constitution. This proves the dainger of chuseing Senetors or men into office for 6 or even four years, for it was known & published in Ingland long before the treaty arived in Amarica that 20 of our Senetors had agreed to sign the treaty before they see it.

The conduct of the president in his apointing men to office & turning out those that are faithfull to their trust, as he did in turning out Mr. Munro & others, proves the dainger & folly of trusting men with such grate powers, that are elected so sildom into office. When the patriotick State of Virginia moved for amendments to the Constitution so as to have the time shortned for the election of Senetors & another tribunal for the tryol of impeachments, I thought & am still confident that their might be corts erected in each district to try impeachments & remove from & appoint to all offices within the same, & every man be well paid for his services with less cost than we are now at. For it appears very unreasonable & absurd for a hole Legeslature or any branch of it to be detained on a tryal of impeachment & witnesses to travel 500 Miles when the hole issew is ondly the loss of a pety office, when their is hundreds stand ready to fill them that can sarve the publick better than those removed. Some may say that if such corts ware erected it would discorage men from undertaking in offices, but I dare say that if the duties of officers ware made as plain as they might be by the Legeslature & a single blunder in an officer was made Death, their would be anough of defitient abilityes that would undertake for halfe the pay some of them receiv now. But these alterations never will take place without better meens of knowledge amongue the peopel.

4
MAJORITY RULE

All, too, will bear in mind this sacred principle, that though the will of the majority is in all cases to prevail, that will to be rightful must be reasonable; that the minority possess their equal rights, which equal laws must protect, and to violate would be oppression.

THOMAS JEFFERSON, First Inaugural Address, 1801

The first principle of our system—THAT THE MAJORITY IS TO GOVERN . . . as few impediments as possible should exist to the free operation of the public will.

ANDREW JACKSON, First Message to Congress, 1829

The ratification of the Constitution may have completed the American "founding," but it did not answer serious questions concerning the nature of a nation "so conceived and so dedicated." Americans are indebted to a Frenchman, Alexis de Tocqueville, for the first comprehensive attempt to answer these questions and to show how the principles of liberty and equality operate in American society. In *Democracy in America,* Tocqueville analyzed social conditions in America with a view toward understanding their causes—physical, historical, and philosophical—and potential effects. What he discovered was a society characterized by almost total acceptance of the principles of the Declaration of Independence, with an especial emphasis on equality. This discovery is indicative of Tocqueville's discerning eye but, more importantly, is also indicative of the force of the principles of the Declaration. The country which Tocqueville visited—Jacksonian America—had, in large degree, borne out the promises of its founding. Young in years, it was mature in the sense of its political principles. As Professors Mason and Meyers suggest, it was "the" place to study the interplay of equality and liberty:

Barring slavery, America in the second quarter of the nineteenth century may well have come closer to realizing the ideals of our Declaration of Independence than at any time before or since.

When the Jacksonian movement formed in the late 1820's, America was far
out upon a democratic course. . . . Government by the people was largely
a matter of consensus and of wont. Basic principles and institutions were
firmly settled; only their legal elaboration . . . was recent and still in
progress.[1]

Tocqueville was fortunate. He had set out to study democracy and, in
America, discovered a place where the "democratic revolution" was
practically complete.

I confess that in America I saw more than America; I sought the image of
democracy itself, with its inclinations, its character, its prejudices, and
its passions, in order to learn what we have to fear or to hope from
its progress.[2]

He was not disappointed; in America evidence existed to support both
fear and hope for the future of democracy. The ultimate response would
depend on how the relationship of the democratic impulses toward
equality and liberty developed.

     According to *Democracy in America* the very fact that equality
of social condition is almost universal in America is the source of the
fear for America's future. Egalitarian principle wedded to egalitarian
social conditions tends to endanger liberty and individuality. The
democratic urge for equality is never satisfied. Indeed, as one approaches
equality, both the urge for more and the frustration with its denial
increase in strength. The slave may be happy for an additional piece of
bread but men possessed by the idea of equality will be satisfied with
nothing less than that which their neighbors have, even if it means
depriving their neighbors of liberty. Thus, general equality of conditions
is especially dangerous to liberty for it places in the hands of the
majority of men the power to reduce those who are somehow different
to the level of the majority. Ironically, the very triumph of egalitarianism
in America, the triumph which is the basis of democratic hope, leads to
the possibility of sacrificing liberty to the egalitarian urge, the basis of
democratic fear. America's triumph, in short, makes possible an even
greater tragedy.

There is . . . a manly and lawful passion for equality which excites men to
wish all to be powerful and honoured. This passion tends to elevate the
humble to the rank of the great; but there exists also in the human heart a

[1] Alphaus Mason, ed., *Free Government in the Making* (New York: Oxford University
Press, 1965), p. 445; Marvin Meyers, *The Jacksonian Persuasion* (Stanford: Stanford
University Press, 1960), p. 7.
[2] Alexis de Tocqueville, *Democracy in America* (New York: Schocken Books, 1961),
Vol. I, p. lxxxii.

depraved taste for equality, which impels the weak to attempt to lower
the powerful to their own level, and reduces men to prefer equality in
slavery to inequality with freedom. Not that those nations whose social
condition is democratic naturally despise liberty; on the contrary they have
an instinctive love for it. But liberty is not the chief and constant object
of their desires; equality is their idol: they make rapid and sudden efforts
to obtain liberty; and if they miss their aim, resign themselves to their
disappointments, but nothing can satisfy them except equality, and rather
than lose it they resolve to perish.[3]

Happily, Tocqueville found that Americans had not yet succumbed
to such temptation. They had been spared the worst manifestations of
the egalitarian impulse because of the strength and stability of certain of
their political institutions—e.g., decentralized administration—and,
most significantly, the political and religious ideas they had inherited from
their British forebears. Such ideas, incorporated in the young country's
fundamental principles, were cause for hope that American resistance to
the excesses of egalitarian passions might continue.

The remarks I have made will suffice to display the character of Anglo-
American civilization in its true light. It is the result (and this should be
constantly present to the mind) of two distinct elements, which in
other places have been in frequent hostility, but which in America have
been admirably incorporated and combined with one another. I allude
to the spirit of Religion, and the spirit of Liberty.[4]

The dangers, however, would always remain. A continual tension
between equality and liberty is the condition of democratic life, in
America as well as other democracies. The tension is controllable but
never extinguishable, short of extinguishing liberty. And even such
control, Tocqueville continues, is not accomplished without cost. A stable
and free community built upon an egalitarian base is achieved by way of
a kind of conformity and uniformity of opinion which is uncomfortable
for the man who, in Thoreau's phrase, "hears a different drummer." [5]
This, Tocqueville seems to suggest, is a high price but not as high as the

[3] *Ibid.*, p. 46.
[4] *Ibid.*, p. 32.
[5] Henry David Thoreau, *Walden* (New York: New American Library, 1942), p. 216. It
is out of such concerns that Tocqueville develops the famous doctrine of the "tyranny
of the majority," a tyranny most terrifying not for its use of naked force but for
the manner in which it submerges individuality in the name of public sentiment or
public opinion. The most notable example of disenchantment with such majority force
during this period is, of course, Henry David Thoreau. For reasons of space and
because of their ready availability elsewhere, we have chosen not to include selections
from Thoreau in this chapter. However, for a fine example of what we have referred
to above as democratic "discomfort," the reader is directed to *Walden* and
"Civil Disobedience."

alternative. An intelligent democratic citizen must be ready to bear discomfort and worse to preserve his freedom. He must realize that equality is never perfect and that individual views cannot always stand before public sentiment.

The selections which follow ought to be read within the context of the problems that Tocqueville describes. Washington's "Farewell" and Jefferson's "Inaugural" are political expressions of men who presided over the initiation of the political order which Tocqueville later examines. Both are concerned about the future of a country beset by some of the stresses Tocqueville identifies. Harriet Martineau's *Society in America* is, in effect, a companion piece to *Democracy in America*. She visits America at approximately the same time as Tocqueville and offers another perspective on the young democracy, one which strikingly bears out Tocqueville's themes.

George Washington

FAREWELL ADDRESS
(1796)

Friends, and Fellow-Citizens: The period for a new election of a Citizen, to Administer the Executive government of the United States, being not far distant, and the time actually arrived, when your thoughts must be employed in designating the person, who is to be cloathed with that important trust, it appears to me proper, especially as it may conduce to a more distinct expression of the public voice, that I should now apprise you of the resolution I have formed, to decline being considered among the number of those, out of whom a choice is to be made.

I beg you, at the same time, to do me the justice to be assured, that this resolution has not been taken, without a strict regard to all the considerations appertaining to the relation, which binds a dutiful citizen to his country, and that, in with drawing the tender of service which silence in my situation might imply, I am influenced by no diminution of zeal for your future interest, no deficiency of grateful respect for your past kindness; but am supported by a full conviction that the step is compatible with both.

The acceptance of, and continuance hitherto in, the office to which your Suffrages have twice called me, have been a uniform sacrifice of inclination to the opinion of duty, and to a deference for what appeared to be your desire. I constantly hoped, that it would have been much earlier in my power, consistently with motives, which I was not at liberty to disregard, to return to that retirement, from which I had been reluctantly drawn. The strength of my inclination to do this, previous to the last Election, had even led to the preparation of an address to declare it to you; but mature reflection on the then perplexed and critical posture of our Affairs with foreign Nations, and the unanimous advice of persons entitled to my confidence, impelled me to abandon the idea.

I rejoice, that the state of your concerns, external as well as internal, no longer renders the pursuit of inclination incompatible with the senti-

Messages and Papers of the Presidents, 1789–1897, J. D. Richardson, ed. (Washington, D.C.: U. S. Government Printing Office, 1897), Vol. I, pp. 213 ff.

ment of duty, or propriety; and am persuaded whatever partiality may be retained for my services, that in the present circumstances of our country, you will not disapprove my determination to retire.

The impressions, with which I first undertook the arduous trust, were explained on the proper occasion. In the discharge of this trust, I will only say, that I have, with good intentions, contributed towards the Organization and Administration of the government, the best exertions of which a very fallible judgment was capable. Not unconscious, in the outset, of the inferiority of my qualifications, experience in my own eyes, perhaps still more in the eyes of others, has strengthened the motives to diffidence of myself; and every day the increasing weight of years admonishes me more and more, that the shade of retirement is as necessary to me as it will be welcome. Satisfied that if any circumstances have given peculiar value to my services, they were temporary, I have the consolation to believe, that while choice and prudence invite me to quit the political scene, patriotism does not forbid it.

In looking forward to the moment, which is intended to terminate the career of my public life, my feelings do not permit me to suspend the deep acknowledgment of that debt of gratitude which I owe to my beloved country, for the many honors it has conferred upon me; still more for the stedfast confidence with which it has supported me; and for the opportunities I have thence enjoyed of manifesting my inviolable attachment, by services faithful and persevering, though in usefulness unequal to my zeal. If benefits have resulted to our country from these services, let it always be remembered to your praise, and as an instructive example in our annals, that, under circumstances in which the Passions agitated in every direction were liable to mislead, amidst appearances sometimes dubious, vicissitudes of fortune often discouraging, in situations in which not unfrequently want of Success has countenanced the spirit of criticism, the constancy of your support was the essential prop of the efforts, and a guarantee of the plans by which they were effected. Profoundly penetrated with this idea, I shall carry it with me to my grave, as a strong incitement to unceasing vows that Heaven may continue to you the choicest tokens of its beneficence; that your Union and brotherly affection may be perpetual; that the free constitution, which is the work of your hands, may be sacredly maintained; that its Administration in every department may be stamped with wisdom and Virtue; that, in fine, the happiness of the people of these States, under the auspices of liberty, may be made complete, by so careful a preservation and so prudent a use of this blessing as will acquire to them the glory of recommending it to the applause, the affection, and adoption of every nation which is yet a stranger to it

Here, perhaps, I ought to stop. But a solicitude for your welfare, which cannot end but with my life, and the apprehension of danger, natural to that solicitude, urge me on an occasion like the present, to offer to your solemn contemplation, and to recommend to your frequent review, some sentiments; which are the result of much reflection, of no inconsiderable observation, and which appear to me all important to the permanency of your felicity as a People. These will be offered to you with the more freedom, as you can only see in them the disinterested warnings of a parting friend, who can possibly have no personal motive to bias his counsel. Nor can I forget, as an encouragement to it, your indulgent reception of my sentiments on a former and not dissimilar occasion.

Interwoven as is the love of liberty with every ligament of your hearts, no recommendation of mine is necessary to fortify or confirm the attachment.

The Unity of Government which constitutes you one people is also now dear to you. It is justly so; for it is a main Pillar in the Edifice of your real independence, the support of your tranquillity at home; your peace abroad; of your safety; of your prosperity; of that very Liberty which you so highly prize. But as it is easy to foresee, that from different causes and from different quarters, much pains will be taken, many artifices employed, to weaken in your minds the conviction of this truth; as this is the point in your political fortress against which the batteries of internal and external enemies will be most constantly and actively (though often covertly and insidiously) directed, it is of infinite moment, that you should properly estimate the immense value of your national Union to your collective and individual happiness; that you should cherish a cordial, habitual and immoveable attachment to it; accustoming yourselves to think and speak of it as of the Palladium of your political safety and prosperity; watching for its preservation with jealous anxiety; discountenancing whatever may suggest even a suspicion that it can in any event be abandoned, and indignantly frowning upon the first dawning of every attempt to alienate any portion of our Country from the rest, or to enfeeble the sacred ties which now link together the various parts.

For this you have every inducement of sympathy and interest. Citizens by birth or choice, of a common country, that country has a right to concentrate your affections. The name of AMERICAN, which belongs to you, in your national capacity, must always exalt the just pride of Patriotism, more than any appellation derived from local discriminations. With slight shades of difference, you have the same Religion, Manners, Habits and political Principles. You have in a common cause fought and triumphed together. The independence and liberty you possess are the work of joint councils, and joint efforts; of common dangers, sufferings and successes.

But these considerations, however powerfully they address themselves to your sensibility, are greatly outweighed by those which apply more immediately to your Interest. Here every portion of our country finds the most commanding motives for carefully guarding and preserving the Union of the whole.

The *North*, in an unrestrained intercourse with the *South*, protected by the equal Laws of a common government, finds in the productions of the latter, great additional resources of Maritime and commercial enterprise and precious materials of manufacturing industry. The *South* in the same Intercourse, benefitting by the Agency of the *North*, sees its agriculture grow and its commerce expand. Turning partly into its own channels the seamen of the *North*, it finds its particular navigation envigorated; and while it contributes, in different ways, to nourish and increase the general mass of the National navigation, it looks forward to the protection of a Maritime strength, to which itself is unequally adapted. The *East*, in a like intercourse with the *West*, already finds, and in the progressive improvement of interior communications, by land and water, will more and more find a valuable vent for the commodities which it brings from abroad, or manufactures at home. The *West* derives from the *East* supplies requisite to its growth and comfort, and what is perhaps of still greater consequence, it must of necessity owe the *secure* enjoyment of indispensable *outlets* for its own productions to the weight, influence, and the future Maritime strength of the Atlantic side of the Union, directed by an indissoluble community of Interest as *one Nation*. Any other tenure by which the *West* can hold this essential advantage, whether derived from its own separate strength, or from an apostate and unnatural connection with any foreign Power, must be intrinsically precarious.

While then every part of our country thus feels an immediate and particular Interest in Union, all the parts combined cannot fail to find in the united mass of means and efforts greater strength, greater resource, proportionably greater security from external danger, a less frequent interruption of their Peace by foreign Nations; and, what is of inestimable value! they must derive from Union an exemption from those broils and Wars between themselves, which so frequently afflict neighbouring countries, not tied together by the same government; which their own rivalships alone would be sufficient to produce, but which opposite foreign alliances, attachments and intrigues would stimulate and imbitter. Hence likewise they will avoid the necessity of those overgrown Military establishments, which under any form of Government are inauspicious to liberty, and which are to be regarded as particularly hostile to Republican Liberty.

In this sense it is, that your Union ought to be considered as a main prop of your liberty, and that the love of the one ought to endear to you the preservation of the other.

These considerations speak a persuasive language to every reflecting and virtuous mind, and exhibit the continuance of the Union as a primary object of Patriotic desire. Is there a doubt, whether a common government can embrace so large a sphere? Let experience solve it. To listen to mere speculation in such a case were criminal. We are authorized to hope that a proper organization of the whole, with the auxiliary agency of governments for the respective Subdivisions, will afford a happy issue to the experiment. 'Tis well worth a fair and full experiment. With such powerful and obvious motives to Union, affecting all parts of our country, while experience shall not have demonstrated its impracticability, there will always be reason, to distrust the patriotism of those, who in any quarter may endeavor to weaken its bands.

In contemplating the causes which may disturb our Union, it occurs as matter of serious concern, that any ground should have been furnished for characterizing parties by *Geographical* discriminations: *Northern* and *Southern; Atlantic* and *Western;* whence designing men may endeavor to excite a belief that there is a real difference of local interests and views. One of the expedients of Party to acquire influence, within particular districts, is to misrepresent the opinions and aims of other Districts. You cannot shield yourselves too much against the jealousies and heart burnings which spring from these misrepresentations. They tend to render Alien to each other those who ought to be bound together by fraternal affection. The Inhabitants of our Western country have lately had a useful lesson on this head. They have seen, in the Negociation by the Executive, and in the unanimous ratification by the Senate, of the Treaty with Spain, and in the universal satisfaction at that event, throughout the United States, a decisive proof how unfounded were the suspicions propagated among them of a policy in the General Government and in the Atlantic States unfriendly to their Interests in regard to the Mississippi. They have been witnesses to the formation of two Treaties, that with G: Britain and that with Spain, which secure to them every thing they could desire, in respect to our Foreign relations, towards confirming their prosperity. Will it not be their wisdom to rely for the preservation of these advantages on the Union by which they were procured? Will they not henceforth be deaf to those advisers, if such there are, who would sever them from their Brethren and connect them with Aliens?

To the efficacy and permanency of Your Union, a Government for the whole is indispensable. No Alliances however strict between the parts can be an adequate substitute. They must inevitably experience the infractions and interruptions which all Alliances in all times have experienced. Sensible of this momentous truth, you have improved upon your first essay, by the adoption of a Constitution of Government, better calculated than your former for an intimate Union, and for the efficacious management of your common concerns. This government, the offspring of our own choice uninfluenced and unawed, adopted upon full investigation and mature deliberation, completely free in its principles, in the distribution of its powers, uniting security with energy, and containing within itself a provision for its own amendment, has a just claim to your confidence and your support. Respect for its authority, compliance with its Laws, acquiescence in its measures, are duties enjoined by the fundamental maxims of true Liberty. The basis of our political systems is the right of the people to make and to alter their Constitutions of Government. But the Constitution which at any time exists, 'till changed by an explicit and authentic act of the whole People, is sacredly obligatory upon all. The very idea of the power and the right of the People to establish Government presupposes the duty of every Individual to obey the established Government.

All obstructions to the execution of the Laws, all combinations and Associations, under whatever plausible character, with the real design to direct, control, counteract, or awe the regular deliberation and action of the Constituted authorities are destructive of this fundamental principle and of fatal tendency. They serve to organize faction, to give it an artificial and extraordinary force; to put in the place of the delegated will of the Nation, the will of a party; often a small but artful and enterprising minority of the Community; and, according to the alternate triumphs of different parties, to make the public administration the Mirror of the ill concerted and incongruous projects of faction, rather than the organ of consistent and wholesome plans digested by common councils and modified by mutual interests. However combinations or Associations of the above description may now and then answer popular ends, they are likely, in the course of time and things, to become potent engines, by which cunning, ambitious and unprincipled men will be enabled to subvert the Power of the People, and to usurp for themselves the reins of Government; destroying afterwards the very engines which have lifted them to unjust dominion.

Towards the preservation of your Government and the permanency of your present happy state, it is requisite, not only that you steadily discountenance irregular oppositions to its acknowledged authority, but also that you resist with care the spirit of innovation upon its principles however specious the pretexts. One method of assault may be to effect, in the forms of the Constitution, alterations which will impair the energy of the system, and thus to undermine what cannot be directly overthrown. In all the changes to which you may be invited, remember that time and habit are at least as necessary to fix the true character of Governments, as of other human institutions; that experience is the surest standard, by which to test the real tendency of the existing Constitution of a country; that facility in changes upon the credit of mere hypotheses and opinion exposes to perpetual change, from the endless variety of hypotheses and opinion: and remember, especially, that for the efficient management of your common interests, in a country so extensive as ours, a Government of as much vigour as is consistent with the perfect security of Liberty is indispensable. Liberty itself will find in such a Government, with powers properly distributed and adjusted, its surest Guardian. It is indeed little else than a name, where the Government is too feeble to withstand the enterprises of faction, to confine each member of the Society within the limits prescribed by the laws and to maintain all in the secure and tranquil enjoyment of the rights of person and property.

I have already intimated to you the danger of Parties in the State, with particular reference to the founding of them on Geographical discriminations. Let me now take a more comprehensive view, and warn you in the most solemn manner against the baneful effects of the Spirit of Party, generally.

This spirit, unfortunately, is inseparable from our nature, having its root in the strongest passions of the human Mind. It exists under different shapes in all Governments, more or less stifled, controlled, or repressed; but, in those of the popular form it is seen in its greatest rankness and is truly their worst enemy.

The alternate domination of one faction over another, sharpened by the spirit of revenge natural to party dissension, which in different ages and countries has perpetrated the most horrid enormities, is itself a frightful despotism. But this leads at length to a more formal and permanent despotism. The disorders and miseries, which result, gradually incline the minds of men to seek security and repose in the absolute power of an Individual: and sooner or later the chief of some prevailing faction more able or more fortunate than his competitors, turns this disposition to the purposes of his own elevation, on the ruins of Public Liberty.

Without looking forward to an extremity of this kind (which nevertheless ought not to be entirely out of sight) the common and continual mischiefs of the spirit of Party are sufficient to make it the interest and the duty of a wise People to discourage and restrain it.

It serves always to distract the Public Councils and enfeeble the Public administration. It agitates the Community with ill founded jealousies and false alarms, kindles the animosity of one part against another, foments occasionally riot and insurrection. It opens the door to foreign influence and corruption, which find a facilitated access to the government itself through the channels of party passions. Thus the policy and the will of one country, are subjected to the policy and will of another.

There is an opinion that parties in free countries are useful checks upon the Administration of the Government and serve to keep alive the spirit of Liberty. This within certain limits is probably true, and in Governments of a Monarchical cast Patriotism may look with indulgence, if not with favour, upon the spirit of party. But in those of the popular character, in Governments purely elective, it is a spirit not to be encouraged. From their natural tendency, it is certain there will always be enough of that spirit for every salutary purpose. And there being constant danger of excess, the effort ought to be, by force of public opinion, to mitigate and assuage it. A fire not to be quenched, it demands a uniform vigilance to prevent its bursting into a flame, lest instead of warming it should consume.

It is important, likewise, that the habits of thinking in a free Country should inspire caution in those entrusted with its administration, to confine themselves within their respective Constitutional spheres; avoiding in the exercise of the Powers of one department to encroach upon another. The spirit of encroachment tends to consolidate the powers of all the departments in one, and thus to create whatever the form of government, a real despotism. A just estimate of that love of power, and proneness to abuse it, which predominates in the human heart is sufficient to satisfy us of the truth of this position. The necessity of reciprocal checks in the exercise of political power, by dividing and distributing it into different depositories, and constituting each the Guardian of the Public Weal against invasions by the others, has been evinced by experiments ancient and modern; some of them in our country and under our own eyes. To preserve them must be as necessary as to institute them. If in the opinion of the People, the distribution or modification of the Constitutional powers be in any particular wrong, let it be corrected by an amendment in the way which the Constitution designates. But let there be no change by usurpation; for though this, in one instance, may be the instrument of good, it is the customary weapon by which free governments are destroyed. The precedent must always greatly overbalance in permanent evil any partial or transient benefit which the use can at any time yield.

Of all the dispositions and habits which lead to political prosperity, Religion and morality are indispensable supports. In vain would that man claim the tribute of Patriotism, who should labour to subvert these great Pillars of human happiness, these firmest props of the duties of Men and citizens. The mere Politician, equally with the pious man ought to respect and to cherish them. A volume could not trace all their connections with private and public felicity. Let it simply be asked where is the security for property, for reputation, for life, if the sense of religious obligation *desert* the oaths, which are the instruments of investigation in Courts of Justice? And let us with caution indulge the supposition, that morality can be maintained without religion. Whatever may be conceded to the influence of refined education on minds of peculiar structure, reason and experience both forbid us to expect that National morality can prevail in exclusion of religious principle.

'Tis substantially true, that virtue or morality is a necessary spring of popular government. The rule indeed extends with more or less force to every species of free Government. Who that is a sincere friend to it, can look with indifference upon attempts to shake the foundation of the fabric?

Promote then as an object of primary importance, Institutions for the general diffusion of knowledge. In proportion as the structure of a government gives force to public opinion, it is essential that public opinion should be enlightened. . . .

Observe good faith and justice towards all Nations. Cultivate peace and harmony with all. Religion and morality enjoin this conduct; and can it be that good policy does not equally enjoin it? It will be worthy of a free, enlightened, and, at no distant period, a great Nation, to give to mankind the magnanimous and too novel example of a People always guided by an exalted justice and benevolence. Who can doubt that in the course of time and things the fruits of such a plan would richly repay any temporary advantages which might be lost by a steady adherence to it? Can it be, that Providence has not connected the permanent felicity of a Nation with its virtue? The experiment, at least, is recommended by every sentiment which ennobles human Nature. Alas! is it rendered impossible by its vices?

In the execution of such a plan nothing is more essential than that permanent, inveterate antipathies against particular Nations and passionate attachments for others should be excluded; and that in place of them just and amicable feelings towards all should be cultivated. The Nation, which indulges towards another an habitual hatred, or an habitual fondness, is in some degree a slave. It is a slave to its animosity or to its affection, either of which is sufficient to lead it astray from its duty and its interest. Antipathy in one Nation against another, disposes each more readily to offer insult and injury, to lay hold of slight causes of umbrage, and to be haughty and intractable, when accidental or trifling occasions of dispute occur. Hence frequent collisions, obstinate envenomed and bloody contests. The Nation, prompted by ill will and resentment sometimes impels to War the Government, contrary to the best calculations of policy. The Government sometimes participates in the national propensity, and adopts through passion what reason would reject; at other times, it makes the animosity of the Nation subservient to projects of hostility instigated by pride, ambition and other sinister and pernicious motives. The peace often, sometimes perhaps the Liberty, of Nations has been the victim.

So likewise, a passionate attachment of one Nation for another produces a variety of evils. Sympathy for the favourite nation, facilitating the illusion of an imaginary common interest, in cases where no real common interest exists, and infusing into one the enmities of the other, betrays the former into a participation in the quarrels and Wars of the latter, without adequate inducement or justification. It leads also to concessions to the favourite Nation of privileges denied to others, which is apt doubly to injure the Nation making the concessions; by unnecessarily parting with what ought to have been retained; and by exciting jealousy, ill will, and a disposition to retaliate, in the parties from whom equal privileges are withheld. And it gives to ambitious, corrupted, or deluded citizens (who devote themselves to the favourite Nation) facility to betray, or sacrifice the interests of their own country, without odium, sometimes even with popularity; gilding with the appearances of a virtuous sense of obligation a commendable deference for public opinion, or a laudable zeal for public good, the base or foolish compliances of ambition, corruption, or infatuation.

As avenues to foreign influence in innumerable ways, such attachments are particularly alarming to the truly enlightened and independent Patriot. How many opportunities do they afford to tamper with domestic factions, to practice the arts of seduction, to mislead public opinion, to influence or awe the public Councils! Such an attachment of a small or weak, towards a great and powerful Nation, dooms the former to be the satellite of the latter.

Against the insidious wiles of foreign influence, (I conjure you to believe me fellow citizens) the jealousy of a free people ought to be *constantly* awake; since history and experience prove that foreign influence is one of the most baneful foes of Republican Government. But that jealousy to be useful must be impartial; else it becomes the instrument of the very influence to be avoided, instead of a defence against it. Excessive partiality for one foreign nation and excessive dislike of another, cause those whom they actuate to see danger only on one side, and serve to veil and even second the arts of influence on the other. Real Patriots, who may resist the intrigues of the favourite, are liable to become suspected and odious; while its tools and dupes usurp the applause and confidence of the people, to surrender their interests.

The Great rule of conduct for us, in regard to foreign Nations is in extending our commercial relations to have with them as little *political* connection as possible. So far as we have already formed engagements let them be fulfilled, with perfect good faith. Here let us stop. . . .

Relying on its kindness in this as in other things, and actuated by that fervent love towards it, which is so natural to a Man, who views in it the native soil of himself and his progenitors for several Generations; I anticipate with pleasing expectation that retreat, in which I promise myself to realize, without alloy, the sweet enjoyment of partaking, in the midst of my fellow Citizens, the benign influence of good Laws under a free Government, the ever favourite object of my heart, and the happy reward, as I trust, of our mutual cares, labours and dangers.

FIRST INAUGURAL ADDRESS
(1801)

Friends and Fellow-Citizens:

Called upon to undertake the duties of the first executive office of our country, I avail myself of the presence of that portion of my fellow-citizens which is here assembled to express my grateful thanks for the favor with which they have been pleased to look toward me, to declare a sincere consciousness that the task is above my talents, and that I approach it with those anxious and awful presentiments which the greatness of the charge and the weakness of my powers so justly inspire. A rising nation, spread over a wide and fruitful land, traversing all the seas with the rich productions of their industry, engaged in commerce with nations who feel power and forget right, advancing rapidly to destinies beyond the reach of mortal eye—when I contemplate these transcendent objects, and see the honor, the happiness, and the hopes of this beloved country committed to the issue, and the auspices of this day, I shrink from the contemplation, and humble myself before the magnitude of the under-taking. Utterly, indeed, should I despair did not the presence of many whom I here see remind me that in the other high authorities provided by our Constitution I shall find resources of wisdom, of virtue, and of zeal on which to rely under all difficulties. To you, then, gentlemen, who are charged with the sovereign functions of legislation, and to those associated with you, I look with encouragement for that guidance and support which may enable us to steer with safety the vessel in which we are all embarked amidst the conflicting elements of a troubled world.

During the contest of opinion through which we have passed the animation of discussions and of exertions has sometimes worn an aspect which might impose on strangers unused to think freely and to speak and to write what they think; but this being now decided by the voice of the nation, announced according to the rules of the Constitution, all will, of course, arrange themselves under the will of the law, and unite in common efforts for the common good. All, too, will bear in mind this sacred

Messages and Papers of the Presidents, 1789–1902, Richardson, ed., Vol. I, p. 322 ff.

principle, that though the will of the majority is in all cases to prevail, that will to be rightful must be reasonable; that the minority possess their equal rights, which equal laws must protect, and to violate would be oppression. Let us, then, fellow-citizens, unite with one heart and one mind. Let us restore to social intercourse that harmony and affection without which liberty and even life itself are but dreary things. And let us reflect that, having banished from our land that religious intolerance under which mankind so long bled and suffered, we have yet gained little if we countenance a political intolerance as despotic, as wicked, and capable of as bitter and bloody persecutions. During the throes and convulsions of the ancient world, during the agonizing spasms of infuriated man, seeking through blood and slaughter his long-lost liberty, it was not wonderful that the agitation of the billows should reach even this distant and peaceful shore; that this should be more felt and feared by some and less by others, and should divide opinions as to measures of safety. But every difference of opinion is not a difference of principle. We have called by different names brethren of the same principle. We are all Republicans, we are all Federalists. If there be any among us who would wish to dissolve this Union or to change its republican form, let them stand undisturbed as monuments of the safety with which error of opinion may be tolerated where reason is left free to combat it. I know, indeed, that some honest men fear that a republican government can not be strong, that this Government is not strong enough; but would the honest patriot, in the full tide of successful experiment, abandon a government which has so far kept us free and firm on the theoretic and visionary fear that this Government, the world's best hope, may by possibility want energy to preserve itself? I trust not. I believe this, on the contrary, the strongest Government on earth. I believe it the only one where every man, at the call of the law, would fly to the standard of the law, and would meet invasions of the public order as his own personal concern. Sometimes it is said that man can not be trusted with the government of himself. Can he, then, be trusted with the government of others? Or have we found angels in the forms of kings to govern him? Let history answer this question.

Let us, then, with courage and confidence pursue our own Federal and Republican principles, our attachment to union and representative government. Kindly separated by nature and a wide ocean from the exterminating havoc of one quarter of the globe; too high-minded to endure the degradations of the others; possessing a chosen country, with room enough for our descendants to the thousandth and thousandth generation; entertaining a due sense of our equal right to the use of our own faculties, to the acquisitions of our own industry, to honor and confidence from our fellow-citizens, resulting not from birth, but from our actions and their sense of them; enlightened by a benign religion, professed, indeed, and practiced in various forms, yet all of them inculcating honesty, truth, temperance, gratitude, and the love of man; acknowledging and adoring an overruling Providence, which by all its dispensations proves that it delights in the happiness of man here and his greater happiness hereafter—with all these blessings, what more is necessary to make us a happy and a prosperous people? Still one thing more, fellow-citizens—a wise and frugal Government, which shall restrain men from injuring one another, shall leave them otherwise free to regulate their own pursuits of industry and improvement, and shall not take from the mouth of labor the bread it has earned. This is the sum of good government, and this is necessary to close the circle of our felicities.

About to enter, fellow-citizens, on the exercise of duties which comprehend everything dear and valuable to you, it is proper you should understand what I deem the essential principles of our Government, and consequently those which ought to shape its Administration. I will compress them within the narrowest compass they will bear, stating the general principle, but not all its limitations. Equal and exact justice to all men, of whatever state or persuasion, religious or political; peace, commerce, and honest friendship with all nations, entangling alliances with none; the support of the State governments in all their rights, as the most competent administrations for our domestic concerns and the surest bulwarks against antirepublican tendencies; the preservation of the General Government in its whole constitutional vigor, as the sheet anchor of our peace at home and safety abroad; a jealous care of the right of election by the people—a mild and safe corrective of abuses which are lopped by the sword of revolution where peaceable remedies are unprovided; absolute acquiescence in the decisions of the majority, the vital principle of republics, from which is no appeal but to force, the vital principle and immediate parent of despotism; a well-disciplined militia, our best reliance in peace and for the first moments of war, till regulars may relieve them; the supremacy of the civil over the military authority; economy in the public expense, that labor may be lightly burthened; the honest payment of our debts and sacred preservation of the public faith; encouragement of agriculture, and of commerce as its handmaid; the diffusion of information and arraignment of all abuses at the bar of the public reason; freedom of religion; freedom of the press, and freedom of person under the protection of the habeas corpus, and trial by juries impartially selected. These principles form the bright constellation which has gone before us and guided our steps through an age of revolution and reformation. The wisdom of our sages and blood of our heroes have been devoted to their attainment. They should be the creed of our political faith, the text of civic instruction, the touchstone by which to try the services of those we trust; and should we wander from them in moments of error or of alarm, let us hasten to retrace our steps and to regain the road which alone leads to peace, liberty, and safety.

I repair, then, fellow-citizens, to the post you have assigned me. With experience enough in subordinate offices to have seen the difficulties of this the greatest of all, I have learnt to expect that it will rarely fall to the lot of imperfect man to retire from this station with the reputation and the favor which bring him into it. Without pretentions to that high confidence you reposed in our first and greatest revolutionary character, whose preeminent services had entitled him to the first place in his country's love and destined for him the fairest page in the volume of faithful history, I ask so much confidence only as may give firmness and effect to the legal administration of your affairs. I shall often go wrong through defect of judgment. When right, I shall often be thought wrong by those whose positions will not command a view of the whole ground. I ask your indulgence for my own errors, which will never be intentional, and your support against the errors of others, who may condemn what they would not if seen in all its parts. The approbation implied by your suffrage is a great consolation to me for the past, and my future solicitude will be to retain the good opinion of those who have bestowed it in advance, to conciliate that of others by doing them all the good in my power, and to be instrumental to the happiness and freedom of all.

Relying, then, on the patronage of your good will, I advance with obedience to the work, ready to retire from it whenever you become sensible how much better choice it is in your power to make. And may that Infinite Power which rules the destinies of the universe lead our councils to what is best, and give them a favorable issue for your peace and prosperity.

Alexis de Tocqueville

DEMOCRACY IN AMERICA

INTRODUCTORY CHAPTER

Amongst the novel objects that attracted my attention during my stay in the United States, nothing struck me more forcibly than the general equality of conditions. I readily discovered the prodigious influence which this primary fact exercises on the whole course of society, by giving a certain direction to public opinion, and a certain tenor to the laws; by imparting new maxims to the governing powers, and peculiar habits to the governed.

I speedily perceived that the influence of this fact extends far beyond the political character and the laws of the country, and that it has no less empire over civil society than over the Government; it creates opinions, engenders sentiments, suggests the ordinary practices of life, and modifies whatever it does not produce.

The more I advanced in the study of American society, the more I perceived that the equality of conditions is the fundamental fact from which all others seem to be derived, and the central point at which all my observations constantly terminated.

I then turned my thoughts to our own hemisphere, where I imagined that I discerned something analogous to the spectacle which the New World presented to me. I observed that the equality of conditions is daily progressing towards those extreme limits which it seems to have reached in the United States; and that the democracy which governs the American communities appears to be rapidly rising into power in Europe.

I hence conceived the idea of the book which is now before the reader.

It is evident to all alike that a great democratic revolution is going on amongst us; but there are two opinions as to its nature and consequences. To some it appears to be a novel accident, which as such may still be checked; to others, it seems irresistible, because it is the most

Henry Reeve translation, Schocken Books Edition, 1961.

uniform, the most ancient, and the most permanent tendency which is to be found in history. . . .

From the time when the exercise of the intellect became the source of strength and of wealth, it is impossible not to consider every addition to science, every fresh truth, and every new idea as a germ of power placed within the reach of the people. Poetry, eloquence, and memory, the grace of wit, the glow of imagination, the depth of thought, and all the gifts which are bestowed by Providence with an equal hand, turned to the advantage of the democracy; and even when they were in the possession of its adversaries, they still served its cause by throwing into relief the natural greatness of man; its conquests spread, therefore, with those of civilization and knowledge; and literature became an arsenal, where the poorest and the weakest could always find weapons to their hand.

In perusing the pages of our history, we shall scarcely meet with a single great event, in the lapse of seven hundred years, which has not turned to the advantage of equality. . . .

There is a country in the world where the great revolution which I am speaking of seems nearly to have reached its natural limits; it has been effected with ease and simplicity, say rather that this country has attained the consequences of the democratic revolution which we are undergoing, without having experienced the revolution itself.

The emigrants who fixed themselves on the shores of America in the beginning of the seventeenth century, severed the democratic principle from all the principles which repressed it in the old communities of Europe, and transplanted it unalloyed to the New World. It has there been allowed to spread in perfect freedom, and to put forth its consequences in the laws by influencing the manners of the country.

It appears to me beyond a doubt that sooner or later we shall arrive, like the Americans, at an almost complete equality of conditions. But I do not conclude from this, that we shall ever be necessarily led to draw the same political consequences which the Americans have derived from a similar social organization. I am far from supposing that they have chosen the only form of government which a democracy may adopt; but the identity of the efficient cause of laws and manners in the two countries is sufficient to account for the immense interest we have in becoming acquainted with its effects in each of them.

It is not, then, merely to satisfy a legitimate curiosity that I have examined America; my wish has been to find instruction by which we may ourselves profit. Whoever should imagine that I have intended to write a panegyric would be strangely mistaken, and on reading this book he will perceive that such was not my design: nor has it been my object to advocate any form of government in particular, for I am of opinion that absolute excellence is rarely to be found in any legislation; I have not even affected to discuss whether the social revolution, which I believe to be irresistible, is advantageous or prejudicial to mankind; I have acknowledged this revolution as a fact already accomplished or on the eve of its accomplishment; and I have selected the nation, from amongst those which have undergone it, in which its development has been the most peaceful and the most complete, in order to discern its natural consequences, and, if it be possible, to distinguish the means by which it may be rendered profitable. I confess that in America I saw more than America; I sought the image of democracy itself, with its inclinations, its character, its prejudices, and its passions, in order to learn what we have to fear or to hope from its progress.

Social Condition of the Anglo-Americans

A social condition is commonly the result of circumstances, sometimes of laws, oftener still of these two causes united; but wherever it exists, it may justly be considered as the source of almost all the laws, the usages, and the ideas which regulate the conduct of nations: whatever it does not produce it modifies.

It is therefore necessary, if we would become acquainted with the legislation and the manners of a nation, to begin by the study of its social condition.

The Striking Characteristic of the Social Condition of the Anglo-Americans Is Its Essential Democracy

Many important observations suggest themselves upon the social condition of the Anglo-Americans; but there is one which takes precedence of all the rest. The social condition of the Americans is eminently democratic; this was its character at the foundation of the Colonies, and is still more strongly marked at the present day. . . .

The democratic principle, on the contrary, has gained so much strength by time, by events, and by legislation, as to have become not only predominant but all-powerful. There is no family or corporate authority, and it is rare to find even the influence of individual character enjoy any durability.

America, then, exhibits in her social state a most extraordinary phænomenon. Men are there seen on a greater equality in point of fortune and intellect, or, in other words, more equal in their strength, than in any other country of the world, or in any age of which history has preserved the remembrance.

Political Consequences of the Social Condition of the Anglo-Americans

The political consequences of such a social condition as this are easily deducible.

It is impossible to believe that equality will not eventually find its way into the political world as it does everywhere else. To conceive of men remaining for ever unequal upon one single point, yet equal on all others, is impossible; they must come in the end to be equal upon all.

Now I know of only two methods of establishing equality in the political world; every citizen must be put in possession of his rights, or rights must be granted to no one. For nations which are arrived at the same stage of social existence as the Anglo-Americans, it is therefore very difficult to discover a medium between the sovereignty of all and the absolute power of one man: and it would be vain to deny that the social condition which I have been describing is equally liable to each of these consequences.

There is, in fact, a manly and lawful passion for equality which excites men to wish all to be powerful and honoured. This passion tends to elevate the humble to the rank of the great; but there exists also in the human heart a depraved taste for equality, which impels the weak to attempt to lower the powerful to their own level, and reduces men to prefer equality in slavery to inequality with freedom. Not that those nations whose social condition is democratic naturally despise liberty; on the contrary, they have an instinctive love of it. But liberty is not the chief and constant object of their desires; equality is their idol: they make rapid and sudden efforts to obtain liberty; and if they miss their aim, resign themselves to their disappointment; but nothing can satisfy them except equality, and rather than lose it they resolve to perish.

On the other hand, in a State where the citizens are nearly on an equality, it becomes difficult for them to preserve their independence against the aggressions of power. No one among them being strong enough to engage in the struggle with advantage, nothing but a general combination can protect their liberty. And such a union is not always to be found.

From the same social position, then, nations may derive one or the other of two great political results; these results are extremely different from each other, but they may both proceed from the same cause.

The Anglo-Americans are the first nations who, having been exposed to this formidable alternative, have been happy enough to escape the dominion of absolute power. They have been allowed by their circumstances, their origin, their intelligence, and especially by their moral feeling, to establish and maintain the sovereignty of the people....

Unlimited Power of the Majority in the United States, and Its Consequences

The very essence of democratic government consists in the absolute sovereignty of the majority; for there is nothing in democratic states which is capable of resisting it. Most of the American Constitutions have sought to increase this natural strength of the majority by artificial means.

The legislature is, of all political institutions, the one which is most easily swayed by the wishes of the majority. The Americans determined that the members of the legislature should be elected by the people immediately, and for a very brief term, in order to subject them, not only to the general convictions, but even to the daily passions of their constituents. The members of both Houses are taken from the same class in society, and are nominated in the same manner; so that the modifications of the legislative bodies are almost as rapid and quite as irresistible as those of a single assembly. It is to a legislature thus constituted, that almost all the authority of the government has been entrusted.

But whilst the law increased the strength of those authorities which of themselves were strong, it enfeebled more and more those which were naturally weak. It deprived the representatives of the executive of all stability and independence; and by subjecting them completely to the caprices of the legislature, it robbed them of the slender influence which the nature of a democratic government might have allowed them to retain. In several States, the judicial power was also submitted to the elective discretion of the majority; and in all of them its existence was made to depend on the pleasure of the legislative authority, since the representatives were empowered annually to regulate the stipend of the judges.

Custom, however, has done even more than law. A proceeding which will in the end set all the guarantees of representative government at naught, is becoming more and more general in the United States: it frequently happens that the electors, who choose a delegate, point out a certain line of conduct to him, and impose upon him a certain number of positive obligations which he is pledged to fulfil. With the exception of the tumult, this comes to the same thing as if the majority of the populace held its deliberations in the market-place.

Several other circumstances concur in rendering the power of the majority in America not only preponderant, but irresistible. The moral authority of the majority is partly based upon the notion, that there is more intelligence and more wisdom in a great number of men collected together than in a single individual, and that the quantity of legislators is more important than their quality. The theory of equality is in fact applied to the intellect of man; and human pride is thus assailed in its last retreat, by a doctrine which the minority hesitate to admit, and in which they very slowly concur. Like all other powers, and perhaps more than all other powers, the authority of the many requires the sanction of time; at first it enforces obedience by constraint; but its laws are not respected until they have long been maintained.

The right of governing society, which the majority supposes itself to derive from its superior intelligence, was introduced into the United States by the first settlers; and this idea, which would be sufficient of itself to create a free nation, has now been amalgamated with the manners of the people, and the minor incidents of social intercourse.

The French, under the old monarchy, held it for a maxim, (which is still a fundamental principle of the English Constitution), that the King could do no wrong; and if he did do wrong, the blame was imputed to his advisers. This notion was highly favourable to habits of obedience; and it enabled the subject to complain of the law, without ceasing to love and honour the lawgiver. The Americans entertain the same opinion with respect to the majority.

The moral power of the majority is founded upon yet another principle, which is, that the interests of the many are to be preferred to those of the few. It will readily be perceived that the respect here professed for the rights of the majority must naturally increase or diminish according to the state of parties. When a nation is divided into several irreconcilable factions, the privilege of the majority is often overlooked, because it is intolerable to comply with its demands.

If there existed in America a class of citizens whom the legislating majority sought to deprive of exclusive privileges, which they had possessed for ages, and to bring down from an elevated station to the level of the ranks of the multitude, it is probable that the minority would be less ready to comply with its laws. But as the United States were colonized by men holding equal rank amongst themselves, there is as yet no natural or permanent source of dissension between the interests of its different inhabitants.

There are certain communities in which the persons who constitute the minority can never hope to draw over the majority to their side, because they must then give up the very point which is at issue between them. Thus, an aristocracy can never become a majority whilst it retains its exclusive privileges, and it cannot cede its privileges without ceasing to be an aristocracy.

In the United States, political questions cannot be taken up in so general and absolute a manner; and all parties are willing to recognize the rights of the majority, because they all hope to turn those rights to their own advantage at some future time. The majority therefore in that country exercises a prodigious actual authority, and a moral influence which is scarcely less preponderant; no obstacles exist which can impede, or so much as retard its progress, or which can induce it to heed the complaints of those whom it crushes upon its path. This state of things is fatal in itself and dangerous for the future.

How the Unlimited Power of the Majority Increases in America, the Instability of Legislation and the Administration Inherent in Democracy

I have already spoken of the natural defects of democratic institutions, and they all of them increase at the exact ratio of the power of the majority. To begin with the most evident of them all; the mutability of the laws is an evil inherent in democratic government, because it is natural to democracies to raise men to power in very rapid succession. But this evil is more or less sensible in proportion to the authority and the means of action which the legislature possesses.

In America the authority exercised by the legislative bodies is supreme; nothing prevents them from accomplishing their wishes with celerity, and with irresistible power, whilst they are supplied by new representatives every year. That is to say, the circumstances which contribute most powerfully to democratic instability, and which admit of the free application of caprice to every object in the State, are here in full operation. In conformity with this principle, America is, at the present day, the country in the world where laws last the shortest time. Almost all the American constitutions have been amended within the course of thirty years: there is therefore not a single American State which has not modified the principles of its legislation in that lapse of time. As for the laws themselves, a single glance upon the archives of the different States of the Union suffices to convince one, that in America the activity of the legislator never slackens. Not that the American democracy is naturally less stable than any other, but that it is allowed to follow its capricious propensities in the formation of the laws.

The omnipotence of the majority, and the rapid as well as absolute manner in which its decisions are executed in the United States, has not only the effect of rendering the law unstable, but it exercises the same influence upon the execution of the law and the conduct of the public administration. As the majority is the only power which it is important to court, all its projects are taken up with the greatest ardour; but no sooner is its attention distracted, than all this ardour ceases; whilst in the free states of Europe, the administration is at once independent and secure, so that the projects of the legislature are put into execution, although its immediate attention may be directed to other objects.

In America certain ameliorations are undertaken with much more zeal and activity than elsewhere; in Europe the same ends are promoted by much less social effort, more continuously applied.

Some years ago several pious individuals undertook to ameliorate the conditions of the prisons. The public was excited by the statements which they put forward, and the regeneration of criminals became a very popular undertaking. New prisons were built; and, for the first time, the idea of reforming as well as of punishing the delinquent, formed a part of prison discipline. But this happy alteration, in which the public had taken so hearty an interest, and which the exertions of the citizens had irresistibly accelerated, could not be completed in a moment. Whilst the new penitentiaries were being erected, (and it was the pleasure of the majority that they should be terminated with all possible celerity,) the old prisons existed, which still contained a great number of offenders. These gaols became more unwholesome and more corrupt in proportion as the new establishments were beautified and improved, forming a contrast which may readily be understood. The majority was so eagerly employed in founding the new prisons, that those which already existed were forgotten; and as the general attention was diverted to a novel object, the care which had hitherto been bestowed upon the others ceased. The salutary regulations of discipline were first relaxed, and afterwards broken; so that in the immediate neighbourhood of a prison which bore witness to the mild and enlightened spirit of our time, dungeons might be met with which reminded the visitor of the barbarity of the Middle Ages.

Tyranny of the Majority

I hold it to be an impious and an execrable maxim that, politically speaking, a people has a right to do whatsoever it pleases; and yet I have asserted that all authority originates in the will of the majority. Am I, then, in contradiction with myself?

A general law—which bears the name of Justice—has been made and sanctioned, not only by a majority of this or that people, but by a majority of mankind. The rights of every people are consequently confined within the limits of what is just. A nation may be considered in the light of a jury which is empowered to represent society at large, and to apply the great and general law of Justice. Ought such a jury, which represents society, to have more power than the society in which the laws it applies originate?

When I refuse to obey an unjust law, I do not contest the right which the majority has of commanding, but I simply appeal from the sovereignty of the people to the sovereignty of mankind. It has been asserted that a people can never entirely outstep the boundaries of justice and of reason in those affairs which are more peculiarly its own; and that consequently full power may fearlessly be given to the majority by which it is represented. But this language is that of a slave.

A majority taken collectively may be regarded as a being whose opinions, and most frequently whose interests, are opposed to those of another being, which is styled a minority. If it be admitted that a man, possessing absolute power, may misuse that power by wronging his adversaries, why should a majority not be liable to the same reproach? Men are not apt to change their characters by agglomeration; nor does their patience in the presence of obstacles increase with the consciousness of their strength. And for these reasons I can never willingly invest any number of my fellow-creatures with that unlimited authority which I should refuse to any one of them.

I do not think that it is possible to combine several principles in the same government, so as at the same time to maintain freedom, and really to oppose them to one another. The form of government which is usually termed *mixed* has always appeared to me to be a mere chimera. Accurately speaking there is no such thing as a mixed government, (with the meaning usually given to that word,) because in all communities some one principle of action may be discovered, which preponderates over the others. England in the last century, which has been more especially cited as an example of this form of government, was in point of fact an essentially aristocratic state, although it comprised very powerful elements of democracy: for the laws and customs of the country were such, that the aristocracy could not but preponderate in the end, and subject the direction of public affairs to its own will. The error arose from too much attention being paid to the actual struggle which was going on between the nobles and the people, without considering the probable issue of the contest, which was in reality the important point. When a community really has a mixed government, that is to say, when it is equally divided between two adverse principles, it must either pass through a revolution, or fall into complete dissolution.

I am therefore of opinion that some one social power must always be made to predominate over the others; but I think that liberty is endangered when this power is checked by no obstacles which may retard its course, and force it to moderate its own vehemence.

Unlimited power is in itself a bad and dangerous thing; human beings are not competent to exercise it with discretion; and God alone can be omnipotent, because his wisdom and his justice are always equal to his power. But no power upon earth is so worthy of honour for itself, or of reverential obedience to the rights which it represents, that I would consent to admit its uncontrolled and all-predominant authority. When

I see that the right and the means of absolute command are conferred on a people or upon a king, upon an aristocracy or a democracy, a monarchy or a republic, I recognize the germ of tyranny, and I journey onwards to a land of more hopeful institutions.

In my opinion the main evil of the present democratic institutions of the United States does not arise, as is often asserted in Europe, from their weakness, but from their overpowering strength; and I am not so much alarmed at the excessive liberty which reigns in that country, as at the very inadequate securities which exist against tyranny.

When an individual or a party is wronged in the United States, to whom can he apply for redress? If to public opinion, public opinion constitutes the majority; if to the legislature, it represents the majority, and implicitly obeys its injunctions; if to the executive power, it is appointed by the majority and remains a passive tool in its hands; the public troops consist of the majority under arms; the jury is the majority invested with the right of hearing judicial cases; and in certain States even the judges are elected by the majority. However iniquitous or absurd the evil of which you complain may be, you must submit to it as well as you can.

If, on the other hand, a legislative power could be so constituted as to represent the majority without necessarily being the slave of its passions; an executive, so as to retain a certain degree of uncontrolled authority; and a judiciary, so as to remain independent of the two other powers; a government would be formed which would still be democratic without incurring any risk of tyrannical abuse.

I do not say that tyrannical abuses frequently occur in America at the present day; but I maintain that no sure barrier is established against them, and that the causes which mitigate the government are to be found in the circumstances and the manners of the country more than in its laws.

Effects of the Unlimited Power of the Majority upon the Arbitrary Authority of the American Public Officers

A distinction must be drawn between tyranny and arbitrary power. Tyranny may be exercised by means of the law, and in that case it is not arbitrary: arbitrary power may be exercised for the good of the community at large, in which case it is not tyrannical. Tyranny usually employs arbitrary means, but, if necessary, it can rule without them.

In the United States the unbounded power of the majority, which is favourable to the legal despotism of the legislature, is likewise favourable to the arbitrary authority of the magistrate. The majority has an entire control over the law when it is made and when it is executed; and as it possesses an equal authority over those who are in power, and the community at large, it considers public officers as its passive agents, and readily confides the task of serving its designs to their vigilance. The details of their office and the privileges which they are to enjoy are rarely defined beforehand; but the majority treats them, as a master does his servants, when they are always at work in his sight, and he has the power of directing or reprimanding them at every instant.

In general the American functionaries are far more independent than the French civil officers within the sphere which is prescribed to them. Sometimes, even, they are allowed by the popular authority to exceed those bounds; and as they are protected by the opinion, and backed by the cooperation, of the majority, they venture upon such manifestations of their power as astonish a European. By this means habits are formed in the heart of a free country which may some day prove fatal to its liberties.

Power Exercised by the Majority in America upon Opinion

It is in the examination of the display of public opinion in the United States, that we clearly perceive how far the power of the majority surpasses all the powers with which we are acquainted in Europe. Intellectual principles exercise an influence which is so invisible and often so inappreciable, that they baffle the toils of oppression. At the present time the most absolute monarchs in Europe are unable to prevent certain notions, which are opposed to their authority, from circulating in secret throughout their dominions, and even in their courts. Such is not the case in America; as long as the majority is still undecided, discussion is carried on; but as soon as its decision is irrevocably pronounced, a submissive silence is observed; and the friends, as well as the opponents, of the measure, unite in assenting to propriety. The reason of this is perfectly clear: no monarch is so absolute as to combine all the powers of society in his own hands, and to conquer all opposition, with the energy of a majority, which is invested with the right of making and of executing the laws.

The authority of a king is purely physical, and it controls the actions of the subject without subduing his private will; but the majority possesses a power which is physical and moral at the same time; it acts upon the will as well as upon the actions of men, and it represses not only all contest, but all controversy.

I know no country in which there is so little true independence of mind and freedom of discussion as in America. In any constitutional state in Europe every sort of religious and political theory may be advocated and propagated abroad; for there is no country in Europe so subdued by any single authority, as not to contain citizens who are ready to protect the man who raises his voice in the cause of truth, from the consequences of his hardihood. If he is unfortunate enough to live under an absolute government, the people is upon his side; if he inhabits a free country, he may find a shelter behind the authority of the throne, if he require one. The aristocratic part of society supports him in some countries, and the democracy in others. But in a nation where democratic institutions exist, organized like those of the United States, there is but one sole authority, one single element of strength and of success, with nothing beyond it.

In America, the majority raises very formidable barriers to the liberty of opinion: within these barriers an author may write whatever he pleases, but he will repent it if he ever step beyond them. Not that he is exposed to the terrors of an auto-da-fé, but he is tormented by the slights and persecutions of daily obloquy. His political career is closed for ever, since he has offended the only authority which is able to promote his success. Every sort of compensation, even that of celebrity, is refused to him. Before he published his opinions, he imagined that he held them in common with many others; but no sooner has he declared them openly, than he is loudly censured by his overbearing opponents, whilst those who think, without having the courage to speak, like him, abandon him in silence. He yields at length, oppressed by the daily efforts he has been making, and he subsides into silence, as if he was tormented by remorse for having spoken the truth.

Fetters and headsmen were the coarse instruments which tyranny formerly employed; but the civilization of our age has refined the arts of despotism, which seemed however to have been sufficiently perfected before. The excesses of monarchical power had devised a variety of physical means of oppression: the democratic republics of the present day have rendered it as entirely an affair of the mind, as that will which it is intended to coerce. Under the absolute sway of an individual despot, the body was attacked in order to subdue the soul; and the soul escaped the blows which were directed against it, and rose superior to the attempt; but such is not the course adopted by tyranny in democratic republics; there the body is left free, and the soul is enslaved. The sovereign can no longer say, "You shall think as I do on pain of death;" but he says, "You are free to think differently from me, and to retain your life, your property, and all that you possess; but if such be your determination, you are henceforth an alien among your people. You may retain your civil rights, but they will be useless to you, for you will never be chosen by your fellow-citizens if you solicit their suffrages; and they will affect to scorn you, if you solicit their esteem. You will remain among men, but you will be deprived of the rights of mankind. Your fellow-creatures will shun you like an impure being; and those who are most persuaded of your innocence will abandon you too, lest they should be shunned in their turn. Go in peace! I have given you your life, but it is an existence incomparably worse than death."

Monarchical institutions have thrown an odium upon despotism; let us beware lest democratic republics should restore oppression, and should render it less odious and less degrading in the eyes of the many, by making it still more onerous to the few.

Works have been published in the proudest nations of the Old World, expressly intended to censure the vices and deride the follies of the times: Labruyère inhabited the palace of Louis XIV. when he composed his chapter upon the Great, and Molière criticized the courtiers in the very pieces which were acted before the Court. But the ruling power in the United States is not to be made game of; the smallest reproach irritates its sensibility, and the slightest joke which has any foundation in truth renders it indignant; from the style of its language to the more solid virtues of its character, everything must be made the subject of encomium. No writer, whatever be his eminence, can escape from this tribute of adulation to his fellow-citizens. The majority lives in the perpetual practice of self-applause; and there are certain truths which the Americans can only learn from strangers or from experience.

If great writers have not at present existed in America, the reason is very simply given in these facts; there can be no literary genius without freedom of opinion, and freedom of opinion does not exist in America. The Inquisition has never been able to prevent a vast number of anti-religious books from circulating in Spain. The empire of the majority succeeds much better in the United States, since it actually removes the wish of publishing them. Unbelievers are to be met with in America, but, to say the truth, there is no public organ of infidelity. Attempts have been made by some governments to protect the morality of nations by prohibiting licentious books. In the United States no one is punished for this sort of works, but no one is induced to write them; not because all the citizens are immaculate in their manners, but because the majority of the community is decent and orderly.

In these cases the advantages derived from the exercise of this power are unquestionable; and I am simply discussing the nature of the power itself. This irresistible authority is a constant fact, and its judicious exercise is an accidental occurrence.

Effects of the Tyranny of the Majority upon the National Character of the Americans

The tendencies which I have just alluded to are as yet very slightly perceptible in political society; but they already begin to exercise an unfavourable influence upon the national character of the Americans. I am inclined to attribute the singular paucity of distinguished political characters to the ever-increasing activity of the despotism of the majority in the United States.

When the American Revolution broke out, they arose in great numbers; for public opinion then served, not to tyrannize over, but to direct the exertions of individuals. Those celebrated men took a full part in the general agitation of mind common at that period, and they attained a high degree of personal fame, which was reflected back upon the nation, but which was by no means borrowed from it.

In absolute governments, the great nobles who are nearest to the throne flatter the passions of the sovereign, and voluntarily truckle to his caprices. But the mass of the nation does not degrade itself by servitude; it often submits from weakness, from habit, or from ignorance, and sometimes from loyalty. Some nations have been known to sacrifice their own desires to those of the sovereign with pleasure and with pride; thus exhibiting a sort of independence in the very act of submission. These peoples are miserable, but they are not degraded. There is a great difference between doing what one does not approve, and feigning to approve what one does; the one is the necessary case of a weak person, the other befits the temper of a lacquey.

In free countries, where every one is more or less called upon to give his opinion in the affairs of state; in democratic republics, where public life is incessantly commingled with domestic affairs, where the sovereign authority is accessible on every side, and where its attention can almost always be attracted by vociferation, more persons are to be met with who speculate upon its foibles, and live at the cost of its passions, than in absolute monarchies. Not because men are naturally worse in these States than elsewhere, but the temptation is stronger, and of easier access at the same time. The result is a far more extensive debasement of the characters of citizens.

Democratic republics extend the practice of currying favour with the many, and they introduce it into a greater number of classes at once: this is one of the most serious reproaches that can be addressed to them. In democratic States organized on the principles of the American republics, this is more especially the case, where the authority of the majority is so absolute and so irresistible, that a man must give up his rights as a citizen, and almost abjure his quality as a human being, if he intends to stray from the track which it lays down.

In that immense crowd which throngs the avenues to power in the United States, I found very few men who displayed any of that manly candour, and that masculine independence of opinion which frequently distinguished the Americans in former times, and which constitutes the leading feature in distinguished characters wheresoever they may be found. It seems, at first sight, as if all the minds of the Americans were formed upon one model, so accurately do they correspond in their manner of judging. A stranger does, indeed, sometimes meet with Americans who dissent from these rigorous formularies; with men who deplore the defects of the laws, the mutability and the ignorance of democracy; who even go so far as to observe the evil tendencies which impair the national character, and to point out such remedies as it might be possible to apply; but no one is there to hear these things besides yourself, and you, to whom these secret reflections are confided, are a stranger and a bird of passage. They are very ready to communicate truths which are useless to you, but they continue to hold a different language in public.

If ever these lines are read in America, I am well assured of two things: in the first place, that all who peruse them will raise their voices to condemn me; and in the second place, that very many of them will acquit me at the bottom of their conscience.

I have heard of patriotism in the United States, and it is a virtue which may be found among the people, but never among the leaders of the people. This may be explained by analogy; despotism debases the oppressed much more than the oppressor: in absolute monarchies the king has often great virtues, but the courtiers are invariably servile. It is true that the American courtiers do not say "Sire," or "Your Majesty" —a distinction without a difference. They are for ever talking of the natural intelligence of the populace they serve; they do not debate the question as to which of the virtues of their master is pre-eminently worthy of admiration; for they assure him that he possesses all the virtues under heaven without having acquired them, or without caring to acquire them; they do not give him their daughters and their wives to be raised at his pleasure to the rank of his concubines, but, by sacrificing their opinions, they prostitute themselves. Moralists and philosophers in America are not obliged to conceal their opinions under the veil of allegory; but, before they venture upon a harsh truth, they say, "We are aware that the people which we are addressing is too superior to all the weaknesses of human nature to lose the command of its temper for an instant; and we should not hold this language if we were not speaking to men, whom their virtues and their intelligence render more worthy of freedom than all the rest of the world."

It would have been impossible for the sycophants of Louis XIV. to flatter more dexterously. For my part, I am persuaded that in all governments, whatever their nature may be, servility will cower to force, and adulation will cling to power. The only means of preventing men from degrading themselves, is to invest no one with that unlimited authority which is the surest method of debasing them.

The Greatest Dangers of the American Republics Proceed from the Unlimited Power of the Majority

Governments usually fall a sacrifice to impotence or to tyranny. In the former case their power escapes from them; it is wrested from their grasp in the latter. Many observers, who have witnessed the anarchy of democratic States, have imagined that the government of those States was naturally weak and impotent. The truth is, that when once hostilities are begun between parties, the government loses its control over society. But I do not think that a democratic power is naturally without force or without resources: say rather, that it is almost always by the abuse of its force, and the misemployment of its resources, that a democratic government fails. Anarchy is almost always produced by its tyranny or its mistakes, but not by its want of strength.

It is important not to confound stability with force, or the greatness of a thing with its duration. In democratic republics, the power which directs society is not stable; for it often changes hands and assumes a new direction. But whichever way it turns, its force is almost irresistible. The Governments of the American republics appear to me to be as much centralized as those of the absolute monarchies of Europe, and more energetic than they are. I do not, therefore, imagine that they will perish from weakness.

If ever the free institutions of America are destroyed, that event may be attributed to the unlimited authority of the majority, which may at some future time urge the minorities to desperation, and oblige them to have recourse to physical force. Anarchy will then be the result, but it will have been brought about by despotism.

Mr. Hamilton expresses the same opinion in the Federalist, No. 51. "It is of great importance in a republic not only to guard the society against the oppression of its rulers, but to guard one part of the society against the injustice of the other part. Justice is the end of government. It is the end of civil society. It ever has been, and ever will be pursued until it be obtained, or until liberty be lost in the pursuit. In a society, under the forms of which the stronger faction can readily unite and oppress the weaker, anarchy may as truly be said to reign as in a state of nature, where the weaker individual is not secured against the violence of the stronger: and as in the latter state even the stronger individuals are prompted by the uncertainty of their condition to submit to a government which may protect the weak as well as themselves, so in the former state will the more powerful factions be gradually induced by a like motive to wish for a government which will protect all parties, the weaker as well as the more powerful. It can be little doubted, that if the State of Rhode Island was separated from the Confederacy and left to itself, the insecurity of right under the popular form of government within such narrow limits, would be displayed by such reiterated oppressions of the factious majorities, that some power altogether independent of the people would soon be called for by the voice of the very factions whose misrule had proved the necessity of it."

Jefferson has also thus expressed himself in a letter to Madison: "The executive power in our Government is not the only, perhaps not even the principal object of my solicitude. The tyranny of the legislature is really the danger most to be feared, and will continue to be so for many years to come. The tyranny of the executive power will come in its turn, but at a more distant period."

I am glad to cite the opinion of Jefferson upon this subject rather than that of another, because I consider him to be the most powerful advocate democracy has ever sent forth. . . .

Why Democratic Nations Show a More Ardent and Enduring Love of Equality Than of Liberty

The first and most intense passion which is engendered by the equality of conditions is, I need hardly say, the love of that same equality. My readers will therefore not be surprised that I speak of it before all others.

Everybody has remarked, that in our time, and especially in France, this passion for equality is every day gaining ground in the human heart. It has been said a hundred times that our contemporaries are far more ardently and tenaciously attached to equality than to freedom; but, as I do not find that the causes of the fact have been sufficiently analysed, I shall endeavour to point them out.

It is possible to imagine an extreme point at which freedom and equality would meet and be confounded together. Let us suppose that all the members of the community take a part in the government, and that each one of them has an equal right to take a part in it. As none is different from his fellows, none can exercise a tyrannical power: men will be perfectly free, because they will all be entirely equal; and they will all be perfectly equal, because they will be entirely free To this ideal state democratic nations tend. Such is the completest form that equality can assume upon earth; but there are a thousand others which, without being equally perfect, are not less cherished by those nations.

The principle of equality may be established in civil society, without prevailing in the political world. Equal rights may exist of indulging in the same pleasures, of entering the same professions, of frequenting the same places—in a word, of living in the same manner and seeking wealth by the same means, although all men do not take an equal share in the government.

A kind of equality may even be established in the political world, though there should be no political freedom there. A man may be the equal of all his countrymen save one, who is the master of all without distinction, and who selects equally from among them all the agents of his power.

Several other combinations might be easily imagined, by which very great equality would be united to institutions more or less free, or even to institutions wholly without freedom.

Although men cannot become absolutely equal unless they be entirely free, and consequently equality, pushed to its furthest extent, may be confounded with freedom, yet there is good reason for distinguishing the one from the other. The taste which men have for liberty, and that which they feel for equality, are, in fact, two different things; and I am not afraid to add, that, amongst democratic nations, they are two unequal things.

Upon close inspection, it will be seen that there is in every age some peculiar and preponderating fact with which all others are connected; this fact almost always gives birth to some pregnant idea or some ruling passion, which attracts to itself, and bears away in its course, all the feelings and opinions of the time: it is like a great stream, towards which each of the surrounding rivulets seems to flow.

Freedom has appeared in the world at different times and under various forms; it has not been exclusively bound to any social condition, and it is not confined to democracies. Freedom cannot, therefore, form the distinguishing characteristic of democratic ages. The peculiar and preponderating fact which marks those ages as its own is the equality of conditions; the ruling passion of men in those periods is the love of this equality. Ask not what singular charm the men of democratic ages find in being equal, or what special reasons they may have for clinging so tenaciously to equality rather than to the other advantages which society holds out to them: equality is the distinguishing characteristic of the age they live in; that, of itself, is enough to explain that they prefer it to all the rest.

But independently of this reason there are several others, which will at all times habitually lead men to prefer equality to freedom.

If a people could ever succeed in destroying, or even in diminishing, the equality which prevails in its own body, this could only be accomplished by long and laborious efforts. Its social condition must be modified, its laws abolished, its opinions superseded, its habits changed, its manners corrupted. But political liberty is more easily lost; to neglect to hold it fast, is to allow it to escape.

Men therefore not only cling to equality because it is dear to them; they also adhere to it because they think it will last for ever.

That political freedom may compromise in its excesses the tranquillity, the property, the lives of individuals, is obvious to the narrowest and most unthinking minds. But, on the contrary, none but attentive and clear-sighted men perceive the perils with which equality threatens us, and they commonly avoid pointing them out. They know that the calamities they apprehend are remote, and flatter themselves that they will only fall upon future generations, for which the present generation takes but little thought. The evils which freedom sometimes brings with it are immediate; they are apparent to all, and all are more or less affected by them. The evils which extreme equality may produce are slowly disclosed; they creep gradually into the social frame; they are only seen at intervals, and at the moment at which they become most violent, habit already causes them to be no longer felt.

The advantages which freedom brings are only shown by length of time; and it is always easy to mistake the cause in which they originate. The advantages of equality are instantaneous, and they may constantly be traced from their source.

Political liberty bestows exalted pleasures, from time to time, upon a certain number of citizens. Equality every day confers a number of small enjoyments on every man. The charms of equality are every instant felt, and are within the reach of all; the noblest hearts are not insensible to them, and the most vulgar souls exult in them. The passion which equality engenders must therefore be at once strong and general. Men cannot enjoy political liberty unpurchased by some sacrifices, and they never obtain it without great exertions. But the pleasures of equality are self-proffered: each of the petty incidents of life seems to occasion them, and in order to taste them nothing is required but to live.

Democratic nations are at all times fond of equality, but there are certain epochs at which the passion they entertain for it swells to the height of fury. This occurs at the moment when the old social system, long menaced, completes its own destruction after a last intestine struggle, and when the barriers of rank are at length thrown down. At such times men pounce upon equality as their booty, and they cling to it as to some precious treasure which they fear to lose. The passion for equality penetrates on every side into men's hearts, expands there, and fills them entirely. Tell them not that by this blind surrender of themselves to an exclusive passion, they risk their dearest interests: they are deaf. Show them not freedom escaping from their grasp, whilst they are looking another way: they are blind—or rather, they can discern but one sole object to be desired in the universe.

What I have said is applicable to all democratic nations: what I am about to say concerns the French alone. Amongst most modern nations, and especially amongst all those of the continent of Europe, the taste and the idea of freedom only began to exist and to extend itself at the time when social conditions were tending to equality, and as a consequence of that very equality. Absolute kings were the most efficient levellers of ranks amongst their subjects. Amongst these nations equality preceded freedom: equality was therefore a fact of some standing, when freedom was still a novelty: the one had already created customs, opinions, and laws belonging to it, when the other, alone and for the first time, came into actual existence. Thus the latter was still only an affair of opinion and of taste, whilst the former had already crept into the habits of the people, possessed itself of their manners, and given a particular turn to the smallest actions in their lives. Can it be wondered that the men of our own time prefer the one to the other?

I think that democratic communities have a natural taste for freedom: left to themselves, they will seek it, cherish it, and view any privation of it with regret. But for equality, their passion is ardent, insatiable, incessant, invincible: they call for equality in freedom; and if they cannot obtain that, they still call for equality in slavery. They will endure poverty, servitude, barbarism,—but they will not endure aristocracy.

This is true at all times, and especially true in our own. All men and all powers seeking to cope with this irresistible passion, will be overthrown and destroyed by it. In our age, freedom cannot be established without it, and despotism itself cannot reign without its support.

Harriet Martineau

SOCIETY IN AMERICA

Politics are morals, all the world over; that is, politics universally implicate the duty and happiness of man. Every branch of morals is, and ought to be considered, a universal concern. Under despotic governments, there is a pretension, more or less sincere, on the part of the rulers, to moral regards; but from these the bulk of the people are, by common consent, cut off. If the bulk of the people saw the truth, that the principles of politics affect them,—are the message of their Maker (as principles are) to them, as well as to their rulers, they would become moral agents in regard to politics, and despotism would be at an end. As it is, they pay their taxes, and go out to war when they are bid, are thankful when they are left unmolested by their government, and sorry or angry when they feel themselves oppressed; and there they end. It is owing to their ignorance of politics being morals—*i. e.* matters of equal concern to all—that this truth is not made manifest in action in every country on the globe that has any government at all.

The same is the case of the unrepresented under governments which are not called despotic. According to the principles professed by the United States, there is there a rectification of this mighty error—a correction of this grand oversight. In that self-governing nation, all are held to have an equal interest in the principles of its institutions, and to be bound in equal duty to watch their workings. Politics there are universal duty. None are exempted from obligation but the unrepresented; and they, in theory, are none. However various may be the tribes of inhabitants in those States, whatever part of the world may have been their birthplace, or that of their fathers, however broken may be their language, however noble or servile their employments, however exalted or despised their state, all are declared to be bound together by equal political obligation, as firmly as under any other law of personal or social duty. The president, the senator, the governor, may take upon himself some additional responsibility, as the physician and lawyer do in other departments of office; but they are under precisely the same political obligation as

Harriet Martineau, *Society in America* (London: Saunders and Otley, 1837), Vol. I, pp. 6–8, 27–34, 58, 110–112, 158–162; Vol. III, pp. 5–9, 67–70.

the German settler, whose axe echoes through the lonely forest; and the Southern planter, who is occupied with his hospitalities; and the New England merchant, whose thoughts are on the sea; and the Irishman, in his shanty on the canal-bank; and the negro, hoeing cotton in the hot field, or basking away his sabbath on the shore of the Mississippi. Genius, knowledge, wealth, may in other affairs set a man above his fellows; but not in this. Weakness, ignorance, poverty may exempt a man from other obligations; but not from this. The theory of the government of the United States has grasped and embodied the mighty principle, that politics are morals;—that is, a matter of universal and equal concern. We shall have to see whether this principle is fully acted out.

Implicated with this is the theory, that the majority will be in the right, both as to the choice of principles which are to govern particular cases, and the agents who are to work them. This theory, obviously just as it appears, as long as it is applied to matters of universal and equal concern, cannot be set aside without overthrowing all with which it is involved. We shall have to see, also, whether this principle is effectually carried out. . . .

One sunny October morning I was taking a drive, with my party, along the shores of the pretty Owasco Lake, in New York state, and conversing on the condition of the country with a gentleman who thought the political prospect less bright than the landscape. I had been less than three weeks in the country, and was in a state of something like awe at the prevalence of, not only external competence, but intellectual ability. The striking effect upon a stranger of witnessing, for the first time, the absence of poverty, of gross ignorance, of all servility, of all insolence of manner, cannot be exaggerated in description. I had seen every man in the towns an independent citizen; every man in the country a land-owner. I had seen that the villages had their newspapers, the factory girls their libraries. I had witnessed the controversies between candidates for office on some difficult subjects, of which the people were to be the judges. With all these things in my mind, and with every evidence of prosperity about me in the comfortable homesteads which every turn in the road, and every reach of the lake, brought into view, I was thrown into a painful amazement by being told that the grand question of the time was "whether the people should be encouraged to govern themselves, or whether the wise should save them from themselves." The confusion of inconsistencies was here so great as to defy argument: the patronage among equals that was implied; the assumption as to who were the wise; and the conclusion that all the rest must be foolish. This one sentence seemed to be the most extraordinary combination that could proceed from the lips of a republican.

The expressions of fear vary according to the pursuits, or habits of mind of those who entertain them: but all are inconsistent with the theory that the majority are right. One fears the influence in the national councils of the "Tartar population" of the west, observing that men retrograde in civilisation when thinly settled in a fruitful country. But the representatives from these regions will be few while they are thinly settled, and will be in the minority when in the wrong. When these representatives become numerous, from the thick settlement of those regions, their character will have ceased to become Tartar-like and formidable: even supposing that a Tartar-like character could co-exist with the commerce of the Mississippi. Another tells me that the State has been, again and again, "on a lee shore, and a flaw has blown it off, and postponed the danger; but this cannot go on for ever." The fact here is true; and it would seem to lead to a directly contrary inference. "The flaw" is the will of the majority, which might be better indicated by a figure of something more stable. "The majority is right." It has thus far preserved the safety of the state; and this is the best ground for supposing that it will continue to be a safeguard.

One of the most painful apprehensions seems to be that the poorer will heavily tax the richer members of society; the rich being always a small class. If it be true, as all parties appear to suppose, that rulers in general are prone to use their power for selfish purposes, there remains the alternative, whether the poor shall over-tax the rich, or whether the rich shall over-tax the poor: and, if one of these evils were necessary, few would doubt which would be the least. But the danger appears much diminished on the consideration that, in the country under our notice, there are not, nor are likely to be, the wide differences in property which exist in old countries. There is no class of hereditary rich or poor. Few are very wealthy; few are poor; and every man has a fair chance of being rich. No such unequal taxation has yet been ordained by the sovereign people; nor does there appear to be any danger of it, while the total amount of taxation is so very small as in the United States, and the interest that every one has in the protection of property is so great. A friend in the South, while eulogizing to me the state of society there, spoke with compassion of his northern fellow citizens, who were exposed to the risks of "a perpetual struggle between pauperism and property." To which a northern friend replied, that it is true that there is a perpetual struggle everywhere between pauperism and property. The question is, which succeeds. In the United States, the prospect is that each will succeed. Paupers may obtain what they want, and proprietors will keep that which they have. As a mere matter of convenience, it is shorter and easier to obtain property by enterprise and labour in the United States, than by pulling down the wealthy. Even the most desponding do not consider the case as very urgent, at present. I asked one of my wealthy friends, who was predicting that in thirty years his children would be living under a despotism, why he did not remove. "Where," said he, with a countenance of perplexity, "could I be better off?"—which appeared to me a truly reasonable question.

In a country, the fundamental principle of whose politics is, that its "rulers derive their just powers from the consent of the governed," it is clear that there can be no narrowing of the suffrage. However earnestly some may desire this, no one hopes it. But it does not follow that the apprehensive minority has nothing left but discontent. The enlightenment of society remains not only matter for hope, but for achievement. The prudent speak of the benefits of education as a matter of policy, while the philanthropic promote it as a matter of justice. Security of person and property follows naturally upon a knowledge of rights. However the aristocracy of wealth, learning, and talent may differ among themselves, as to what is the most valuable kind of knowledge, all will agree that every kind will strengthen the bonds of society. In this direction must the aristocracy work for their own security. If they sufficiently provide the means of knowledge to the community, they may dismiss their fears, and rest assured that the great theory of their government will bear any test; and that "the majority will be in the right."

If the fears of the aristocracy are inconsistent with the theory of the government under which they live, so is much of the practice of the democracy. Their hopefulness is reasonable; their reliance on the majority is reasonable. But there are evils attendant on their practice of their true theories which may account for the propounding of worse theories by their opponents.

Learning by experience is slow work. However sure it may be, it is slow; and great is the faith and patience required by men who are in advance of a nation on a point which they feel that they could carry, if they had not to wait the pleasure of the majority. Though the majority be right in respect of the whole of politics, there is scarcely a sensible man who may not be more in the right than the majority with regard to some one point; and no allowance can be too great for the perpetual discouragement hence arising. The majority eventually wills the best; but, in the present imperfection of knowledge, the will is long in exhibiting itself; and the ultimate demonstration often crowns a series of mistakes and failures. From this fact arises the complaint of many federalists that the democratic party is apt to adopt their measures, after railing both at those measures, and at the men who framed them. This is often true: and it is true that, if the people had only had the requisite knowledge, they would have done wisely to have accepted good measures from the beginning, without any railing at all. But the knowledge was wanting. The next best thing that can happen is, that which does happen: that the people learn, and act upon their learning. If they are not wise enough to adopt a good measure at first, it would be no improvement of the case that they should be too obstinate to accept it at last. The case proves only that out of ignorance come knowledge, conviction, and action; and the majority is ultimately in the right. Whenever there is less of ignorance to begin with, there will be less of the railing, which is childish enough, whether as a mere imputation, or as a reality.

The great theory presumes that the majority not only will the best measures, but choose the best men. This is far from being true in practice. In no respect, perhaps, are the people more behind their theory than in this. The noble set of public servants with which the people were blessed in their revolutionary period seems to have inspired them at first with a somewhat romantic faith in men who profess strong attachment to whatever has been erected into a glory of the nation; and, from that time to this, the federal party has, from causes which will be hereafter explained, furnished a far superior set of men to the public service than the democratic party. I found this fact almost universally admitted by the wisest adherents of democracy; and out of it has arisen the mournful question, whether an honest man with false political principles be not more dangerous as a ruler than an unscrupulous man with true political principles. I have heard the case put thus: "There is not yet a sufficiency of real friends of the people willing to be their servants. They must take either a somewhat better set of men whose politics they disapprove, or a somewhat worse set of men to make tools of. They take the tools, use them, and throw them away."

This is true; and a melancholy truth it is; since it is certain that whenever the people shall pertinaciously require honest servants, and take due pains to ascertain their honesty, true men will be forthcoming. Under God's providence, the work never waits for the workman. . . .

Nothing can be more striking to a stranger than the experience gained, after some residence in the United States, of the ultimate ascendency of the will of the majority—*i. e.* of the right—in defiance of all appearances to the contrary. The review of what I witnessed of this kind, in the course of two years, with regard to the conduct of Congress alone, surprises and cheers me. It is true that I see several wrongs unredressed; several wounds inflicted on the people's liberties yet unhealed; but these are cases in which the people do not yet understand what has been done; or have not yet roused themselves to show that they do. . . .

Under a pure despotism, the morals of politics would make but a very short chapter. Mercy in the ruler; obedience in his officers, with, perhaps, an occasional stroke of remonstrance; and tax-paying in the people, would comprehend the whole. Among a self-governing people, who profess to take human equality for their great common principle, and the golden rule for their political vow, a long chapter of many sections is required.

The morals of politics are not too familiar anywhere. The clergy are apt to leave out its topics from their list of subjects for the pulpit. Writers on morals make that chapter as brief as if they lived under the pure despotism, supposed above. An honest newspaper, here and there, or a newspaper honest for some particular occasion, and therefore uninfluential in its temporary honesty, are the only speakers on the morals of politics. The only speakers; but not the only exhibitors. Scattered here and there, through a vast reach of ages, and expanse of communities, there may be found, to bless his race, an honest statesman. Statesmen, free from the gross vices of peculation, sordid, selfish ambition, cruelty and tergiversation, are not uncommon. But the last degree of honesty has always been, and is still, considered incompatible with statesmanship. To hunger and thirst after righteousness has been naturally, as it were, supposed a disqualification for affairs; and a man, living for truth, and in a spirit of love, "pure in the last recesses of the mind," who should propose to seek truth through political action, and exercise love in the use of political influence, and refine his purity by disinfecting the political atmosphere of its corruptions, would hear it reported on every hand that he had a demon. Yet one who is aware of the enthusiasm with which the Germans hail the words of Posa at every representation of Don Carlos; one who has seen how American officials are supported by the people, on the supposition that they are great men, (however small such men may really be,) one who has watched the acceleration, within our own time, of the retribution which overtakes untrustworthy public men, whatever may be their talents and their knowledge, in contrast with the comparative stability of less able, but more honest men, can doubt no longer that the time is at hand for the advent of political principle. The hour is come when dwellers in the old world should require integrity of their rulers; and dwellers in the new world, each in his turn a servant of society, should require it of each other and of themselves. The people of the United States are seeking after this, feebly and dimly. They have retained one wise saying of the fathers to whom they owe so much; that the letter of laws and constitutions is a mere instrument; with no vitality; no power to protect and bless; and that the spirit is all in all. They have been far from acting upon this with such steadiness as to show that they understand and believe it. But the saying is in their minds; and, like every other true thing that lies there, it will in time exhibit itself in the appointed mode—the will of the majority.

A public man told me that it would be a great point gained, if every citizen could be induced to vote, at least once a year. So far is it from being true that all Americans are the bustling politicians the English have been apt to suppose. If such political bustle should be absurd, the actual apathy is something worse. If it were only borne in mind that rulers derive their just powers from the consent of the governed, surely all conscientious men would see the guilt of any man acquiescing in the rule of governors whom he disapproves, by not having recorded his dissent. Or, if he should be in the majority, the case is no better. He has omitted to bear his testimony to what he esteems the true principles of government. He has not appointed his rulers; and, in as far as he accepts their protection, he takes without having given, he reaps without having sown; he deprives his just rulers of a portion of the authority which is their due—of a portion of the consent of the governed.

There is another cause for the reluctance to vote which is complained of by the best friends of the people; but it is almost too humbling and painful to be discussed. Some are afraid to vote!

This happens not in the country, nor among the strength of the population in the towns: but among the feeble aristocracy. There is not, in the United States, as with us, a system of intimidation exercised by the rich over the poor. In the country, there are no landlords and tenants at will. In the towns, the tradesmen do not stand in need of the patronage of the rich. Though they vote by ballot, and any man who chooses it may vote secretly, (and many do upon occasion,) there is rarely any need of such protection. But there is no reason why the gentry, who may be afraid of hurting one another's feelings, should not use their power of secret voting, rather than neglect the duty of giving their suffrage. If the educated and principled men of the community, as they are esteemed, fall back into idleness and silence, when the time comes for a struggle for principles, and there is a danger of disappointing expectations, and hurting feelings, their country has little to thank them for. They are the men from whom the open discharge of duty is looked for; they are the men who should show that political obligation is above private regards. If they have not the virtue to do this, and take the consequences, let them avail themselves of the secrecy of the ballot-box, which in England is desired for the protection of those whom bad arrangements have made dependent for bread on the rich and powerful. At all events, let them vote, or be ashamed to accept the privileges of citizenship without having discharged the duties.

The fear of opinion sometimes takes the form of an almost insane dread of responsibility. There are occasions when public men, unable to judge for themselves of particular classes of circumstances, are obliged to ask advice of their friends and supporters. Happy he who obtains a full and true answer from any one! The chances against this are in proportion to the importance of the case. I knew of one such instance, the result of which more than one is, I trust, now grieving over in his inmost heart. An eminent statesman was hesitating whether to offer himself as a candidate for a very high office. He requested the opinion and advice of a number of gentlemen in public life, his supporters. All were of the same opinion; that he should not stand. No one of them chose to take the responsibility of telling him so. Some of them wrote ambiguous answers, hoping that he would infer that they thought ill of his chance. Others rather encouraged the enterprise. The illustrative details which might be given,—showing the general uniformity, with particular diversity, of the conduct of the advisers,—would be amusing if they were not too sad. Suffice it that no one, as far as I could learn, could get over his fear of responsibility so as to be faithful. They allowed their idol to make a fool of himself. If he should henceforth be sunk in political scepticism, perhaps these gentlemen may find that in shunning one kind of responsibility, they have incurred another, far heavier.

It is felt, and understood, in the United States, that their near future in politics is indiscernible. Odd, unexpected circumstances, determining the present, are perpetually turning up. Almost every man has his convictions as to what the state of affairs will be, in the gross, a century hence. Scarcely any man will venture a conjecture as to what will have happened next spring. This is the very condition, if the people could but see it, for the exercise of faith in principles. With a dark and shifting near future, and a bright and fixed ultimate destiny, what is the true, the only wisdom? Not to pry into the fogs and thickets round about, or to stand still for fear of what may next occur in the path; but to look from Eden gate behind to heaven gate before, and press on to the certain future. In his political as in his moral life, man should, in the depth of his ignorance and the fallibility of his judgment, throw himself, in a full sense of security, upon principles; and then he is safe from being depressed by opposition, or scared by uncertainty, or depraved by responsibility. . . .

While the republics of North America are new, the ideas of the people are old. While these republics were colonies, they contained an old people, living under old institutions, in a new country. Now they are a mixed people, infant as a nation, with a constant accession of minds from old countries, living in a new country, under institutions newly combined out of old elements. It is a case so singular, that the old world may well have patience for some time, to see what will arise. The old world must have patience; for the Americans have no national character yet; nor can have, for a length of years. It matters not that they think they have: or it matters only so far as it shows to what they tend. Their veneration of Washington has led them to suppose that he is the type of their nation. Their patriotic feelings are so far associated with him that they conclude the nation is growing up in his likeness. If any American were trusted by his countrymen to delineate what they call their national character, it would infallibly come out a perfect likeness of Washington. But there is a mistake here. There were influences prior to Washington, and there are circumstances which have survived him, that cause some images to lie deeper down in the hearts of Americans than Washington himself. His character is a grand and very prevalent idea among them: but there are others which take the precedence, from being more general still. Wealth and opinion were practically worshipped before Washington opened his eyes on the sun which was to light him to his deeds; and the worship of Opinion is, at this day, the established religion of the United States.

If the prevalent idea of society did not arise out of circumstances over which the mutations of outward events exercise but a small immediate influence, it is clear that, in this case, the idea should arise out of the characters of the benefactors who achieved the revolution, and must be consistent with the solemn words in which they conveyed their united Declaration. The principles of truth, and the rule of justice, according to which that Declaration was framed, and that revolutionary struggle undertaken and conducted, should, but for prior influences, have been the spirit inspiring the whole civilisation of the American people. There should then have been the utmost social as well as political freedom. The pursuit of wealth might then have been subordinated at pleasure: fear of injury, alike from opinion and from violence, should have been banished; and as noble facilities afforded for the progression of the inward, as for the enjoyment of the outward, man. But this was not given. Instead of it there was ordained a mingling of old and new influences, from which a somewhat new kind of civilisation has arisen.

The old-world estimation of wealth has remained among them, though, I believe and trust, somewhat diminished in strength. Though every man works for it in America, and not quite every man does so in England, it seems to me that it is not so absolutely the foreground object in all views of life, the one subject of care, speculation, inquiry, and supposition, that it is in England. It is in America clearly subordinate to another idea, still an idol, but of a higher order than the former. The worship of Opinion certainly takes precedence of that of wealth.

In a country where the will of the majority decides all political affairs, there is a temptation to belong to the majority, except where strong interests, or probabilities of the speedy supremacy of the minority, countervail. The minority, in such a case, must be possessed of a strong will, to be a minority. A strong will is dreaded by the weaker, who have so little faith as to believe that such a will endangers the political equality which is the fundamental principle of their institutions. This dread occasions persecution, or at least opprobrium: opprobrium becomes a real danger; and, like all dangers, is much more feared than it deserves, the longer it lasts, and the more it is dwelt upon. Thus, from a want of faith in the infallible operation of the principles of truth and the rule of justice, these last become "hollow words" in the States of the new, as in the kingdoms of the old world; and the infant nation, which was expected to begin a fresh and higher social life, is acting out in its civilisation an idea but little more exalted than those which have operated among nations far less favoured than herself in regard to political freedom. . . .

If I am not much mistaken, society in the new world is wakening up, under the stimulus of the slave-question, to a sense of its want of practical freedom, owing to its too great regard to opinion. The examples of those who can and do assert and maintain their liberty in these times of fiery trial, are venerable and beautiful in the eyes of the young. Those in the cities who have grown old in the practice of mistrust are unconscious of the extent of their privations: but the free yeomanry, and the youth of the towns, have an eye for the right, and a heart for the true, amid the mists and subtleties in which truth and liberty have been of late involved. The young men of Boston, especially, seem to be roused: and it is all-important that they should be. Boston is looked to throughout the Union, as the superior city she believes herself to be: and nowhere is the entrance upon life more perilous to the honesty and consistency of young aspirants after the public service. Massachusetts is the head-quarters of federalism. Federalism is receding before democracy, even there; but that State has still a federal majority. A Massachusetts man has little chance of success in public life, unless he starts a federalist: and he has no chance of rising above a certain low point, unless, when he reaches that point, he makes a transition into democracy. The trial is too great for the moral independence of most ambitious men: and it fixes the eyes of the world on the youth of Boston. They are watched, that it may be seen whether they who now burn with ardour for complete freedom will hereafter "reverence the dreams of their youth," or sink down into cowardice, apathy, and intolerance, as they reach the middle of life.

If they will only try, they will find how great are the ease and peace attendant on the full exercise of rights, even though it should shut the career of politics, and possibly of wealth, against them for a time. If they will look in the faces of the few who dare to live in the midst of Boston as freely as if they were in the centre of the prairies, they will see in those countenances a brightness and serenity which a sense of mere safety could never impart. The pursuit of safety,—safety from outward detriment,—is of all in this world the most hopeless. The only attainable safety is that which usually bears another name,—repose in absolute truth. Where there is a transparency of character which defies misrepresentation, a faith in men which disarms suspicion, an intrepidity which overawes malice, and a spirit of love which wins confidence, there is safety; and in nothing short of all these. If any of them are deficient, in the same proportion does safety give place to danger; and no substitution of prudence will be of more than temporary avail. Prudence is now reigning supreme over the elderly classes of Boston generally, and too many of the young. Independence is animating the rest. It remains to be seen which will have succumbed when the present youth of the city shall have become her legislators, magistrates, and social representatives.

As a specimen of the thoughts and feelings of some on the spot, I give the following.

"Liberty of thought and opinion is strenuously maintained: in this proud land it has become almost a wearisome cant: our speeches and journals, religious and political, are made nauseous by the vapid and vain-glorious reiteration. But does it, after all, *characterise any community among us?* Is there any one to which a qualified observer shall point, and say, *There* opinion is free? On the contrary, is it not a fact, a sad and deplorable fact, that in no land on this earth is the mind more fettered than it is here? that here what we call public opinion has set up a despotism, such as exists nowhere else? Public opinion,—a tyrant, sitting in the dark, wrapt up in mystification and vague terrors of obscurity; deriving power no one knows from whom; like an Asian monarch, unapproachable, unimpeachable, undethronable, perhaps illegitimate,—but irresistible in its power to quell thought, to repress action, to silence conviction, —and bringing the timid perpetually under an unworthy bondage of mean fear to some impostor opinion, some noisy judgment, which gets astride on the popular breath for a day, and controls, through the lips of impudent folly, the speech and actions of the wise. From this influence and rule, from this bondage to opinion, no community, as such, is free; though doubtless individuals are. But your community, brethren, based on the principles which you profess, is bound to be so."

5
RIGHTS OF THE STATES

If any one proposition could command the universal assent of mankind, we might expect it would be this—that the government of the Union, though limited in its powers, is supreme within its sphere of action. This would seem to result necessarily from its nature. It is the government of all; its powers are delegated by all; it represents all, and acts for all. Though any one state may be willing to control its operations, no state is willing to let others control them. The nation, on those subjects on which it can act, must necessarily bind its component parts. . . . The government of the United States, then, though limited in its powers, is supreme; and its laws when made in pursuance of the constitution, form the supreme law of the land, anything in the constitution or laws of any state to the contrary notwithstanding.

JOHN MARSHALL, *McCulloch* v. *Maryland*, 1819

Successive toasts at a Jefferson Day Dinner, Washington, D.C., 1830:

Our Federal Union! It must be preserved!

PRESIDENT ANDREW JACKSON

The Union, after our liberty most dear.

VICE-PRESIDENT JOHN C. CALHOUN

Few issues in American history have so consistently led Americans to recall and evaluate their political origins than that of "states' rights." From Patrick Henry's challenge to the framers of the Constitution

Who authorized them to speak the language, "We, the people," instead of "We, the states?" States are the characteristics and soul of a confederation. If the states be not the agents of this compact, it must be one great, consolidated, national government of the people of all the states.

to a contemporary plea for preservation of state power

The power centers of the states protect our liberty from the possible tyranny of the national government, just as the power of the national government protects each citizen from the tyranny of the states.

the question of the correct relationship which ought to exist between
the states and the national government has been a recurring theme
in American life.[1]

Because it arises out of problems created by American political
principles, it forces a reconsideration of those principles. The fact that the
question endures is one of those ironies created by the inherent tensions
in American political principles. The irony is that what rights states have
is supposedly long since decided. Why, we must ask, do we argue
over a "dead" issue? As Henry suggested, once "We, the people," and not
"We, the states," were accepted as the founders of American government,
there was no recourse but to formulate "one great, consolidated,
national government of the people of all the states." Recognition of
the supremacy of the people necessitated recognition of the need for a
supreme national authority. Henry was right: the principle of popular
rule demands that the people be able to speak with a single voice.
Any lesser authority—i.e., a state or local government—which seeks to deny
that voice—i.e., the central government—stands opposed to the concept
of popular government enunciated in the Declaration of Independence
and embodied in the Constitution. Accepting "We, the people"
as sovereign in America meant that state and local authorities would
forever be subservient in the American constitutional order.[2] Yet, Henry's
arguments still reverberate through history and states' rights disputes
still provoke serious and divisive quarrels. Why this is so and how
the quarrels force a reconsideration of American principles are the
questions to which this chapter is directed.

The continued assertion of the states' rights position is, in the main,
attributable to a common end held by almost all of its defenders.[3]
They seek to protect individual and minority liberties from the enormous
power the national government can bring to bear as the spokesman of
"the people." Indeed, those who argue for the states may generally
be said to be suspicious of governments in general. Rarely, if ever, do
they claim that state and local authorities are better or more virtuous than

---

[1] Jonathan Elliot, *Debates on the Adoption of the Federal Constitution* (New York:
Burt Franklin, from the edition of 1888), Vol. III, p. 22; Terry Sanford, *Storm over the
States* (New York: McGraw-Hill, 1967), p. 8. Sanford was governor of North Carolina
from 1961–1965. More recent and striking evidence of such rhetoric is discovered
in the speeches of George Wallace during the 1968 Presidential campaign.
[2] The question has long been settled in respect to Constitutional law. The
seminal case is *McCulloch* v. *Maryland*, 4 Wheat. 316 (1819).
[3] We use the phrase "states' rights position" in a rather comprehensive sense. At present,
men argue as forcefully—perhaps, more forcefully—for the rights of governing units
even smaller than the states. Thus, serious proposals advancing the rights of cities,
municipalities, counties, and other governing units are made. All such arguments,
we believe, are derivative of the original states' rights arguments and our discussion
may be extended to them all.

their national counterpart. The claim is not so much that the lesser governments are good as that the national government is potentially more evil because of its greater powers and distance from the people. In this sense, states' rights defenders tacitly accept the fact of popular government and the problematic position which states hold under such government. States' rights arguments may often sound rebellious simply because those who hold the position understand their lack of legal and Constitutional support. Daniel Webster stated the situation quite clearly in his famous reply to Senator Hayne of South Carolina. States might rebel but legally they had little recourse but to obey the directives of the national authority. There were no other alternatives.

I cannot conceive that there can be a middle course, between submission to the laws, when regularly pronounced Constitutional, on the one hand, and open resistance, which is a revolution or rebellion, on the other. I say, the right of a State to annul a law of Congress cannot be maintained, but on the ground of an inalienable right of man to resist oppression; that is to say, upon the ground of revolution. I admit that there is an ultimate violent remedy, above the Constitution and in defiance of the Constitution, which may be resorted to when a revolution is to be justified. But I do not admit, that, under the Constitution and in conformity with it, there is any mode in which a State government, as a member of the Union, can interfere and stop the progress of the general government, by force of her own laws, under any circumstances whatever.[4]

The people having asserted their sovereignty in the national government, Webster continues, denial of the government constitutes a denial of the people's ultimate sovereignty and is unacceptable.

The people of the United States have declared this Constitution shall be the supreme law. We must either admit the proposition or dispute their authority; . . . the fact is, that the people of the United States have chosen to impose control on State sovereignties. . . . There are those, doubtless, who wish they had been left without restraint; but the Constitution has ordered the matter differently.[5]

Webster's arguments were, and are, compelling in a legal consideration of the place of the states within the union. But, as suggested above, legal niceties do not explain the influence of states' rights claims in America. Their appeal is extralegal; it rests upon the continuing response of Americans to limitations upon liberty. Opposition to the popular will expressed through the national

[4] *Writings and Speeches of Daniel Webster* (Boston: Little, Brown, 1903, National Edition), Vol. VI, pp. 53–54.
[5] *Ibid.*, pp. 54–55.

government is a libertarian response to the excesses possible in popular, egalitarian governing. The dichotomy between liberty and equality is therefore basic to the states' rights discussion. Once again Webster is instructive in making this issue explicit. The clash is between individual liberty and the egalitarian urge towards popular rule. The problem, as he describes it, is how far liberty can be supported without doing irreparable harm to the egalitarian supports of popular government.

In one sense, indeed, Sir, this is assuming an attitude of open resistance in favor of liberty. But what sort of liberty? The liberty of establishing their own opinions, in defiance of the opinions of others; the liberty of judging and of deciding exclusively themselves, in a matter in which others have as much right to judge and decide as they; the liberty of placing their own opinions above the judgment of all others, above the laws, and above the Constitution. This is their liberty, and this is the fair result of the proposition contended for by the honorable gentleman. Or, it may be more properly said, it is identical with it, rather than a result of it.[6]

The irony of the states' rights dispute, then, is resolved when it is seen that for all its legal phraseology the argument reflects the same issue which appeared during America's founding, the potential conflict between egalitarianism and libertarianism. The question of states' rights *per se* is decided in the strictly Constitutional sense. It continues because of the continuing tensions implicit in American principles. The states' rights position, in short, is one of the traditional American vehicles for defending minority rights and liberties— especially sectional minorities. In this sense, the position is better appreciated in respect to its cause than in respect to the internal validity of the arguments used in its support. Such a perspective, for example, begins to explain how James Madison, perhaps the most influential member of the Constitutional Convention, and Thomas Jefferson, who unabashedly used the full extent of national power during his Presidency, could have been the moving forces behind the Virginia and Kentucky Resolutions. Their advocacy of national power in other contexts did not stop them from urging state interposition and nullification of Congressional directives when they saw, as they believed, traditional American liberty being endangered by the Alien and Sedition Laws. Such behavior was no more contradictory than the original American political principles. Those who most warmly endorse popular government are not beyond urging restraints upon it when they see individual rights threatened.

[6]*Ibid.*, p. 57.

When extended, however, advocacy of individual and minority liberty may deny the legitimacy of popular government. That is, if pushed to the extreme, states' rights libertarianism can be decidely antiegalitarian. And it should be added that there is such a strain of political thinking in America that denies the tenets of popular government. The primary American exponent of this view was John C. Calhoun. As senator from South Carolina and vice president of the United States, Calhoun publicly fought for the principle that personal liberty takes precedence to allegiance to any kind of political order, even one based upon the sovereignty of "the people." Essentially, Calhoun feared governmental despotism of any variety, including popular. His goal was to arrange governmental structures which would provide protection for individual security and liberty, no matter what the source of sovereignty.

To perfect society it is necessary to develop the faculties, intellectual and moral, with which man is endowed. But the mainspring to the development and, through this, to progress, improvement, and civilization, with all their blessings, is the desire of individuals to better their conditions. For this purpose liberty and security are indispensable. Liberty leaves each free to pursue the course he may deem best to promote his interest and happiness, as far as it may be compatible with the primary end for which government is ordained, while security gives assurance to each that he shall not be deprived of the fruits of his exertions to better his condition.[1]

To accomplish this, Calhoun devises a system in which sovereign activity may be thwarted by an interested and opposing minority. In effect, he proposes that a minority—he calls it the "concurrent majority"— be given veto power over the acts of majorities. Such a system, however, is antithetical to egalitarian rule that is effective only when the majority will moves the government. It follows that Calhoun and those who adopt his position stand apart from accepted American political tradition in placing liberty in so privileged a position that it denies equality. Perhaps it was for this reason that Calhoun's fully worked out political philosophy, *A Disquisition on Government*, was not published until after his death. In its failure to provide a secure base for popular rule, it is unacceptable to the egalitarian strain of American political thought. In America one can argue for equality and liberty or for the primacy of equality, but it is difficult to argue for liberty at the expense of equality. The hope is that the two may coexist. Webster's closing words to Hayne are more than rhetorical flourish.

[1] Richard Crallé, ed., *The Works of John C. Calhoun* (New York: D. Appleton and Co., 1854), Vol. I, p. 52.

"Liberty *and* Union, now and for ever, one and inseparable!" [8] The emphasis was Webster's. It would take a civil war to finally decide the issue, but on the level of principle the question had been answered by the Declaration of Independence and the Constitution.

The selections which follow underline these issues. Included are the Virginia and Kentucky Resolutions, selections from Webster's reply to Hayne, and selections from Calhoun's *Disquisition*.

[8] *Writings and Speeches of Daniel Webster*, Vol. VI, p. 75.

THE KENTUCKY AND VIRGINIA RESOLUTIONS

KENTUCKY LEGISLATURE
IN THE HOUSE OF REPRESENTATIVES
(NOVEMBER 10TH, 1798)

Resolved, that the several States composing the United States of America, are not united on the principles of unlimited submission to their General Government; but that by compact under the style and title of a Constitution for the United States and of amendments thereto, they constituted a General Government for special purposes, delegated to that Government certain definite powers, reserving each State to itself, the residuary mass of right to their own self Government; and that whensoever the General Government assumes undelegated powers, its acts are unauthoritative, void, and of no force: That to this compact each State acceded as a State, and is an integral party, its co-States forming as to itself, the other party: That the Government created by this compact was not made the exclusive or final *judge* of the extent of the powers delegated to itself; since that would have made its discretion, and not the Constitution, the measure of its powers; but that as in all other cases of compact among parties having no common Judge, each party has an equal right to judge for itself, as well of infractions as of the mode and measure of redress.

II. Resolved, that the Constitution of the United States having delegated to Congress a power to punish treason, counterfeiting the securities and current coin of the United States, piracies and felonies committed on the High Seas, and offenses against the laws of nations, and no other crimes whatever, and it being true as a general principle, and one of the amendments to the Constitution having also declared, "that the powers not delegated to the United States by the Constitution, nor prohibited by it to the States, are reserved to the States respectively, or to the people," therefore also the same act of Congress passed on the 14th day of July, 1798, and entitled "An act in addition to the act entitled an act for the punishment of certain crimes against the United

The Kentucky-Virginia Resolutions and Mr. Madison's Report of 1799, reprinted and distributed by the Virginia Commission on Constitutional Government (1960).

States," as also the act passed by them on the 27th day of June, 1798, entitled "An act to punish frauds committed on the Bank of the United States" (and all other their acts which assume to create, define, or punish crimes other than those enumerated in the Constitution) are altogether void and of no force, and that the power to create, define, and punish such other crimes is reserved, and of right appertains solely and exclusively to the respective States, each within its own Territory.

III. Resolved, that it is true as a general principle, and is also expressly declared by one of the amendments to the Constitution that "the powers not delegated to the United States by the Constitution, nor prohibited by it to the States, are reserved to the States respectively or to the people;" and that no power over the freedom of religion, freedom of speech, or freedom of the press being delegated to the United States by the Constitution, nor prohibited by it to the States, all lawful powers respecting the same did of right remain, and were reserved to the States, or to the people: That thus was manifested their determination to retain to themselves the right of judging how far the licentiousness of speech and of the press may be abridged without lessening their useful freedom, and how far those abuses which cannot be separated from their use, should be tolerated rather than the use be destroyed; and thus also they guarded against all abridgement by the United States of the freedom of religious opinions and exercises, and retained to themselves the right of protecting the same, as this state by a Law passed on the general demand of its Citizens, had already protected them from all human restraint or interference: And that in addition to this general principle and express declaration, another and more special provision has been made by one of the amendments to the Constitution which expressly declares, that "Congress shall make no law respecting an Establishment of religion, or prohibiting the free exercise thereof, or abridging the freedom of speech, or the press," thereby guarding in the same sentence, and under the same words, the freedom of religion, of speech, and of the press, insomuch, that whatever violates either, throws down the sanctuary which covers the others, and that libels, falsehoods, and defamation, equally with heresy and false religion, are withheld from the cognizance of the federal tribunals. That therefore the act of the Congress of the United States passed on the 14th day of July 1798, entitled "An act in addition to the act for the punishment of certain crimes against the United States," which does abridge the freedom of the press, is not law, but is altogether void and of no effect.

IV. Resolved, that alien friends are under the jurisdiction and protection of the laws of the State wherein they are; that no power over them has been delegated to the United States, nor prohibited to the individual States distinct from their power over citizens; and it being true as a general principle, and one of the amendments to the Constitution having also declared, that "the powers not delegated to the United States by the Constitution nor prohibited by it to the States are reserved to the States respectively or to the people," the act of the Congress of the United States passed on the 22d day of June, 1798, entitled "An act concerning aliens," which assumes power over alien friends not delegated by the Constitution, is not law, but is altogether void and of no force.

V. Resolved, that in addition to the general principle as well as the express declaration, that powers not delegated are reserved, another and more special provision inserted in the Constitution from abundant caution has declared, "that the *migration* or importation of such persons as any of the States now existing shall think proper to admit, shall not be prohibited by the Congress prior to the year 1808." That this Commonwealth does admit the migration of alien friends described as the subject of the said act concerning aliens; that a provision against prohibiting their migration, is a provision against all acts equivalent thereto, or it would be nugatory; that to remove them when migrated is equivalent to a prohibition of their migration, and is therefore contrary to the said provision of the Constitution and void.

VI. Resolved, that the imprisonment of a person under the protection of the Laws of this Commonwealth on his failure to obey the simple *order* of the President to depart out of the United States, as is undertaken by the said act entitled "An act concerning Aliens," is contrary to the Constitution, one amendment to which has provided, that "no person shall be deprived of liberty without due process of law," and that another having provided "that in all criminal prosecutions, the accused shall enjoy the right to a public trial by an impartial jury, to be informed of the nature and cause of the accusation, to be confronted with the witnesses against him, to have compulsory process for obtaining witnesses in his favour, and to have the assistance of counsel for his defence," the same act undertaking to authorize the President to remove a person out of the United States who is under the protection of the Law, on his own suspicion, without accusation, without jury, without public trial, without confrontation of the witnesses against him, without having witnesses in his favour, without defence, without counsel, is contrary to these provisions also of the Constitution, is therefore not law but utterly void and of no force.

That transferring the power of judging any person who is under the protection of the laws, from the Courts to the President of the United States, as is undertaken by the same act concerning Aliens, is against the article of the Constitution which provides, that "the judicial power of the United States shall be vested in Courts, the Judges of which shall hold their offices during good behaviour," and that the said act is void for that reason also; and it is further to be noted, that this transfer of Judiciary power is to that magistrate of the General Government who already possesses all the Executive, and a qualified negative in all the Legislative powers.

VII. Resolved, that the construction applied by the General Government (as is evinced by sundry of their proceedings) to those parts of the Constitution of the United States which delegate to Congress a power to lay and collect taxes, duties, imposts, and excises; to pay the debts, and provide for the common defence, and general welfare of the United States, and to make all laws which shall be necessary and proper for carrying into execution the powers vested by the Constitution in the Government of the United States, or any department thereof, goes to the destruction of all the limits prescribed to their power by the Constitution—That words meant by that instrument to be subsiduary only to the execution of the limited powers, ought not to be so construed as themselves to give unlimited powers, nor a part so to be taken, as to destroy the whole residue of the instrument: That the proceedings of the General Government under colour of these articles, will be a fit and necessary subject for revisal and correction at a time of greater tranquility, while those specified in the preceding resolutions call for immediate redress.

VIII. Resolved, that the preceeding Resolutions be transmitted to the Senators and Representatives in Congress from this Commonwealth, who are hereby enjoined to present the same to their respective Houses, and to use their best endeavours to procure at the next session of Congress, a repeal of the aforesaid unconstitutional and obnoxious acts.

IX. Resolved lastly, that the Governor of this Commonwealth be, and is hereby authorised and requested to communicate the preceding Resolutions to the Legislatures of the several States, to assure them that this Commonwealth considers Union for specified National purposes, and particularly for those specified in their late Federal Compact, to be friendly to the peace, happiness, and prosperity of all the States: that faithful to that compact, according to the plain intent and meaning in which it was understood and acceded to by the several parties, it is sincerely anxious for its preservation: that it does also believe, that to take from the States all the powers of self government, and transfer them to a general and consolidated Government, without regard to the special delegations and reservations solemnly agreed to in that compact, is not for the peace, happiness, or prosperity of these States: And that therefore, this Commonwealth is determined, as it doubts not its co-States are, tamely to submit to undelegated & consequently unlimited powers in no man or body of men on earth: that if the acts before specified should stand, these conclusions would flow from them; that the General Government may place any act they think proper on the list of crimes & punish it themselves, whether enumerated or not enumerated by the Constitution as cognizable by them: that they may transfer its cognizance to the President or any other person, who may himself be the accuser, counsel, judge, and jury, whose *suspicions* may be the evidence, his order the sentence, his officer the executioner, and his breast the sole record of the transaction: that a very numerous and valuable description of the inhabitants of these States, being by this precedent reduced as outlaws to the absolute dominion of one man and the barrier of the Constitution thus swept away from us all, no rampart now remains against the passions and the power of a majority of Congress, to protect from a like exportation or other more grievous punishment the minority of the same body, the Legislatures, Judges, Governors, & Counsellors of the States, nor their other peaceable inhabitants who may venture to reclaim the constitutional rights & liberties of the States & people, or who for other causes, good or bad, may be obnoxious to the views or marked by the suspicions of the President, or be thought dangerous to his or their elections or other interests public or personal: that the friendless alien has indeed been selected as the safest subject of a first experiment: but the citizen will soon follow, or rather has already followed; for, already has a Sedition Act marked him as its prey: that these and successive acts of the same character, unless arrested on the threshold, may tend to drive these States into revolution and blood, and will furnish new calumnies against Republican Governments, and new pretexts for those who wish it to be believed, that man cannot be governed but by a rod of iron: that it would be a dangerous delusion were a confidence in the men of our choice to silence our fears for the safety of our rights: that confidence is every where the parent of despotism: free government is founded in jealousy and not in confidence; it is jealousy and not confidence which prescribes limited Constitutions to bind down those whom we are obliged to trust with power: that our Constitution has accordingly fixed the limits to which and no further our confidence may go; and let the honest advocate of confidence read the Alien and Sedition Acts, and say if the Constitution has not been wise in fixing limits to the Government it created, and whether we should be wise in destroying those limits? Let him say what the Government is if it be not a tyranny, which the men of our choice have conferred on the President, and the President of our choice has assented to and accepted over the friendly strangers, to whom the mild spirit of our Country and its laws had pledged hospitality and protection: that the men of our choice have more respected the bare suspicions of the President than the solid rights of innocence, the claims of justification, the sacred force of truth, and the forms & substance of law and justice. In questions of power then let no more be heard of confidence in man, but bind him down from mischief by the chains of the Constitution. That this Commonwealth does therefore call on its co-States for an expression of their sentiments on the acts concerning Aliens, and for the punishment of certain crimes herein before specified, plainly declaring whether these acts are or are not authorized by the Federal Compact? And it doubts not that their sense will be so announced as to prove their attachment unaltered to limited Government, whether general or particular, and that the rights and liberties of their co-States will be exposed to no dangers by remaining embarked on a common bottom with their own: That they will concur with this Commonwealth in considering the said acts as so palpably against the Constitution as to amount to an undisguised declaration, that the Compact is not meant to be the measure of the powers of the General Government, but that it will proceed in the exercise over these States of all powers whatsoever: That they will view this as seizing the rights of the States and consolidating them in the hands of the General Government with a power assumed to bind the States (not merely in cases made federal) but in all cases whatsoever, by laws made, not with their consent, but by others against their consent: That this would be to surrender the form of Government we have chosen, and to live under one deriving its powers from its own will, and not from our authority; and that the co-States recurring to their natural right in cases not made federal, will concur in declaring these acts void and of no force, and will each unite with this Commonwealth in requesting their repeal at the next session of Congress.

THE GENERAL ASSEMBLY OF VIRGINIA
IN THE HOUSE OF DELEGATES
(FRIDAY, DECEMBER 21, 1798)

Resolved, That the General Assembly of Virginia, doth unequivocally express a firm resolution to maintain and defend the Constitution of the United States, and the Constitution of this State, against every aggression either foreign or domestic, and that they will support the government of the United States in all measures warranted by the former.

That this Assembly most solemnly declares a warm attachment to the Union of the States, to maintain which it pledges all its powers; and that for this end, it is their duty to watch over and oppose every infraction of those principles which constitute the only basis of that Union, because a faithful observance of them, can alone secure its existence and the public happiness.

That this Assembly doth explicitly and peremptorily declare, that it views the powers of the federal government, as resulting from the compact, to which the States are parties; as limited by the plain sense and intention of the instrument constituting that compact; as no further valid than they are authorized by the grants enumerated in that compact; and that in case of a deliberate, palpable, and dangerous exercise of other powers, not granted by the said compact, the States who are parties thereto, have the right, and are in duty bound, to interpose for arresting the progress of the evil, and for maintaining within their respective limits, the authorities, rights and liberties appertaining to them.

That the General Assembly doth also express its deep regret, that a spirit has in sundry instances, been manifested by the federal government, to enlarge its powers by forced constructions of the constitutional charter which defines them; and that indications have appeared of a design to expound certain general phrases (which having been copied from the very limited grant of powers in the former articles of confederation were the less liable to be misconstrued) so as to destroy the meaning and effect, of the particular enumeration which necessarily explains and limits the general phrases; and so as to consolidate the States by degrees, into one sovereignty, the obvious tendency and inevitable consequence of which would be, to transform the present republican system of the United States, into an absolute, or at best a mixed monarchy.

That the General Assembly doth particularly protest against the palpable and alarming infractions of the Constitution, in the two late cases of the "Alien and Sedition Acts" passed at the last session of Congress; the first of which exercises a power nowhere delegated to the federal government, and which by uniting legislative and judicial powers to those of executive, subverts the general principles of free government, as well as the particular organization, and positive provisions of the federal Constitution; and the other of which acts, exercises in like manner, a power not delegated by the Constitution, but on the contrary, expressly and positively forbidden by one of the amendments thereto;—a power, which more than any other, ought to produce universal alarm, because it is leveled against that right of freely examining public characters and measures, and of free communication among the people thereon, which has ever been justly deemed, the only effectual guardian of every other right.

That this State having by its Convention, which ratified the Federal Constitution, expressly declared, that among other essential rights, "the Liberty of Conscience and of the Press cannot be cancelled, abridged, restrained, or modified by any authority of the United States," and from its extreme anxiety to guard these rights from every possible attack of sophistry or ambition, having with other States, recommended an amendment for that purpose, which amendment was, in due time, annexed to the Constitution; it would mark a reproachful inconsistency, and criminal degeneracy, if an indifference were now shewn, to the most palpable violation of one of the Rights, thus declared and secured; and to the establishment of a precedent which may be fatal to the other.

That the good people of this Commonwealth, having ever felt, and continuing to feel, the most sincere affection for their brethren of the other States; the truest anxiety for establishing and perpetuating the union of all; and the most scrupulous fidelity to that Constitution, which is the pledge of mutual friendship, and the instrument of mutual happiness, the General Assembly doth solemnly appeal to the like dispositions of the other States, in confidence that they will concur with this Commonwealth in declaring, as it does hereby declare, that the acts aforesaid, are unconstitutional; and that the necessary and proper measures will be taken by each, for cooperating with this State, in maintaining the Authorities, Rights, and Liberties, reserved to the States respectively, or to the People.

That the Governor be desired, to transmit a copy of the foregoing Resolutions to the executive authority of each of the other States, with a request that the same may be communicated to the Legislature thereof; and that a copy be furnished to each of the Senators and Representatives representing this State in the Congress of the United States.

Daniel Webster

REPLY TO HAYNE
(1830)

This leads, Sir, to the real and wide difference in political opinion between the honorable gentleman and myself. On my part, I look upon all these objects as connected with the common good, fairly embraced in its object and its terms; he, on the contrary, deems them all, if good at all, only local good. This is our difference. The interrogatory which he proceeded to put, at once explains this difference. "What interest," asks he, "has South Carolina in a canal in Ohio?" Sir, this very question is full of significance. It develops the gentleman's whole political system; and its answer expounds mine. Here we differ. I look upon a road over the Alleghanies, a canal round the falls of the Ohio, or a canal or railway from the Atlantic to the Western waters, as being an object large and extensive enough to be fairly said to be for the common benefit. The gentleman thinks otherwise, and this is the key to his construction of the powers of the government. He may well ask what interest has South Carolina in a canal in Ohio. On his system, it is true, she has no interest. On that system, Ohio and Carolina are different governments and different countries; connected here, it is true, by some slight and ill-defined bond of union, but in all main respects separate and diverse. On that system, Carolina has no more interest in a canal in Ohio than in Mexico. The gentleman, therefore, only follows out his own principles; he does no more than arrive at the natural conclusions of his own doctrines; he only announces the true results of that creed which he has adopted himself, and would persuade others to adopt, when he thus declares that South Carolina has no interest in a public work in Ohio.

Sir, we narrow-minded people of New England do not reason thus. Our *notion* of things is entirely different. We look upon the States, not as separated, but as united. We love to dwell on that union, and on the mutual happiness which it has so much promoted, and the common

Daniel Webster, "Second Speech on Foot's Resolution" (1830), reprinted in *The Writings and Speeches of Daniel Webster*, National Edition (Boston: Little, Brown and Co., 1903), Vol. VI, pp. 3–75

renown which it has so greatly contributed to acquire. In our contemplation, Carolina and Ohio are parts of the same country; States, united
under the same general government, having interests, common, associated,
intermingled. In whatever is within the proper sphere of the constitutional power of this government, we look upon the States as one. We
do not impose geographical limits to our patriotic feeling or regard;
we do not follow rivers and mountains, and lines of latitude, to find
boundaries, beyond which public improvements do not benefit us. We
who come here, as agents and representatives of these narrow-minded and
selfish men of New England, consider ourselves as bound to regard with
an equal eye the good of the whole, in whatever is within our powers of
legislation. Sir, if a railroad or canal, beginning in South Carolina and
ending in South Carolina, appeared to me to be of national importance
and national magnitude, believing, as I do, that the power of government
extends to the encouragement of works of that description, if I were to
stand up here and ask, What interest has Massachusetts in a railroad in
South Carolina? I should not be willing to face my constituents. These
same narrow-minded men would tell me, that they had sent me to act
for the whole country, and that one who possessed too little comprehension, either of intellect or feeling, one who was not large enough, both
in mind and in heart, to embrace the whole, was not fit to be intrusted
with the interest of any part.

Sir, I do not desire to enlarge the powers of the government by
unjustifiable construction, nor to exercise any not within a fair interpretation. But when it is believed that a power does exist, then it is, in my
judgment, to be exercised for the general benefit of the whole. So far as
respects the exercise of such a power, the States are one. It was the very
object of the Constitution to create unity of interests to the extent of
the powers of the general government. In war and peace we are one; in
commerce, one; because the authority of the general government reaches
to war and peace, and to the regulation of commerce. I have never seen
any more difficulty in erecting lighthouses on the lakes, than on the ocean;
in improving the harbors of inland seas, than if they were within the ebb
and flow of the tide; or in removing obstructions in the vast streams of the
West, more than in any work to facilitate commerce on the Atlantic
coast. If there be any power for one, there is power also for the other; and
they are all and equally for the common good of the country.

There are other objects, apparently more local, or the benefit of
which is less general, towards which, nevertheless, I have concurred with
others, to give aid by donations of land. It is proposed to construct a road,
in or through one of the new States, in which this government possesses
large quantities of land. Have the United States no right, or, as a great
and untaxed proprietor, are they under no obligation to contribute to an

object thus calculated to promote the common good of all the proprietors, themselves included? And even with respect to education, which is the extreme case, let the question be considered. In the first place, as we have seen, it was made matter of compact with these States, that they should do their part to promote education. In the next place, our whole system of land laws proceeds on the idea that education is for the common good; because, in every division, a certain portion is uniformly reserved and appropriated for the use of schools. And, finally, have not these new States singularly strong claims, founded on the ground already stated, that the government is a great untaxed proprietor, in the ownership of the soil? It is a consideration of great importance, that probably there is in no part of the country, or the world, so great call for the means of education, as in these new States, owing to the vast numbers of persons within those ages in which education and instruction are usually received if received at all. This is the natural consequence of recency of settlement and rapid increase. The census of these States shows how great a porportion of the whole population occupies the classes between infancy and manhood. These are the wide fields, and here is the deep and quick soil for the seeds of knowledge and virtue; and this is the favored season, the very spring-time for sowing them. Let them be disseminated without stint. Let them be scattered with a bountiful hand, broadcast. Whatever the government can fairly do towards these objects, in my opinion, ought to be done. . . .

There yet remains to be performed, Mr. President, by far the most grave and important duty, which I feel to be devolved on me by this occasion. It is to state, and to defend, what I conceive to be the true principles of the Constitution under which we are here assembled. I might well have desired that so weighty a task should have fallen into other and abler hands. I could have wished that it should have been executed by those whose character and experience give weight and influence to their opinions, such as cannot possibly belong to mine. But, Sir, I have met the occasion, not sought it; and I shall proceed to state by my own sentiments, without challenging for them any particular regard, with studied plainness, and as much precision as possible.

I understand the honorable gentleman from South Carolina to maintain, that it is a right of the State legislatures to interfere, whenever, in their judgment, this government transcends its constitutional limits, and to arrest the operation of its laws.

I understand him to maintain this right, as a right existing *under* the Constitution, not as a right to overthrow it on the ground of extreme necessity, such as would justify violent revolution.

I understand him to maintain an authority, on the part of the States, thus to interfere, for the purpose of correcting the exercise of power by the general government, of checking it, and of compelling it to conform to their opinion of the extent of its powers.

I understand him to maintain, that the ultimate power of judging of the constitutional extent of its own authority is not lodged exclusively in the general government, or any branch of it; but that, on the contrary, the States may lawfully decide for themselves, and each State for itself, whether, in a given case, the act of the general government transcends its power.

I understand him to insist, that, if the exigency of the case, in the opinion of any State government, require it, such State government may, by its own sovereign authority, annul an act of the general government which it deems plainly and palpably unconstitutional.

This is the sum of what I understand from him to be the South Carolina doctrine, and the doctrine which he maintains. I propose to consider it, and compare it with the Constitution. Allow me to say, as a preliminary remark, that I call this the South Carolina doctrine only because the gentleman himself has so denominated it. I do not feel at liberty to say that South Carolina, as a State, has ever advanced these sentiments. I hope she has not, and never may. That a great majority of her people are opposed to the tariff laws, is doubtless true. That a majority, somewhat less than that just mentioned, conscientiously believe these laws unconstitutional, may probably also be true. But that any majority holds to the right of direct State interference at State discretion, the right of nullifying acts of Congress by acts of State legislation, is more than I know, and what I shall be slow to believe.

That there are individuals besides the honorable gentleman who do maintain these opinions, is quite certain. I recollect the recent expression of a sentiment, which circumstances attending its utterance and publication justify us in supposing was not unpremeditated. "The sovereignty of the State,—never to be controlled, construed, or decided on, but by her own feelings of honorable justice."

> Mr. Hayne here rose and said, that, for the purpose of being clearly understood, he would state that his proposition was in the words of the Virginia resolution, as follows:—

> "That this assembly doth explicitly and peremptorily declare, that it views the powers of the federal government, as resulting from the compact to which the States are parties, as limited by the plain sense and intention of the instrument constituting that compact, as no farther valid than they are authorized by the grants enumerated in that compact; and that, in case of a deliberate, palpable, and dangerous exercise of other powers, not granted by the said compact, the States who are parties thereto have the right, and are in duty bound, to interpose, for arresting the progress of the

evil, and for maintaining within their respective limits the authorities, rights, and liberties appertaining to them."

Mr. Webster resumed:—

I am quite aware, Mr. President, of the existence of the resolution which the gentleman read, and has now repeated, and that he relies on it as his authority. I know the source, too, from which it is understood to have proceeded. I need not say that I have much respect for the constitutional opinions of Mr. Madison; they would weigh greatly with me always. But before the authority of his opinion be vouched for the gentleman's proposition, it will be proper to consider what is the fair interpretation of that resolution, to which Mr. Madison is understood to have given his sanction. As the gentleman construes it, it is an authority for him. Possibly, he may not have adopted the right construction. That resolution declares, that, *in the case of the dangerous exercise of powers not granted by the general government, the States may interpose to arrest the progress of the evil.* But how interpose, and what does this declaration purport? Does it mean no more than that there may be extreme cases, in which the people, in any mode of assembling, may resist usurpation, and relieve themselves from a tyrannical government? No one will deny this. Such resistance is not only acknowledged to be just in America, but in England also. Blackstone admits as much, in the theory, and practice, too, of the English constitution. We, Sir, who oppose the Carolina doctrine, do not deny that the people may, if they choose, throw off any government when it becomes oppressive and intolerable, and erect a better in its stead. We all know that civil institutions are established for the public benefit, and that when they cease to answer the ends of their existence they may be changed. But I do not understand the doctrine now contended for to be that, which, for the sake of distinction, we may call the right of revolution. I understand the gentleman to maintain, that, without revolution, without civil commotion, without rebellion, a remedy for supposed abuse and transgression of the powers of the general government lies in a direct appeal to the interference of the State governments.

Mr. Hayne here rose and said: He did not contend for the mere right of revolution, but for the right of constitutional resistance. What he maintained was, that in case of a plain, palpable violation of the Constitution by the general government, a State may interpose; and that this interposition is constitutional.

Mr. Webster resumed:—

So, Sir, I understood the gentleman, and am happy to find that I did not misunderstand him. What he contends for is, that it is constitutional to interrupt the administration of the Constitution itself, in the hands of those who are chosen and sworn to administer it, by the direct interference, in form of law, of the States, in virtue of their sovereign capacity. The inherent right in the people to reform their government I do not deny; and they have another right, and that is, to resist unconstitutional laws, without overturning the government. It is no doctrine of mine that unconstitutional laws bind the people. The great question is, Whose prerogative is it to decide on the constitutionality or unconstitutionality of the laws? On that, the main debate hinges. The proposition, that, in case of a supposed violation of the Constitution by Congress, the States have a constitutional right to interfere and annul the law of Congress, is the proposition of the gentleman. I do not admit it. If the gentleman had intended no more than to assert the right of revolution for justifiable cause, he would have said only what all agree to. But I cannot conceive that there can be a middle course, between submission to the laws, when regularly pronounced constitutional, on the one hand, and open resistance, which is revolution or rebellion, on the other. I say, the right of a State to annul a law of Congress cannot be maintained, but on the ground of the inalienable right of man to resist oppression; that is to say, upon the ground of revolution. I admit that there is an ultimate violent remedy, above the Constitution and in defiance of the Constitution, which may be resorted to when a revolution is to be justified. But I do not admit, that, under the Constitution and in conformity with it, there is any mode in which a State government, as a member of the Union, can interfere and stop the progress of the general government, by force of her own laws, under any circumstances whatever.

This leads us to inquire into the origin of this government and the source of its power. Whose agent is it? Is it the creature of the State legislatures, or the creature of the people? If the government of the United States be the agent of the State governments, then they may control it, provided they can agree in the manner of controlling it; if it be the agent of the people, then the people alone can control it, restrain it, modify, or reform it. It is observable enough, that the doctrine for which the honorable gentleman contends leads him to the necessity of maintaining, not only that this general government is the creature of the States, but that it is the creature of each of the States severally, so that each may assert the power for itself of determining whether it acts within the limits of its authority. It is the servant of four-and-twenty masters, of different wills and different purposes, and yet bound to obey all. This absurdity (for it seems no less) arises from a misconception as to the origin of this government and its true character. It is, Sir, the people's Constitution, the people's government, made for the people, made by the people, and answerable to the people. The people of the United States have declared that this Constitution shall be the supreme law. We must either admit the proposition, or dispute their authority. The States are, unquestionably, sovereign, so far as their sovereignty is not affected by this supreme law. But the State legislatures, as political bodies, however sovereign, are yet not sovereign over the people. So far as the people have given power to the general government, so far the grant is unquestionably good, and the government holds of the people, and not of the State governments. We are all agents of the same supreme power, the people. The general government and the State governments derive their authority from the same source. Neither can, in relation to the other, be called primary, though one is definite and restricted, and the other general and residuary. The national government possesses those powers which it can be shown the people have conferred on it, and no more. All the rest belongs to the State governments, or to the people themselves. So far as the people have restrained State sovereignty, by the expression of their will, in the Constitution of the United States, so far, it must be admitted, State sovereignty is effectually controlled. I do not contend that it is, or ought to be, controlled farther. The sentiment to which I have referred propounds that State sovereignty is only to be controlled by its own "feeling of justice"; that is to say, it is not to be controlled at all, for one who is to follow his own feelings is under no legal control. Now, however men may think this ought to be, the fact is, that the people of the United States have chosen to impose control on State sovereignties. There are those, doubtless, who wish they had been left without restraint; but the Constitution has ordered the matter differently. To make war, for instance, is an exercise of sovereignty; but the Constitution declares that no State shall make war. To coin money is another exercise of sovereign power; but no State is at liberty to coin money. Again, the Constitution says that no sovereign State shall be so sovereign as to make a treaty. These prohibitions, it must be confessed, are a control on the State sovereignty of South Carolina, as well as of the other States, which does not arise "from her own feelings of honorable justice." The opinion referred to, therefore, is in defiance of the plainest provisions of the Constitution. . . .

In another of the South Carolina addresses, having premised that the crisis requires "all the concentrated energy of passion," an attitude of open resistance to the laws of the Union is advised. Open resistance to the laws, then, is the constitutional remedy, the conservative power of the State, which the South Carolina doctrines teach for the redress of political evils, real or imaginary. And its authors further say, that, appealing with confidence to the Constitution itself, to justify their opinions, they cannot consent to try their accuracy by the courts of justice. In one sense, indeed, Sir, this is assuming an attitude of open resistance in favor of liberty. But what sort of liberty? The liberty of establishing their own opinions, in defiance of the opinions of all others; the liberty of judging and of deciding exclusively themselves, in a matter in which others have as much right to judge and decide as they; the liberty of placing their own opinions above the judgment of all others, above the laws, and above the Constitution. This is their liberty, and this is the fair result of the proposition contended for by the honorable gentleman. Or, it may be more properly said, it is identical with it, rather than a result from it. . . .

I must now beg to ask, Sir, Whence is this supposed right of the States derived? Where do they find the power to interfere with the laws of the Union? Sir, the opinion which the honorable gentleman maintains is a notion founded in a total misapprehension, in my judgment, of the origin of this government, and of the foundation on which it stands. I hold it to be a popular government, erected by the people; those who administer it, responsible to the people; and itself capable of being amended and modified, just as the people may choose it should be. It is as popular, just as truly emanating from the people, as the State governments. It is created for one purpose; the State governments for another. It has its own powers; they have theirs. There is no more authority with them to arrest the operation of a law of Congress, than with Congress to arrest the operation of their laws. We are here to administer a Constitution emanating immediately from the people, and trusted by them to our administration. It is not the creature of the State governments. It is of no moment to the argument, that certain acts of the State legislatures are necessary to fill our seats in this body. That is not one of their original State powers, a part of the sovereignty of the State. It is a duty which the people, by the Constitution itself, have imposed on the State legislatures; and which they might have left to be performed elsewhere, if they had seen fit. So they have left the choice of President with electors; but all this does not affect the proposition that this whole government, President, Senate, and House of Representatives, is a popular government. It leaves it still all its popular character. The governor of a State (in some of the States) is chosen, not directly by the people, but by those who are chosen by the people, for the purpose of performing, among other duties, that of electing a governor. Is the government of the State, on that account, not a popular government? This government, Sir, is the independent offspring of the popular will. It is not the creature of State legislatures; nay, more, if the whole truth must be told, the people brought it into existence, established it, and have hitherto supported it, for the very purpose, amongst others, of imposing certain salutary restraints on State sovereignties. The States cannot now make war; they cannot contract alliances; they cannot make, each for itself, separate regulations of commerce; they cannot lay imposts; they cannot coin money. If this Constitution, Sir, be the creature of State legislatures, it must be admitted that it has obtained a strange control over the volitions of its creators.

The people, then, Sir, erected this government. They gave it a Constitution, and in that Constitution they have enumerated the powers which they bestow on it. They have made it a limited government. They have defined its authority. They have restrained it to the exercise of such powers as are granted; and all others, they declare, are reserved to the States or the people. But, Sir, they have not stopped here. If they had, they would have accomplished but half their work. No definition can be so clear, as to avoid possibility of doubt; no limitation so precise, as to exclude all uncertainty. Who, then, shall construe this grant of the people? Who shall interpret their will, where it may be supposed they have left it doubtful? With whom do they repose this ultimate right of deciding on the powers of the government? Sir, they have settled all this in the fullest manner. They have left it with the government itself, in its appropriate branches. Sir, the very chief end, the main design, for which the whole Constitution was framed and adopted, was to establish a government that should not be obliged to act through State agency, or depend on State opinion and State discretion. The people had had quite enough of that kind of government under the Confederation. Under that system, the legal action, the application of law to individuals, belonged exclusively to the States. Congress could only recommend; their acts were not of binding force, till the States had adopted and sanctioned them. Are we in that condition still? Are we yet at the mercy of State discretion and State construction? Sir, if we are, then vain will be our attempt to maintain the Constitution under which we sit.

But, Sir, the people have wisely provided, in the Constitution itself, a proper, suitable mode and tribunal for settling questions of constitutional law. There are in the Constitution grants of powers to Congress, and restrictions on these powers. There are, also, prohibitions on the States. Some authority must, therefore, necessarily exist, having the ultimate jurisdiction to fix and ascertain the interpretation of these grants, restrictions, and prohibitions. The Constitution has itself pointed out, ordained, and established that authority. How has it accomplished this great and essential end? By declaring, Sir, that *"the Constitution, and the laws of the United States made in pursuance thereof, shall be the supreme law of the land, any thing in the constitution or laws of any State to the contrary notwithstanding."*

This, Sir, was the first great step. By this the supremacy of the Constitution and laws of the United States is declared. The people so will it. No State law is to be valid which comes in conflict with the Constitution, or any law of the United States passed in pursuance of it. But who shall decide this question of interference? To whom lies the last appeal? This,

Sir, the Constitution itself decides also, by declaring, *"that the judicial power shall extend to all cases arising under the Constitution and laws of the United States."* These two provisions cover the whole ground. They are, in truth, the keystone of the arch! With these it is a government; without them it is a confederation. In pursuance of these clear and express provisions, Congress established, at its very first session, in the judicial act, a mode for carrying them into full effect, and for bringing all questions of constitutional power to the final decision of the Supreme Court. It then, Sir, became a government. It then had the means of self-protection; and but for this, it would, in all probability, have been now among things which are past. Having constituted the government, and declared its powers, the people have further said, that, since somebody must decide on the extent of these powers, the government shall itself decide; subject, always, like other popular governments, to its responsibility to the people. And now, Sir, I repeat, how is it that a State legislature acquires any power to interfere? Who, or what, gives them the right to say to the people,"We, who are your agents and servants for one purpose, will undertake to decide, that your other agents and servants, appointed by you for another purpose, have transcended the authority you gave them!" The reply would be, I think, not impertinent,—"Who made you a judge over another's servants? To their own masters they stand or fall."

Sir, I deny this power of State legislatures altogether. It cannot stand the test of examination. Gentlemen may say, that, in an extreme case, a State government might protect the people from intolerable oppression. Sir, in such a case, the people might protect themselves, without the aid of the State governments. Such a case warrants revolution. It must make, when it comes, a law for itself. A nullifying act of a State legislature cannot alter the case, nor make resistance any more lawful. In maintaining these sentiments, Sir, I am but asserting the rights of the people. I state what they have declared, and insist on their right to declare it. They have chosen to repose this power in the general government, and I think it my duty to support it, like other constitutional powers.

For myself, Sir, I do not admit the competency of South Carolina, or any other State, to prescribe my constitutional duty; or to settle, between me and the people, the validity of laws of Congress, for which I have voted. I decline her umpirage. I have not sworn to support the Constitution according to her construction of its clauses. I have not stipulated, by my oath of office or otherwise, to come under any responsibility, except to the people, and those whom they have appointed to pass upon the question, whether laws, supported by my votes, conform to the Constitution of the country. And, Sir, if we look to the general nature of the case, could any thing have been more preposterous, than to make a government for the whole Union, and yet leave its powers subject, not to one interpretation, but to thirteen or twenty-four interpretations? Instead

of one tribunal, established by all, responsible to all, with power to decide for all, shall constitutional questions be left to four-and-twenty popular bodies, each at liberty to decide for itself, and none bound to respect
the decisions of others; and each at liberty, too, to give a new construction
on every new election of its own members? Would any thing, with such
a principle in it, or rather with such a destitution of all principle, be fit
to be called a government? No, Sir. It should not be denominated a
Constitution. It should be called, rather, a collection of topics for everlasting controversy; heads of debate for a disputatious people. It would
not be a government. It would not be adequate to any practical good, or
fit for any country to live under. . . .

If any thing be found in the national Constitution, either by original
provision or subsequent interpretation, which ought not to be in it, the
people know how to get rid of it. If any construction, unacceptable to
them, be established, so as to become practically a part of the Constitution, they will amend it, at their own sovereign pleasure. But while the
people choose to maintain it as it is, while they are satisfied with it, and
refuse to change it, who has given, or who can give, to the State legislatures a right to alter it, either by interference, construction, or otherwise?
Gentlemen do not seem to recollect that the people have any power to
do any thing for themselves. They imagine there is no safety for them,
any longer than they are under the close guardianship of the State legislatures. Sir, the people have not trusted their safety, in regard to the
general Constitution, to those hands. They have required other security,
and taken other bonds. They have chosen to trust themselves, first, to the
plain words of the instrument, and to such construction as the government
themselves, in doubtful cases, should put on their own powers, under
their oaths of office, and subject to their responsibility to them; just as
the people of a State trust their own State governments with a similar
power. Secondly, they have reposed their trust in the efficacy of frequent
elections, and in their own power to remove their own servants and agents
whenever they see cause. Thirdly, they have reposed trust in the judicial
power, which, in order that it might be trustworthy, they have made as
respectable, as disinterested, and as independent as was practicable.
Fourthly, they have seen fit to rely, in case of necessity, or high expediency, on their known and admitted power to alter or amend the Constitution, peaceably and quietly, whenever experience shall point out defects
or imperfections. And, finally, the people of the United States have at
no time, in no way, directly or indirectly, authorized any State legislature
to construe or interpret *their* high instrument of government; much less,
to interfere, by their own power, to arrest its course and operation.

If, Sir, the people in these respects had done otherwise than they
have done, their constitution could neither have been preserved, nor
would it have been worth preserving. And if its plain provisions shall

now be disregarded, and these new doctrines interpolated in it, it will become as feeble and helpless a being as its enemies, whether early or more recent, could possibly desire. It will exist in every State but as a poor dependent on State permission. It must borrow leave to be; and will be, no longer than State pleasure, or State discretion, sees fit to grant the indulgence, and to prolong its poor existence.

But, Sir, although there are fears, there are hopes also. The people have preserved this, their own chosen Constitution, for forty years, and have seen their happiness, prosperity, and renown grow with its growth, and strengthen with its strength. They are now, generally, strongly attached to it. Overthrown by direct assault, it cannot be; evaded, undermined, NULLIFIED, it will not be, if we, and those who shall succeed us here, as agents and representatives of the people, shall conscientiously and vigilantly discharge the two great branches of our public trust, faithfully to preserve, and wisely to administer it.

Mr. President, I have thus stated the reasons of my dissent to the doctrines which have been advanced and maintained. I am conscious of having detained you and the Senate much too long. I was drawn into the debate with no previous deliberation, such as is suited to the discussion of so grave and important a subject. But it is a subject of which my heart is full, and I have not been willing to suppress the utterance of its spontaneous sentiments. I cannot, even now, persuade myself to relinquish it, without expressing once more my deep conviction, that, since it respects nothing less than the Union of the States, it is of most vital and essential importance to the public happiness. I profess, Sir, in my career hitherto, to have kept steadily in view the prosperity and honor of the whole country, and the preservation of our Federal Union. It is to that Union we owe our safety at home, and our consideration and dignity abroad. It is to that Union that we are chiefly indebted for whatever makes us most proud of our country. That Union we reached only by the discipline of our virtues in the severe school of adversity. It had its origin in the necessities of disordered finance, prostrate commerce, and ruined credit. Under its benign influences, these great interests immediately awoke, as from the dead, and sprang forth with newness of life. Every year of its duration has teemed with fresh proofs of its utility and its blessings; and although our territory has stretched out wider and wider, and our population spread farther and farther, they have not outrun its protection or its benefits. It has been to us all a copious fountain of national, social, and personal happiness.

I have not allowed myself, Sir, to look beyond the Union, to see what might lie hidden in the dark recess behind. I have not coolly weighed the chances of preserving liberty when the bonds that unite us together shall be broken asunder. I have not accustomed myself to hang over the precipice of disunion, to see whether, with my short sight, I can fathom the depth of the abyss below; nor could I regard him as a safe counsellor in the affairs of this government, whose thoughts should be mainly bent on considering, not how the Union may be best preserved, but how tolerable might be the condition of the people when it should be broken up and destroyed. While the Union lasts, we have high, exciting, gratifying prospects spread out before us, for us and our children. Beyond that I seek not to penetrate the veil. God grant that in my day, at least, that curtain may not rise! God grant that on my vision never may be opened what lies behind! When my eyes shall be turned to behold for the last time the sun in heaven, may I not see him shining on the broken and dishonored fragments of a once glorious Union; on States dissevered, discordant, belligerent; on a land rent with civil feuds, or drenched, it may be, in fraternal blood! Let their last feeble and lingering glance rather behold the gorgeous ensign of the republic, now known and honored throughout the earth, still full high advanced, its arms and trophies streaming in their original lustre, not a stripe erased or polluted, nor a single star obscured, bearing for its motto, no such miserable interrogatory as "What is all this worth?" nor those other words of delusion and folly, "Liberty first and Union afterwards"; but everywhere, spread all over in characters of living light, blazing on all its ample folds, as they float over the sea and over the land, and in every wind under the whole heavens, that other sentiment, dear to every true American heart,—Liberty *and* Union, now and for ever, one and inseparable!"

A DISQUISITION
ON GOVERNMENT

But government, although intended to protect and preserve society, has itself a strong tendency to disorder and abuse of its powers, as all experience and almost every page of history testify. The cause is to be found in the same constitution of our nature which makes government indispensable. The powers which it is necessary for government to possess, in order to repress violence and preserve order, cannot execute themselves. They must be administered by men in whom, like others, the individual are stronger than the social feelings. And hence, the powers vested in them to prevent injustice and oppression on the part of others, will, if left unguarded, be by them converted into instruments to oppress the rest of the community. That, by which this is prevented, by whatever name called, is what is meant by CONSTITUTION, in its most comprehensive sense, when applied to GOVERNMENT.

Having its origin in the same principle of our nature, *constitution* stands to *government*, as *government* stands to *society*; and, as the end for which society is ordained, would be defeated without government, so that for which government is ordained would, in a great measure, be defeated without constitution. But they differ in this striking particular. There is no difficulty in forming government. It is not even a matter of choice, whether there shall be one or not. Like breathing, it is not permitted to depend on our volition. Necessity will force it on all communities in some one form or another. Very different is the case as to constitution. Instead of a matter of necessity, it is one of the most difficult tasks imposed on man to form a constitution worthy of the name; while, to form a perfect one,—one that would completely counteract the tendency of government to oppression and abuse, and hold it strictly to the great ends for which it is ordained,—has thus far exceeded human wisdom, and possibly ever will. From this, another striking difference results. Constitution is the contrivance of man, while government is of Divine

The Works of John C. Calhoun, ed. Richard K. Crallé (New York: D. Appleton and Co., 1854), Vol. I., pp. 1 ff.

ordination. Man is left to perfect what the wisdom of the Infinite ordained, as necessary to preserve the race.

With these remarks, I proceed to the consideration of the important
and difficult question: How is this tendency of government to be coun-
teracted? Or, to express it more fully,—How can those who are invested
with the powers of government be prevented from employing them, as
the means of aggrandizing themselves, instead of using them to protect
and preserve society? ...

There is but one way in which this can possibly be done; and that is,
by such an organism as will furnish the ruled with the means of resisting successfully this tendency on the part of the rulers to oppression
and abuse. Power can only be resisted by power,—and tendency by tendency. Those who exercise power and those subject to its exercise,—the
rulers and the ruled,—stand in antagonistic relations to each other. The
same constitution of our nature which leads rulers to oppress the ruled,—
regardless of the object for which government is ordained,—will, with
equal strength, lead the ruled to resist, when possessed of the means of
making peaceable and effective resistance. Such an organism, then, as
will furnish the means by which resistance may be systematically and
peaceably made on the part of the ruled, to oppression and abuse of
power on the part of the rulers, is the first and indispensable step towards
forming a constitutional government. And as this can only be effected
by or through the right of suffrage,—(the right on the part of the ruled
to choose their rulers at proper intervals, and to hold them thereby responsible for their conduct,)—the responsibility of the rulers to the ruled,
through the right of suffrage, is the indispensable and primary principle
in the *foundation* of a constitutional government. When this right is
properly guarded, and the people sufficiently enlightened to understand
their own rights and the interests of the community, and duly to appreciate the motives and conduct of those appointed to make and execute
the laws, it is all-sufficient to give to those who elect, effective control
over those they have elected. ...

But such is not the case. On the contrary, nothing is more difficult
than to equalize the action of the government, in reference to the various
and diversified interests of the community; and nothing more easy than
to pervert its powers into instruments to aggrandize and enrich one or
more interests by oppressing and impoverishing the others; and this too,
under the operation of laws, couched in general terms;—and which, on
their face, appear fair and equal. Nor is this the case in some particular
communities only. It is so in all; the small and the great,—the poor and
the rich,—irrespective of pursuits, productions, or degrees of civilization;
—with, however, this difference, that the more extensive and populous
the country, the more diversified the condition and pursuits of its pop-

ulation, and the richer, more luxurious, and dissimilar the people, the more difficult is it to equalize the action of the government,—and the more easy for one portion of the community to pervert its powers to oppress, and plunder the other.

Such being the case, it necessarily results, that the right of suffrage, by placing the control of the government in the community must, from the same constitution of our nature which makes government necessary to preserve society, lead to conflict among its different interests,—each striving to obtain possession of its powers, as the means of protecting itself against the others;—or of advancing its respective interests, regardless of the interests of others. For this purpose, a struggle will take place between the various interests to obtain a majority, in order to control the government. If no one interest be strong enough, of itself, to obtain it, a combination will be formed between those whose interests are most alike;— each conceding something to the others, until a sufficient number is obtained to make a majority. The process may be slow, and much time may be required before a compact, organized majority can be thus formed; but formed it will be in time, even without preconcert or design, by the sure workings of that principle or constitution of our nature in which government itself originates. When once formed, the community will be divided into two great parties,—a major and minor,—between which there will be incessant struggles on the one side to retain, and on the other to obtain the majority,—and, thereby, the control of the government and the advantages it confers. . . .

The dominant majority, for the time, would, in reality, through the right of suffrage, be the rulers—the controlling, governing, and irresponsible power; and those who make and execute the laws would, for the time, be, in reality, but *their* representatives and agents.

Nor would the fact that the former would constitute a majority of the community, counteract a tendency originating in the constitution of man; and which, as such, cannot depend on the number by whom the powers of the government may be wielded. Be it greater or smaller, a majority or minority, it must equally partake of an attribute inherent in each individual composing it; and, as in each the individual is stronger than the social feelings, the one would have the same tendency as the other to oppression and abuse of power. The reason applies to government in all its forms,—whether it be that of the one, the few, or the many. In each there must, of necessity, be a governing and governed,—a ruling and a subject portion. The one implies the other; and in all, the two bear the same relation to each other;—and have, on the part of the governing portion, the same tendency to oppression and abuse of power. Where the majority is that portion, it matters not how its powers may be exercised;—whether directly by themselves, or indirectly, through representatives or agents. Be it which it may, the minority, for the time, will be as much the governed or subject portion, as are the people in an aristocracy, or the subjects in a monarchy. The only difference in this respect is, that in the government of a majority, the minority may become the majority, and the majority the minority, through the right of suffrage; and thereby change their relative positions, without the intervention of force and revolution. But the duration, or uncertainty of the tenure, by which power is held, cannot, of itself, counteract the tendency inherent in government to oppression and abuse of power. On the contrary, the very uncertainty of the tenure, combined with the violent party warfare which must ever precede a change of parties under such governments, would rather tend to increase than diminish the tendency to oppression.

As, then, the right of suffrage, without some other provision, cannot counteract this tendency of government, the next question for consideration is—What is that other provision? This demands the most serious consideration; for of all the questions embraced in the science of government, it involves a principle, the most important, and the least understood; and when understood, the most difficult of application in practice. It is, indeed, emphatically, that principle which *makes* the constitution, in its strict and limited sense.

From what has been said, it is manifest, that this provision must be of a character calculated to prevent any one interest, or combination of interests, from using the powers of government to aggrandize itself at the expense of the others. Here lies the evil: and just in proportion as it shall prevent, or fail to prevent it, in the same degree it will effect, or fail to effect the end intended to be accomplished. There is but one certain mode in which this result can be secured; and that is, by the adoption of some restriction or limitation, which shall so effectually prevent any one interest, or combination of interests, from obtaining the exclusive control of the government, as to render hopeless all attempts directed to that end. There is, again, but one mode in which this can be effected; and that is, by taking the sense of each interest or portion of the community, which may be unequally and injuriously affected by the action of the government, separately, through its own majority, or in some other way by which its voice may be fairly expressed; and to require the consent of each interest, either to put or to keep the government in action. This, too, can be accomplished only in one way,—and that is, by such an organism of the government,—and, if necessary for the purpose, of the community also,—as will, by dividing and distributing the powers of government, give to each division or interest, through its appropriate organ, either a concurrent voice in making and executing the laws, or a veto on their execution. It is only by such an organism, that the assent of each can be made necessary to put the government in motion; or the power made effectual to arrest its action, when put in motion;—and it is only by the one or the other that the different interests, orders, classes, or portions, into which the community may be divided, can be protected, and all conflict and struggle between them prevented,—by rendering it impossible to put or to keep it in action, without the concurrent consent of all.

Such an organism as this, combined with the right of suffrage, constitutes, in fact, the elements of constitutional government. The one, by rendering those who make and execute the laws responsible to those on whom they operate, prevents the rulers from oppressing the ruled; and the other, by making it impossible for any one interest or combination of interests or class, or order, or portion of the community, to obtain exclusive control, prevents any one of them from oppressing the other. It is clear, that oppression and abuse of power must come, if at all, from the one or the other quarter. From no other can they come. It follows, that the two, suffrage and proper organism combined, are sufficient to counteract the tendency of government to oppression and abuse of power; and to restrict it to the fulfilment of the great ends for which it is ordained. . . .

It results, from what has been said, that there are two different modes in which the sense of the community may be taken; one, simply by the right of suffrage, unaided; the other, by the right through a proper organism. Each collects the sense of the majority. But one regards numbers only, and considers the whole community as a unit, having but one common interest throughout; and collects the sense of the greater number of the whole, as that of the community. The other, on the contrary, regards interests as well as numbers;—considering the community as made up of different and conflicting interests, as far as the action of the government is concerned; and takes the sense of each, through its majority or appropriate organ, and the united sense of all, as the sense of the entire community. The former of these I shall call the numerical, or absolute majority; and the latter, the concurrent, or constitutional majority. . . .

The necessary consequence of taking the sense of the community by the concurrent majority is, as has been explained, to give to each interest or portion of·the community a negative on the others. It is this mutual negative among its various conflicting interests, which invests each with the power of protecting itself;—and places the rights and safety of each, where only they can be securely placed, under its own guardianship. Without this there can be no systematic, peaceful, or effective resistance to the natural tendency of each to come into conflict with the others: and without this there can be no constitution. It is this negative power,—the power of preventing or arresting the action of the government,—be it called by what term it may,—veto, interposition, nullification, check, or balance of power,—which, in fact, forms the constitution. They are all but different names for the negative power. In all its forms, and under all its names, it results from the concurrent majority. Without this there can be no negative; and, without a negative, no constitution. The assertion is true in reference to all constitutional governments, be their forms what they may. It is, indeed, the negative power which makes the constitution,—and the positive which makes the government. The one is the power of acting;—and the other the power of preventing or arresting action. The two, combined, make constitutional governments.

But, as there can be no constitution without the negative power, and no negative power without the concurrent majority;—it follows, necessarily, that where the numerical majority has the sole control of the government, there can be no constitution; as constitution implies limitation or restriction,—and, of course, is inconsistent with the idea of sole or exclusive power. And hence, the numerical, unmixed with the concurrent majority, necessarily forms, in all cases, absolute government.

It is, indeed, the single, or *one power*, which excludes the negative, and constitutes absolute government; and not the *number* in whom the power is vested. The numerical majority is as truly a *single power*, and excludes the negative as completely as the absolute government of one, or of the few. The former is as much the absolute government of the democratic, or popular form, as the latter of the monarchical or aristocratical. It has, accordingly, in common with them, the same tendency to oppression and abuse of power....

The government of the concurrent majority, where the organism is perfect, excludes the possibility of oppression, by giving to each interest, or portion, or order,—where there are established classes,—the means of protecting itself, by its negative, against all measures calculated to advance the peculiar interests of others at its expense. Its effect, then, is, to cause the different interests, portions, or orders,—as the case may be,—to desist from attempting to adopt any measure calculated to promote the prosperity of one, or more, by sacrificing that of others; and thus to force them to unite in such measures only as would promote the prosperity of all, as the only means to prevent the suspension of the action of the government;—and, thereby, to avoid anarchy, the greatest of all evils. It is by means of such authorized and effectual resistance, that oppression is prevented, and the necessity of resorting to force superseded, in governments of the concurrent majority;—and, hence, compromise, instead of force, becomes their conservative principle.

It would, perhaps, be more strictly correct to trace the conservative principle of constitutional governments to the necessity which compels the different interests, or portions, or orders, to compromise,—as the only way to promote their respective prosperity, and to avoid anarchy,—rather than to the compromise itself. No necessity can be more urgent and imperious, than that of avoiding anarchy. It is the same as that which makes government indispensable to preserve society; and is not less imperative than that which compels obedience to superior force. Traced to this source, the voice of a people,—uttered under the necessity of avoiding the greatest of calamities, through the organs of a government so constructed as to suppress the expression of all partial and selfish interests, and to give a full and faithful utterance to the sense of the whole community, in reference to its common welfare,—may, without impiety, be called *the voice of God*. To call any other so, would be impious. . . .

If the two be compared, in reference to the ends for which government is ordained, the superiority of the government of the concurrent majority will not be less striking. These, as has been stated, are twofold; to protect, and to perfect society. But to preserve society, it is necessary to guard the community against injustice, violence, and anarchy within, and against attacks from without. If it fail in either, it would fail in the primary end of government, and would not deserve the name.

To perfect society, it is necessary to develope the faculties, intellectual and moral, with which man is endowed. But the main spring to their development, and, through this, to progress, improvement and civilization, with all their blessings, is the desire of individuals to better their condition. For, this purpose, liberty and security are indispensable. Liberty leaves each free to pursue the course he may deem best to promote his interest and happiness, as far as it may be compatible with the primary end for which government is ordained;—while security gives assurance to each, that he shall not be deprived of the fruits of his exertions to better his condition. These combined, give to his desire the strongest impulse of which it is susceptible. For, to extend liberty beyond the limits assigned, would be to weaken the government and to render it incompetent to fulfil its primary end,—the protection of society against dangers, internal and external. The effect of this would be, insecurity; and, of insecurity,—to weaken the impulse of individuals to better their condition, and thereby retard progress and improvement. On the other hand, to extend the powers of the government, so as to contract the sphere assigned to liberty, would have the same effect, by disabling individuals in their efforts to better their condition.

Herein is to be found the principle which assigns to power and liberty their proper spheres, and reconciles each to the other under all circumstances. For, if power be necessary to secure to liberty the fruits of its exertions, liberty, in turn, repays power with interest, by increased population, wealth, and other advantages, which progress and improvement bestow on the community. By thus assigning to each its appropriate sphere, all conflicts between them cease; and each is made to co-operate with and assist the other, in fulfilling the great ends for which government is ordained.

But the principle, applied to different communities, will assign to them different limits. It will assign a larger sphere to power and a more contracted one to liberty, or the reverse, according to circumstances. To the former, there must ever be allotted, under all circumstances, a sphere sufficiently large to protect the community against danger from without and violence and anarchy within. The residuum belongs to liberty. More cannot be safely or rightly allotted to it. . . .

It follows, from what has been stated, that it is a great and dangerous error to suppose that all people are equally entitled to liberty. It is a reward to be earned, not a blessing to be gratuitously lavished on all alike;—a reward reserved for the intelligent, the patriotic, the virtuous and deserving;—and not a boon to be bestowed on a people too ignorant, degraded and vicious, to be capable either of appreciating or of enjoying it. Nor is it any disparagement to liberty, that such is, and ought to be the case. On the contrary, its greatest praise,—its proudest distinction is, that an all-wise Providence has reserved it, as the noblest and highest reward for the development of our faculties, moral and intellectual. A reward more appropriate than liberty could not be conferred on the deserving;—nor a punishment inflicted on the undeserving more just, than to be subject to lawless and despotic rule. This dispensation seems to be the result of some fixed law;—and every effort to disturb or defeat it, by attempting to elevate a people in the scale of liberty, above the point to which they are entitled to rise, must ever prove abortive, and end in disappointment. The progress of a people rising from a lower to a higher point in the scale of liberty, is necessarily slow;—and by attempting to precipitate, we either retard, or permanently defeat it.

There is another error, not less great and dangerous, usually associated with the one which has just been considered. I refer to the opinion, that liberty and equality are so intimately united, that liberty cannot be perfect without perfect equality.

That they are united to a certain extent,—and that equality of citizens, in the eyes of the law, is essential to liberty in a popular government, is conceded. But to go further, and make equality of *condition* essential to liberty, would be to to destroy both liberty and progress. The reason is, that inequality of condition, while it is a necessary consequence of liberty, is, at the same time, indispensable to progress. In order to understand why this is so, it is necessary to bear in mind, that the main spring to progress is, the desire of individuals to better their condition; and that the strongest impulse which can be given to it is, to leave individuals free to exert themselves in the manner they may deem best for that purpose, as far at least as it can be done consistently with the ends for which government is ordained,—and to secure to all the fruits of their exertions. Now, as individuals differ greatly from each other, in intelligence, sagacity, energy, perseverance, skill, habits of industry and economy, physical power, position and opportunity,—the necessary effect of leaving all free to exert themselves to better their condition, must be a corresponding inequality between those who may possess these qualities and advantages in a high degree, and those who may be deficient in them. The only means by which this result can be prevented are, either to impose such restrictions on the exertions of those who may possess them in a high degree, as will place them on a level with those who do not; or to deprive them of the fruits of their exertions. But to impose such restrictions on them would be destructive of liberty,—while, to deprive them of the fruits of their exertions, would be to destroy the desire of bettering their condition. It is, indeed, this inequality of condition between the front and rear ranks, in the march of progress, which gives so strong an impulse to the former to maintain their position, and to the latter to press forward into their files. This gives to progress its greatest impulse. To force the front rank back to the rear, or attempt to push forward the rear into line with the front, by the interposition of the government, would put an end to the impulse, and effectually arrest the march of progress. . . .

It follows, from all that has been said, that the more perfectly a government combines power and liberty,—that is, the greater its power and the more enlarged and secure the liberty of individuals, the more perfectly it fulfils the ends for which government is ordained. To show, then, that the government of the concurrent majority is better calculated to fulfil them than that of the numerical, it is only necessary to explain why the former is better suited to combine a higher degree of power and a wider scope of liberty than the latter. I shall begin with the former.

The concurrent majority, then, is better suited to enlarge and secure the bounds of liberty, because it is better suited to prevent government from passing beyond its proper limits, and to restrict it to its primary end, —the protection of the community. But in doing this, it leaves, necessarily, all beyond it open and free to individual exertions; and thus enlarges and secures the sphere of liberty to the greatest extent which the condidition of the community will admit, as has been explained. The tendency of government to pass beyond its proper limits is what exposes liberty to danger, and renders its insecure; and it is the strong counteraction of governments of the concurrent majority to this tendency which makes them so favorable to liberty. On the contrary, those of the numerical, instead of opposing and counteracting this tendency, add to it increased strength, in consequence of the violent party struggles incident to them, as has been fully explained. And hence their encroachments on liberty, and the danger to which it is exposed under such governments.

6
TESTING THE PRINCIPLES

I hold that a negro is not and never ought to be a citizen of the United States. I hold that this government was made on the white basis, by white men, for the benefit of white men and their posterity forever, and should be administered by white men and none others. I do not believe that the Almighty made the negro capable of self-government; . . . in my opinion the signers of the Declaration had no reference to the negro whatever when they declared all men to be created equal.

STEPHEN DOUGLAS

What are these arguments? They are the arguments that kings have made for enslaving people in all ages of the world; . . . whether it comes from the mouth of a king, an excuse for enslaving the people of his country, or from the mouth of men of one race as a reason for enslaving the men of another race, it is all the same old serpent, and I hold if that course of argumentation that is made for the purpose of convincing the public mind that we should not care about this, should be granted, it does not stop with the negro. I should like to know if taking this old Declaration of Independence, which declares that all men are equal upon principle and making exceptions to it where will it stop. If one man says it does not mean a negro, why not another say it does not mean some other man?

ABRAHAM LINCOLN

If there is one especially striking paradox about the struggle over slavery in America, it is that both sides in the dispute were, in Louis Hartz' words, within the "mainstream of American Political thought." [1] The Civil War was not a result of the clash of alien philosophies; it was the culmination of tensions produced by the opposing poles of the same political tradition. Attackers and defenders of slavery shared the same political roots. Thus Hartz describes the tortured arguments of Southerners, who attempted to preserve slavery yet remain consistent with "traditional American liberalism," and the passionate pleas of Northerners, who in the midst of the "greatest moral crusade in American

[1] Louis Hartz, "The Reactionary Enlightenment," in John P. Roche, ed., *American Political Thought* (New York: Harper & Row, 1967), p. 86.

history produced practically no original political thought." [2] Because
the disputants represented opposite poles of the same tradition, the Civil
War may be called the most "characteristic" event in American history.[3]
It was the crucible in which the most characteristic of American principles
were tested. What made the test particularly harsh was the issue in
question—slavery. On that issue, hitherto muted passions could no longer
be held in check.

To understand the causes of the Civil War, then, is to understand
the relationship of slavery to American political principles and how
the disputants understood that relationship. Within all the varied and
complex interpretations of the Civil War, this issue is basic. It is
especially borne out in the positions of the more radical defenders
and opponents of slavery. At the level of principle, they understood
the propositions of the Declaration of Independence to be in question.
To abolitionists, for example, slavery was inherently an affront to the
Declaration. William Lloyd Garrison was explicit on the point: the issue
was beyond dispute.

What is the proposition to be discussed? It is this: whether all men are
created free and equal, and have an inalienable right to liberty! I am
urged to argue this with a people who declare it to be a self-evident truth!
Why, such folly belongs to Bedlam.[4]

As their "Declaration of Sentiments" made clear, abolitionists "plant[ed]
[them]selves upon the Declaration of our Independence and the truths
of Divine Revelation, as upon the Everlasting Rock." [5] And no more than
that rock would they be moved. Any argument that a class or race of
men could legitimately be enslaved by another class or race was morally
as well as politically repugnant to them. They considered slavery not
only politically unacceptable but sinful. Moreover, if slavery was sinful,
so too was any regime which suffered its existence. When pushed to
the extreme the abolitionist argument led irrevocably to the sacrifice of
any political order which allowed slavery. Equating the Declaration
with the highest moral truth meant condemning a regime which was
inconsistent with it. To do otherwise would be to pardon immorality of
the worst kind. Yet, the Union created by the Constitution recognized
slavery. For abolitionists, the conclusion was inescapable: in any contest

[2] *Ibid.*, Hartz' conception of what constitutes American liberalism may be found in
pp. 62–73 of his essay.
[3] We borrow this term from Professor Harry Jaffa, whose treatment of these issues is to
the point and exhaustive. *Crisis of the House Divided* (New York: Doubleday, 1959).
[4] *Writings and Speeches of William Lloyd Garrison* (New York: Negro Universities
Press, 1968), p. 127.
[5] *Ibid.*, p. 70.

between extinguishing slavery or perpetuating the Union, it was the Union which had to be sacrificed.

> To say this "covenant with death" shall not be annulled—that this "agreement with hell" shall continue to stand—that this "refuge of lies" shall not be swept away—is to hurl defiance at the eternal throne, and to give the lie to Him who sits thereon. . . . Henceforth, the watchword of every uncompromising abolitionist, of every friend of God and liberty, must be, both in a religious and political sense—"NO UNION WITH SLAVEHOLDERS!"[6]

In short, in the name of the principles of the Declaration, a Constitution which compromised those principles could be destroyed.

Southern radical supporters of slavery were no less explicit than abolitionists in this respect. They too, in the name of principle, were willing to sacrifice the Union. To begin, they viewed the entire progress of their civilization and, therefore, the future of their liberty as dependent upon a slave culture. In other words, they believed that only the continuation of slavery assured them the fulfillment of the promise of liberty provided by the Declaration. Deny them their slaves, the Southerners argued, and their liberty would die. Deny slavery and the republic would cease.

> So when the greatest progress in civil liberty has been made, the enlightened lover of liberty will know that there must remain much inequality, much injustice, much *slavery*, which no human wisdom or virtue will ever be able wholly to prevent or redress.

> Slavery is truly the "corner-stone" and foundation of every well-designed and durable republican edifice.[7]

Southern radicals, therefore, were led to the same conclusions as abolitionists. A political order contrary to what they understood to be basic to their liberty would be unendurable. They would no more consent to the abolition of slavery—and the denial of their rights under the Declaration—than abolitionists would consent to its preservation —and the denial of universal equality.

> We are well content to give up the Union sooner than sacrifice two thousand millions of dollars, and with them all the rights we prize. . . . If the abolitionists are prepared to expand their own treasure and shed their own blood as freely as they ask us to do ours, let them come.

[6] *Ibid.*, pp. 118–119.
[7] *The Pro-Slavery Argument* (Philadelphia: Lippincott, Grambo & Co., 1853), p. 9.

Come what may, we are firmly resolved that OUR SYSTEM OF DOMESTIC
SLAVERY SHALL STAND.[8]

If radicals of both sides were uncompromising, it was because one
point upon which they differed could not be compromised. Either all
men are created equal and slavery was impermissible, or the equality of
the Declaration is not universally applicable and slavery was permissible.
There were no alternatives between these poles. In order to appeal to
libertarian ideals consistent with the Declaration, Southerners had to
argue that slavery was consistent with the Declaration. To accomplish
this, in turn, they had to demonstrate that what abolitionists accepted as
self-evident really was not so evident. Their arguments to this end were
complex—and sometimes devious—but their conclusions were the same.
A defense of slavery consistent with American principles demanded
proof that Negroes were not among those declared to be equal in the
Declaration. And if the Declaration said that all men are created
equal, proof had to be forthcoming that Negroes were less than men.
Southern arguments on this subject differed more in style than in
substance.

It is his mental and moral inferiority which has enslaved, or subjected him
to a superior. . . . They have not that moral courage—the true source of
independence—which would prompt them, like the poor white pioneer,
to sally forth into the wilderness. . . . They feel their inferiority to the
whites, even when nominally free men; and sink into the condition of
serviles, in fact, if not in name, in compliance with their natural
dependence, and unquestionable moral deficiencies.

"Fleas are not *Lobsters*—d--n their souls." Negroes and white men are
essentially distinct in their nature. It is a most *odious* and *odorous*
comparison. The dark complexion, peculiar features, wooly hair and small
skulls of the negroes, are not their only characteristics. Their blood is
not of the temperature of ours by two degrees; and their mental
capacities are a hundred degrees below that of their white "brethren,"
as you [Garrison] are pleased to call us.[9]

This was the fatal issue of the slavery debate. If the equality of the
Declaration was not extendible to Negroes, what effect would such
qualification of that principle have upon the other ideas contained in
the document? In other words, could universal equality be denied
without doing irreparable damage to the source of the American political
tradition? The issue was fatal inasmuch as even moderates in the slavery
debate could not agree upon it. And because such agreement was not

[8] *Ibid.*, pp. 142, 149.
[9] *Ibid.*, pp. 269–270; Truman Nelson, ed., *Documents of Upheaval* (New York: Hill and
Wang, 1966), pp. 50–51.

forthcoming, only arms were left to settle the debate. The best example of this division among nonradicals is provided in the Lincoln-Douglas debates. Abraham Lincoln and Stephen Douglas were both moderates, in the sense that preservation of the Union was their primary goal. They were willing to compromise their positions on slavery to the degree they believed necessary to accomplish that end. For all their willingness to modify their arguments to conform to political necessity, however, there was no moderate course on the essential question. Either all men were equal or they were not.

Douglas argued that a decision that Negroes were unequal was not inconsistent with American political principles, and, therefore, that slavery could be perpetuated in America without ill effects. It was, he insisted, the right of the people to vote slavery up or down in their particular localities. This course, he continued, was the one consistent with American libertarian tradition.

Now, my friends, if we will only act conscientiously and rigidly upon this great principle of popular sovereignty which guarantees to each State and Territory the right to do as it pleases on all things local and domestic instead of Congress interfering, we will continue at peace one with another; ... if we only adhere to that principle, we can go forward increasing in territory, in power, in strength and in glory until the Republic of America shall be the North Star that shall guide the friends of freedom throughout the civilized world. And why can we not adhere to the great principle of self-government, upon which our institutions were originally based.[10]

Douglas' words echoed the sentiments which had long been the basis of states' rights arguments. However, when the immediate issue was slavery, a new problem arose in respect to those arguments. To allow slavery anywhere in America implied that the inferior position of Negroes had to be accepted everywhere. That is, once slavery was accepted in any single state, Negro inferiority had to be allowed in principle in all states and territories. For one state to popularly decide that Negroes were equal men and full citizens with the rights and privileges of citizens, and for another to popularly decide the precise opposite would create an untenable situation. Whether a Negro could be an American citizen had to be a question of national policy. The logic of Douglas' position, in other words, called for a national decision that blacks were not equal to whites within the meaning of the Declaration. Douglas' moderation notwithstanding, his logic was not far removed from that of the Southern radicals. Moreover, his personal feelings appear to have comported quite well with theirs.

[10] Roy Basler, ed., *The Collected Works of Abraham Lincoln* (New Brunswick, N.J.: Rutgers University Press, 1953), Vol. III, pp. 11–12.

For one, I am opposed to negro citizenship in any, and every form. I
believe this government was made on the white basis. I believe it was made
by white men, for the benefit of white men and their posterity for ever,
and I am in favor of confining citizenship to white men, men of European
birth and descent, instead of conferring it upon negroes, Indians, and
other inferior races. . . . I do not believe that the Almighty ever intended
the negro to be the equal of the white man.[11]

It was for these reasons that Douglas welcomed and endorsed the
Supreme Court's decision in the *Dred Scott* case. Chief Justice Taney's
unequivocal declaration that Negroes were not and could not be
included as men in the sense of the Declaration of Independence or as
citizens in the sense of the Constitution offered authoritative support
for Douglas' position. It was proof that blacks were inferior and their
inferiority had to be recognized everywhere.

In the opinion of the court, the legislation and histories of the times, and
the language used in the Declaration of Independence, show, that
neither the class of persons who had been imported as slaves, nor their
descendants, whether they had become free or not, were then acknowledged
as a part of the people, nor intended to be included in the general words
used in that memorable instrument.[12]

For all the rhetoric of popular sovereignty and states' rights, therefore, it
was basic to Taney and Douglas that the perpetuation of slavery assumed
universal recognition that Negroes were not men within the meaning
of the Declaration. Paradoxically, the argument that there ought to be
liberty to decide locally about slavery did not allow any locality the
liberty to establish full Negro equality.

Lincoln's opposition to Douglas was keyed to this point. Having
admitted that the Negro was not included in the "men" of the
Declaration, he asked, how could one be sure that the arguments
would not be extended to men other than black? Arguments by
which the equality of a particular race or class of men was denied
might readily be made applicable to any race or class. The slavery logic
was impossible to check.

If A can prove, however conclusively, that he may, of right, enslave B—
why may not B snatch the same argument, and prove equally, that he may
enslave A?

You say A is white, and B is black. It is *color*, then; the lighter, having the
right to enslave the darker? Take care. By this rule, you are to be slave
to the first man you meet, with a fairer skin than your own. You do not

[11] *Ibid.*, pp. 9–10.
[12] 19 *Howard* 393, p. 407.

mean *color exactly?* You mean the whites are *intellectually* the superiors of
the blacks, and therefore have the right to enslave them? Take care again.
By this rule, you are to be slave to the first man you meet, with an intellect
superior to your own.[13]

According to Lincoln, once the doctrine of equality was compromised, the
entire American political tradition was endangered. He was opposed
to the spread of slavery because it was inimicable to the Union and to
popular egalitarian government in general. As a moderate, Lincoln
was unopposed to allowing slavery to remain within the borders of the
states in which it already existed because such limitation would put
it in the "course of ultimate extinction." [14] He would not, however, allow
its extension and nationalization. That would have unwarranted and
deleterious effects upon American principles. In the American political
order, he concluded, there was no choice but to include all men within
the equality of the Declaration. Equality was not perfect, but all men had
the rights essential to the American political tradition.

There is no reason in the world why the negro is not entitled to all the
rights enumerated in the Declaration of Independence. . . . I hold that he
is as much entitled to these as the white man. I agree with Judge Douglas
that he is not my equal in many respects—certainly not in color,
perhaps, not in moral or intellectual endowment. But in the right to eat
the bread, without the leave of anybody else, which his own hand earns, he
is my equal and the equal of Judge Douglas and the equal of every
living man.[15]

Their moderation, then, did not prevent Lincoln and Douglas from
being as fundamentally opposed as were Southern radicals and
abolitionists. The Civil War, finally, determined the issue. There could
henceforward be no liberty to choose a system which would deny
human equality through chattel slavery. The war's cost was frightful but,
as Lincoln said, it had to be borne if America was to "long endure."
    The following selections include some of the radical arguments in
the slave debate as well as the more moderate positions of Lincoln and
Douglas. There are representative pieces from the Abolitionists—notably
William Lloyd Garrison—from Southern radicals, from the court's
opinion in the *Dred Scott* case, and from the Lincoln-Douglas debates.
And because no set of readings on this subject would be complete
without them, the Gettysburg Address and the 13th, 14th, and 15th
Amendments to the Constitution are included.

[13] Basler, *op. cit.,* Vol. II, pp. 222–223.
[14] *Ibid.,* Vol. III, p. 18. Cf. Lincoln's Springfield Speech for the practical arguments that
he offered to support the point.
[15] *Ibid.,* p. 16.

American Anti-Slavery Society

DECLARATION OF SENTIMENTS

The Convention assembled in the city of Philadelphia, to organize a National Anti-Slavery Society, promptly seize the opportunity to promulgate the following Declaration of Sentiments, as cherished by them in relation to the enslavement of one-sixth portion of the American people.

More than fifty-seven years have elapsed, since a band of patriots convened in this place, to devise measures for the deliverance of this country from a foreign yoke. The corner-stone upon which they founded the Temple of Freedom was broadly this—'that all men are created equal; that they are endowed by their Creator with certain inalienable rights; that among these are life, LIBERTY, and the pursuit of happiness.' At the sound of their trumpet-call, three millions of people rose up as from the sleep of death, and rushed to the strife of blood; deeming it more glorious to die instantly as freemen, than desirable to live one hour as slaves. They were few in number—poor in resources; but the honest conviction that Truth, Justice and Right were on their side, made them invincible.

We have met together for the achievement of an enterprise, without which that of our fathers is incomplete; and which, for its magnitude, solemnity, and probable results upon the destiny of the world, as far transcends theirs as moral truth does physical force.

In purity of motive, in earnestness of zeal, in decision of purpose, in intrepidity of action, in steadfastness of faith, in sincerity of spirit, we would not be inferior to them.

Their principles led them to wage war against their oppressors, and to spill human blood like water, in order to be free. Ours forbid the doing of evil that good may come, and lead us to reject, and to entreat the oppressed to reject, the use of all carnal weapons for deliverance from bondage; relying solely upon those which are spiritual, and mighty through God to the pulling down of strong holds.

Their measures were physical resistance—the marshalling in arms— the hostile array—the mortal encounter. Ours shall be such only as the

Proceedings of the American Anti-Slavery Society . . . (New York: American Anti-Slavery Society, 1864), pp. 17–21.

opposition of moral purity to moral corruption—the destruction of error by the potency of truth—the overthrow of prejudice by the power of love—and the abolition of slavery by the spirit of repentance.

Their grievances, great as they were, were trifling in comparison with the wrongs and sufferings of those for whom we plead. Our fathers were never slaves—never bought and sold like cattle—never shut out from the light of knowledge and religion—never subjected to the lash of brutal taskmasters.

But those, for whose emancipation we are striving—constituting at the present time at least one-sixth part of our countrymen—are recognized by law, and treated by their fellow-beings, as marketable commodities, as goods and chattels, as brute beasts; are plundered daily of the fruits of their toil without redress; really enjoy no constitutional nor legal protection from licentious and murderous outrages upon their persons; and are ruthlessly torn asunder—the tender babe from the arms of its frantic mother—the heart-broken wife from her weeping husband—at the caprice or pleasure of irresponsible tyrants. For the crime of having a dark complexion, they suffer the pangs of hunger, the infliction of stripes, the ignominy of brutal servitude. They are kept in heathenish darkness by laws expressly enacted to make their instruction a criminal offence.

These are the prominent circumstances in the condition of more than two millions of our people, the proof of which may be found in thousands of indisputable facts, and in the laws of the slaveholding States.

Hence we maintain—that, in view of the civil and religious privileges of this nation, the guilt of its oppression is unequalled by any other on the face of the earth; and, therefore, that it is bound to repent instantly, to undo the heavy burdens, and to let the oppressed go free.

We further maintain—that no man has a right to enslave or imbrute his brother—to hold or acknowledge him, for one moment, as a piece of merchandize—to keep back his hire by fraud—or to brutalize his mind, by denying him the means of intellectual, social and moral improvement.

The right to enjoy liberty is inalienable. To invade it is to usurp the prerogative of Jehovah. Every man has a right to his own body—to the products of his own labor—to the protection of law—and to the common advantages of society. It is piracy to buy or steal a native African, and subject him to servitude. Surely, the sin is as great to enslave an American as an African.

Therefore we believe and affirm—that there is no difference, in principle, between the African slave trade and American slavery:

That every American citizen, who detains a human being in involuntary bondage as his property, is, according to Scripture, (Ex. xxi. 16,) a man-stealer:

That the slaves ought instantly to be set free, and brought under the protection of law:

That if they had lived from the time of Pharaoh down to the present period, and had been entailed through successive generations, their right to be free could never have been alienated, but their claims would have constantly risen in solemnity:

That all those laws which are now in force, admitting the right of slavery, are therefore, before God, utterly null and void; being an audacious usurpation of the Divine prerogative, a daring infringement on the law of nature, a base overthrow of the very foundations of the social compact, a complete extinction of all the relations, endearments and obligations of mankind, and a presumptuous transgression of all the holy commandments; and that therefore they ought instantly to be abrogated.

We further believe and affirm—that all persons of color, who possess the qualifications which are demanded of others, ought to be admitted forthwith to the enjoyment of the same privileges, and the exercise of the same prerogatives, as others; and that the paths of preferment, of wealth, and of intelligence, should be opened as widely to them as to persons of a white complexion.

We maintain that no compensation should be given to the planters emancipating their slaves:

Because it would be a surrender of the great fundamental principle, that man cannot hold property in man:

Because slavery is a crime, and therefore is not an article to be sold:

Because the holders of slaves are not the just proprietors of what they claim; freeing the slave is not depriving them of property, but restoring it to its rightful owner; it is not wronging the master, but righting the slave—restoring him to himself:

Because immediate and general emancipation would only destroy nominal, not real property; it would not amputate a limb or break a bone of the slaves, but by infusing motives into their breasts, would make them doubly valuable to the masters as free laborers; and

Because, if compensation is to be given at all, it should be given to the outraged and guiltless slaves, and not to those who have plundered and abused them.

We regard as delusive, cruel and dangerous, any scheme of expatriation which pretends to aid, either directly or indirectly, in the emancipation of the slaves, or to be a substitute for the immediate and total abolition of slavery.

We fully and unanimously recognise the sovereignty of each State, to legislate exclusively on the subject of the slavery which is tolerated within its limits; we concede that Congress, under the present national compact, has no right to interfere with any of the slave States, in relation to this momentous subject:

But we maintain that Congress has a right, and is solemnly bound, to suppress the domestic slave trade between the several States, and to abolish slavery in those portions of our territory which the Constitution has placed under its exclusive jurisdiction.

We also maintain that there are, at the present time, the highest obligations resting upon the people of the free States to remove slavery by moral and political action, as prescribed in the Constitution of the United States. They are now living under a pledge of their tremendous physical force, to fasten the galling fetters of tyranny upon the limbs of millions in the Southern States; they are liable to be called at any moment to suppress a general insurrection of the slaves; they authorize the slave owner to vote for three-fifths of his slaves as property, and thus enable him to perpetuate his oppression; they support a standing army at the South for its protection; and they seize the slave, who has escaped into their territories, and send him back to be tortured by an enraged master or a brutal driver. This relation to slavery is criminal, and full of danger: IT MUST BE BROKEN UP.

These are our views and principles—these our designs and measures. With entire confidence in the overruling justice of God, we plant ourselves upon the Declaration of our Independence and the truths of Divine Revelation, as upon the Everlasting Rock.

We shall organize Anti-Slavery Societies, if possible, in every city, town and village in our land.

We shall send forth agents to lift up the voice of remonstrance, of warning, of entreaty, and of rebuke.

We shall circulate, unsparingly and extensively, antislavery tracts and periodicals.

We shall enlist the pulpit and the press in the cause of the suffering and the dumb.

We shall aim at a purification of the churches from all participation in the guilt of slavery.

We shall encourage the labor of freemen rather than that of slaves, by giving a preference to their productions: and

We shall spare no exertions nor means to bring the whole nation to speedy repentance.

Our trust for victory is solely in God. We may be personally defeated, but our principles never. Truth, Justice, Reason, Humanity, must and will gloriously triumph. Already a host is coming up to the help of the Lord against the mighty, and the prospect before us is full of encouragement.

Submitting this Declaration to the candid examination of the people of this country, and of the friends of liberty throughout the world, we hereby affix our signatures to it; pledging ourselves that, under the guidance and by the help of Almighty God, we will do all that in us lies, consistently with this Declaration of our principles, to overthrow the most execrable system of slavery that has ever been witnessed upon earth; to deliver our land from its deadliest curse; to wipe out the foulest stain which rests upon our national escutcheon; and to secure to the colored population of the United States, all the rights and privileges which belong to them as men, and as Americans—come what may to our persons, our interests, or our reputation—whether we live to witness the triumph of Liberty, Justice and Humanity, or perish untimely as martyrs in this great, benevolent, and holy cause.

Done at Philadelphia, December 6th, A. D. 1833.

William Lloyd Garrison

EVILS OF SLAVERY
(1838)

EXORDIUM—REPUBLICAN CONSISTENCY!

Fellow Citizens: What a glorious day is this! what a glorious people are we! This is the time-honored, wine-honored, toast-drinking, powder-wasting, tyrant-killing fourth of July—consecrated, for the last sixty years, to bombast, to falsehood, to impudence, to hypocrisy. It is the great carnival of republican despotism, and of christian impiety, famous the world over! Since we held it last year, we have kept securely in their chains, the stock of two millions, three hundred thousand slaves we then had on hand, in spite of every effort of fanaticism to emancipate them; and, through the goodness of God, to whom we are infinitely indebted for the divine institution of negro slavery, have been graciously enabled to steal some seventy thousand babes, the increase of that stock, and expect to steal a still greater number before "another glorious" anniversary shall come round! We have again struck down the freedom of speech in Congress, and utterly banished it from one half of the Union, by the aid of pistols, bowie-knives, and lynch-law. We have also renewedly decided, in both houses of Congress, that the right of petition is not to be allowed to those who are the advocates of immediate and universal emancipation. As to the Indian tribes, we have done the best we could to expel and exterminate them; and the blood upon our hands, and the gore upon our garments, show that our success has almost equalled our wishes. We have driven the Cherokees, at the point of the bayonet, into a distant wilderness, from their abodes of civilization—violated the most solemn treaties ever entered into between man and man—and committed nameless and numberless outrages upon the domestic security and personal rights of these hapless victims—all for the laudable purpose of getting their lands, that the "divine institution" of slavery may be extended, and perpetuated to the latest generation, as "the corner-stone of our republican edifice!" We have trampled all law and order under foot, resolved society into

"An Address Delivered in Marlboro Chapel, Boston, July 4, 1838" (Boston: Issac Knapp, 1838).

jacobinical clubs, and filled the land with mobs and riots which have ended in arson and murder, in order to show our abhorrence of those who "plead for justice in the name of humanity, and according to the law of the living God." Hail, Columbia! happy land! Hail, the return of the fourth of July, that we may perjure ourselves afresh, in solemnly invoking heaven and earth to witness, that "we hold these truths to be self-evident— that all men are created equal; that they are endowed by their Creator with certain inalienable rights; that among these are life, LIBERTY, and the pursuit of happiness!" "Sound the trumpet—beat the drum!" Let the bells give their merriest peals to the breeze—unfurl every star-spangled banner —thunder mightily, ye cannon, from every hill-top—and let shouts arise from every plain and valley; for tyrants and their minions shall find no quarter at our hands this day! . . .

IMMEDIATE EMANCIPATION DEMANDED

I present myself as the advocate of my enslaved countrymen, at a time when their claims cannot be shuffled out of sight, and on an occasion which entitles me to a respectful hearing in their behalf. If I am asked to prove their title to liberty, my answer is, that the fourth of July is not a day to be wasted in establishing "self-evident truths." In the name of the God, who has made us of one blood, and in whose image we are created; in the name of the messiah, who came to bind up the broken- hearted, to proclaim liberty to the captives, and the opening of the prison to them that are bound; in the name of the Holy Ghost, whom to despise is to perish; I demand the immediate emancipation of all who are pining in slavery on the American soil, whether they are fattening for the shambles in Maryland and Virginia, or are wasting, as with a pestilent disease, on the cotton and sugar plantations of Alabama and Louisiana; whether they are males or females, young or old, vigorous or infirm. I make this demand, not for the children merely, but the parents also; not for one, but for all; not with restrictions and limitations, but uncondi- tionally. I assert their perfect equality with ourselves, as a part of the human race, and their inalienable right to liberty and the pursuit of happiness. That this demand is founded in justice, and is therefore irresistible, the whole nation is this day acknowledging, as upon oath at the bar of the world. And not until, by a formal vote, the people repudiate the Declaration of Independence as a rotten and dangerous instrument, and cease to keep this festival in honor of liberty, as unworthy of note or remembrance; not until they spike every cannon, and muffle every bell, and disband every procession, and quench every bonfire, and gag every orator; not until they brand Washington, and Adams, and Jefferson, and Hancock, as fanatics and madmen; not until they place themselves again in the condition of colonial subserviency to Great Britain, or transform this republic into an imperial government; not until they cease to point exultingly toward Bunker Hill, and the plains of Concord and Lexington; not, in fine, until they deny the authority of God, and proclaim themselves to be destitute of principle and humanity; will I argue the question, as one of doubtful disputation, on an occasion like this, whether our slaves are entitled to the rights and privileges of freemen. That question is settled irrevocably. There is no man to be found, unless he has a brow of brass and a heart of stone, who will dare to contest it on a day like this. A state of vassalage is pronounced, by universal acclamation, to be such as no man, or body of men, ought to submit to for one moment. I therefore tell the American slaves, that the time for their emancipation is come; that, their own task-masters being witnesses, they are created equal to the rest of mankind, and possess an inalienable right to liberty; and that no man has a right to hold them in bondage. I warn them not to fight for their freedom, both on account of the hopelessness of the effort, and because it is contrary to the will of God; but I tell them, not less emphatically, it is not wrong in them to refuse to wear the yoke of slavery any longer. Let them shed no blood— enter into no conspiracies—raise no murderous revolts; but, whenever and wherever they can break their fetters, God give them the courage to do so! And should they attempt to elope from their house of bondage, and come to the North, may each of them find a covert from the search of the spoiler, and an invincible public sentiment to shield them from the grasp of the kidnapper! Success attend them in their flight to Canada, to touch whose *monarchical* soil insures freedom to every *republican* slave!

SEDITION

Is this preaching sedition? Sedition against what? Not the lives of southern oppressors—for I renew the solemn injunction, "Shed no blood!" —but against unlawful authority, and barbarous usage, and unrequited toil. If slaveholders are still obstinately bent upon plundering and starving their long-suffering victims, why, let them look well to the consequences. To save them from danger, I am not obligated to suppress the truth, or to stop proclaiming liberty "throughout all the land, unto all the inhabitants thereof." No, indeed. There are two important truths, which, as far as practicable, I mean every slave shall be made to understand. The first is, that he has a right to his freedom *now;* the other is, that this is recognized as a self-evident truth in the Declaration of American Independence. Sedition, forsooth! Why, what are the American people doing this day? In *theory,* maintaining the freedom and equality of the human race; and in *practice,* declaring that all tyrants ought to be extirpated from the face of the earth! We are giving to our slaves the following easy sums for solution:—If the principle involved in a three-penny tax on tea, justified a seven years' war, how much blood may be lawfully spilt in resisting the principle, that one human being has a right to the body and soul of another, on account of the color of his skin? Again:—If the impressment of 6000 American *seamen,* by Great Britain, furnished sufficient cause for a bloody struggle with that nation, and the sacrifice of hundreds of millions of capital, in self-defence, how many lives may be taken, by way of retribution, on account of the enslavement of more than two millions of American *laborers?*

DANGER OF INSURRECTION

Oppression and insurrection go hand in hand, as cause and effect are allied together. In what age of the world have tyrants reigned with impunity, or the victims of tyranny not resisted unto blood? Besides our own grand insurrection against the authority of the mother country, there have been many insurrections, during the last two hundred years, in various sections of the land, on the part of the victims of our tyranny, but without the success that attended our own struggle. The last was the memorable one in Southampton, Virginia, headed by a black patriot, nicknamed, in the contemptuous nomenclature of slavery, *Nat* Turner. The name does not strike the ear so harmoniously as that of Washington, or Lafayette, or Hancock, or Warren; but the name is nothing. It is not in the power of all the slaveholders upon earth, to rended odious the memory of that sable chieftain. "Resistance to tyrants is obedience to God," was our revolutionary motto. We acted upon that motto—what more did Nat Turner? Says George McDuffie, "A people who deliberately submit to oppression, with a full knowledge that they are oppressed, are fit only to be slaves. No tyrant ever made a slave—no community, however small, having the spirit of freemen, ever yet had a master. It does not belong to men to count the costs, and calculate the hazards of vindicating their rights, and defending their liberties!"—So reasoned Nat Turner, and acted accordingly. Was he a patriot, or a monster? Do we mean to say to the oppressed of all nations, in the 62d year of our independence, and on the 4th of July, that our example in 1776 was a bad one, and ought not to be followed? As a christian abolitionist, I, for one, am prepared to say so—but are THE PEOPLE ready to say, that no chains ought to be broken by the hand of violence, and no blood spilt in defence of inalienable human rights, in any quarter of the globe? If not, then our slaves will peradventure take us at our word, and there will be given unto us blood to drink, for we are worthy. Why accuse abolitionists of stirring them to insurrection? The charge is false—but what if it were true? If any man has a right to fight for liberty, this right equally extends to all men subjected to bondage. In claiming this right for themselves, the American people necessarily concede it to all mankind. If, therefore, they are found tyrannizing over any part of the human race, they voluntarily seal their own death-warrant, and confess that they deserve to perish.

> What are the banners ye exalt?—the deeds
> That raised your fathers' pyramid of fame?
> Ye show the wound that still in history bleeds,
> And talk exulting of the patriot's name—
> Then, *when your words have waked a kindred flame,*
> And slaves behold the freedom ye adore,
> And deeper feel their sorrow and their shame,
> Ye double all the fetters that they wore,
> And press them down to earth, till hope
>   exults no more!

INCENTIVES TO PERSEVERANCE

A word to those who dare to think for themselves, and to give free utterance to their thoughts—who care not what may be "the prevailing voice and will of the brotherhood" on any subject—the faithful followers of truth, through evil as well as good report—the uncompromising enemies of oppression in every form, technically called abolitionists, but stigmatized as fanatics by an insane multitude. If time had allowed, an animating view of the progress of our sacred cause, since the last national anniversary, in all parts of the free States, might have been drawn, to cheer us in carrying on the conflict another year. New England has almost become one great anti-slavery society. The change that has been wrought in public sentiment, throughout the country, in favor of our principles and measures, calls for devout thanksgiving to God, and is full of encouragement. But, while so much remains to be accomplished,—while we know that a great crisis is at hand, which is to settle the destiny of this republic, —while we perceive that slaveholding despotism is still fearfully in the ascendant, tramping under foot the Declaration of Independence as a seditious instrument, and treating the American Constitution as "a blurred and tattered parchment,"—let us not stop to recount our victories, or to repose in the lap of complacency, but GO FORWARD to surmount new obstacles thrown up in our path, make new assaults upon the execrable system of slavery, and storm other entrenchments of the common enemy of God and man. What an example of tireless effort, of unwearied devotion, of indomitable perseverance, of disinterested philanthropy, of triumphant success, has been set us by the friends of negro emancipation in Great Britain! O, blessings upon them all! Though for years struggling against fearful odds—though a thousand times repulsed on the right hand and on the left—though often deceived and betrayed by faithless representatives in Parliament, and by a corrupt ministry—still they have faltered not, they have doubted not, but pressed onward with almost superhuman energy, with a faith adequate to the removal of mountains, with quenchless zeal and victorious assurance, until they have succeeded in unloosing the chains of eight hundred thousand bondmen, who are soon to go forth and rank among the freest of the free. And their philanthropic labors have been the more remarkable, inasmuch as the victims for whose redemption *they* have so long expended their time, and means, and sympathies, reside in distant islands; while those for whom we plead are on our soil. *They* had no dread of insurrection, saw no stains of blood, heard no clankings of chains or wailings of despair, and beheld no traffic in human flesh, among themselves; but *we* are in constant danger of a servile war in our midst, our soil is red with gore, every breeze from the south is laden with woe, and our shambles are crowded with husbands and wives, parents and children, destined to be torn asunder and sold like dumb beasts to the highest bidders! Having, then, so many stronger inducements to be up and doing than our English brethren have been necessitated to feel—the very existence of our beloved country, with all its precious institutions, being in peril, and our own lives and liberties at stake; having, moreover, not eight hundred thousand, but TWO MILLIONS AND A HALF of slaves to liberate from bondage; shall we be less munificent, less active, or less consecrated to the cause of bleeding humanity, than our transatlantic exemplars? O no! it cannot be—unless our faith is spurious, our profession hypocritical, our sympathy hollow-hearted, our hatred of oppression a fitful spasm, our ardor of spirit a transient glow; unless we hate our own flesh, and desire to see human blood spilt like water, and delight to trample upon our species, and are recreant to the God in whom we live, and move, and have our being!

> Friends of the cause of righteous liberty!
> Shrink not, though you be straitened in your course.
> Even as was Israel at the Red Sea wave.
> Nerve every faculty—call every means,
> And every energy of heart and mind,
> Forth into action—summon up your strength—
> Ply arguments, persuasion, eloquence—
> Your property, time, talents, consecrate—
> Bear patiently with deeply rooted feelings
> of prejudice, self-interest, and all else
> That may have twined round your opponents' hearts:
> Yet combat still—remove and overpower them—
> Until no longer in our favored land

Is heard the voice of tyranny, and all
Who breathe the same pure air alike are free!
so may God bless you! and the franchised slave
Remember only in his grateful prayers,
That he has ever drained Oppression's cup,
And that he owes his liberty to you!

HAMMOND'S LETTERS ON SLAVERY

It is impossible, therefore, to suppose that Slavery is contrary to the will of God. It is equally absurd to say that American Slavery differs in form or principle from that of the chosen people. *We accept the Bible terms as the definition of our Slavery, and its precepts as the guide of our conduct.* We desire nothing more. Even the right to "buffet," which is esteemed so shocking, finds its express license in the gospel. 1 Peter ii. 20. Nay, what is more, God directs the Hebrews to "bore holes in the ears of their brothers" to *mark* them, when under certain circumstances they become *perpetual slaves*. Exodus xxi. 6.

I think, then, I may safely conclude, and I firmly believe, that American Slavery is not only not a sin, but especially commanded by God through Moses, and approved by Christ through his apostles. And here I might close its defence; for what God ordains, and Christ sanctifies, should surely command the respect and toleration of man. But I fear there has grown up in our time a transcendental religion, which is throwing even transcendental philosophy into the shade—a religion too pure and elevated for the Bible; which seeks to erect among men a higher standard of morals than the Almighty has revealed, or our Saviour preached; and which is probably destined to do more to impede the extension of God's kingdom on earth than all the infidels who have ever lived. Error is error. It is as dangerous to deviate to the right hand as the left. And when men, professing to be holy men, and who are by numbers so regarded, declare those things to be sinful which our Creator has expressly authorized and instituted, they do more to destroy his authority among mankind than the most wicked can effect, by proclaiming that to be innocent which he has forbidden. To this self-righteous and self-exalted class belong all the abolitionists whose writings I have read. With them it is no end of the argument to prove your propositions by the text of the Bible, interpreted according to its plain and palpable meaning, and as understood by all mankind for three thousand years before their time. They are more ingenious at construing and interpolating to accommodate it to their new-fangled and etherial code of morals, than ever were Voltaire and Hume in picking it to pieces, to free the world from what they considered

The Pro-Slavery Argument (Philadelphia: Lippincott, Grambo and Co., 1853), pp. 107–111.

a delusion. When the abolitionists proclaim "man-stealing" to be a sin, and show me that it is so written down by God, I admit them to be right, and shudder at the idea of such a crime. But when I show them that to hold "bondmen forever" is ordained by God, *they deny the Bible, and set up in its place a law of their own making.* I must then cease to reason with them on this branch of the question. Our religion differs as widely as our manners. The great judge in our day of final account must decide between us.

Turning from the consideration of slaveholding in its relations to man as an accountable being, let us examine it in its influence on his political and social state. Though, being foreigners to us, you are in no wise entitled to interfere with the civil institutions of this country, it has become quite common for your countrymen to decry Slavery as an enormous political evil to us, and even to declare that our Northern States ought to withdraw from the Confederacy rather than continue to be contaminated by it. The American abolitionists appear to concur fully in these sentiments, and a portion, at least, of them are incessantly threatening to dissolve the Union. Nor should I be at all surprised if they succeed. It would not be difficult, in my opinion, to conjecture which region, the North or South, would suffer most by such an event. For one, I should not object, by any means, to cast my lot in a confederacy of States whose citizens might all be slaveholders.

I endorse without reserve the much abused sentiment of Governor M'Duffie, that "Slavery is the corner-stone of our republican edifice;" while I repudiate, as ridiculously absurd, that much lauded but nowhere accredited dogma of Mr. Jefferson, that "all men are born equal." No society has ever yet existed, and I have already incidentally quoted the highest authority to show that none ever will exist, without a natural variety of classes. The most marked of these must, in a country like ours, be the rich and the poor, the educated and the ignorant. It will scarcely be disputed that the very poor have less leisure to prepare themselves for the proper discharge of public duties than the rich; and that the ignorant are wholly unfit for them at all. In all countries save ours, these two classes, or the poor rather, who are presumed to be necessarily ignorant, are by law expressly excluded from all participation in the management of public affairs. In a Republican Government this cannot be done. Universal suffrage, though not essential in theory, seems to be in fact a necessary appendage to a republican system. Where universal suffrage obtains, it is obvious that the government is in the hands of a numerical majority; and it is hardly necessary to say that in every part of the world more than half the people are ignorant and poor. Though no one can look upon poverty as a crime, and we do not here generally regard it as any objection to a man in his individual capacity, still it must be admitted that it is a wretched and insecure government which is administered by its most ignorant citizens, and those who have the least at stake under it. Though intelligence and wealth have great influence here, as everywhere, in keeping in check reckless and unenlightened numbers, yet it is evident to close observers, if not to all, that these are rapidly usurping all power in the non-slaveholding States, and threaten a fearful crisis in republican institutions there at no remote period. In the slaveholding States, however, nearly one-half of the whole population, and those the poorest and most ignorant, have no political influence whatever, because they are slaves. Of the other half, a large proportion are both educated and independent in their circumstances, while those who unfortunately are not so, being still elevated far above the mass, are higher toned and more deeply interested in preserving a stable and well ordered government, than the same class in any other country. Hence, Slavery is truly the "corner-stone" and foundation of every well-designed and durable "republican edifice."

HARPER'S MEMOIR ON SLAVERY

If anything can be predicated as universally true of uncultivated man, it is that he will not labor beyond what is absolutely necessary to maintain his existence. Labor is pain to those who are unaccustomed to it, and the nature of man is averse to pain. Even with all the training, the helps and motives of civilization, we find that this aversion cannot be overcome in many individuals of the most cultivated societies. The coercion of Slavery alone is adequate to form man to habits of labor. Without it, there can be no accumulation of property, no providence for the future, no tastes for comfort or elegancies, which are the characteristics and essentials of civilization. He who has obtained the command of another's labor, first begins to accumulate and provide for the future, and the foundations of civilization are laid. We find confirmed by experience that which is so evident in theory. Since the existence of man upon the earth, with no exception whatever, either of ancient or modern times, every society which has attained civilization, has advanced to it through this process.

Will those who regard Slavery as immoral, or crime in itself, tell us that man was not intended for civilization, but to roam the earth as a biped brute? That he was not to raise his eyes to heaven, or be conformed in his nobler faculties to the image of his Maker? Or will they say that the Judge of all the earth has done wrong in ordaining the means by which alone that end can be obtained? It is true that the Creator can make the wickedness as well as the wrath of man to praise him, and bring forth the most benevolent results from the most atrocious actions. But in such

The Pro-Slavery Argument, pp. 3–12.

cases, it is the motive of the actor alone which condemns the action. The act itself is good, if it promotes the good purposes of God, and would be approved by him, if that result only were intended. Do they not blaspheme the providence of God who denounce as wickedness and outrage, that which is rendered indispensable to his purposes in the government of the world? Or at what stage of the progress of society will they say that Slavery ceases to be necessary, and its very existence becomes sin and crime? I am aware that such argument would have little effect on those with whom it would be degrading to contend—who pervert the inspired writings—which in some parts expressly sanction Slavery, and throughout indicate most clearly that it is a civil institution, with which religion has no concern—with a shallowness and presumption not less flagrant and shameless than his, who would justify murder from the text, "and Phineas arose and executed judgment."

There seems to be something in this subject which blunts the perceptions, and darkens and confuses the understandings and moral feelings of men. Tell them that, of necessity, in every civilized society, there must be an infinite variety of conditions and employments, from the most eminent and intellectual, to the most servile and laborious; that the negro race, from their temperament and capacity, are peculiarly suited to the situation which they occupy, and not less happy in it than any corresponding class to be found in the world; prove incontestibly that no scheme of emancipation could be carried into effect without the most intolerable mischiefs and calamities to both master and slave, or without probably throwing a large and fertile portion of the earth's surface out of the pale of civilization—and you have done nothing. They reply, that whatever may be the consequence, you are bound to do *right;* that man has a right to himself, and man cannot have property in man; that if the negro race be naturally inferior in mind and character, they are not less entitled to the rights of humanity; that if they are happy in their condition, it affords but the stronger evidence of their degradation, and renders them still more objects of commiseration. They repeat, as the fundamental maxim of our civil policy, that all men are born free and equal, and quote from our Declaration of Independence, "that men are endowed by their Creator with certain inalienable *rights,* among which are life, liberty, and the pursuit of happiness."

It is not the first time that I have had occasion to observe that men may repeat with the utmost confidence, some maxim or sentimental phrase, as self-evident or admitted truth, which is either palpably false, or to which, upon examination, it will be found that they attach no definite idea. Notwithstanding our respect for the important document which declared our independence, yet if any thing be found in it, and especially in what may be regarded rather as its ornament than its substance—false, sophistical or unmeaning, that respect should not screen it from the freest examination.

All men are born free and equal. Is it not palpably nearer the truth to say that no man was ever born free, and that no two men were ever born equal? Man is born in a state of the most helpless dependence on others. He continues subject to the absolute control of others, and remains without many of the civil and all of the political privileges of his society, until the period which the laws have fixed as that at which he is supposed to have attained the maturity of his faculties. Then inequality is further developed, and becomes infinite in every society, and under whatever form of government. Wealth and poverty, fame or obscurity, strength or weakness, knowledge or ignorance, ease or labor, power or subjection, mark the endless diversity in the condition of men.

But we have not arrived at the profundity of the maxim. This inequality is, in a great measure, the result of abuses in the institutions of society. They do not speak of what exists, but of what ought to exist. Every one should be left at liberty to obtain all the advantages of society which he can compass, by the free exertion of his faculties, unimpeded by civil restraints. It may be said that this would not remedy the evils of society which are complained of. The inequalities to which I have referred, with the misery resulting from them, would exist in fact under the freest and most popular form of government that man could devise. But what is the foundation of the bold dogma so confidently announced? Females are human and rational beings. They may be found of better faculties, and better qualified to exercise political privileges, and to attain the distinctions of society, than many men; yet who complains of the order of society by which they are excluded from them? For I do not speak of the few who would desecrate them; do violence to the nature which their Creator has impressed upon them; drag them from the position which they necessarily occupy for the existence of civilized society, and in which they constitute its blessing and ornament—the only position which they have ever occupied in any human society—to place them in a situation in which they would be alike miserable and degraded. Low as we descend in combating the theories of presumptuous dogmatists, it cannot be necessary to stoop to this. A youth of eighteen may have powers which cast into the shade those of any of his more advanced contemporaries. He may be capable of serving or saving his country, and if not permitted to do so now, the occasion may have been lost forever. But he can exercise no political privilege, or aspire to any political distinction. It is said that, of necessity, society must exclude from some civil and political privileges those who are unfitted to exercise them, by infirmity, unsuitableness of character, or defect of discretion; that of necessity there must be some general rule on the subject, and that any rule which can be devised will operate with hardship and injustice on individuals. This is all that can be said, and all that need be said. It is saying, in other words, that the privileges in question are no matter of natural right, but to be settled by convention, as the good and safety of society may require. If society should disfranchise individuals convicted of infamous crimes, would this be an invasion of natural right? Yet this would not be justified on the score of their moral guilt, but that the good of society required or would be promoted by it. We admit the existence of a moral law, binding on societies as on individuals. Society must act in good faith. No man, or body of men, has a right to inflict pain or privation on others, unless with a view, after full and impartial deliberation, to prevent a greater evil. If this deliberation be had, and the decision made in good faith, there can be no imputation of moral guilt. Has any politician contended that the very existence of governments in which there are orders privileged by law, constitutes a violation of morality; that their continuance is a crime, which men are bound to put an end to, without any consideration of the good or evil to result from the change? Yet this is the natural inference from the dogma of the natural equality of men as applied to our institution of Slavery—an equality not to be invaded without injustice and wrong, and requiring to be restored instantly, unqualifiedly, and without reference to consequences.

This is sufficiently common-place, but we are sometimes driven to common-place. It is no less a false and shallow, than a presumptuous philosophy, which theorizes on the affairs of men as of a problem to be solved by some unerring rule of human reason, without reference to the designs of a superior intelligence, so far as he has been pleased to indicate them, in their creation and destiny. Man is born to subjection. Not only during infancy is he dependent, and under the control of others; at all ages, it is the very bias of his nature, that the strong and the wise should control the weak and the ignorant. So it has been since the days of Nimrod. The existence of some form of slavery in all ages and countries, is proof enough of this. He is born to subjection as he is born in sin and ignorance. To make any considerable progress in knowledge, the continued efforts of successive generations and the diligent training and unwearied exertions of the individual, are requisite. To make progress in moral virtue, not less time and effort, aided by superior help, are necessary; and it is only by the matured exercise of his knowledge and his virtue, that he can attain to civil freedom. Of all things, the existence of civil liberty is most the result of artificial institution. The proclivity of the natural man is to domineer or to be subservient. A noble result, indeed, but in the attaining of which, as in the instances of knowledge and virtue, the Creator, for his own purposes, has set a limit beyond which we cannot go.

But he who is most advanced in knowledge, is most sensible of his own ignorance, and how much must forever be unknown to man in his present condition. As I have heard it expressed, the further you extend the circle of light, the wider is the horizon of darkness. He who has made the greatest progress in moral purity, is most sensible of the depravity, not only of the world around him, but of his own heart, and the imperfection of his best motives; and this he knows that men must feel and lament so long as they continue men. So when the greatest progress in civil liberty has been made, the enlightened lover of liberty will know that there must remain much inequality, much injustice, much *slavery*, which no human wisdom or virtue will ever be able wholly to prevent or redress. As I have before had the honor to say to this Society, the condition of our whole existence is but to struggle with evils—to compare them—to choose between them, and, so far as we can, to mitigate them. To say that there is evil in any institution, is only to say that it is human.

And can we doubt but that this long discipline and laborious process, by which men are required to work out the elevation and improvement of their individual nature and their social condition, is imposed for a great and benevolent end? Our faculties are not adequate to the solution of the mystery, why it should be so; but the truth is clear, that the world was not intended for the seat of universal knowledge, or goodness, or happiness, or freedom.

Man has been endowed by his Creator with certain inalienable rights, among which are life, liberty, and the pursuit of happiness. What is meant by the *inalienable* right of liberty? Has any one who has used the words ever asked himself this question? Does it mean that a man has no right to alienate his own liberty—to sell himself and his posterity for slaves? This would seem to be the more obvious meaning. When the word *right* is used, it has reference to some law which sanctions it, and would be violated by its invasion. It must refer either to the general law of morality, or the law of the country—the law of God or the law of man. If the law of any country permitted it, it would of course be absurd to say that the law of that country was violated by such alienation. If it have any meaning in this respect, it must mean that though the law of the country permitted it, the man would be guilty of an immoral act who should thus alienate his liberty. A fit question for schoolmen to discuss, and the consequences resulting from its decision as important as from any of theirs. Yet who will say that the man pressed by famine, and in prospect of death, would be criminal for such an act? Self-preservation, as is truly said, is the first law of nature. High and peculiar characters, by elaborate cultivation, may be taught to prefer death to slavery, but it would be folly to prescribe this as a duty to the mass of mankind.

If any rational meaning can be attributed to the sentence I have quoted, it is this:—That the society, or the individuals who exercise the powers of government, are guilty of a violation of the law of God or of morality, when, by any law or public act, they deprive men of life or liberty, or restrain them in the pursuit of happiness. Yet every government does, and of necessity must, deprive men of life and liberty for offences against society. Restrain them in the pursuit of happiness! Why all the laws of society are intended for nothing else but to restrain men from the pursuit of happiness, according to their own ideas of happiness or advantage—which the phrase must mean if it means any thing. And by what right does society punish by the loss of life or liberty? Not on account of the moral guilt of the criminal—not by impiously and arrogantly assuming the prerogative of the Almighty, to dispense justice or suffering, according to moral desert. It is for its own protection—it is the right of self-defence. If there existed the blackest moral turpitude, which by its example or consequences, could be of no evil to society, government would have nothing to do with that. If an action, the most harmless in its moral character, could be dangerous to the security of society, society would have the perfect right to punish it. If the possession of a black skin would be otherwise dangerous to society, society has the same right to protect itself by disfranchising the possessor of civil privileges, and to continue the disability to his posterity, if the same danger would be incurred by its removal. Society inflicts these forfeitures for the security of the lives of its members; it inflicts them for the security of their property, the great essential of civilization; it inflicts them also for the protection of its political institutions, the forcible attempt to overturn which, has always been justly regarded as the greatest crime; and who has questioned its right so to inflict? "Man cannot have property in man"—a phrase as full of meaning as, "who slays fat oxen should himself be fat." Certainly he may, if the laws of society allow it, and if it be on sufficient grounds, neither he nor society do wrong.

PROFESSOR DEW ON SLAVERY

The great object of government is the protection of property;—from the days of the patriarchs down to the present time, the great desideratum has been to find out the most efficient mode of protecting property. There is not a government at this moment in Christendom, whose peculiar practical character is not the result of the state of property.

No government can exist which does not conform to the state of property; it cannot make the latter conform entirely to the government; an attempt to do it would and ought to revolutionize any state. The great difficulty in forming the government of any country arises almost universally from the state of property, and the necessity of making it to conform to that state; and it was the state of property in Virginia which really constituted the whole difficulty in the late Convention. . . .

The Pro-Slavery Argument, pp. 387, 389–391, 461–462.

If a convention of the whole State of Virginia were called, and in due form the right of slave property were abolished by the votes of Western Virginia alone, does any one think that Eastern Virginia would be bound to yield to the decree? Certainly not. The strong and unjust man in a state of nature robs the weaker, and you establish government to prevent this oppression. Now, only sanction the doctrine of Virginia orators, let one interest in the government (the West) rob another at pleasure (the East); and is there any man who can fail to see that government is systematically producing that very oppression for which it is intended to remedy, and for which alone it is established? In forming the late Constitution of Virginia, the East objected to the "white basis principle," upon the very grounds that it would enable Western to oppress Eastern Virginia, through the medium of slave property. The most solemn asseverations of a total unwillingness, on the part of the West, to meddle with or touch the slave population, beyond the rightful and equitable demands of revenue, were repeatedly made by their orators. And now, what has the lapse of two short years developed? Why, that the West, unmindful of former professions, and regardless of the eternal principles of justice, is urging on an invasion and final abolition of that kind of property which it was solemnly pledged to protect! Is it possible that gentlemen can have reflected upon the consequences which even the avowal of such doctrines are calculated to produce? Are they conciliatory? Can they be taken kindly by the East? Is it not degrading for freemen to stand quailing with the fear of losing that property which they have been accumulating for ages, to stand waiting in fearful anxiety for the capricious edict of the West, which may say to one man, "Sir, you must give up your property, although you have amassed it under the guarantee of the laws and constitution of your State and of the United States;" and to another, who is near him, and has an equal amount of property of a different description, and has no more virtue and no more conscience than the slaveholder, "you may hold yours, because we do not yet consider it a 'nuisance'?" This is language which cannot fail to awaken the people to a sense of their danger. These doctrines, whenever announced in debate, have a tendency to disorganize and unhinge the condition of society, and to produce uncertainty and alarm; to create revulsions of capital; to cause the land of Old Virginia, and real source of wealth, to be abandoned; and her white wealthy population to flee the State, and seek an asylum in a land where they will be protected in the enjoyment of the fruits of their industry. In fine, we would say, these doctrines are 'nuisances,' and if we were disposed to retaliate, would add that they ought to be 'abated.' We will close our remarks on this dangerous doctrine, by calling upon Western Virginia and the non-slaveholders of Eastern Virginia, not to be allured by the syren song. It is as delusive as it may appear fascinating; all the sources of wealth and departments of industry, all the great interests of society, are really interwoven with one another—they form an indissoluble chain; a blow at any part quickly vibrates through the whole length—the destruction of one interest involves another. Destroy agriculture, destroy tillage, and the ruin of the farmer will draw down ruin upon the mechanic, the merchant, the sailor and the manufacturer—they must all flee together from the land of desolation. . . .

It has been contended that slavery is unfavorable to a republican spirit; but the whole history of the world proves that this is far from being the case. In the ancient republics of Greece and Rome, where the spirit of liberty glowed with most intensity, the slaves were more numerous than the freemen. Aristotle, and the great men of antiquity, believed slavery necessary to keep alive the spirit of freedom. In Sparta, the freemen were even forbidden to perform the offices of slaves, lest he might lose the spirit of independence. In modern times, too, liberty has always been more ardently desired by slaveholding communities. "Such" says Burke, "were our Gothic ancestors; such, in our days, were the Poles; and such will be all masters of slaves who are not slaves themselves." "These people of the southern (American) colonies are much more strongly, and with a higher and more stubborn spirit, attached to liberty, than those of the northward." And from the time of Burke down to the present day, the Southern States have always borne the same honorable distinction. Burke says, "it is because freedom is to them not only an enjoyment, but a kind of rank and privilege." Another, and perhaps more efficient cause of this, is the perfect spirit of equality so prevalent among the whites of all the slaveholding States. Jack Cade, the English reformer, wished all mankind to be brought to one common level. We believe slavery in the U. States has accomplished this, in regard to the whites, as nearly as can be expected or even desired in this world. The menial and low offices being all performed by the blacks, there is at once taken away the greatest cause of distinction and separation of the ranks of society. The man to the north will not shake hands familiarly with his servant, and converse, and laugh and dine with him, no matter how honest and respectable he may be. But go to the south, and you will find that no white man feels such inferiority of rank as to be unworthy of association with those around him. Color alone is here the badge of distinction, the true mark of aristocracy, and all who are white are equal in spite of the variety of occupation. The same thing is observed in the West Indies. "Of the character common to the white resident of the West Indies, it appears to me," says Edwards, "that the leading feature is an independent spirit, and a display of *conscious equality* throughout all ranks and conditions. The poorest white person seems to consider himself nearly on a level with the richest; and emboldened by this idea, approaches his employer with extended hand, and a freedom which, in the countries of Europe, is seldom displayed by men in the lower orders of life towards their superiors." And it is this spirit of equality which is both the generator and preserver of the genuine spirit of liberty.

DRED SCOTT v. SANFORD
19 HOW. 393 (1857)

MR. CHIEF JUSTICE TANEY delivered the opinion of the Court:

The question is simply this: can a negro, whose ancestors were imported into this country and sold as slaves, become a member of the political community formed and brought into existence by the Constitution of the United States, and as such become entitled to all the rights, and privileges, and immunities, guarantied by that instrument to the citizen? One of these rights is the privilege of suing in a court of the United States in the cases specified in the Constitution. . . .

The words "people of the United States" and "citizens" are synonymous terms, and mean the same thing. They both describe the political body who, according to our republican institutions, form the sovereignty, and who hold the power and conduct the government through their representatives. They are what we familiarly call the "sovereign people," and every citizen is one of this people, and a constituent member of this sovereignty. The question before us is, whether the class of persons described in the plea in abatement compose a portion of this people, and are constituent members of this sovereignty. We think they are not, and that they are not included, and were not intended to be included, under the word "citizens" in the Constitution, and can, therefore, claim none of the rights and privileges which that instrument provides for and secures to citizens of the United States. On the contrary, they were at that time considered as a subordinate and inferior class of beings, who had been subjugated by the dominant race, and whether emancipated or not, yet remained subject to their authority, and had no rights or privileges but such as those who held the power and the government might choose to grant them. . . .

The question then arises, whether the provisions of the Constitution, in relation to the personal rights and privileges to which the citizen of a state should be entitled, embraced the negro African race, at that time in this country, or who might afterwards be imported, who had then or should afterwards be made free in any State; and to put it in the power of a single State to make him a citizen of the United States, and endue him with the full rights of citizenship in every other State without their consent. Does the Constitution of the United States act upon him whenever he shall be made free under the laws of a State, and raised there to the rank of a citizen, and immediately clothe him with all the privileges of a citizen in every other State, and in its own courts?

The court think the affirmative of these propositions cannot be maintained. And if it cannot, the plaintiff in error could not be a citizen of the State of Missouri, within the meaning of the Constitution of the United States, and, consequently, was not entitled to sue in its courts.

It is true, every person, and every class and description of persons, who were at the time of the adoption of the Constitution recognized as citizens in the several States, became also citizens of this new political body; but none other; it was formed by them, and for them and their posterity, but for no one else. And the personal rights and privileges guarantied to citizens of this new sovereignty were intended to embrace those only who were then members of the several state communities, or who should afterwards, by birthright or otherwise, become members, according to the provisions of the Constitution and the principles on which it was founded. It was the union of those who were at that time members of distinct and separate political communities into one political family, whose power, for certain specified purposes, was to extend over the whole territory of the United States. And it gave to each citizen rights and privileges outside of his State which he did not before possess, and placed him in every other State upon a perfect equality with its own citizens as to rights of person and rights of property; it made him a citizen of the United States.

It becomes necessary, therefore, to determine who were citizens of the several States when the Constitution was adopted. And in order to do this, we must recur to the governments and institutions of the thirteen Colonies, when they separated from Great Britain and formed new sovereignties, and took their places in the family of independent nations. We must inquire who, at that time, were recognized as the people or citizens of a State, whose rights and liberties had been outraged by the English Government; and who declared their independence, and assumed the powers of government to defend their rights by force of arms.

In the opinion of the court, the legislation and histories of the times, and the language used in the Declaration of Independence, show, that neither the class of persons who had been imported as slaves, nor their descendants, whether they had become free or not, were then acknowledged as a part of the people, nor intended to be included in the general words used in that memorable instrument.

It is difficult at this day to realize the state of public opinion in relation to that unfortunate race, which prevailed in the civilized and enlightened portions of the world at the time of the Declaration of Independence, and when the Constitution of the United States was framed and adopted. But the public history of every European nation displays it in a manner too plain to be mistaken.

They had for more than a century before been regarded as beings of an inferior order, and altogether unfit to associate with the white race, either in social or political relations; and so far inferior, that they had no rights which the white man was bound to respect; and that the negro might justly and lawfully be reduced to slavery for his benefit. He was bought and sold, and treated as an ordinary article of merchandise and traffic, whenever a profit could be made by it. This opinion was at that time fixed and universal in the civilized portion of the white race. It was regarded as an axiom in morals as well as in politics, which no one thought of disputing, or supposed to be open to dispute; and men in every grade and position in society daily and habitually acted upon it in their private pursuits, as well as in matters of public concern, without doubting for a moment the correctness of this opinion.

And in no nation was this opinion more firmly fixed or more uniformly acted upon than by the English Government and English people. They not only seized them on the coast of Africa, and sold them or held them in slavery for their own use; but they took them as ordinary articles of merchandise to every country where they could make a profit on them, and were far more extensively engaged in this commerce than any other nation in the world.

The opinion thus entertained and acted upon in England was naturally impressed upon the colonies they founded on this side of the Atlantic. And, accordingly, a negro of the African race was regarded by them as an article of property, and held, and bought and sold as such, in every one of the thirteen colonies which united in the Declaration of Independence, and afterwards formed the Constitution of the United States. The slaves were more or less numerous in the different colonies, as slave labor was found more or less profitable. But no one seems to have doubted the correctness of the prevailing opinion of the time.

The legislation of the different colonies furnishes positive and indisputable proof of this fact.

The language of the Declaration of Independence is equally conclusive:

It begins by declaring that, "when in the course of human events it becomes necessary for one people to dissolve the political bands which have connected them with another, and to assume among the powers of the earth the separate and equal station to which the laws of nature and nature's God entitle them, a decent respect for the opinions of mankind requires that they should declare the causes which impel them to the separation."

It then proceeds to say: "We hold these truths to be self-evident: that all men are created equal; that they are endowed by their Creator with certain unalienable rights; that among them is life, liberty, and the pursuit of happiness; that to secure these rights, Governments are instituted, deriving their just powers from the consent of the governed."

The general words above quoted would seem to embrace the whole human family, and if they were used in a similar instrument at this day would be so understood. But it is too clear for dispute, that the enslaved African race were not intended to be included, and formed no part of the people who framed and adopted this declaration; for if the language, as understood in that day, would embrace them, the conduct of the distinguished men who framed the Declaration of Independence would have been utterly and flagrantly inconsistent with the principles they asserted; and instead of the sympathy of mankind, to which they so confidently appealed, they would have deserved and received universal rebuke and reprobation.

Yet the men who framed this declaration were great men—high in literary acquirements—high in their sense of honor, and incapable of asserting principles inconsistent with those on which they were acting. They perfectly understood the meaning of the language they used, and how it would be understood by others; and they knew that it would not in any part of the civilized world be supposed to embrace the negro race, which, by common consent, had been excluded from civilized Governments and the family of nations, and doomed to slavery. They spoke and acted according to the then established doctrines and principles, and in the ordinary language of the day, and no one misunderstood them. The unhappy black race were separated from the white by indelible marks, and laws long before established, and were never thought of or spoken of except as property, and when the claims of the owner or the profit of the trader were supposed to need protection.

This state of public opinion had undergone no change when the Constitution was adopted, as is equally evident from its provisions and language.

The brief preamble sets forth by whom it was formed, for what purposes, and for whose benefit and protection. It declares that it is formed by the *people* of the United States; that is to say, by those who were members of the different political communities in the several States; and its great object is declared to be to secure the blessings of liberty to themselves and their posterity. It speaks in general terms of the *people* of the United States, and of *citizens* of the several States, when it is providing for the exercise of the powers granted or the privileges secured to the citizen. It does not define what description of persons are intended to be included under these terms, or who shall be regarded as a citizen and one of the people. It uses them as terms so well understood, that no further description or definition was necessary.

But there are two clauses in the Constitution which point directly and specifically to the negro race as a separate class of persons, and show clearly that they were not regarded as a portion of the people or citizens of the Government then formed. . . .

The legislation of the States therefore shows, in a manner not to be mistaken, the inferior and subject condition of that race at the time the Constitution was adopted, and long afterwards, throughout the thirteen States by which that instrument was framed; and it is hardly consistent with the respect due to these States, to suppose that they regarded at that time, as fellow citizens and members of the sovereignty, a class of beings whom they had thus stigmatized; whom, as we are bound, out of respect to the State sovereignties, to assume they had deemed it just and necessary thus to stigmatize, and upon whom they had impressed such deep and enduring marks of inferiority and degradation; or that when they met in convention to form the Constitution, they looked upon them as a portion of their constituents, or designed to include them in the provisions so carefully inserted for the security and protection of the liberties and rights of their citizens. It cannot be supposed that they intended to secure to them rights, and privileges, and rank, in the new political body throughout the Union, which every one of them denied within the limits of its own dominion. More especially, it cannot be believed that the large slaveholding States regarded them as included in the word "citizens," or would have consented to a constitution which might compel them to receive them in that character from another State. For if they were so received, and entitled to the privileges and immunities of citizens, it would exempt them from the operation of the special laws and from the police regulations which they considered to be necessary for their own safety. It would give to persons of the negro race, who were recognized as citizens in any one State of the Union, the right to enter every other State when-ever they pleased, singly or in companies, without pass or passport, and without obstruction, to sojourn there as long as they pleased, to go where they pleased at every hour of the day or night without molestation, unless they committed some violation of law for which a white man would be punished; and it would give them the full liberty of speech in public and in private upon all subjects which its own citizens might speak; to hold public meetings upon political affairs, and to keep and carry arms wher-ever they went. And all of this would be done in the face of the subject race of the same color, both free and slaves, inevitably producing discontent and insubordination among them, and endangering the peace and safety of the State. . . .

To all this mass of proof we have still to add, that Congress has repeatedly legislated upon the same construction of the Constitution that we have given. Three laws, two of which were passed almost immediately after the Government went into operation, will be abundantly sufficient to show this. The two first are particularly worthy of notice, because many of the men who assisted in framing the Constitution, and took an active part in procuring its adoption, were then in the halls of legislation, and certainly understood what they meant when they used the words "people of the United States" and "citizen" in that well-considered instrument.

The first of these acts is the naturalization law, which was passed at the second session of the first Congress, March 26, 1790, and confines the right of becoming citizens *"to aliens being free white persons."* . . .

Another of the early laws of which we have spoken, is the first militia law, which was passed in 1792, at the first session of the second Congress. The language of this law is equally plain and significant with the one just mentioned. It directs that every "free able-bodied white male citizen" shall be enrolled in the militia. The word *white* is evidently used to exclude the African race, and the word "citizen" to exclude unnaturalized foreigners; the latter forming no part of the sovereignty, owing it no allegiance, and therefore under no obligation to defend it. The African race, however, born in the country, did owe allegiance to the Government, whether they were slave or free; but it is repudiated, and rejected from the duties and obligations of citizenship in marked language. . . .

No one, we presume, supposes that any change in public opinion or feeling, in relation to this unfortunate race, in the civilized nations of Europe or in this country, should induce the court to give to the words of the Constitution a more liberal construction in their favor than they were intended to bear when the instrument was framed and adopted. Such an argument would be altogether inadmissible in any tribunal called on to interpret it. If any of its provisions are deemed unjust, there is a mode prescribed in the instrument itself by which it may be amended; but while it remains unaltered, it must be construed now as it was understood at the time of its adoption. It is not only the same in words, but the same in meaning, and delegates the same powers to the Government, and reserves and secures the same rights and privileges to the citizen; and as long as it continues to exist in its present form, it speaks not only in the same words, but with the same meaning and intent with which it spoke when it came from the hands of its framers, and was voted on and adopted by the people of the United States. Any other rule of construction would abrogate the judicial character of this court, and make it the mere reflex of the popular opinion or passion of the day. This court was not created by the Constitution for such purposes. Higher and graver trusts have been confided to it, and it must not falter in the path of duty.

What the construction was at that time, we think can hardly admit of doubt. We have the language of the Declaration of Independence and of the Articles of Confederation, in addition to the plain words of the Constitution itself; we have the legislation of the different States, before, about the time, and since, the Constitution was adopted; we have the legislation of Congress, from the time of its adoption to a recent period; and we have the constant and uniform action of the Executive Department, all concurring together, and leading to the same result. And if anything in relation to the construction of the Constitution can be regarded as settled, it is that which we now give to the word "citizen" and the word "people."

And upon a full and careful consideration of the subject, the court is of opinion that, upon the facts stated in the plea in abatement, Dred Scott was not a citizen of Missouri with the meaning of the Constitution of the United States, and not entitled as such to sue in its courts; and, consequently, that the Circuit Court has no jurisdiction of the case, and that the judgment on the plea in abatement is erroneous. . . .

The powers over person and property of which we speak are not only not granted to Congress, but are in express terms denied, and they are forbidden to exercise them. And this prohibition is not confined to the States, but the words are general, and extend to the whole territory over which the Constitution gives it power to legislate, including those portions of it remaining under territorial government as well as that covered by States. It is a total absence of power everywhere within the dominion of the United States, and places the citizens of a territory, so far as the rights are concerned, on the same footing with citizens of the States, and guards them as firmly and plainly against any inroads which the general government might attempt, under the plea of implied or incidental powers. And if Congress itself cannot do this—if it is beyond the powers conferred on the Federal Government—it will be admitted, we presume, that it could not authorize a territorial government to exercise them. It could confer no power on any local government, established by its authority, to violate the provisions of the Constitution.

It seems, however, to be supposed, that there is a difference between property in a slave and other property, and that different rules may be applied to it in expounding the Constitution of the United States. And the laws and usages of nations, and the writings of eminent jurists upon the relation of master and slave and their mutual rights and duties, and the powers which governments may exercise over it, have been dwelt upon in the argument. . . .

Now, as we have already said in an earlier part of this opinion, upon a different point, *the right of property in a slave is distinctly and expressly affirmed in the Constitution.* The right to traffic in it, like an ordinary article of merchandise and property, was guaranteed to the citizens of the United States, in every State that might desire it, for twenty years. And the government in express terms is pledged to protect it in all future time, if the slave escapes from his owner. This is done in plain words—too plain to be misunderstood. And no word can be found in the Constitution which gives Congress a greater power over slave property, or which entitles property of that kind to less protection than property of any other description. The only power conferred is the power coupled with the duty of guarding and protecting the owner in his rights.

Upon these considerations, it is the opinion of the court that the Act of Congress which prohibited a citizen from holding and owning property of this kind in the territory of the United States north of the line therein mentioned, is not warranted by the Constitution, and is therefore void; and that neither Dred Scott himself, nor any of his family, were made free by being carried into this territory; even if they have been carried there by the owner, with the intention of becoming a permanent resident.

Lincoln-Douglas Debates (1858)

MR. DOUGLAS' SPEECH

Ladies and gentlemen: I appear before you to-day for the purpose of discussing the leading political topics which now agitate the public mind. By an arrangement between Mr. Lincoln and myself, we are present here to-day for the purpose of having a joint discussion as the representatives of the two great political parties of the State and Union, upon the principles in issue between these parties and this vast concourse of people, shows the deep feeling which pervades the public mind in regard to the questions dividing us.

Prior to 1854 this country was divided into two great political parties, known as the Whig and Democratic parties. Both were national and patriotic, advocating principles that were universal in their application. An old line Whig could proclaim his principles in Louisiana and Massachusetts alike. Whig principles had no boundary sectional line, they were not limited by the Ohio river, nor by the Potomac, nor by the line of the free and slave States, but applied and were proclaimed wherever the Constitution ruled or the American flag waved over the American soil. (Hear him, and three cheers.) . . .

Having formed this new party for the benefit of deserters from Whiggery, and deserters from Democracy, and having laid down the Abolition platform which I have read, Lincoln now takes his stand and proclaims his Abolition doctrines. Let me read a part of them. In his speech at Springfield to the convention which nominated him for the Senate, he said:

> In my opinion it will not cease until a crisis shall have been reached and passed. "A house divided against itself cannot stand." I believe this Government *cannot endure permanently half Slave and half Free.* I do not expect the Union to be dissolved—I do not expect the house to fall—*but I do expect it will cease to be divided.* It will become all one thing, or all the other. Either the opponents of Slavery *will arrest the further spread of it,* and place it where the public mind shall rest in the belief *that it is in the course of ultimate extinction;* or its advocates *will push it forward*

First Debate at Ottawa, Illinois. From Roy P. Basler, ed., *The Collected Works of Abraham Lincoln* (New Brunswick, N.J.: Rutgers University Press, 1953), Vol. III, pp. 1–37.

till it shall become alike lawful in all the States—old as well as new, North as well as South.

("Good," "good," and cheers.)

I am delighted to hear you Black Republicans say "good." (Laughter and cheers.) I have no doubt that doctrine expresses your sentiments ("hit them again," "that's it,") and I will prove to you now, if you will listen to me, that it is revolutionary and destructive of the existence of this Government. ("Hurrah for Douglas," "good," and cheers.) Mr. Lincoln, in the extract from which I have read, says that this Government cannot endure permanently in the same condition in which it was made by its framers—divided into free and slave States. He says that it has existed for about seventy years thus divided, and yet he tells you that it cannot endure permanently on the same principles and in the same relative condition in which our fathers made it. ("Neither can it.") Why can it not exist divided into free and slave States? Washington, Jefferson, Franklin, Madison, Hamilton, Jay, and the great men of that day, made this Government divided into free States and slave States, and left each State perfectly free to do as it pleased on the subject of slavery. ("Right, right.") Why can it not exist on the same principles on which our fathers made it? ("It can.") They knew when they framed the Constitution that in a country as wide and broad as this, with such a variety of climate, production and interest, the people necessarily required different laws and institutions in different localities. They knew that the laws and regulations which would suit the granite hills of New Hampshire would be unsuited to the rice plantations of South Carolina, ("right, right,") and they, therefore, provided that each State should retain its own Legislature, and its own sovereignty with the full and complete power to do as it pleased within its own limits, in all that was local and not national. (Applause.) One of the reserved rights of the States, was the right to regulate the relations between Master and Servant, on the slavery question. At the time the Constitution was formed, there were thirteen States in the Union, twelve of which were slaveholding States and one a free State. Suppose this doctrine of uniformity preached by Mr. Lincoln, that the States should all be free or all be slave had prevailed and what would have been the result? Of course, the twelve slaveholding States would have overruled the one free State, and slavery would have been fastened by a Constitutional provision on every inch of the American Republic, instead of being left as our fathers wisely left it, to each State to decide for itself. ("Good, good," and three cheers for Douglas.) Here I assert that uniformity in the local laws and institutions of the different States is neither possible or desirable. If uniformity had been adopted when the government was established, it must inevitably have been uniformity of slavery everywhere, or else the uniformity of negro citizenship and negro equality everywhere.

We are told by Lincoln that he is utterly opposed to the Dred Scott decision, and will not submit to it, for the reason that he says it deprives the negro of the rights and privileges of citizenship. (Laughter and applause.) That is the first and main reason which he assigns for his warfare on the Supreme Court of the United States and its decision. I ask you, are you in favor of conferring upon the negro the rights and privileges of citizenship? ("No, no.") Do you desire to strike out of our State Constitution that clause which keeps slaves and free negroes out of the State, and allow the free negroes to flow in, ("never,") and cover your prairies with black settlements? Do you desire to turn this beautiful State into a free negro colony, ("no, no,") in order that when Missouri abolishes slavery she can send one hundred thousand emancipated slaves into Illinois, to become citizens and voters, on an equality with yourselves? ("Never," "no.") If you desire negro citizenship, if you desire to allow them to come into the State and settle with the white man, if you desire them to vote on an equality with yourselves, and to make them eligible to office, to serve on juries, and to adjudge your rights, then support Mr. Lincoln and the Black Republican party, who are in favor of the citizenship of the negro. ("Never, never.") For one, I am opposed to negro citizenship in any and every form. (Cheers.) I believe this government was made on the white basis. ("Good.") I believe it was made by white men, for the benefit of white men and their posterity for ever, and I am in favor of confining citizenship to white men, men of European birth and descent, instead of conferring it upon negroes, Indians and other inferior races. ("Good for you." "Douglas forever.")

Mr. Lincoln, following the example and lead of all the little Abolition orators, who go around and lecture in the basements of schools and churches, reads from the Declaration of Independence, that all men were created equal, and then asks how can you deprive a negro of that equality which God and the Declaration of Independence awards to him. He and they maintain that negro equality is guarantied by the laws of God, and that it is asserted in the Declaration of Independence. If they think so, of course they have a right to say so, and so vote. I do not question Mr. Lincoln's conscientious belief that the negro was made his equal, and hence is his brother, (laughter,) but for my own part, I do not regard the negro as my equal, and positively deny that he is my brother or any kin to me whatever. ("Never." "Hit him again," and cheers.) Lincoln has evidently learned by heart Parson Lovejoy's catechism. (Laughter and applause.) He can repeat it as well as Farnsworth, and he is worthy of a medal from father Giddings and Fred Douglass for his Abolitionism. (Laughter.) He holds that the negro was born his equal and yours, and that he was endowed with equality by the Almighty, and that no human law can deprive him of these rights which were guarantied to him by the Supreme ruler of the Universe. Now, I do not believe that the Almighty ever intended the negro to be the equal of the white man. ("Never, never.") If he did, he has been a long time demonstrating the fact. (Cheers.) For thousands of years the negro has been a race upon the earth, and during all that time, in all latitudes and climates, wherever he has wandered or been taken, he has been inferior to the race which he has there met. He belongs to an inferior race, and must always occupy an inferior position. ("Good," "that's so," &c.) I do not hold that because the negro is our inferior that therefore he ought to be a slave. By no means can such a conclusion be drawn from what I have said. On the contrary, I hold that humanity and christianity both require that the negro shall have and enjoy every right, every privilege, and every immunity consistent with the safety of the society in which he lives. ("That's so.") On that point, I presume, there can be no diversity of opinion. You and I are bound to extend to our inferior and dependent being every right, every privilege, every facility and immunity consistent with the public good. The question then arises what rights and privileges are consistent with the public good. This is a question which each State and each Territory must decide for itself—Illinois has decided it for herself. We have provided that the negro shall not be a slave, and we have also provided that he shall not be a citizen, but protect him in his civil rights, in his life, his person and his property, only depriving him of all political rights whatsoever, and re- fusing to put him on an equality with the white man. ("Good.") That policy of Illinois is satisfactory to the Democratic party and to me, and if it were to the Republicans, there would then be no question upon the subject; but the Republicans say that he ought to be made a citizen, and when he becomes a citizen he becomes your equal, with all your rights and privileges. ("He never shall.") They assert the Dred Scott decision to be monstrous because it denies that the negro is or can be a citizen under the Constitution. Now, I hold that Illinois had a right to abolish and prohibit slavery as she did, and I hold that Kentucky has the same right to continue and protect slavery that Illinois had to abolish it. I hold that New York had as much right to abolish slavery as Virginia has to continue it, and that each and every State of this Union is a sovereign power, with the right to do as it pleases upon this question of slavery, and upon all its domestic institutions. Slavery is not the only question which comes up in this controversy. There is a far more important one to you, and that is, what shall be done with the free negro? We have settled the slavery question as far as we are concerned; we have prohibited it in Illinois forever, and in doing so, I think we have done wisely, and there is no man in the State who would be more strenuous in his opposition to the introduction of slavery than I would; (cheers) but when we settled it for ourselves, we exhausted all our power over that subject. We have done our whole duty, and can do no more. We must leave each and every other State to decide for itself the same question. In relation to the policy to be pursued towards the free negroes, we have said that they shall not vote; whilst Maine, on the other hand, has said that they shall vote. Maine is a sovereign State, and has the power to regulate the qualifications of voters within her limits. I would never consent to confer the right of voting and of citizenship upon a negro, but still I am not going to quarrel with Maine for differing from me in opinion. Let Maine take care of her own negroes and fix the qualifications of her own voters to suit herself, without interfering with Illinois, and Illinois will not interfere with Maine. So with the State of New York. She allows the negro to vote provided he owns two hundred and fifty dollars' worth of property, but not otherwise. While I would not make any distinction whatever between a negro who held property and one who did not; yet if the sovereign State of New York chooses to make that distinction it is her business and not mine, and I will not quarrel with her for it. She can do as she pleases on this question if she minds her own business, and we will do the same thing. Now, my friends, if we will only act conscientiously and rigidly upon this great principle of popular sovereignty which guarantees to each State and Territory the right to do as it pleases on all things local and domestic instead of Congress interfering, we will continue at peace one with another. Why should Illinois be at war with Missouri, or Kentucky with Ohio, or Virginia with New York, merely because their institutions differ? Our fathers intended that our institutions should differ. They knew that the North and the South having different climates, productions and interests, required different institutions. This doctrine of Mr. Lincoln's of uniformity among the institutions of the different States is a new doctrine, never dreamed of by Washington, Madison, or the framers of this Government. Mr. Lincoln and the Republican party set themselves up as wiser than these men who made this government, which has flourished for seventy years under the principle of popular sovereignty, recognizing the right of each State to do as it pleased. Under that principle, we have grown from a nation of three or four millions to a nation of about thirty millions of people; we have crossed the Allegheny mountains and filled up the whole North West, turning the prairie into a garden, and building up churches and schools, thus spreading civilization and christianity where before there was nothing but savage-barbarism. Under that principle we have become from a feeble nation, the most powerful on the face of the earth, and if we only adhere to that principle, we can go forward increasing in territory, in power, in strength and in glory until the Republic of America shall be the North

Star that shall guide the friends of freedom throughout the civilized world. ("Long may you live," and great applause.) And why can we not adhere to the great principle of self-government, upon which our institutions were originally based. ("We can.") I believe that this new doctrine preached by Mr. Lincoln and his party will dissolve the Union if it succeeds. They are trying to array all the Northern States in one body against the South, to excite a sectional war between the free States and the slave States, in order that the one or the other may be driven to the wall.

I am told that my time is out. Mr. Lincoln will now address you for an hour and a half, and I will then occupy a half hour in replying to him. (Three times three cheers were here given for Douglas.)

MR. LINCOLN'S REPLY

Mr. Lincoln then came forward and was greeted with loud and protracted cheers from fully two-thirds of the audience. This was admitted by the Douglas men on the platform. It was some minutes before he could make himself heard, even by those on the stand. . . .

Anything that argues me into his idea of perfect social and political equality with the negro, is but a specious and fantastic arrangement of words, by which a man can prove a horse chestnut to be a chestnut horse. [Laughter.] I will say here, while upon this subject, that I have no purpose directly or indirectly to interfere with the institution of slavery in the States where it exists. I believe I have no lawful right to do so, and I have no inclination to do so. I have no purpose to introduce political and social equality between the white and the black races. There is a physical difference between the two, which in my judgment will probably forever forbid their living together upon the footing of perfect equality, and inasmuch as it becomes a necessity that there must be a difference, I, as well as Judge Douglas, am in favor of the race to which I belong, having the superior position. I have never said anything to the contrary, but I hold that notwithstanding all this, there is no reason in the world why the negro is not entitled to all the natural rights enumerated in the Declaration of Independence, the right to life, liberty and the pursuit of happiness. [Loud cheers.] I hold that he is as much entitled to these as the white man. I agree with Judge Douglas he is not my equal in many respects— certainly not in color, perhaps not in moral or intellectual endowment. But in the right to eat the bread, without leave of anybody else, which his own hand earns, *he is my equal and the equal of Judge Douglas, and the equal of every living man.* [Great applause.] . . .

As I have not used up so much of my time as I had supposed, I will dwell a little longer upon one or two of these minor topics upon which the Judge has spoken. He has read from my speech in Springfield, in which I say that "a house divided against itself cannot stand." Does the Judge say it *can* stand? [Laughter.] I don't know whether he does or not. The Judge does not seem to be attending to me just now, but I would like to know if it is his opinion that a house divided against itself *can stand*. If he does, then there is a question of veracity, not between him and me, but between the Judge and an authority of a somewhat higher character. [Laughter and applause.]

Now, my friends, I ask your attention to this matter for the purpose of saying something seriously. I know that the Judge may readily enough agree with me that the maxim which was put forth by the Saviour is true, but he may allege that I misapply it; and the Judge has a right to urge that, in my application, I do misapply it, and then I have a right to show that I do *not* misapply it. When he undertakes to say that because I think this nation, so far as the question of Slavery is concerned, will all become one thing or all the other, I am in favor of bringing about a dead uniformity in the various States, in all their institutions, he argues erroneously. The great variety of the local institutions in the States, springing from differences in the soil, differences in the face of the country, and in the climate, are bonds of Union. They do not make "a house divided against itself," but they make a house united. If they produce in one section of the country what is called for by the wants of another section, and this other section can supply the wants of the first, they are not matters of discord but bonds of union, true bonds of union. But can this question of slavery be considered as among *these* varieties in the institutions of the country? I leave it to you to say whether, in the history of our government, this institution of slavery has not always failed to be a bond of union, and, on the contrary, been an apple of discord and an element of division in the house. [Cries of "Yes, yes," and applause.] I ask you to consider whether, so long as the moral constitution of men's minds shall continue to be the same, after this generation and assemblage shall sink into the grave, and another race shall arise, with the same moral and intellectual development we have—whether, if that institution is standing in the same irritating position in which it now is, it will not continue an element of division? [Cries of "Yes, yes."] If so, then I have a right to say that in regard to this question, the Union is a house divided against itself, and when the Judge reminds me that I have often said to him that the institution of slavery has existed for eighty years in some States, and yet it does not exist in some others, I agree to the fact, and I account for it by looking at the position in which our fathers originally placed it—restricting it from the new Territories where it had not gone, and legislating to cut off its source by the abrogation of the slave trade, thus putting the seal of legislation *against its spread*. The public mind *did* rest in the belief that it was in the course of ultimate extinction. [Cries of "Yes, yes."] But lately, I think—and in this I charge nothing on the Judge's motives—lately, I think, that he, and those acting with him, have placed that institution on a new basis, which looks to the *perpetuity and nationalization of slavery*. [Loud cheers.] And while it is placed upon this new basis, I say, and I have said, that I believe we shall not have peace upon the question until the opponents of slavery arrest the further spread of it, and place it where the public mind shall rest in the belief that it is in the course of ultimate extinction; or, on the other hand, that its advocates will push it forward until it shall become alike lawful in all the States, old as well as new, North as well as South. Now, I believe if we could arrest the spread, and place it where Washington, and Jefferson, and Madison placed it, it *would be* in the course of ultimate extinction, and the public mind *would* as for eighty years past, believe that it was in the course of ultimate extinction. The crisis would be past and the institution might be let alone for a hundred years, if it should live so long, in the States where it exists, yet it would be going out of existence in the way best for both the black and the white races. [Great cheering.]

A VOICE—Then do you repudiate Popular Sovereignty?

MR. LINCOLN—Well, then, let us talk about Popular Sovereignty! [Laughter.] What is Popular Sovereignty? [Cries of "A humbug," "a humbug."] Is it the right of the people to have Slavery or not have it, as they see fit, in the territories? I will state—and I have an able man to watch me—my understanding is that Popular Sovereignty, as now applied to the question of Slavery, does allow the people of a Territory to have Slavery if they want to, but does not allow them *not* to have it if they *do not* want it. [Applause and laughter.] I do not mean that if this vast concourse of people were in a Territory of the United States, any one of them would be obliged to have a slave if he did not want one; but I do say that, as I understand the Dred Scott decision, if any one man wants slaves, all the rest have no way of keeping that one man from holding them.

When I made my speech at Springfield, of which the Judge complains, and from which he quotes, I really was not thinking of the things which he ascribes to me at all. I had no thought in the world that I was doing anything to bring about a war between the free and slave States. I had no thought in the world that I was doing anything to bring about a political and social equality of the black and white races. It never occurred to me that I was doing anything or favoring anything to reduce to a dead uniformity all the local institutions of the various States. But I must say, in all fairness to him, if he thinks I am doing something which leads to these bad results, it is none the better that I did not mean it. It is just as fatal to the country, if I have any influence in producing it, whether I intend it or not. But can it be true, that placing this institution upon the original basis—the basis upon which our fathers placed it—can have any tendency to set the Northern and the Southern States at war with one another, or that it can have any tendency to make the people of Vermont raise sugar cane, because they raise it in Louisiana, or that it can compel the people of Illinois to cut pine logs on the Grand Prairie, where they will not grow, because they cut pine logs in Maine, where they do grow? [Laughter.] The Judge says this is a new principle started in regard to this question. Does the Judge claim that he is working on the plan of the founders of government? I think he says in some of his speeches—indeed I have one here now—that he saw evidence of a policy to allow slavery to be south of a certain line, while north of it it should be excluded, and he saw an indisposition on the part of the country to stand upon that policy, and therefore he set about studying the subject upon *original principles,* and upon *original principles* he got up the Nebraska bill! I am fighting it upon these "original principles"—fighting it in the Jeffersonian, Washingtonian, and Madisonian fashion. [Laughter and applause.] . . .

Now my friends, I have but one branch of the subject, in the little time I have left, to which to call your attention, and as I shall come to a close at the end of that branch, it is probable that I shall not occupy quite all the time allotted to me. Although on these questions I would like to talk twice as long as I have, I could not enter upon another head and discuss it properly without running over my time. I ask the attention of the people here assembled and elsewhere, to the course that Judge Douglas is pursuing every day as bearing upon this question of making slavery national. Not going back to the records but taking the speeches he makes, the speeches he made yesterday and day before and makes constantly all over the country—I ask your attention to them. In the first place what is necessary to make the institution national? Not war. There is no danger that the people of Kentucky will shoulder their muskets and with a young nigger stuck on every bayonet march into Illinois and force them upon us. There is no danger of our going over there and making war upon them. Then what is necessary for the nationalization of slavery? It is simply the next Dred Scott decision. It is merely for the Supreme Court to decide that no *State* under the Constitution can exclude it, just as they have already decided that under the Constitution neither Congress nor the Territorial Legislature can do it. When that is decided and acquiesced in, the whole thing is done. This being true, and this being the way as I think that slavery is to be made national, let us consider what Judge Douglas is doing every day to that end. In the first place, let us see what influence he is exerting on public sentiment. In this and like communities, public sentiment is everything. With public sentiment, nothing can fail; without it nothing can succeed. Consequently he who moulds public sentiment, goes deeper than he who enacts statutes or pronounces decisions. He makes statutes and decisions possible or impossible to be executed. This must be borne in mind, as also the additional fact that Judge Douglas is a man of vast influence, so great that it is enough for many men to profess to believe anything, when they once find out that Judge Douglas professes to believe it. . . .

Henry Clay, my beau ideal of a statesman, the man for whom I fought all my humble life—Henry Clay once said of a class of men who would repress all tendencies to liberty and ultimate emancipation, that they must, if they would do this, go back to the era of our Independence, and muzzle the cannon which thunders its annual joyous return; they must blow out the moral lights around us; they must penetrate the human soul, and eradicate there the love of liberty; and then and not till then, could they perpetuate slavery in this country! [Loud cheers.] To my thinking, Judge Douglas is, by his example and vast influence, doing that very thing in this community, [cheers,] when he says that the negro has nothing in the Declaration of Independence. Henry Clay plainly understood the contrary. Judge Douglas is going back to the era of our Revolution, and to the extent of his ability, muzzling the cannon which thunders its annual joyous return. When he invites any people willing to have slavery, to establish it, he is blowing out the moral lights around us. [Cheers.] When he says he "cares not whether slavery is voted down or voted up,"—that it is a sacred right of self government—he is in my judgment penetrating the human soul and eradicating the light of reason and the love of liberty in this American people. [Enthusiastic and continued applause.] And now I will only say that when, by all these means and appliances, Judge Douglas shall succeed in bringing public sentiment to an exact accordance with his own views—when these vast assemblages shall echo back all these sentiments—when they shall come to repeat his views and to avow his principles, and to say all that he says on these mighty questions—then it needs only the formality of the second Dred Scott decision, which he endorses in advance, to make Slavery alike lawful in all the States—old as well as new, North as well as South.

GETTYSBURG ADDRESS

Four score and seven years ago our fathers brought forth on this continent, a new nation, conceived in Liberty, and dedicated to the proposition that all men are created equal.

Now we are engaged in a great civil war, testing whether that nation, or any nation so conceived and so dedicated, can long endure. We are met on a great battle-field of that war. We have come to dedicate a portion of that field, as a final resting place for those who here gave their lives that that nation might live. It is altogether fitting and proper that we should do this.

But, in a larger sense, we can not dedicate—we can not consecrate—we can not hallow—this ground. The brave men, living and dead, who struggled here, have consecrated it, far above our poor power to add or detract. The world will little note, nor long remember what we say here, but it can never forget what they did here. It is for us the living, rather, to be dedicated here to the unfinished work which they who fought here have thus far so nobly advanced. It is rather for us to be here dedicated to the great task remaining before us—that from these honored dead we take increased devotion to that cause for which they gave the last full measure of devotion—that we here highly resolve that these dead shall not have died in vain—that this nation, under God, shall have a new birth of freedom—and that government of the people, by the people, for the people, shall not perish from the earth.

November 19, 1863.   ABRAHAM LINCOLN

CIVIL WAR AMENDMENTS

ARTICLE XIII (1865)

Section 1. Neither slavery nor involuntary servitude, except as a punishment for crime whereof the party shall have been duly convicted, shall exist within the United States, or any place subject to their jurisdiction.

Section 2. Congress shall have power to enforce this article by appropriate legislation.

ARTICLE XIV (1868)

Section 1. All persons born or naturalized in the United States, and subject to the jurisdiction thereof, are citizens of the United States and of the State wherein they reside. No State shall make or enforce any law which shall abridge the privileges or immunities of citizens of the United States; nor shall any State deprive any person of life, liberty, or property, without due process of law; nor deny to any person within its jurisdiction the equal protection of the laws.

Section 2. Representatives shall be apportioned among the several States according to their respective numbers, counting the whole number of persons in each State, excluding Indians not taxed. But when the right to vote at an election for the choice of electors for President and Vice President of the United States, Representatives in Congress, the Executive and Judicial officers of a State, or the members of the Legislature thereof, is denied to any of the male inhabitants of such State, being twenty-one years of age, and citizens of the United States, or in any way abridged, except for participation in rebellion, or other crime, the basis of representation therein shall be reduced in the proportion which the number of such male citizens shall bear to the whole number of male citizens twenty-one years of age in such State.

Section 3. No person shall be a Senator or Representative in Congress, or elector of President and Vice President, or hold any office, civil or military, under the United States, or under any State, who, having previously taken an oath, as a member of Congress, or as an officer of the United States, or as a member of any State legislature, or as an executive or judicial officer of any State, to support the Constitution of the United

States, shall have engaged in insurrection or rebellion against the same, or given aid or comfort to the enemies thereof. But Congress may by a vote of two-thirds of each House, remove such disability.

Section 4. The validity of the public debt of the United States, authorized by law, including debts incurred for payment of pensions and bounties for services in suppressing insurrection or rebellion, shall not be questioned. But neither the United States nor any State shall assume or pay any debt or obligation incurred in aid of insurrection or rebellion against the United States, or any claim for the loss or emancipation of any slave; but all such debts, obligations and claims shall be held illegal and void.

Section 5. The Congress shall have power to enforce, by appropriate legislation, the provisions of this article.

ARTICLE XV (1870)

Section 1. The right of citizens of the United States to vote shall not be denied or abridged by the United States or by any State on account of race, color, or previous condition of servitude.

Section 2. The Congress shall have power to enforce this article by appropriate legislation.

7
THE LIBERAL ERA

Millionaires are a product of natural selection, acting on the whole body of men, to pick out those who can meet the requirement of certain work to be done.... They may fairly be regarded as the naturally selected agents of society of certain work. They get high wages and live in luxury, but the bargain is a good one for society....

WILLIAM GRAHAM SUMNER

The primal principle of democracy is the worth and dignity of the individual. That dignity, consisting in the quality of human nature, is essentially the same in all individuals, and therefore equality is the vital principle of democracy. To this intrinsic and equal dignity of the individual all material conditions must be made subservient, and personal accidents and attributes subordinated.

EDWARD BELLAMY

A prevailing tenet of American politics is that adherence to American principles leads to material prosperity as well as political well-being. For a principled argument to be successful in America, a demonstration that it is consistent with the "pursuit of happiness" must be forthcoming. And such demonstration is traditionally offered in material terms. As Tocqueville pointed out, happiness in America is commonly considered synonymous with material or physical wealth.

In America the passion for physical well-being is not always exclusive, but it is general; and if all do not feel it in the same manner, yet it is felt by all. . . .If I were to inquire what passion is most natural to men who are stimulated and circumscribed by the obscurity of their birth or the mediocrity of their fortune, I could discover none more peculiarly appropriate to their condition than this love of physical prosperity. . . . The love of well-being is now become the predominant taste of the nation; the great current of man's passions runs in that channel, and sweeps everything along in its course.[1]

[1] Alexis de Tocqueville, *Democracy in America* (New York: Schocken Books, 1961), Vol. II, pp. 153–155

In short, effective principled arguments in America are wedded to advances in the general prosperity. This creates another perspective from which to investigate the theme of this volume, the tension in American political thought between equality and liberty. Discussions of what best promotes public prosperity often reflect that tension and a bias towards liberty or equality often is defended as arising out of devotion to the public happiness. These American political traits are the subject of this chapter.

Perhaps the best example of the tension between liberty and equality as it relates to matters of public prosperity occurs in the latter half of the nineteenth century. The major argument of the period, in terms of our themes, was whether public prosperity and progress was best served by allowing individuals enormous latitude to act in economic matters or whether there ought to be governmental restraints upon such liberty. The period was the heyday of what is known as traditional American liberalism.[2] Fundamental to the liberal position was the belief that the activity of free unfettered individuals is the key to human progress in general and economic prosperity in particular. In their more extreme formulations—which were the mode in the late 1800s— liberals accepted virtually no curtailment of liberty in economic matters. Nor were they disturbed that liberty of this type might strain American egalitarian principle. Indeed, a tenet of the liberal faith was that equality is a fiction which blocks human progress. The classic American expression of this view is that of William Graham Sumner, the most notable of early American sociologists. Sumner's ideas were derived from those of Herbert Spencer, an Englishman who had applied evolutionary biological theories to human social development. Using the concept of "survival of the fittest" in conjunction with social history, Spencer argued that society developed as the strongest and most capable men came to the fore, just as the fittest were the survivors and leaders in biological evolution. For Spencer and his followers, as Professor Alan Grimes puts it, "Life was a ruthless competitive struggle for survival in which some were crushed and some were elevated to the top of the heap; but one always had the consolation that the breed was improving as each generation eliminated the unfit."[3] It followed that individual liberty was a prerequisite for the most efficient progress, inasmuch as it allowed the fullest development of the competitive struggle. In economics, the result of this idea was *laissez-faire*, i.e., the theory that men ought to be

[2] This was the liberalism to which Professor Hartz referred in the comment in the preceding chapter.
[3] Alan Grimes, *American Political Thought* (New York: Henry Holt & Co., 1955), p. 305. Grimes' short description of Spencer, Sumner, and other liberals is well done; cf. especially Chapter 13.

left alone in economic affairs, that social interference in economics
could only delay the progress of society.

To Sumner, the implications of this theory in the American context
were clear. First, individual liberty had to be placed in a Constitutionally
preferred position. Government could not be allowed to interfere in
the economic activities of its citizens.

What we mean by liberty is civil liberty, or liberty under law; and this
means the guarantee of law that a man shall not be interfered with,
while using his own powers for his own benefit. It is, therefore, a civil and
political status; and that nation has the freest institutions in which the
guarantees of peace for the laborer and security for the capitalist are the
highest.[4]

Liberty, Sumner continued, permitted men to accumulate capital, and
capital provided the fuel for progress. The argument was straightforward:
liberty was the condition of capital accumulation, and capital
accumulation was the condition of human advancement.

Capital is labor raised to a higher power by being constantly multiplied
into itself. Nature has been more and more subjugated by the human
race through the power of capital, and every human being now living
shares the improved status of the race to a degree which neither he nor any
one else can measure, and for which he pays nothing.[5]

Liberal doctrine, then, tied the advance of humanity to the principle
of individual liberty. However, a further question remained: Could the
American egalitarian tradition survive where liberty was so preferred?
Sumner's answer was negative and blunt.

The assertion that all men are equal is perhaps the purest of falsehoods
in dogmas that was ever put into human language; five minutes'
observation of facts will show that men are unequal through a very wide
range of variation.[6]

In this manner liberal devotion to liberty paralleled a deemphasis or
even a denial of equality. The "pursuit of happiness" would be won only
at the expense of equality.

As might be expected, liberal ideas provoked an egalitarian
response, although liberal views prevailed until the early 1900s.
Throughout the 1880s and '90s, opposition to liberal economic and

[4] A. G. Keller and M. Davie, eds., *Essays of William Graham Sumner* (New Haven: Yale
University Press, 1934), Vol. II, p. 96.
[5] *Ibid.*, Vol. II, p. 91.
[6] *Ibid.*, Vol. I, p. 422.

political doctrine developed. Initially, such opposition—Henry George, Edward Bellamy, Populists, Grangers, et al.—was disunified and politically unsuccessful, but the strength and appeal of the egalitarian viewpoint won many adherents and had considerable effect after the turn of the century.[7] Fundamentally, those of an egalitarian persuasion held liberalism to be subversive of equality and a check upon meaningful public happiness. Edward Bellamy provides a good example of the position. In his most famous book, *Looking Backward*, and its sequel, *Equality*, he argued that liberal denial of equality was doubly destructive of the Declaration of Independence. It worked against equality and destroyed the only possible basis for the "pursuit of happiness," common sharing of material wealth. General happiness, Bellamy insisted, demanded that all men be able to partake equally of the fruits of progress. And if his logic led to the proposition that government control of economic affairs was the only adequate protection against artificial economic distinctions among men, Bellamy was as ready to take that step as Sumner was to forbid it.

The corner stone of our state is economic equality, and is not that the obvious, necessary, and only adequate pledge of these three birthrights— life, liberty, and happiness? What is life without its material basis, and what is an equal right to life but a right to an equal material basis for it? What is liberty? How can men be free who must ask the right to labor and to live from their fellow-men and seek their bread from the hands of others? How else can any government guarantee liberty to men save by providing them a means of labor and of life coupled with independence; and how could that be done unless the government conducted the economic system upon which employment and maintenance depend.[8]

These ideas were basic to Bellamy and others who opposed liberalism. *Laissez-faire* economics and liberal philosophy had been used to justify the accumulation of vast fortunes. An egalitarian people, reformers urged, could not be asked to suffer the inequities of such a system. For example, the Populist movement—an attempt to join farmers and urban laborers in a unified political party—sought to rearrange the American economic structure to provide equality and promote a more popular understanding of happiness. Thus, their 1892 platform called for policies that would return the government to the "people."

The fruits of the toil of millions are boldly stolen to build up colossal fortunes for a few . . . [and] breed the two great classes—tramps and

[7] Twentieth-century progressivism, which supplanted liberalism, clearly has roots in the nineteenth-century arguments against liberal theory.
[8] Edward Bellamy, *Equality* (New York: D. Appleton & Co., 1897), p. 17.

millionaires; . . . we seek to restore the government of the Republic to
the hands of "the plain people," with which class it originated. . . .
We believe that the power of government—in other words, of the people—
should be expanded . . . as rapidly and as far as the good sense of an
intelligent people and the teachings of experience shall justify; . . . the
forces of reform this day organized will never cease to move forward
until every wrong is remedied and equal privileges securely established
for all the men and women of this country.[9]

In the same manner, William Jennings Bryan's famous "Cross of Gold
Speech"—which borrowed a good deal of the Populist rhetoric and
policy and won Bryan the Democratic Presidential nomination in 1896—
urged equal treatment for all men as the precondition of real prosperity.

There are two ideas of government. There are those who believe that,
if you will only legislate to make the well-to-do prosperous, their prosperity
will leak through to those below. The Democratic idea, however, has been
that if you legislate to make the masses prosperous, their prosperity will find
its way up through every class which rests upon them.[10]

Such arguments gave rise to some of the clearest expressions of the
continuing tension between liberty and equality in American life in
the late nineteenth century. The argument over whether liberty
or equality would lead Americans to prosperity and happiness exposes,
once again, how liberty and equality serve as the poles in American
political debate. The selections in this chapter ought to be read in this
light. Included are statements from Sumner and Bellamy, the "Populist
Platform of 1892," and Bryan's "Cross of Gold Speech." Finally,
portions of the opinions in the Supreme Court decision in the case of
Lochner v. *New York* are added. The opinions very nicely express
the dichotomy between liberal sentiment on economic matters and the
thought of those not similarly disposed. In this particular example,
Justice Peckham speaks for the court and the idea that only unavoidable
government interference in economic matters is allowable; Justice
Holmes dissents, challenging the presumption that uncompromising
protection for economic liberty ought to be a ruling principle in America.

[9] *The World Almanac* (1893).
[10] William Jennings Bryan, *The First Battle* (Chicago: W. B. Conky Co., 1896), p. 205.

William Graham Sumner

THE CHALLENGE
OF FACTS

Socialism is no new thing. In one form or another it is to be found throughout all history. It arises from an observation of certain harsh facts in the lot of man on earth, the concrete expression of which is poverty and misery. These facts challenge us. It is folly to try to shut our eyes to them. We have first to notice what they are, and then to face them squarely.

Man is born under the necessity of sustaining the existence he has received by an onerous struggle against nature, both to win what is essential to his life and to ward off what is prejudicial to it. He is born under a burden and a necessity. Nature holds what is essential to him, but she offers nothing gratuitously. He may win for his use what she holds, if he can. Only the most meager and inadequate supply for human needs can be obtained directly from nature. There are trees which may be used for fuel and for dwellings, but labor is required to fit them for this use. There are ores in the ground, but labor is necessary to get out the metals and make tools or weapons. For any real satisfaction, labor is necessary to fit the products of nature for human use. In this struggle every individual is under the pressure of the necessities for food, clothing, shelter, fuel, and every individual brings with him more or less energy for the conflict necessary to supply his needs. The relation, therefore, between each man's needs and each man's energy, or "individualism," is the first fact of human life.

It is not without reason, however, that we speak of a "man" as the individual in question, for women (mothers) and children have special disabilities for the struggle with nature, and these disabilities grow greater and last longer as civilization advances. The perpetuation of the race in health and vigor, and its success as a whole in its struggle to expand and develop human life on earth, therefore, require that the head of the

Essays of William Graham Sumner, Albert Keller and Maurice Davie, eds., Vol. II (New Haven: Yale University Press, 1934). Reprinted by permission of Yale University Press, copyright © 1934.

family shall, by his energy, be able to supply not only his own needs, but those of the organisms which are dependent upon him. The history of the human race shows a great variety of experiments in the relation of the sexes and in the organization of the family. These experiments have been controlled by economic circumstances, but, as man has gained more and more control over economic circumstances, monogamy and the family education of children have been more and more sharply developed. If there is one thing in regard to which the student of history and sociology can affirm with confidence that social institutions have made "progress" or grown "better," it is in this arrangement of marriage and the family. All experience proves that monogamy, pure and strict, is the sex relation which conduces most to the vigor and intelligence of the race, and that the family education of children is the institution by which the race as a whole advances most rapidly, from generation to generation, in the struggle with nature. Love of man and wife, as we understand it, is a modern sentiment. The devotion and sacrifice of parents for children is a sentiment which has been developed steadily and is now more intense and far more widely practiced throughout society than in earlier times. The relation is also coming to be regarded in a light quite different from that in which it was formerly viewed. It used to be believed that the parent had unlimited claims on the child and rights over him. In a truer view of the matter, we are coming to see that the rights are on the side of the child and the duties on the side of the parent. Existence is not a boon for which the child owes all subjection to the parent. It is a responsibility assumed by the parent towards the child without the child's consent, and the consequence of it is that the parent owes all possible devotion to the child to enable him to make his existence happy and successful.

The value and importance of the family sentiments, from a social point of view, cannot be exaggerated. They impose self-control and prudence in their most important social bearings, and tend more than any other forces to hold the individual up to the virtues which make the sound man and the valuable member of society. The race is bound, from generation to generation, in an unbroken chain of vice and penalty, virtue and reward. The sins of the fathers are visited upon the children, while, on the other hand, health, vigor, talent, genius, and skill are, so far as we can discover, the results of high physical vigor and wise early training. The popular language bears witness to the universal observation of these facts, although general social and political dogmas have come into fashion which contradict or ignore them. There is no other such punishment for a life of vice and self-indulgence as to see children grow up cursed with the penalties of it, and no such reward for self-denial and virtue as to see children born and grow up vigorous in mind and body. It is time that the true import of these observations for moral and educational purposes was developed, and it may well be questioned whether we do not go too far in our reticence in regard to all these matters when we leave it to romances and poems to do almost all the educational work that is done in the way of spreading ideas about them. The defense of marriage and the family, if their sociological value were better understood, would be not only instinctive but rational. The struggle for existence with which we have to deal must be understood, then, to be that of a man for himself, his wife, and his children.

The next great fact we have to notice in regard to the struggle of human life is that labor which is spent in a direct struggle with nature is severe in the extreme and is but slightly productive. To subjugate nature, man needs weapons and tools. These, however cannot be won unless the food and clothing and other prime and direct necessities are supplied in such amount that they can be consumed while tools and weapons are being made, for the tools and weapons themselves satisfy no needs directly. A man who tills the ground with his fingers or with a pointed stick picked up without labor will get a small crop. To fashion even the rudest spade or hoe will cost time, during which the laborer must still eat and drink and wear, but the tool, when obtained, will multiply immensely the power to produce. Such products of labor, used to assist production, have a function so peculiar in the nature of things that we need to distinguish them. We call them capital. A lever is capital, and the advantage of lifting a weight with a lever over lifting it by direct exertion is only a feeble illustration of the power of capital in production. The origin of capital lies in the darkness before history, and it is probably impossible for us to imagine the slow and painful steps by which the race began the formation of it. Since then it has gone on rising to higher and higher powers by a ceaseless involution, if I may use a mathematical expression. Capital is labor raised to a higher power by being constantly multiplied into itself. Nature has been more and more subjugated by the human race through the power of capital, and every human being now living shares the improved status of the race to a degree which neither he nor any one else can measure, and for which he pays nothing.

Let us understand this point, because our subject will require future reference to it. It is the most short-sighted ignorance not to see that, in a civilized community, all the advantage of capital except a small fraction is gratuitously enjoyed by the community. For instance, suppose the case of a man utterly destitute of tools, who is trying to till the ground with a pointed stick. He could get something out of it. If now he should obtain a spade with which to till the ground, let us suppose, for illustration, that he could get twenty times as great a product. Could, then, the owner of a spade in a civilized state demand, as its price, from the man who had no spade, nineteen-twentieths of the product which could be produced by the use of it? Certainly not. The price of a spade is fixed by the supply and demand of products in the community. A spade is bought for a dollar and the gain from the use of it is an inheritance of knowledge, experience, and skill which every man who lives in a civilized state gets for nothing. What we pay for steam transportation is no trifle, but imagine, if you can, eastern Massachusetts cut off from steam connection with the rest of the world, turnpikes and sailing vessels remaining. The cost of food would rise so high that a quarter of the population would starve to death and another quarter would have to emigrate. To-day every man here gets an enormous advantage from the status of a society on a level of steam transportation, telegraph, and machinery, for which he pays nothing.

So far as I have yet spoken, we have before us the struggle of man with nature, but the social problems, strictly speaking, arise at the next step. Each man carries on the struggle to win his support for himself, but there are others by his side engaged in the same struggle. If the stores of nature were unlimited, or if the last unit of the supply she offers could be won as easily as the first, there would be no social problem. If a square mile of land could support an indefinite number of human beings, or if it cost only twice as much labor to get forty bushels of wheat from an acre as to get twenty, we should have no social problem. If a square mile of land could support millions, no one would ever emigrate and there would be no trade or commerce. If it cost only twice as much labor to get forty bushels as twenty, there would be no advance in the arts. The fact is far otherwise. So long as the population is low in proportion to the amount of land, on a given stage of the arts, life is easy and the competition of man with man is weak. When more persons are trying to live on a square mile than it can support, on the existing stage of the arts, life is hard and the competition of man with man is intense. In the former case, industry and prudence may be on a low grade; the penalties are not severe, or certain, or speedy. In the latter case, each individual needs to exert on his own behalf every force, original or acquired, which he can command. In the former case, the average condition will be one of comfort and the population will be all nearly on the average. In the latter case, the average condition will not be one of comfort, but the population will cover wide extremes of comfort and misery. Each will find his place according to his ability and his effort. The former society will be democratic; the latter will be aristocratic.

The constant tendency of population to outstrip the means of subsistence is the force which has distributed population over the world, and produced all advance in civilization. To this day the two means of escape for an overpopulated country are emigration and an advance in the arts. The former wins more land for the same people; the latter makes the same land support more persons. If, however, either of these means opens a chance for an increase of population, it is evident that the advantage so won may be speedily exhausted if the increase takes place. The social difficulty has only undergone a temporary amelioration, and when the conditions of pressure and competition are renewed, misery and poverty reappear. The victims of them are those who have inherited disease and depraved appetites, or have been brought up in vice and ignorance, or have themselves yielded to vice, extravagance, idleness, and imprudence. In the last analysis, therefore, we come back to vice, in its original and hereditary forms, as the correlative of misery and poverty.

The condition for the complete and regular action of the force of competition is liberty. Liberty means the security given to each man that, if he employs his energies to sustain the struggle on behalf of himself and those he cares for, he shall dispose of the product exclusively as he chooses. It is impossible to know whence any definition or criterion of justice can be derived, if it is not deduced from this view of things; or if it is not the definition of justice that each shall enjoy the fruit of his own labor and self-denial, and of injustice that the idle and the industrious, the self-indulgent and the self-denying, shall share equally in the product. Aside from the *a priori* speculations of philosophers who have tried to make equality an essential element in justice, the human race has recognized, from the earliest times, the above conception of justice as the true one, and has founded upon it the right of property. The right of property, with marriage and the family, gives the right of bequest.

Monogamic marriage, however, is the most exclusive of social institutions. It contains, as essential principles, preference, superiority, selection, devotion. It would not be at all what it is if it were not for these characteristic traits, and it always degenerates when these traits are not present. For instance, if a man should not have a distinct preference for the woman he married, and if he did not select her as superior to others, the marriage would be an imperfect one according to the standard of true monogamic marriage. The family under monogamy, also, is a closed group, having special interests and estimating privacy and reserve as valuable advantages for family development. We grant high prerogatives, in our society, to parents, although our observation teaches us that thousands of human beings are unfit to be parents or to be entrusted with the care of children. It follows, therefore, from the organization of marriage and the family, under monogamy, that great inequalities must exist in a society based on those institutions. The son of wise parents cannot start on a level with the son of foolish ones, and the man who has had no home discipline cannot be equal to the man who has had home discipline. If the contrary were true, we could rid ourselves at once of the wearing labor of inculcating sound morals and manners in our children.

Private property, also, which we have seen to be a feature of society organized in accordance with the natural conditions of the struggle for existence produces inequalities between men. The struggle for existence is aimed against nature. It is from her niggardly hand that we have to wrest the satisfactions for our needs, but our fellow-men are our competitors for the meager supply. Competition, therefore, is a law of nature. Nature is entirely neutral; she submits to him who most energetically and resolutely assails her. She grants her rewards to the fittest, therefore, without regard to other considerations of any kind. If, then, there be liberty, men get from her just in proportion to their works, and their having and enjoying are just in proportion to their being and their doing. Such is the system of nature. If we do not like it, if we try to amend it, there is only one way in which we can do it. We can take from the better and give to the worse. We can deflect the penalties of those who have done ill and throw them on those who have done better. We can take the rewards from those who have done better and give them to those who have done worse. We shall thus lessen the inequalities. We shall favor the survival of the unfittest, and we shall accomplish this by destroying liberty. Let it be understood that we cannot go outside of this alternative: liberty, inequality, survival of the fittest, not-liberty, equality, survival of the unfittest. The former carries society forward and favors all its best members; the latter carries society downwards and favors all its worst members.

For three hundred years now men have been trying to understand and realize liberty. Liberty is not the right or chance to do what we choose; there is no such liberty as that on earth. No man can do as he chooses: the autocrat of Russia or the King of Dahomey has limits to his arbitrary will; the savage in the wilderness, whom some people think free, is the slave of routine, tradition, and superstitious fears; the civilized man must earn his living, or take care of his property, or concede his own will to the rights and claims of his parents, his wife, his children, and all the persons with whom he is connected by the ties and contracts of civilized life.

What we mean by liberty is civil liberty, or liberty under law; and this means the guarantees of law that a man shall not be interfered with while using his own powers for his own welfare. It is, therefore, a civil and a political status; and that nation has the freest institutions in which the guarantees of peace for the laborer and security for the capitalist are the highest. Liberty, therefore, does not by any means do away with the struggle for existence. We might as well try to do away with the need of eating, for that would, in effect, be the same thing. What civil liberty does is to turn the competition of man with man from violence and brute force into an industrial competition under which men vie with one another for the acquisition of material goods by industry, energy, skill, frugality, prudence, temperance, and other industrial virtues. Under this changed order of things the inequalities are not done away with. Nature still grants her rewards of having and enjoying, according to our being and doing, but it is now the man of the highest training and not the man of the heaviest fist who gains the highest reward. It is impossible that the man with capital and the man without capital should be equal. To affirm that they are equal would be to say that a man who has no tool can get as much food out of the ground as the man who has a spade or a plough; or that the man who has no weapon can defend himself as well against hostile beasts or hostile men as the man who has a weapon. If that were so, none of us would work any more. We work and deny ourselves to get capital just because, other things being equal, the man who has it is superior, for attaining all the ends of life, to the man who has it not. Considering the eagerness with which we all seek capital and the estimate we put upon it, either in cherishing it if we have it, or envying others who have it while we have it not, it is very strange what platitudes pass current about it in our society so soon as we begin to generalize about it. If our young people really believed some of the teachings they hear, it would not be amiss to preach them a sermon once in a while to reassure them, setting forth that it is not wicked to be rich, nay even, that it is not wicked to be richer than your neighbor.

It follows from what we have observed that it is the utmost folly to denounce capital. To do so is to undermine civilization, for capital is the first requisite of every social gain, educational, ecclesiastical, political, æsthetic, or other. . . .

I have shown how men emerge from barbarism only by the use of capital and why it is that, as soon as they begin to use capital, if there is liberty, there will be inequality. The socialist looking at these facts says that it is capital which produces the inequality. It is the inequality of men in what they get out of life which shocks the socialist. He finds enough to criticize in the products of past dogmatism and bad statesmanship to which I have alluded, and the program of reforms to be accomplished and abuses to be rectified which the socialists have set up have often been admirable. It is their analysis of the situation which is at fault. Their diagnosis of the social disease is founded on sectarian assumptions, not on the scientific study of the structure and functions of the social body. In attacking capital they are simply attacking the foundations of civilization, and every socialistic scheme which has ever been proposed, so far as it has lessened the motives to saving or the security of capital, is anti-social and anti-civilizing. . . .

It is a matter of course that a reactionary party should arise to declare that universal suffrage, popular education, machinery, free trade, and all the other innovations of the last hundred years are all a mistake. If any one ever believed that these innovations were so many clear strides towards the millennium, that they involve no evils or abuses of their own, that they tend to emancipate mankind from the need for prudence, caution, forethought, vigilance—in short, from the eternal struggle against evil—it is not strange that he should be disappointed. If any one ever believed that some "form of government" could be found which would run itself and turn out the pure results of abstract peace, justice, and righteousness without any trouble to anybody, he may well be dissatisfied. To talk of turning back, however, is only to enhance still further the confusion and danger of our position. The world cannot go back. Its destiny is to go forward and to meet the new problems which are continually arising. Under our so-called progress evil only alters its forms, and we must esteem it a grand advance if we can believe that, on the whole, and over a wide view of human affairs, good has gained a hair's breadth over evil in a century. Popular institutions have their own abuses and dangers just as much as monarchical or aristocratic institutions. We are only just finding out what they are. All the institutions which we have inherited were invented to guard liberty against the encroachments of a powerful monarch or aristocracy, when these classes possessed land and the possession of land was the greatest social power. Institutions must now be devised to guard civil liberty against popular majorities, and this necessity arises first in regard to the protection of property, the first and greatest function of government and element in civil liberty. There is no escape from any dangers involved in this or any other social struggle save in going forward and working out the development. It will cost a struggle and will demand the highest wisdom of this and the next generation. It is very probable that some nations—those, namely, which come up to this problem with the least preparation, with the least intelligent comprehension of the problem, and under the most inefficient leadership —will suffer a severe check in their development and prosperity; it is very probable that in some nations the development may lead through revolution and bloodshed; it is very probable that in some nations the consequence may be a reaction towards arbitrary power. In every view we take of it, it is clear that the general abolition of slavery has only cleared the way for a new social problem of far wider scope and far greater difficulty. It seems to me, in fact, that this must always be the case. The conquest of one difficulty will only open the way to another; the solution of one problem will only bring man face to face with another. Man wins by the fight, not by the victory, and therefore the possibilities of growth are unlimited, for the fight has no end.

EQUALITY

Edith meditated in silence for some moments. Finally she said: "Your contemporaries were not madmen nor fools; surely there is something you have not told me; there must be some explanation or at least color of excuse why the people not only abdicated the power of controling their most vital and important interests, but turned them over to a class which did not even pretend any interest in their welfare, and whose government completely failed to secure it."

"Oh, yes," I said, "there was an explanation, and a very fine-sounding one. It was in the name of individual liberty, industrial freedom, and individual initiative that the economic government of the country was surrendered to the capitalists."

"Do you mean that a form of government which seems to have been the most irresponsible and despotic possible was defended in the name of liberty?"

"Certainly; the liberty of economic initiative by the individual."

"But did you not just tell me that economic initiative and business opportunity in your day were practically monopolized by the capitalists themselves?"

"Certainly. It was admitted that there was no opening for any but capitalists in business, and it was rapidly becoming so that only the greatest of the capitalists themselves had any power of initiative."

"And yet you say that the reason given for abandoning industry to capitalist government was the promotion of industrial freedom and individual initiative among the people at large."

"Certainly. The people were taught that they would individually enjoy greater liberty and freedom of action in industrial matters under the dominion of the capitalists than if they collectively conducted the industrial system for their own benefit; that the capitalists would, moreover, look out for their welfare more wisely and kindly than they could possibly do it themselves, so that they would be able to provide for them-

Edward Bellamy, *Equality* (New York: D. Appleton and Co., 1897), pp. 8–10, 14, 15–23.

selves more bountifully out of such portion of their product as the capitalists might be disposed to give them than they possibly could do if they
became their own employers and divided the whole product among
themselves."

"But that was mere mockery; it was adding insult to injury."

"It sounds so, doesn't it? But I assure you it was considered the
soundest sort of political economy in my time. Those who questioned it
were set down as dangerous visionaries."

"But I suppose the people's government, the government they voted
for, must have done something. There must have been some odds and
ends of things which the capitalists left the political government to attend to."

"Oh, yes, indeed. It had its hands full keeping the peace among the
people. That was the main part of the business of political governments
in my day."

"Why did the peace require such a great amount of keeping? Why
didn't it keep itself, as it does now?"

"On account of the inequality of conditions which prevailed. The
strife for wealth and desperation of want kept in quenchless blaze a hell
of greed and envy, fear, lust, hate, revenge, and every foul passion of the
pit. To keep this general frenzy in some restraint, so that the entire social
system should not resolve itself into a general massacre, required an army
of soldiers, police, judges, and jailers, and endless law-making to settle
the quarrels. Add to these elements of discord a horde of outcasts degraded and desperate, made enemies of society by their sufferings and
requiring to be kept in check, and you will readily admit there was
enough for the people's government to do."

"So far as I can see," said Edith, "the main business of the people's
government was to struggle with the social chaos which resulted from
its failure to take hold of the economic system and regulate it on a basis
of justice."

"That is exactly so. You could not state the whole case more adequately if you wrote a book." . . .

Absorbed in our talk, we had not heard the steps of Dr. Leete as
he approached. . . .

"Really, doctor," I said, "you ought to be greatly obliged to your
daughter. She has saved you lots of time and effort."

"How so, precisely?"

"By rendering it unnecessary for you to trouble yourself to explain
to me any further how and why you came to set up your nationalized
industrial system and your economic equality. If you have ever seen a
desert or sea mirage, you remember that, while the picture in the sky is
very clear and distinct in itself, its unreality is betrayed by a lack of detail,

a sort of blur, where it blends with the foreground on which you are standing. Do you know that this new social order of which I have so strangely become a witness has hitherto had something of this mirage effect? In itself it is a scheme precise, orderly, and very reasonable, but I could see no way by which it could have naturally grown out of the utterly different conditions of the nineteenth century. I could only imagine that this world transformation must have been the result of new ideas and forces that had come into action since my day. I had a volume of questions all ready to ask you on the subject, but now we shall be able to use the time in talking of other things, for Edith has shown me in ten minutes' time that the only wonderful thing about your organization of the industrial system as public business is not that it has taken place, but that it waited so long before taking place, that a nation of rational beings consented to remain economic serfs of irresponsible masters for more than a century after coming into possession of absolute power to change at pleasure all social institutions which inconvenienced them."

"Really," said the doctor, "Edith has shown herself a very efficient teacher, if an involuntary one. She has succeeded at one stroke in giving you the modern point of view as to your period. As we look at it, the immortal preamble of the American Declaration of Independence, away back in 1776, logically contained the entire statement of the doctrine of universal economic equality guaranteed by the nation collectively to its members individually. You remember how the words run:

"'We hold these truths to be self-evident; that all men are created equal, with certain inalienable rights; that among these are life, liberty, and the pursuit of happiness; that to secure these rights governments are instituted among men, deriving their just powers from the consent of the governed; that whenever any form of government becomes destructive of these rights it is the right of the people to alter or to abolish it and institute a new government, laying its foundations on such principles and organizing its powers in such form as may seem most likely to effect their safety and happiness.'

"Is it possible, Julian, to imagine any governmental system less adequate than ours which could possibly realize this great ideal of what a true people's government should be? The corner stone of our state is economic equality, and is not that the obvious, necessary, and only adequate pledge of these three birthrights—life, liberty, and happiness? What is life without its material basis, and what is an equal right to life but a right to an equal material basis for it? What is liberty? How can men be free who must ask the right to labor and to live from their fellow-men and seek their bread from the hands of others? How else can any government guarantee liberty to men save by providing them a means of labor and of life coupled with independence; and how could that be done unless the government conducted the economic system upon which employment and maintenance depend? Finally, what is implied in the equal right of all to the pursuit of happiness? What form of happiness, so far as it depends at all on material facts, is not bound up with economic conditions; and how shall an equal opportunity for the pursuit of happiness be guaranteed to all save by a guarantee of economic equality?"

"Yes," I said, "it is indeed all there, but why were we so long in seeing it?"

"Let us make ourselves comfortable on this bench," said the doctor, "and I will tell you what is the modern answer to the very interesting question you raise. At first glance, certainly the delay of the world in general, and especially of the American people, to realize that democracy logically meant the substitution of popular government for the rule of the rich in regulating the production and distribution of wealth seems incomprehensible, not only because it was so plain an inference from the idea of popular government, but also because it was one which the masses of the people were so directly interested in carrying out. Edith's conclusion that people who were not capable of so simple a process of reasoning as that did not deserve much sympathy for the afflictions they might so easily have remedied, is a very natural first impression.

"On reflection, however, I think we shall conclude that the time taken by the world in general and the Americans in particular in finding out the full meaning of democracy as an economic as well as a political proposition was not greater than might have been expected, considering the vastness of the conclusions involved. It is the democratic idea that all human beings are peers in rights and dignity, and that the sole just excuse and end of human governments is, therefore, the maintenance and furtherance of the common welfare on the equal terms. This idea was the greatest social conception that the human mind had up to that time ever formed. It contained, when first conceived, the promise and potency of a complete transformation of all then existing social institutions, one and all of which had hitherto been based and formed on the principle of personal and class privilege and authority and the domination and selfish use of the many by the few. But it was simply inconsistent with the limitations of the human intellect that the implications of an idea so prodigious should at once have been taken in. The idea must absolutely have time to grow. The entire present order of economic democracy and equality was indeed logically bound up in the first full statement of the democratic idea, but only as the full-grown tree is in the seed: in the one case, as in the other, time was an essential element in the evolution of the result.

"We divide the history of the evolution of the democratic idea into two broadly contrasted phases. The first of these we call the phase of negative democracy. To understand it we must consider how the democratic idea originated. Ideas are born of previous ideas and are long in outgrowing the characteristics and limitations impressed on them by the circumstances under which they came into existence. The idea of popular government, in the case of America as in previous republican experiments in general, was a protest against royal government and its abuses. Nothing is more certain than that the signers of the immortal Declaration had no idea that democracy necessarily meant anything more than a device for getting along without kings. They conceived of it as a change in the forms of government only, and not at all in the principles and purposes of government.

"They were not, indeed, wholly without misgivings lest it might some time occur to the sovereign people that, being sovereign, it would be a good idea to use their sovereignty to improve their own condition. In fact, they seem to have given some serious thought to that possibility, but so little were they yet able to appreciate the logic and force of the democratic idea that they believed it possible by ingenious clauses in paper Constitutions to prevent the people from using their power to help themselves even if they should wish to.

"This first phase of the evolution of democracy, during which it was conceived of solely as a substitute for royalty, includes all the so-called republican experiments up to the beginning of the twentieth century, of which, of course, the American Republic was the most important. During this period the democratic idea remained a mere protest against a previous form of government, absolutely without any new positive or vital principle of its own. Although the people had deposed the king as driver of the social chariot, and taken the reins into their own hands, they did not think as yet of anything but keeping the vehicle in the old ruts and naturally the passengers scarcely noticed the change.

"The second phase in the evolution of the democratic idea began with the awakening of the people to the perception that the deposing of kings, instead of being the main end and mission of democracy, was merely preliminary to its real programme, which was the use of the collective social machinery for the indefinite promotion of the welfare of the people at large.

"It is an interesting fact that the people began to think of applying their political power to the improvement of their material condition in Europe earlier than in America, although democratic forms had found much less acceptance there. This was, of course, on account of the perennial economic distress of the masses in the old countries, which prompted them to think first about the bearing any new idea might have on the question of livelihood. On the other hand, the general prosperity of the masses in America and the comparative ease of making a living up to the beginning of the last quarter of the nineteenth century account for the fact that it was not till then that the American people began to think seriously of improving their economic condition by collective action.

"During the negative phase of democracy it had been considered as differing from monarchy only as two machines might differ, the general use and purpose of which were the same. With the evolution of the democratic idea into the second or positive phase, it was recognized that the transfer of the supreme power from king and nobles to people meant not merely a change in the forms of government, but a fundamental revolution in the whole idea of government, its motives, purposes, and functions—a revolution equivalent to a reversal of polarity of the entire social system, carrying, so to speak, the entire compass card with it, and making north south, and east west. Then was seen what seems so plain to us that it is hard to understand why it was not always seen, that instead of its being proper for the sovereign people to confine themselves to the functions which the kings and classes had discharged when they were in power, the presumption was, on the contrary, since the interest of kings and classes had always been exactly opposed to those of the people, that whatever the previous governments had done, the people as rulers ought not to do, and whatever the previous governments had not done, it would be presumably for the interest of the people to do; and that the main use and function of popular government was properly one which no previous government had ever paid any attention to, namely, the use of the power of the social organization to raise the material and moral welfare of the whole body of the sovereign people to the highest possible point at which the same degree of welfare could be secured to all—that is to say, an equal level. The democracy of the second or positive phase triumphed in the great Revolution, and has since been the only form of government known in the world."

"Which amounts to saying," I observed, "that there never was a democratic government properly so called before the twentieth century."

"Just so," assented the doctor. "The so-called republics of the first phase we class as pseudo-republics or negative democracies. They were not, of course, in any sense, truly popular governments at all, but merely masks for plutocracy, under which the rich were the real though irresponsible rulers! You will readily see that they could have been nothing else. The masses from the beginning of the world had been the subjects and servants of the rich, but the kings had been above the rich, and constituted a check on their dominion. The overthrow of the kings left no check at all on the power of the rich, which became supreme. The people, indeed, nominally were sovereigns; but as these sovereigns were individually and as a class the economic serfs of the rich, and lived at their mercy, the so-called popular government became the mere stalking-horse of the capitalists.

"Regarded as necessary steps in the evolution of society from pure monarchy to pure democracy, these republics of the negative phase mark a stage of progress; but if regarded as finalities they were a type far less admirable on the whole than decent monarchies. In respect especially to their susceptibility to corruption and plutocratic subversion they were the worst kind of government possible. The nineteenth century, during which this crop of pseudo-democracies ripened for the sickle of the great Revolution, seems to the modern view nothing but a dreary interregnum of nondescript, *fainéant* government intervening between the decadence of virile monarchy in the eighteenth century and the rise of positive democracy in the twentieth. The period may be compared to that of the minority of a king, during which the royal power is abused by wicked stewards. The people had been proclaimed as sovereign, but they had not yet assumed the sceptre."

"And yet," said I, "during the latter part of the nineteenth century, when, as you say, the world had not yet seen a single specimen of popular government, our wise men were telling us that the democratic system had been fully tested and was ready to be judged on its results. Not a few of them, indeed, went so far as to say that the democratic experiment had proved a failure when, in point of fact, it seems that no experiment in democracy, properly understood, had as yet ever been so much as attempted."

The doctor shrugged his shoulders.

"It is a very sympathetic task," he said, "to explain the slowness of the masses in feeling their way to a comprehension of all that the democratic idea meant for them, but it is one equally difficult and thankless to account for the blank failure of the philosophers, historians, and statesmen of your day to arrive at an intelligent estimate of the logical content of democracy and to forecast its outcome. Surely the very smallness of the practical results thus far achieved by the democratic movement as compared with the magnitude of its proposition and the forces behind it ought to have suggested to them that its evolution was yet but in the first stage. How could intelligent men delude themselves with the notion that the most portentous and revolutionary idea of all time had exhausted its influence and fulfilled its mission in changing the title of the executive of a nation from king to President, and the name of the national Legislature from Parliament to Congress? If your pedagogues, college professors and presidents, and others who were responsible for your education, had been worth their salt, you would have found nothing in the present order of economic equality that would in the least have surprised you. You would have said at once that it was just what you had been taught must necessarily be the next phase in the inevitable evolution of the democratic idea."

Edith beckoned from the door and we rose from our seat.

"The revolutionary party in the great Revolution," said the doctor, as we sauntered toward the house, "carried on the work of agitation and propaganda under various names more or less grotesque and ill-fitting as political party names were apt to be, but the one word democracy, with its various equivalents and derivatives, more accurately and completely expressed, explained, and justified their method, reason, and purpose than a library of books could do. The American people fancied that they had set up a popular government when they separated from England, but they were deluded. In conquering the political power formerly exercised by the king, the people had but taken the outworks of the fortress of tyranny. The economic system which was the citadel and commanded every part of the social structure remained in possession of private and irresponsible rulers, and so long as it was so held, the possession of the outworks was of no use to the people, and only retained by the sufferance of the garrison of the citadel. The Revolution came when the people saw that they must either take the citadel or evacuate the outworks. They must either complete the work of establishing popular government which had been barely begun by their fathers, or abandon all that their fathers had accomplished."

POPULIST PLATFORM
OF 1892

Assembled upon the 116th anniversary of the Declaration of Independence, the People's Party of America, in their first national convention, invoking upon their action the blessing of Almighty God, put forth in the name and on behalf of the people of this country, the following preamble and declaration of principles:

PREAMBLE

The conditions which surround us best justify our co-operation; we meet in the midst of a nation brought to the verge of moral, political, and material ruin. Corruption dominates the ballot-box, the Legislatures, the Congress, and touches even the ermine of the bench. The people are demoralized; most of the States have been compelled to isolate the voters at the polling places to prevent universal intimidation and bribery. The newspapers are largely subsidized or muzzled, public opinion silenced, business prostrated, homes covered with mortgages, labor impoverished, and the land concentrating in the hands of capitalists. The urban workmen are denied the right to organize for self-protection, imported pauperized labor beats down their wages, a hireling standing army, unrecognized by our laws, is established to shoot them down, and they are rapidly degenerating into European conditions. The fruits of the toil of millions are boldly stolen to build up colossal fortunes for a few, unprecedented in the history of mankind; and the possessors of those, in turn, despise the Republic and endanger liberty. From the same prolific womb of governmental injustice we breed the two great classes—tramps and millionaires.

The national power to create money is appropriated to enrich bondholders; a vast public debt payable in legal tender currency has been funded into gold-bearing bonds, thereby adding millions to the burdens of the people.

Edward McPherson, *A Handbook of Politics for 1892* (Washington, D.C.: James J. Chapman, 1892), pp. 269 ff.

Silver, which has been accepted as coin since the dawn of history, has been demonetized to add to the purchasing power of gold by decreasing the value of all forms of property as well as human labor, and the supply of currency is purposely abridged to fatten usurers, bankrupt enterprise, and enslave industry. A vast conspiracy against mankind has been organized on two continents, and it is rapidly taking possession of the world. If not met and overthrown at once it forebodes terrible social convulsions, the destruction of civilization, or the establishment of an absolute despotism.

We have witnessed for more than a quarter of a century the struggles of the two great political parties for power and plunder, while grievous wrongs have been inflicted upon the suffering people. We charge that the controlling influences dominating both these parties have permitted the existing dreadful conditions to develop without serious effort to prevent or restrain them. Neither do they now promise us any substantial reform. They have agreed together to ignore, in the coming campaign, every issue but one. They propose to drown the outcries of a plundered people with the uproar of a sham battle over the tariff, so that capitalists, corporations, national banks, rings, trusts, watered stock, the demonetization of silver and the oppressions of the usurers may all be lost sight of. They propose to sacrifice our homes, lives, and children on the altar of mammon; to destroy the multitude in order to secure corruption funds from the millionaires.

Assembled on the anniversary of the birthday of the nation, and filled with the spirit of the grand general and chief who established our independence, we seek to restore the government of the Republic to the hands of "the plain people," with which class it originated. We assert our purposes to be identical with the purposes of the National Constitution; to form a more perfect union and establish justice, insure domestic tranquillity, provide for the common defence; promote the general welfare, and secure the blessings of liberty for ourselves and our posterity.

We declare that this Republic can only endure as a free government while built upon the love of the whole people for each other and for the nation; that it cannot be pinned together by bayonets; that the civil war is over, and that every passion and resentment which grew out of it must die with it, and that we must be in fact, as we are in name, one united brotherhood of free men.

Our country finds itself confronted by conditions for which there is no precedent in the history of the world; our annual agricultural productions amount to billions of dollars in value, which must, within a few weeks or months, be exchanged for billions of dollars' worth of commodities consumed in their production; the existing currency supply is wholly inadequate to make this exchange; the results are falling prices, the formation of combines and rings, the impoverishment of the producing class. We pledge ourselves that if given power we will labor to correct these evils by wise and reasonable legislation, in accordance with the terms of our platform.

We believe that the power of government—in other words, of the people—should be expanded (as in the case of the postal service) as rapidly and as far as the good sense of an intelligent people and the teachings of experience shall justify, to the end that oppression, injustice, and poverty shall eventually cease in the land.

While our sympathies as a party of reform are naturally upon the side of every proposition which will tend to make men intelligent, virtuous, and temperate, we nevertheless regard these questions, important as they are, as secondary to the great issues now pressing for solution, and upon which not only our individual prosperity but the very existence of free institutions depend; and we ask all men to first help us to determine whether we are to have a republic to administer before we differ as to the conditions upon which it is to be administered, believing that the forces of reform this day organized will never cease to move forward until every wrong is remedied and equal rights and equal privileges securely established for all the men and women of this country.

PLATFORM

We declare, therefore—

First.—That the union of the labor forces of the United States this day consummated shall be permanent and perpetual; may its spirit enter into all hearts for the salvation of the Republic and the uplifting of mankind.

Second.—Wealth belongs to him who creates it, and every dollar taken from industry without an equivalent is robbery. "If any will not work, neither shall he eat." The interests of rural and civic labor are the same; their enemies are identical.

Third.—We believe that the time has come when the railroad corporations will either own the people or the people must own the railroads, and should the government enter upon the work of owning and managing all railroads, we should favor an amendment to the Constitution by which all persons engaged in the government service shall be placed under a civil-service regulation of the most rigid character, so as to prevent the increase of the power of the national administration by the use of such additional government employees.

Finance.—We demand a national currency, safe, sound, and flexible, issued by the general government only, a full legal tender for all debts, public and private, and that without the use of banking corporations, a just, equitable, and efficient means of distribution direct to the people, at a tax not to exceed 2 per cent per annum, to be provided, as set forth in the sub-treasury plan of the Farmers' Alliance, or a better system; also by payments in discharge of its obligations for public improvements.

1. We demand free and unlimited coinage of silver and gold at the present legal ratio of 16 to 1.

2. We demand that the amount of circulating medium be speedily increased to not less than $50 per capita.

3. We demand a graduated income tax.

4. We believe that the money of the country should be kept as much as possible in the hands of the people, and hence we demand that all State and national revenues shall be limited to the necessary expenses of the government, economically and honestly administered.

5. We demand that postal savings banks be established by the government for the safe deposit of the earnings of the people and to facilitate exchange.

Transportation.—Transportation being a means of exchange and a public necessity, the government should own and operate the railroads in the interest of the people. The telegraph, telephone, like the post-office system, being a necessity for the transmission of news, should be owned and operated by the government in the interest of the people.

Land.—The land, including all the natural sources of wealth, is the heritage of the people, and should not be monopolized for speculative purposes, and alien ownership of land should be prohibited. All land now held by railroads and other corporations in excess of their actual needs, and all lands now owned by aliens should be reclaimed by the government and held for actual settlers only.

William Jennings Bryan

CROSS OF GOLD SPEECH
(1896)

Mr. Chairman and Gentlemen of the Convention: I would be presumptuous, indeed, to present myself against the distinguished gentlemen to whom you have listened if this were a mere measuring of abilities; but this is not a contest between persons. The humblest citizen in all the land, when clad in the armor of a righteous cause, is stronger than all the hosts of error. I come to speak to you in defense of a cause as holy as the cause of liberty—the cause of humanity.

When this debate is concluded, a motion will be made to lay upon the table the resolution offered in commendation of the administration, and also the resoluton offered in condemnation of the administration. We object to bringing this question down to the level of persons. The individual is but an atom; he is born, he acts, he dies; but principles are eternal; and this has been a contest over a principle.

Never before in the history of this country has there been witnessed such a contest as that through which we have just passed. Never before in the history of American politics has a great issue been fought out as this issue has been, by the voters of a great party. On the fourth of March, 1895, a few Democrats, most of them members of Congress, issued an address to the Democrats of the nation, asserting that the money question was the paramount issue of the hour; declaring that a majority of the Democratic party had the right to control the action of the party on this paramount issue; and concluding with the request that the believers in the free coinage of silver in the Democratic party should organize, take charge of, and control the policy of the Democratic party. Three months later, at Memphis, an organization was perfected, and the silver Democrats went forth openly and courageously proclaiming their belief, and declaring that, if successful, they would crystallize into a platform the declaration which they had made. Then began the conflict. With a zeal

William J. Bryan, *The First Battle* (Chicago: W. B. Conkey Co., 1896), pp. 199–206.

approaching the zeal which inspired the crusaders who followed Peter the Hermit, our silver Democrats went forth from victory unto victory until they are now assembled, not to discuss, not to debate, but to enter up the judgment already rendered by the plain people of this country. In this contest brother has been arrayed against brother, father against son. The warmest ties of love, acquaintance and association have been disregarded; old leaders have been cast aside when they have refused to give expression to the sentiments of those whom they would lead, and new leaders have sprung up to give direction to this cause of truth. Thus has the contest been waged, and we have assembled here under as binding and solemn instructions as were ever imposed upon representatives of the people.

We do not come as individuals. As individuals we might have been glad to compliment the gentleman from New York (Senator Hill), but we know that the people for whom we speak would never be willing to put him in a position where he could thwart the will of the Democratic party. I say it was not a question of persons; it was a question of principle, and it is not with gladness, my friends, that we find ourselves brought into conflict with those who are now arrayed on the other side.

The gentleman who preceded me (ex-Governor Russell) spoke of the State of Massachusetts; let me assure him that not one present in all this convention entertains the least hostility to the people of the State of Massachusetts, but we stand here representing people who are the equals, before the law, of the greatest citizens in the State of Massachusetts. When you (turning to the gold delegates) come before us and tell us that we are about to disturb your business interests, we reply that you have disturbed our business interests by your course.

We say to you that you have made the definition of a business man too limited in its application. The man who is employed for wages is as much a business man as his employer; the attorney in a country town is as much a business man as the corporation counsel in a great metropolis; the merchant at the cross-roads store is as much a business man as the merchant of New York; the farmer who goes forth in the morning and toils all day—who begins in the spring and toils all summer—and who by the application of brain and muscle to the natural resources of the country creates wealth, is as much a business man as the man who goes upon the board of trade and bets upon the price of grain; the miners who go down a thousand feet into the earth, or climb two thousand feet upon the cliffs, and bring forth from their hiding places the precious metals to be poured into the channels of trade are as much business men as the few financial magnates who, in a back room, corner the money of the world. We come to speak for this broader class of business men.

Ah, my friends, we say not one word against those who live upon the Atlantic coast, but the hardy pioneers who have braved all the dangers of the wilderness, who have made the desert to blossom as the rose—the pioneers away out there (pointing to the West), who rear their children near to Nature's heart, where they can mingle their voices with the voices of the birds—out there where they have erected schoolhouses for the education of their young, churches where they praise their Creator, and cemeteries where rest the ashes of their dead—these people, we say, are as deserving of the consideration of our party as any people in this country. It is for these that we speak. We do not come as aggressors. Our war is not a war of conquest; we are fighting in the defense of our homes, our families, and posterity. We have petitioned and our petitions have been scorned; we have entreated, and our entreaties have been disregarded; we have begged, and they have mocked when our calamity came. We beg no longer; we entreat no more; we petition no more. We defy them.

The gentleman from Wisconsin has said that he fears a Robespierre. My friends, in this land of the free you need not fear that a tyrant will spring up from among the people. What we need is an Andrew Jackson to stand, as Jackson stood, against the encroachments of organized wealth.

They tell us that this platform was made to catch votes. We reply to them that changing conditions make new issues; that the principles upon which Democracy rests are as everlasting as the hills, but that they must be applied to new conditions as they arise. Conditions have arisen, and we are here to meet those conditions. They tell us that the income tax ought not to be brought in here; that it is a new idea. They criticise us for our criticism of the Supreme Court of the United States. My friends, we have not criticised; we have simply called attention to what you already know. If you want criticisms, read the dissenting opinions of the court. There you will find criticisms. They say that we passed an unconstitutional law; we deny it. The income tax law was not unconstitutional when it was passed; it was not unconstitutional when it went before the Supreme Court for the first time; it did not become unconstitutional until one of the judges changed his mind, and we cannot be expected to know when a judge will change his mind. The income tax is just. It simply intends to put the burdens of government justly upon the backs of the people. I am in favor of an income tax. When I find a man who is not willing to bear his share of the burdens of the government which protects him, I find a man who is unworthy to enjoy the blessings of a government like ours.

They say that we are opposing national bank currency; it is true. If you will read what Thomas Benton said, you will find he said that, in searching history, he could find but one parallel to Andrew Jackson; that was Cicero, who destroyed the conspiracy of Cataline and saved Rome. Benton said that Cicero only did for Rome what Jackson did for us when he destroyed the bank conspiracy and saved America. We say in our platform that we believe that the right to coin and issue money is a function of government.

We believe that it is a part of sovereignty, and can no more with safety be delegated to private individuals than we could afford to delegate to private individuals the power to make penal statutes or levy taxes. Mr. Jefferson, who was once regarded as good Democratic authority, seems to have differed in opinion from the gentleman who has addressed us on the part of the minority. Those who are opposed to this proposition tell us that the issue of paper money is a function of the bank, and that the Government ought to go out of the banking business. I stand with Jefferson rather than with them, and tell them, as he did, that the issue of money is a function of government, and that the banks ought to go out of the governing business.

They complain about the plank which declares against life tenure in office. They have tried to strain it to mean that which it does not mean. What we oppose by that plank is the life tenure which is being built up in Washington, and which excludes from participation in official benefits the humbler members of society.

Let me call your attention to two or three important things. The gentleman from New York says that he will propose an amendment to the platform providing that the proposed change in our monetary system shall not effect contracts already made. Let me remind you that there is no intention of affecting those contracts which according to present laws are made payable in gold; but if he means to say that we cannot change our monetary system without protecting those who have loaned money before the change was made, I desire to ask him where, in law or in morals, he can find justification for not protecting the debtors when the act of 1873 was passed, if he now insists that we must protect the creditors.

He says he will also propose an amendment which will provide for the suspension of free coinage if we fail to maintain the parity within a year. We reply that when we advocate a policy which we believe will be successful, we are not compelled to raise a doubt as to our own sincerity by suggesting what we shall do if we fail. I ask him, if he would apply his logic to us, why he does not apply it to himself. He says he wants this country to try to secure an international agreement. Why does he not tell us what he is going to do if he fails to secure an international agreement? There is more reason for him to do that than there is for us to provide against the failure to maintain the parity. Our opponents have tried for twenty years to secure an international agreement, and those are waiting for it most patiently who do not want it at all.

And now, my friends, let me come to the paramount issue. If they ask us why it is that we say more on the money question than we say upon the tariff question, I reply that, if protection has slain its thousands, the gold standard has slain its tens of thousands. If they ask us why we do not embody in our platform all the things that we believe in, we reply that when we have restored the money of the Constitution all other necessary reforms will be possible; but that until this is done there is no other reform that can be accomplished. . . .

Mr. Carlisle said in 1878 that this was a struggle between "the idle holders of idle capital" and "the struggling masses, who produce the wealth and pay the taxes of the country;" and, my friends, the question we are to decide is: Upon which side will the Democratic party fight; upon the side of "the idle holders of idle capital" or upon the side of "the struggling masses?" That is the question which the party must answer first, and then it must be answered by each individual hereafter. The sympathies of the Democratic party, as shown by the platform, are on the side of the struggling masses who have ever been the foundation of the Democratic party. There are two ideas of government. There are those who believe that, if you will only legislate to make the well-to-do prosperous, their prosperity will leak through on those below. The Democratic idea, however, has been that if you legislate to make the masses prosperous, their prosperity will find its way up through every class which rests upon them.

You come to us and tell us that the great cities are in favor of the gold standard; we reply that the great cities rest upon our broad and fertile prairies. Burn down your cities and leave our farms, and your cities will spring up again as if by magic; but destroy our farms and the grass will grow in the streets of every city in the country.

My friends, we declare that this nation is able to legislate for its own people on every question, without waiting for the aid or consent of any other nation on earth; and upon that issue we expect to carry every State in the Union. I shall not slander the inhabitants of the fair State of Massachusetts nor the inhabitants of the State of New York by saying that, when they are confronted with the proposition, they will declare that this nation is not able to attend to its own business. It is the issue of 1776 over again. Our ancestors, when but three millions in number, had the courage to declare their political independence of every other nation; shall we, their descendants, when we have grown to seventy millions, declare that we are less independent than our forefathers? No, my friends, that will never be the verdict of our people. Therefore, we care not upon what lines the battle is fought. If they say bimetallism is good, but that we cannot have it until other nations help us, we reply that, instead of having a gold standard because England has, we will restore bimetallism, and then let England have bimetallism because the United States has it. If they dare to come out in the open field and defend the gold standard as a good thing, we will fight them to the uttermost. Having behind us the producing masses of this nation and the world, supported by the commercial interests, the laboring interests, and the toilers everywhere, we will answer their demand for a gold standard by saying to them: You shall not press down upon the brow of labor this crown of thorns, you shall not crucify mankind upon a cross of gold.

LOCHNER v. NEW YORK
198 U.S. 45 (1905)

MR. JUSTICE PECKHAM, after making the foregoing statement of the facts, delivered the opinion of the court:

The indictment, it will be seen, charges that the plaintiff in error violated the 110th section of article 8, chapter 415, of the Laws of 1897, known as the labor law of the state of New York, in that he wrongfully and unlawfully required and permitted an employee working for him to work more than sixty hours in one week. . . .

The mandate of the statute, that "no employee shall be required or permitted to work," is the substantial equivalent of an enactment that "no employee shall contract or agree to work," more than ten hours per day; and, as there is no provision for special emergencies, the statute is mandatory in all cases. It is not an act merely fixing the number of hours which shall constitute a legal day's work, but an absolute prohibition upon the employer permitting, under any circumstances, more than ten hours' work to be done in his establishment. The employee may desire to earn the extra money which would arise from his working more than the prescribed time, but this statute forbids the employer from permitting the employee to earn it.

The statute necessarily interferes with the right of contract between the employer and employees, concerning the number of hours in which the latter may labor in the bakery of the employer. The general right to make a contract in relation to his business is part of the liberty of the individual protected by the 14th Amendment of the Federal Constitution. . . .

Under that provision no state can deprive any person of life, liberty, or property without due process of law. The right to purchase or sell labor is part of the liberty protected by this amendment, unless there are circumstances which exclude the right. There are, however, certain powers, existing in the sovereignty of each state in the Union, somewhat vaguely termed police powers, the exact description and limitation of which have not been attempted by the courts. Those powers, broadly stated, and without, at present, any attempt at a more specific limitation, relate to the safety, health, morals, and general welfare of the public. Both property and liberty are held on such reasonable conditions as may be imposed by the governing power of the state in the exercise of those powers, and with such conditions the 14th Amendment was not designed to interfere. . . .

The state, therefore, has power to prevent the individual from making certain kinds of contracts, and in regard to them the Federal Constitution offers no protection. If the contract be one which the state, in the legitimate exercise of its police power, has the right to prohibit, it is not prevented from prohibiting it by the 14th Amendment. Contracts in violation of a statute, either of the Federal or state government, or a contract to let one's property for immoral purposes, or to do any other unlawful act, could obtain no protection from the Federal Constitution, as coming under the liberty of person or of free contract. Therefore, when the state, by its legislature, in the assumed exercise of its police powers, has passed an act which seriously limits the right to labor or the right of contract in regard to their means of livelihood between persons who are *sui juris* (both employer and employee), it becomes of great importance to determine which shall prevail,—the right of the individual to labor for such time as he may choose, or the right of the state to prevent the individual from laboring, or from entering into any contract to labor, beyond a certain time prescribed by the state. . . .

It must, of course, be conceded that there is a limit to the valid exercise of the police power by the state. There is no dispute concerning this general proposition. Otherwise the 14th Amendment would have no efficacy and the legislatures of the states would have unbounded power, and it would be enough to say that any piece of legislation was enacted to conserve the morals, the health, or the safety of the people; such legislation would be valid, no matter how absolutely without foundation the claim might be. The claim of the police power would be a mere pretext,—become another and delusive name for the supreme sovereignty of the state to be exercised free from constitutional restraint. This is not contended for. In every case that comes before this court, therefore, where legislation of this character is concerned, and where the protection of the Federal Constitution is sought, the question necessarily arises: Is this a fair, reasonable, and appropriate exercise of the police power of the state, or is it an unreasonable, unnecessary, and arbitrary interference with the right of the individual to his personal liberty, or to enter into those contracts in relation to labor which may seem to him appropriate or necessary for the support of himself and his family? Of course the liberty of contract relating to labor includes both parties to it. The one has as much right to purchase as the other to sell labor.

This is not a question of substituting the judgment of the court for that of the legislature. If the act be within the power of the state it is valid, although the judgment of the court might be totally opposed to the enactment of such a law. But the question would still remain: Is it within the police power of the state? and that question must be answered by the court.

The question whether this act is valid as a labor law, pure and simple, may be dismissed in a few words. There is no reasonable ground for interfering with the liberty of person or the right of free contract, by determining the hours of labor, in the occupation of a baker. There is no contention that bakers as a class are not equal in intelligence and capacity to men in other trades or manual occupations, or that they are not able to assert their rights and care for themselves without the protecting arm of the state, interfering with their independence of judgment and of action. They are in no sense wards of the state. Viewed in the light of a purely labor law, with no reference whatever to the question of health, we think that a law like the one before us involves neither the safety, the morals, nor the welfare, of the public, and that the interest of the public is not in the slightest degree affected by such an act. The law must be upheld, if at all, as a law pertaining to the health of the individual engaged in the occupation of a baker. It does not affect any other portion of the public than those who are engaged in that occupation. Clean and wholesome bread does not depend upon whether the baker works but ten hours per day or only sixty hours a week. The limitation of the hours of labor does not come within the police power on that ground.

It is a question of which of two powers or rights shall prevail,—the power of the state to legislate or the right of the individual to liberty of person and freedom of contract. The mere assertion that the subject relates, though but in a remote degree, to the public health, does not necessarily render the enactment valid. The act must have a more direct relation, as a means to an end, and the end itself must be appropriate and legitimate, before an act can be held to be valid which interferes with the general right of an individual to be free in his person and his power to contract in relation to his own labor. . . .

We think the limit of the police power has been reached and passed in this case. There is, in our judgment, no reasonable foundation for holding this to be necessary or appropriate as a health law to safeguard the public health, or the health of the individuals who are following the trade of a baker. If this statute be valid, and if, therefore, a proper case is made out in which to deny the right of an individual, *sui juris*, as employer or employee, to make contracts for the labor of the latter under the protection of the provisions of the Federal Constitution, there would seem to be no length to which legislation of this nature might not go. . . .

We do not believe in the soundness of the views which uphold this law. On the contrary, we think that such a law as this, although passed in the assumed exercise of the police power, and as relating to the public health, or the health of the employees named, is not within that power, and is invalid. The act is not, within any fair meaning of the term, a health law, but is an illegal interference with the rights of individuals, both employers and employees, to make contracts regarding labor upon such terms as they may think best, or which they may agree upon with the other parties to such contracts. Statutes of the nature of that under review, limiting the hours in which grown and intelligent men may labor to earn their living, are mere meddlesome interferences with the rights of the individual, and they are not saved from condemnation by the claim that they are passed in the exercise of the police power and upon the subject of the health of the individual whose rights are interfered with, unless there be some fair ground, reasonable in and of itself, to say that there is material danger to the public health, or to the health of the employees, if the hours of labor are not curtailed. If this be not clearly the case, the individuals whose rights are thus made the subject of legislative interference are under the protection of the Federal Constitution regarding their liberty of contract as well as of person; and the legislature of the state has no power to limit their right as proposed in this statute. . . .

It is manifest to us that the limitation of the hours of labor as provided for in this section of the statute under which the indictment was found, and the plaintiff in error convicted, has no such direct relation to, and no such substantial effect upon, the health of the employee, as to justify us in regarding the section as really a health law. It seems to us that the real object and purpose were simply to regulate the hours of labor between the master and his employees (all being men, *sui juris*), in a private business, not dangerous in any degree to morals, or in any real and substantial degree to the health of the employees. Under such circumstances the freedom of master and employee to contract with each other in relation to their employment, and in defining the same, cannot be prohibited or interfered with, without violating the Federal Constitution. . . .

Reversed.

MR. JUSTICE HOLMES dissenting:

I regret sincerely that I am unable to agree with the judgment in this case, and that I think it my duty to express my dissent.

This case is decided upon an economic theory which a large part of the country does not entertain. If it were a question whether I agreed with that theory, I should desire to study it further and long before making up my mind. But I do not conceive that to be my duty, because I strongly believe that my agreement or disagreement has nothing to do with the right of a majority to embody their opinions in law. It is settled by various decisions of this court that state constitutions and state laws may regulate life in many ways which we as legislators might think as injudicious, or if you like as tyrannical, as this, and which, equally with this, interfere with the liberty to contract. Sunday laws and usury laws are ancient examples. A more modern one is the prohibition of lotteries. The liberty of the citizen to do as he likes so long as he does not interfere with the liberty of others to do the same, which has been a shibboleth for some well-known writers, is interfered with by school laws, by the Postoffice, by every state or municipal institution which takes his money for purposes thought desirable, whether he likes it or not. The 14th Amendment does not enact Mr. Herbert Spencer's Social Statics. . . .

A Constitution is not intended to embody a particular economic theory, whether of paternalism and the organic relation of the citizen to the state or of *laissez faire*. It is made for people of fundamentally differing views, and the accident of our finding certain opinions natural and familiar, or novel, and even shocking, ought not to conclude our judgment upon the question whether statutes embodying them conflict with the Constitution of the United States.

General propositions do not decide concrete cases. The decision will depend on a judgment or intuition more subtle than any articulate major premise. But I think that the proposition just stated, if it is accepted, will carry us far toward the end. Every opinion tends to become a law. I think that the word "liberty," in the 14th Amendment, is perverted when it is held to prevent the natural outcome of a dominant opinion, unless it can be said that a rational and fair man necessarily would admit that the statute proposed would infringe fundamental principles as they have been understood by the traditions of our people and our law. It does not need research to show that no such sweeping condemnation can be passed upon the statute before us. A reasonable man might think it a proper measure on the score of health. Men whom I certainly could not pronounce unreasonable would uphold it as a first instalment of a general regulation of the hours of work. Whether in the latter aspect it would be open to the charge of inequality I think it unnecessary to discuss.

8

THE BLACK STRUGGLE

All I ask . . . in regard to blacks, is that whatever rule you adopt, whether of intelligence or wealth as the condition of voting, you shall apply it equally to the black man. Do that, and I am satisfied, and eternal justice is satisfied; liberty, fraternity, equality, are satisfied; and the country will move on harmoniously.

FREDERICK DOUGLASS, 1863

Neither slavery nor involuntary servitude, except as a punishment for crime whereof the party shall have been duly convicted, shall exist within the United States, or any place subject to their jurisdiction.

Amendment XIII, Section 1, 1865

All persons born or naturalized in the United States, and subject to the jurisdiction thereof, are citizens of the United States and of the State wherein they reside. No State shall make or enforce any law which shall abridge the privileges or immunities of citizens of the United States; nor shall any state deprive any person of life, liberty, or property, without due process of law; nor deny to any person within its jurisdiction the equal protection of the laws.

Amendment XIV, Section 1, 1868

The right of citizens of the United States to vote shall not be denied or abridged by the United States or by any State on account of race, color, or previous condition of servitude.

Amendment XV, Section 1, 1870

Since the Civil War, American black people have been confronted by what has been called the "American Dilemma." [1] On the one hand, they

---

[1] "The 'American Dilemma' is the ever raging conflict between, on the one hand, the valuations preserved on the general plane which we shall call 'the American Creed,' where the American thinks, talks, and acts under the influence of high national and Christian precepts, and, on the other hand, the valuations on specific planes of individual and group living, where personal and local interests; economic, social, and sexual jealousies; group prejudice against persons or types of people; and all sorts of miscellaneous wants, impulses, and habits dominate his outlook." Gunnar Myrdal, *An American Dilemma: The Negro Problem and Modern Democracy* (New York: Harper & Row, 1962), p. lxxi. [Original italics removed.]

are legally recognized as full citizens within the meaning of the Declaration of Independence and the Constitution. On the other, such recognition has not led to their acceptance as equals within American society. In short, the realization of legal equality for black people was not followed by any general acceptance that they are social and political equals as well. Consequently, the history of black Americans for much of the last century has revolved around their efforts to secure the rights guaranteed them as American citizens—when those rights were unconstitutionally denied—*and* to achieve the kind of social and political equality which make such rights meaningful. This task has been doubly difficult. It is complicated not only by the omnipresent tensions between equality and liberty, but also by the black struggle to reach a position from which to handle that tension. From this perspective, black discontent in America is all too understandable. First, they have to fight for the rights supposedly given to all Americans at birth. Then, if the fight is successful, they find themselves being asked to temper their desires in respect of the rights of those with whom they have just fought. The successful pursuit of equality and liberty brings them face to face with the tensions that arise in America whenever equality and liberty are at issue.

Civil rights activity of the last hundred years, in this sense, reflects both the attempts of black people to win the rights promised all Americans and the problems which typify the interplay of equality and liberty. To understand black politics in America, these differing but related perspectives ought to be recognized. In this chapter, some of the more prominent figures and events in the civil rights struggle will be considered. It is important to keep in mind, however, that these figures and events are part of the American political experience as a whole, not only the black political experience. The broader issues of American political thought are inseparable from the concerns which have always impelled civil rights movements in America. This fact becomes apparent shortly after the Civil War Amendments abolished slavery and extended Constitutional rights to the former slaves and their descendants. The force of these Amendments, as well as several civil rights acts passed by the "Radical Congress," was lost as a result of Supreme Court decisions that illustrate how traditional American problems and particular black concerns are related.

The Civil Rights Act of 1875 was designed to protect Negroes from discriminatory laws which had been passed in several states. The law, in effect, prevented state legislatures from denying equal rights on the basis of color or race and was based upon an assumption that the 14th Amendment provided Congress with the power to protect citizens from discriminatory acts of states and private persons. The Supreme Court, however, disagreed. Delivering the opinion of the Court in the *Civil Rights Cases* in 1883, Justice Bradley argued that Congress could only correct the legislation of states when the states expressly violated provisions of the 14th Amendment. Specifically, he said that Congress had no power to enact "primary and direct" legislation; it could not preempt the state power to govern the relations of the people who lived there. This argument removed one of the chief protections that the newly enfranchised Negroes had been afforded and placed the question of their protection in a greater sphere—the relationship that ought to exist between states and the national government. Without reexamining the "states' rights" dispute, it is notable how efforts to provide Constitutional safeguards for blacks were, from the first, intertwined with the traditional problems of American political thought.

Negro leaders recognized this immediately. The most influential black spokesman before and immediately after the Civil War, Frederick Douglass, criticized the *Civil Rights Cases* as jeopardizing the very basis of American political life. Echoing Lincoln, he declared that whites were no more immune to its consequences than blacks:

No man can put a chain about the ankle of his fellow man, without at last finding the other end of it fastened about his own neck.

The lesson of all the ages on this point is that a wrong done to one man is a wrong done to all men. It may not be felt at the moment, and the evil day may be long delayed, but so sure as there is a moral government of the universe, so sure will the harvest of evil come.[2]

The Negro purpose, then, was double-edged. In working for their own rights, Douglass and his people would be securing the promises of the Declaration for all Americans. Anyone who distinguished social equality from other American rights, according to Douglass, failed to understand how liberty and equality are related in America. Social discrimination on racial grounds meant a denial of liberty on the same grounds:

When a colored man is in the same room or in the carriage with white people, as a servant, there is no talk of social equality, but if he is there as a man and a gentleman, he is an offense. What makes the difference? It is not color, for his color is unchanged. The whole essence of the thing is a studied purpose to degrade and stamp out the liberties of a race.[3]

And, he continued, a denial of liberty on that basis might be infinitely extended. Once liberty was refused one group because of their race,

[2] "Civil Rights Case," in *Proceedings of the Civil Rights Mass Meeting Held at Lincoln Hall, October, 1883: Speeches of Hon. Frederick Douglass and Robert G. Ingersoll*, Washington, D.C., 1883.   [Pamphlet]
[3] *Ibid.*

refusal to other groups on a like basis was unavoidable. Thus, there could be no liberty to discriminate in America upon racial grounds. To try to single out the "Negro problem" for special treatment, in this respect, was to mistake the entire meaning of the American political tradition:

I deny and utterly scout the idea that there is now, properly speaking, any such thing as a Negro problem now before the American people. It is not the Negro . . . who is on trial. . . . The real problem lies in the other direction. . . . The real question, the all-commanding question, is whether American justice, American liberty, American civilization, American law and American Christianity can be made to include and protect alike and forever all American citizens in the rights which, in a generous moment in the nation's life, have been guaranteed to them by the organic and fundamental law of the land.[4]

A failure to respond to its black minority, therefore, could have disastrous consequences for America as a whole.

The most immediate problem for black people, however, was not concerned with abstract principles. How, they had to decide, were they to deal with the outright denial of their liberties? The manner in which they answer this question distinguishes black leaders from the Reconstruction to the present. All agree that equality and liberty must be forthcoming. But how? Douglass taught that blacks had to immediately claim the political liberty promised in the Declaration and Constitution. His position was not universally accepted, however. Another ex-slave, for example, took a different and more moderate course. Booker T. Washington, noting the condition of most of his newly freed people and the prevailing views of whites, urged Negroes to find their way into the hearts and communities of whites through moral and economic achievement. By education, hard work, and success, Negroes would prove themselves worthy of the rights they desired. The leap from slavery to freedom was perilous, Washington declared in a speech at the Atlanta Exposition in 1895. Care had to be taken in making it:

Our greatest danger is that, in the great leap from slavery to freedom, we may overlook the fact that the masses of us are to live by the productions of our hands and fail to keep in mind that we shall prosper in proportion as we learn to dignify and glorify common labor, and put brains and skill into the common occupations of life. It is at the bottom of life we must begin, and not at the top. Nor should we permit our grievances to overshadow our opportunities.[5]

[4] "The Nation's Problem," speech delivered before the Bethel Literary and Historical Society in Washington, D.C., April 16, 1889, Washington, D.C., 1889. [Pamphlet]
[5] "Atlanta Exposition Address," delivered at the opening of the Cotton States and International Exposition at Atlanta, Georgia, September 18, 1895.

The difficulty of this position, as other blacks—and sympathetic whites—observed, was that in an egalitarian society, the acceptance of social inequality marks one as inferior in other areas as well. An egalitarian people encouraged to view a group as somehow less dignified than the mass tends to limit the group's entry into any part of society. Divisions in egalitarian societies are invariably accompanied by differentiation: social segregation of any portion of the society argues for that portion's inferiority and, hence, is followed by arguments in favor of their political inferiority also. To be different in an egalitarian community is to be unequal. For blacks, this meant being "second class." Whereas Douglass had fought for immediate integration, Washington's arguments seemed to invite greater separation. His stand had the virtue of encouraging Negro independence, of developing Negro skills and economic self-sufficiency, and of providing Negroes the opportunity to be dignified in their own right. But from the perspective of Douglass and others, it had the drawback of inviting whites to look upon blacks as less than themselves, which was an invitation to even more severe deprivation for blacks.

This possibility became actuality only one year after Washington's Atlanta address. In the case of *Plessy* v. *Ferguson,* the Supreme Court ruled that the legal establishment of segregation by states was Constitutional. Racial segregation, in short, was elevated to the level of Constitutional principle. Separate but equal facilities—in the *Plessy* case the direct issue was segregated railway cars—were said to be entirely compatible with the concept of equality before the law. Division did not necessarily entail inferiority:

We consider the underlying fallacy of the plaintiff's argument to consist in the assumption that enforced separation of the two races stamps the colored race with a badge of inferiority. If this be so, it is not by reason of anything found in the act, but solely because the colored race chooses to put that construction on it.[6]

But how, it followed, is one to differentiate without some recognition of differences which mark the distinguished class of people as unequal? Justice Harlan dissented in the *Plessy* case on just these grounds. The law, he urged—prematurely for his day—must be color blind. For it to recognize differences based upon color was unallowable according to the tenets of the Declaration:

The law regards man as man, and takes no account of his surroundings or of his color when his civil rights as guaranteed by the supreme law of the land are involved.[7]

[6] 163 U.S. 537 (1896).
[7] *Ibid.*

It was no surprise to Harlan that "Jim Crow" laws and open racial discrimination would proliferate and flourish once racial discrimination was acknowledged as legal principle. Thus, the end of the nineteenth and the beginning of the twentieth centuries saw a positive decline in the position of black people in America, rather than an improvement.[8]

And as the position of blacks deteriorated, more radical and embittered black leaders arose. In the late 1890s, for example, W. E. B. Du Bois challenged Washington's views and his leadership of the black community. The first black to obtain a Ph.D. from Harvard and afterward a noted sociologist, Du Bois became the generally acknowledged leading black intellectual when he published *The Souls of Black Folk* in 1903. As he made clear, the political consequences of delaying the demand for civil rights were tragic for black men. Replying to Washington, he argued that to entrust the black future to the gains which would follow self-help efforts would absolve whites of their responsibility to see that America lived up to its principles. Like Douglass before him, Du Bois pointed to the American nature of the black problem:

His [Washington's] doctrine has tended to make the whites, North and South, shift the burden of the Negro problem to the Negro's shoulders and stand aside as critical and rather pessimistic spectators; when in fact the burden belongs to the nation, and the hands of none of us are clean if we bend not our energies to righting these great wrongs.[9]

Thus, Du Bois stressed the importance of reminding whites that they must remain true to the principles upon which their nation was founded. And if this meant a greater degree of militance than had formerly been true of blacks, Du Bois was ready to take such a step:

By every civilized and peaceful method we must strive for the rights which the world accords men, clinging unwaveringly to those great words which the sons of the Fathers would fain forget: "We hold these truths to be self-evident: That all men are created equal; that they are endowed by their Creator with certain unalienable rights; that among these are life, liberty and the pursuit of happiness."[10]

Du Bois, consequently, was instrumental in organizing blacks politically. He initiated the Niagara Movement—which eventually evolved into the N.A.A.C.P.—a group of more than twenty persons who were unified in their criticism of Washington and their belief in civil rights activism. The two major documents of the Movement—"Declaration of Principles

[8] Cf. C. Vann Woodward, *The Strange Career of Jim Crow* (New York: Oxford University Press, 1957), especially Chapter II.
[9] "Of Mr. Booker T. Washington and Others," in *The Souls of Black Folk* (New York: Allograph Press Corp., 1903), p. 58.
[10] *Ibid.*, p. 59.

(1905)" and "Resolutions (1906)"— indicate the difference between
the self-help doctrine and the newer position. The thrust of the documents
is that the wrongs done to blacks must be corrected and that all black
men must join in demanding that such corrections be made. Blacks were
asked to become intimately and immediately involved in politics and
to force themselves upon white society if that society were slow to
acknowledge them. Essentially, then, Du Bois initiated the civil rights
movements of the twentieth century.

If Du Bois was pessimistic about Washington's solution to black
problems, there were those who were pessimistic about the possibility of
any solution at all. Marcus Garvey, for one, doubted that white
Americans would ever accept the black minority as equals. And Garvey
himself would not accept that blacks should "make do" with lesser
citizenship and discrimination. He would rather, he suggested, move
elsewhere. Hence Garvey took the early lead in urging black separatism.
Since "the white man of America will not, to any organized extent, assimilate the Negro, because in so doing, he feels that he will be committing
racial suicide," the two races would have to formally and finally separate.[11]
For Garvey, the "true solution of the Negro problem" could only be the
creation of Negro nations. To continue as a minority without full civil
rights would be ruinous, he held, for his people:

If the Negro were to live in this Western Hemisphere for another five
hundred years he would still be outnumbered by other races who are
prejudiced against him. He cannot resort to the government for protection
for government will be in the hands of the majority of the people on
the ballot and his industrial progress alone, will be hopeless as it does not
help him when he is lynched, burned, jim-crowed and segregated. The
future of the Negro, therefore, outside of Africa, spells ruin and disaster.[12]

With Garvey, the cycle of Negro comments upon the way to deal
with the unequal treatment given Negroes in America was complete.
Subsequent black spokesmen echo in differing degrees the civil rights
positions of Douglass and Du Bois, the self-improvement doctrines of
Washington, or the separatism of Garvey. Moreover, all these ideas
are part of the American tradition inasmuch as they attempt to treat the
problem of achieving equality in an egalitarian regime that is not
always disposed to grant it. This dilemma offers a fresh perspective on the
American political tradition but does not remove black discontent
from that tradition. If, on the one hand, it demonstrates how minorities
struggle to harmonize America's practical politics with its ideals, on

[11] "Racial Assimilation," in Amy Jacques-Garvey, ed., *Philosophy and Opinions of
Marcus Garvey* (New York: Universal Publishing House, 1923), p. 26.
[12] "The True Solution of the Negro Problem," *ibid.*, p. 53.

the other it demonstrates that minorities are committed to the same American ideals which, in other ways, move the majority. Thus, the American problem, as such, becomes how to harmonize minority and majority commitments to the same principles, and to assure that commitments to these principles are not lost. This is by no means a new situation in America, but it is no less crucial for being long established. The question remains as to whether blacks and whites can accomplish their ends and yet modify their desires and demands to the degree that will allow them to peacefully take part in American political life.

The following selections include statements of some of the more important of the early black spokesmen and selections from three Supreme Court cases which had particularly large effect on the position of Negroes in America after the Civil War. The black spokesmen are represented by Frederick Douglass, Booker T. Washington, W. E. B. Du Bois (and statements from "The Niagara Movement"), and Marcus Garvey. (More recent black leaders will be considered in the next chapter.) The court cases included are the *Civil Rights Cases, Plessy* v. *Ferguson,* and *Brown* v. *Board of Education.* This last selection fittingly concludes the chapter for it is the decision which overturns the doctrines put forth in the *Plessy* case. "Separate but equal," after *Brown* v. *Board of Ed.,* is no longer admissible doctrine in American courts or in American law. Recognizing principles that had been elucidated by Lincoln and Frederick Douglass, Chief Justice Warren—speaking for a unanimous court—made clear that segregated schools were "inherently unequal." And although the case was focused on educational facilities, its implication is that equal citizenship is incompatible with separation along racial lines. Returning to basic principles, Americans can no longer legally argue that racial segregation and equality can coexist.

FOURTH OF JULY ORATION
(1852)

Ladies and gentlemen, the distance between this platform and the slave plantation, from which I escaped, is considerable—and the difficulties to be overcome in getting from the latter to the former, are by no means slight. That I am here to-day, is, to me, a matter of astonishment as well as of gratitude. You will not, therefore, be surprised, if in what I have to say, I evince no elaborate preparation, nor grace my speech with any high sounding exordium. With little experience and less learning, I have been able to throw my thoughts hastily and imperfectly together; and trusting to your patient and generous indulgence, I will proceed to lay them before you.

This, for the purpose of this celebration, is the 4th of July. It is the birthday of your National Independence, and of your political freedom. This, to you, is what the Passover was to the emancipated people of God. It carries your minds back to the day, and to the act of your great deliverance; and to the signs, and to the wonders, associated with that act, and that day. This celebration also marks the beginning of another year of your national life; and reminds you that the Republic of America is now 76 years old. I am glad, fellow-citizens, that your nation is so young. Seventy-six years, though a good old age for a man, is but a mere speck in the life of a nation. Three score years and ten is the allotted time for individual men; but nations number their years by thousands. According to this fact, you are, even now only in the beginning of your national career, still lingering in the period of childhood. I repeat, I am glad this is so. There is hope in the thought, and hope is much needed, under the dark clouds which lower above the horizon. The eye of the reformer is met with angry flashes, portending disastrous times; but his heart may well beat lighter at the thought that America is young, and that she is still in the impressible stage of her existence. May he not hope that high

"Oration Delivered in Corinthian Hall, Rochester, New York, July 5, 1852," printed by Lee, Mann and Co., 1852. Reprinted in Herbert J. Storing, ed., *What Country Have I? Political Writings by Black Americans* (New York: St. Martin's Press, 1970), p. 28.

lessons of wisdom, of justice and of truth, will yet give direction to her destiny? Were the nation older, the patriot's heart might be sadder, and the reformer's brow heavier. Its future might be shrouded in gloom, and the hope of its prophets go out in sorrow. There is consolation in the thought, that America is young.—Great streams are not easily turned from channels, worn deep in the course of ages. They may sometimes rise in quiet and stately majesty, and inundate the land, refreshing and fertilizing the earth with their mysterious properties. They may also rise in wrath and fury, and bear away, on their angry waves, the accumulated wealth of years of toil and hardship. They, however, gradually flow back to the same old channel, and flow on as serenely as ever. But, while the river may not be turned aside, it may dry up, and leave nothing behind but the withered branch, and the unsightly rock, to howl in the abyss-sweeping wind, the sad tale of departed glory. As with rivers so with nations.

Fellow Citizens, I am not wanting in respect for the fathers of this republic. The signers of the Declaration of Independence were brave men. They were great men too—great enough to give fame to a great age. It does not often happen to a nation to raise, at one time, such a number of truly great men. The point from which I am compelled to view them is not, certainly the most favorable; and yet I cannot contemplate their great deeds with less than admiration. They were statesmen, patriots and heroes, and for the good they did, and the principles they contended for, I will unite with you to honor their memory.

They loved their country better than their own private interests; and, though this is not the highest form of human excellence, all will concede that it is a rare virtue, and that when it is exhibited, it ought to command respect. He who will, intelligently, lay down his life for his country, is a man whom it is not in human nature to despise. Your fathers staked their lives, their fortunes, and their sacred honor, on the cause of their country. In their admiration of liberty, they lost sight of all other interests.

They were peace men; but they preferred revolution to peaceful submission to bondage. They were quiet men; but they did not shrink from agitating against oppression. They showed forbearance; but that they knew its limits. They believed in order; but not in the order of tyranny. With them, nothing was *"settled"* that was not right. With them, justice, liberty and humanity were *"final;"* not slavery and oppression. You may well cherish the memory of such men. They were great in their day and generation. Their solid manhood stands out the more as we contrast it with these degenerate times.

How circumspect, exact and proportionate were all their movements! How unlike the politicians of an hour! Their statesmanship looked beyond the passing moment, and stretched away in strength into the distant future. They seized upon eternal principles, and set a glorious example in their defence. Mark them!

Fully appreciating the hardships to be encountered, firmly believing in the right of their cause, honorably inviting the scrutiny of an on-looking world, reverently appealing to heaven to attest their sincerity, soundly comprehending the solemn responsibility they were about to assume, wisely measuring the terrible odds against them, your fathers, the fathers of this republic, did, most deliberately, under the inspiration of a glorious patriotism, and with a sublime faith in the great principles of justice and freedom, lay deep, the corner-stone of the national superstructure, which has risen and still rises in grandeur around you.

Of this fundamental work, this day is the anniversary. Our eyes are met with demonstrations of joyous enthusiasm. Banners and penants wave exultingly on the breeze. The din of business, too, is hushed. Even mammon seems to have quitted his grasp on this day. The ear-piercing fife and the stirring drum unite their accents with the ascending peal of a thousand church bells. Prayers are made, hymns are sung, and sermons are preached in honor of this day; while the quick martial tramp of a great and multitudinous nation, echoed back by all the hills, valleys and mountains of a vast continent, bespeak the occasion one of thrilling and universal interest—a nation's jubilee.

Friends and citizens, I need not enter further into the causes which led to this anniversary. Many of you understand them better than I do. You could instruct me in regard to them. That is a branch of knowledge in which you feel, perhaps, a much deeper interest than your speaker. The causes which led to the separation of the colonies from the British crown have never lacked for a tongue. They have all been taught in your common schools, narrated at your firesides, unfolded from your pulpits, and thundered from your legislative halls, and are as familiar to you as household words. They form the staple of your national poetry and eloquence.

I remember, also, that, as a people, Americans are remarkably familiar with all facts which make in their own favor. This is esteemed by some as a national trait—perhaps a national weakness. It is a fact, that whatever makes for the wealth or for the reputation of Americans, and can be had *cheap!* will be found by Americans. I shall not be charged with slandering Americans, if I say I think the American side of any question may be safely left in American hands.

I leave, therefore, the great deeds of your fathers to other gentlemen whose claim to have been regularly descended will be less likely to be disputed than mine.

My business, if I have any here to-day, is with the present. The accepted time with God and his cause is the ever-living now.

> Trust no future, however pleasant,
>   Let the dead past bury its dead;
> Act, act in the living present,
>   Heart within, and God overhead.

We have to do with the past only as we can make it useful to the present and to the future. To all inspiring motives, to noble deeds which can be gained from the past, we are welcome. But now is the time, the important time. Your fathers have lived, died, and have done their work, and have done much of it well. You live and must die, and you must do your work. You have no right to enjoy a child's share in the labor of your fathers, unless your children are to be blest by your labors. You have no right to wear out and waste the hard-earned fame of your fathers to cover your indolence. Sydney Smith tells us that men seldom eulogize the wisdom and virtues of their fathers, but to excuse some folly or wickedness of their own. This truth is not a doubtful one. There are illustrations of it near and remote, ancient and modern. It was fashionable, hundreds of years ago, for the children of Jacob to boast, we have "Abraham to our father," when they had long lost Abraham's faith and spirit. That people contented themselves under the shadow of Abraham's great name, while they repudiated the deeds which made the name great. Need I remind you that a similar thing is being done all over this country to-day? Need I tell you that the Jews are not the only people who built the tombs of the prophets, and garnished the sepulchres of the righteous? Washington could not die till he had broken the chains of his slaves. Yet his monument is built up by the price of human blood, and the traders in the bodies and souls of men, shout—"We have Washington to *"our father."*—Alas! that it should be so; yet so it is.

> The evil that men do, lives after them,
> The good is oft' interred with their bones.

Fellow-citizens, pardon me, allow me to ask, why am I called upon to speak here to-day? What have I, or those I represent, to do with your national independence? Are the great principles of political freedom and of natural justice, embodied in that Declaration of Independence, extended to us? and am I, therefore, called upon to bring our humble offering to the national altar, and to confess the benefits and express devout gratitude for the blessings resulting from your independence to us?

Would to God, both for your sakes and ours, that an affirmative answer could be truthfully returned to these questions! Then would my task be light, and my burden easy and delightful. For *who* is there so cold, that a nation's sympathy could not warm him? Who so obdurate and dead to the claims of gratitude, that would not thankfully acknowledge such priceless benefits? Who so stolid and selfish, that would not give his voice to swell the hallelujahs of a nation's jubilee, when the chains of servitude had been torn from his limbs? I am not that man. In a case like that, the dumb might eloquently speak, and the "lame man leap as an hart."

But, such is not the state of the case. I say it with a sad sense of the disparity between us. I am not included within the pale of this glorious anniversary! Your high independence only reveals the immeasurable distance between us. The blessings in which you, this day, rejoice, are not enjoyed in common.—The rich inheritance of justice, liberty, prosperity and independence, bequeathed by your fathers, is shared by you, not by me. The sunlight that brought life and healing to you, has brought stripes and death to me. This Fourth July is *yours,* not *mine. You* may rejoice, *I* must mourn. To drag a man in fetters into the grand illuminated temple of liberty, and call upon him to join you in joyous anthems, were inhuman mockery and sacrilegious irony. Do you mean, citizens, to mock me, by asking me to speak to-day? If so, there is a parallel to your conduct. And let me warn you that it is dangerous to copy the example of a nation whose crimes, towering up to heaven, were thrown down by the breath of the Almighty, burying that nation in irrecoverable ruin! I can today take up the plaintive lament of a peeled and woe-smitten people!

"By the rivers of Babylon, there we sat down. Yea! we wept when we remembered Zion. We hanged our harps upon the willows in the midst thereof. For there, they that carried us away captive, required of us a song; and they who wasted us required of us mirth, saying, Sing us one of the songs of Zion. How can we sing the Lord's song in a strange land? If I forget thee, O Jerusalem, let my right hand forget her cunning. If I do not remember thee, let my tongue cleave to the roof of my mouth."

Fellow-citizens; above your national, tumultous joy, I hear the mournful wail of millions! whose chains, heavy and grievous yesterday, are, to-day, rendered more intolerable by the jubilee shouts that reach them. If I do forget, if I do not faithfully remember those bleeding children of sorrow this day, "may my right hand forget her cunning, and may my tongue cleave to the roof of my mouth!" To forget them, to pass lightly over their wrongs, and to chime in with the popular theme, would be treason most scandalous and shocking, and would make me a reproach before God and the world. My subject, then, fellow-citizens, is AMERICAN SLAVERY. I shall see, this day, and its popular characteristics, from the slave's point of view. Standing there, identified with the American bondman, making his wrongs mine, I do not hesitate to declare, with all my soul, that the character and conduct of this nation never looked blacker to me than on this 4th of July! Whether we turn to the declarations of the past, or to the professions of the present, the conduct of the nation seems equally hideous and revolting. America is false to the past, false to the present, and solemnly binds herself to be false to the future. Standing with God and the crushed and bleeding slave on this occasion, I will, in the name of humanity which is outraged, in the name of liberty which is fettered, in the name of the constitution and the Bible, which are disregarded and trampled upon, dare to call in question and to denounce, with all the emphasis I can command, everything that serves to perpetuate slavery—the great sin and shame of America! "I will not equivocate; I will not excuse;" I will use the severest language I can command; and yet not one word shall escape me that any man, whose judgment is not binded by prejudice, or who is not at heart a slaveholder, shall not confess to be right and just.

But I fancy I hear some one of my audience say, it is just in this circumstance that you and your brother abolitionists fail to make a favorable impression on the public mind. Would you argue more, and denounce less, would you persuade more, and rebuke less, your cause would be much more likely to succeed. But, I submit, where all is plain there is nothing to be argued. What point in the anti-slavery creed would you have me argue? On what branch of the subject do the people of this country need light? Must I undertake to prove that the slave is a man? That point is conceded already. Nobody doubts it. The slaveholders themselves acknowledge it in the enactment of laws for their government. They acknowledge it when they punish disobedience on the part of the slave. There are seventy-two crimes in the State of Virginia, which, if committed by a black man (no matter how ignorant he be), subject him to the punishment of death; while only two of the same crimes will subject a white man to the like punishment.—What is this but the acknowledgement that the slave is a moral, intellectual and responsible being. The manhood of the slave is conceded. It is admitted in the fact that Southern statute books are covered with enactments forbidding, under severe fines and penalties, the teaching of the slave to read or to write.—When you can point to any such laws, in reference to the beasts of the field, then I may consent to argue the manhood of the slave. When the dogs in your streets, when the fowls of the air, when the cattle on your hills, when the fish of the sea, and the reptiles that crawl, shall be unable to distinguish the slave from a brute, *then* will I argue with you that the slave is a man!

For the present, it is enough to affirm the equal manhood of the negro race. Is it not astonishing that, while we are ploughing, planting and reaping, using all kinds of mechanical tools, erecting houses, constructing bridges, building ships, working in metals of brass, iron, copper, silver and gold; that, while we are reading, writing and cyphering, acting as clerks, merchants and secretaries, having among us lawyers, doctors, ministers, poets, authors, editors, orators and teachers; that, while we are engaged in all manner of enterprises common to other men, digging gold in California, capturing the whale in the Pacific, feeding sheep and cattle on the hill-side, living, moving, acting, thinking, planning, living in families as husbands, wives and children, and, above all, confessing and worshipping the Christian's God, and looking hopefully for life and immortality beyond the grave, we are called upon to prove that we are men!

Would you have me argue that man is entitled to liberty? that he is the rightful owner of his own body? You have already declared it. Must I argue that wrongfulness of slavery? Is that a question for Republicans? Is it to be settled by the rules of logic and argumentation, as a matter beset with great difficulty, involving a doubtful application of the principle of justice, hard to be understood? How should I look to-day, in the presence of Americans, dividing, and subdividing a discourse, to show that men have a natural right to freedom? speaking of it relatively, and positively, negatively, and affirmatively. To do so, would be to make myself ridiculous, and to offer an insult to your understanding.—There is not a man beneath the canopy of heaven, that does not know that slavery is wrong *for him.*

What, am I to argue that it is wrong to make men brutes, to rob them of their liberty, to work them without wages, to keep them ignorant of their relations to their fellow men, to beat them with sticks, to flay their flesh with the lash, to load their limbs with irons, to hunt them with dogs, to sell them at auction, to sunder their families, to knock out their teeth, to burn their flesh, to starve them into obedience and submission to their masters? Must I argue that a system thus marked with blood, and stained with pollution, is *wrong?* No! I will not. I have better employment for my time and strength, than such arguments would imply.

What, then, remains to be argued? Is it that slavery is not divine; that God did not establish it; that our doctors of divinity are mistaken? There is blasphemy in the thought. That which is inhuman, cannot be divine! *Who* can reason on such a proposition? They that can, may; I cannot. The time for such argument is past.

At a time like this, scorching irony, not convincing argument, is needed. O! had I the ability, and could I reach the nation's ear, I would, to-day, pour out a fiery stream of biting ridicule, blasting reproach, withering sarcasm, and stern rebuke. For it is not light that is needed, but fire; it is not the gentle shower, but thunder. We need the storm, the whirlwind, and the earthquake. The feeling of the nation must be quickened; the conscience of the nation must be roused; the propriety of the nation must be startled; the hypocrisy of the nation must be exposed; and its crimes against God and man must be proclaimed and denounced.

What, to the American slave, is your 4th of July? I answer; a day that reveals to him, more than all other days in the year, the gross injustice and cruelty to which he is the constant victim. To him, your celebration is a sham; your boasted liberty, an unholy license; your national greatness, swelling vanity; your sounds of rejoicing are empty and heartless; your denunciations of tyrants, brass fronted impudence; your shouts of liberty and equality, hollow mockery; your prayers and hymns, your sermons and thanksgivings, with all your religious parade, and solemnity, are, to him, mere bombast, fraud, deception, impiety, and hypocrisy—a thin veil to cover up crimes which would disgrace a nation of savages. There is not a nation on the earth guilty of practices, more shocking and bloody, than are the people of these United States, at this very hour.

Go where you may, search where you will, roam through all the monarchies and despotisms of the old world, travel through South America, search out every abuse, and when you have found the last, lay your facts by the side of the every day practices of this nation, and you will say with me, that, for revolting barbarity and shameless hypocrisy, America reigns without a rival. . . .

Americans! your republican politics, not less than your republican religion, are flagrantly inconsistent. You boast of your love of liberty, your superior civilization, and your pure christianity, while the whole political power of the nation, as embodied in the two great political parties, is solemnly pledged to support and perpetuate the enslavement of three millions of your countrymen. You hurl your anathemas at the crowned headed tyrants of Russia and Austria, and pride yourselves on your Democratic institutions, while you yourselves consent to be the mere *tools* and *body-guards* of the tyrants of Virginia and Carolina. You invite to your shores fugitives of oppression from abroad, honor them with banquets, greet them with ovations, cheer them, toast them, salute them, protect them, and pour out your money to them like water; but the fugitives from your own land, you advertise, hunt, arrest, shoot and kill. You glory in your refinement, and your universal education; yet you maintain a system as barbarous and dreadful, as ever stained the character of a nation—a system begun in avarice, supported in pride, and perpetuated in cruelty. You shed tears over fallen Hungary, and make the sad story of her wrongs the theme of your poets, statesmen and orators, till your gallant sons are ready to fly to arms to vindicate her cause against her oppressors; but, in regard to the ten thousand wrongs of the American slave, you would enforce the strictest silence, and would hail him as an enemy of the nation who dares to make those wrongs the subject of public discourse! You are all on fire at the mention of liberty for France or for Ireland; but are as cold as an iceberg at the thought of liberty for the enslaved of America.—You discourse eloquently on the dignity of labor; yet, you sustain a system which, in its very essence, casts a stigma upon labor. You can bare your bosom to the storm of British artillery, to throw off a three-penny tax on tea; and yet wring the last hard earned farthing from the grasp of the black laborers of your country. You profess to believe "that, of one blood, God made all nations of men to dwell on the face of all the earth," and hath commanded all men, everywhere to love one another; yet you notoriously hate, (and glory in your hatred,) all men whose skins are not colored like your own. You declare, before the world, and are understood by the world to declare, that you *"hold these truths to be self evident, that all men are created equal; and are endowed by their Creator with certain inalienable rights; and that, among these are, life, liberty, and the pursuit of happiness;"* and yet, you hold securely, in a bondage, which according to your own Thomas Jefferson, *"is worse than ages of that which your fathers rose in rebellion to oppose,"* a *seventh part* of the inhabitants of your country.

Fellow-citizens! I will not enlarge further on your national inconsistencies. The existence of slavery in this country brands your republicanism as a sham, your humanity as a base pretence, and your christianity as a lie. It destroys your moral power abroad [;] it corrupts your politicians at home. It saps the foundation of religion; it makes your name a hissing, and a bye-word to a mocking earth. It is the antagonistic force in your government, the only thing that seriously disturbs and endangers your *Union*. It fetters your progress; it is the enemy of improvement, the deadly foe of education; it fosters pride; it breeds insolence; it promotes vice; it shelters crime; it is a curse to the earth that supports it; and yet, you cling to it, as if it were the sheet anchor of all your hopes. Oh! be warned! be warned! a horrible reptile is coiled up in your nation's bosom; the venomous creature is nursing at the tender breast of your youthful republic; *for the love of God, tear away,* and fling from you the hidious monster, and *let the weight of twenty millions, crush and destroy it forever!*

But it is answered in reply to all this, that precisely what I have now denounced is, in fact, guaranteed and sanctioned by the Constitution of the United States; that, the right to hold, and to hunt slaves is a part of that Constitution framed by the illustrious Fathers of this Republic.

Then, I dare to affirm, notwithstanding all I have said before, your fathers stooped, basely stooped

> To palter with us in a double sense:
> And keep the word of promise to the ear,
> But break it to the heart.

And instead of being the honest men I have before declared them to be, they were the veriest imposters that ever practised on mankind. *This* is the inevitable conclusion, and from it there is no escape; but I differ from those who charge this baseness on the framers of the Constitution of the United States. *It is a slander upon their memory,* at least, so I believe. There is not time now to argue the constitutional question at length; nor have I the ability to discuss it as it ought to be discussed. The subject has been handled with masterly power by Lysander Spooner, Esq., by William Goodell, by Samuel E. Sewall, Esq., and last, though not least, by Gerritt Smith, Esq. These gentlemen have, as I think, fully and clearly vindicated the Constitution from any design to support slavery for an hour.

Fellow-citizens! there is no matter in respect to which, the people of the North have allowed themselves to be so ruinously imposed upon, as that of the pro-slavery character of the Constitution. In *that* instrument I hold there is neither warrant, license, nor sanction of the hateful thing; but interpreted, as it *ought* to be interpreted, the Constitution is a GLORIOUS LIBERTY DOCUMENT. Read its preamble, consider its purposes. Is slavery among them? Is it at the gateway? or is it in the temple? it is neither. While I do not intend to argue this question on the present occasion, let me ask, if it be not somewhat singular that, if the Constitution were intended to be, by its framers and adopters, a slaveholding instrument, why neither *slavery, slaveholding,* nor *slave* can anywhere be found in it. What would be thought of an instrument, drawn up, *legally* drawn up, for the purpose of entitling the city of Rochester to a track of land, in which no mention of land was made? Now, there are certain rules of interpretation, for the proper understanding of all legal instruments. These rules are well established. They are plain, common-sense rules, such as you and I, and all of us, can understand and apply, without having passed years in the study of law. I scout the idea that the question of the constitutionality, or unconstitutionality of slavery, is not a question for the people. I hold that every American citizen has a right to form an opinion of the constitution, and to propagate that opinion, and to use all honorable means to make his opinion the prevailing one. Without this right, the liberty of an American citizen would be as insecure as that of a Frenchman. Ex-Vice-President Dallas tells us that the constitution is an object to which no American mind can be too attentive, and no American heart too devoted. He further says, the constitution, in its words, is plain and intelligible, and is meant for the home-bred, unsophisticated understandings of our fellow-citizens. Senator Berrien tells us that the Constitution is the fundamental law, that which controls all others. The charter of our liberties, which every citizen has a personal interest in understanding thoroughly. The testimony of Senator Breese, Lewis Cass, and many others that might be named, who are everywhere esteemed as sound lawyers, so regard the constitution. I take it, therefore, that it is not presumption in a private citizen to form an opinion of that instrument.

Now, take the constitution according to its plain reading, and I defy the presentation of a single pro-slavery clause in it. On the other hand it will be found to contain principles and purposes, entirely hostile to the existence of slavery.

I have detained my audience entirely too long already. At some future period I will gladly avail myself of an opportunity to give this subject a full and fair discussion.

Allow me to say, in conclusion, notwithstanding the dark picture I have this day presented, of the state of the nation, I do not despair of this country. There are forces in operation, which must inevitably, work the downfall of slavery. *"The arm of the Lord is not shortened,"* and the doom of slavery is certain. I, therefore, leave off where I began, with *hope*. While drawing encouragement from "the Declaration of Independence," the great principles it contains, and the genius of American Institutions, my spirit is also cheered by the obvious tendencies of the age. Nations do not now stand in the same relation to each other that they did ages ago. No nation can now shut itself up, from the surrounding world, and trot round in the same old path of its fathers without interference. The time *was* when such could be done. Long established customs of hurtful character could formerly fence themselves in, and do their evil work with social impunity. Knowledge was then confined and enjoyed by the privileged few, and the multitude walked on in mental darkness. But a change has now come over the affairs of mankind. Walled cities and empires have become unfashionable. The arm of commerce has borne away the gates of the strong city. Intelligence is penetrating the darkest corners of the globe. It makes its pathway over and under the sea, as well as on the earth. Wind, steam, and lightning are its chartered agents. Oceans no longer divide, but link nations together. From Boston to London is now a holiday excursion. Space is comparatively annihilated.—Thoughts expressed on one side of the Atlantic, are distinctly heard on the other.

The far off and almost fabulous Pacific rolls in grandeur at our feet. The Celestial Empire, the mystery of ages, is being solved. The fiat of the Almighty, *"Let there be Light,"* has not yet spent its force. No abuse, no outrage whether in taste, sport or avarice, can now hide itself from the all-pervading light. The iron shoe, and crippled foot of China must be seen, in contrast with nature. *Africa must rise and put on her yet unwoven garment. "Ethiopia shall stretch out her hand unto God.".* .

CIVIL RIGHTS CASES
109 U.S. 3 (1883)

Mr. Justice Bradley delivered the opinion of the Court:

It is obvious that the primary and important question in all the cases, is the constitutionality of the law; for if the law is unconstitutional, none of the prosecutions can stand. . . .

Are [Sections 1 and 2 of the Civil Rights Act of 1875] constitutional? The first section, which is the principal one, cannot be fairly understood without attending to the last clause, which qualifies the preceding part.

The essence of the law is, not to declare broadly that all persons shall be entitled to the full and equal enjoyment of the accommodations, advantages, facilities, and privileges of inns, public conveyances, and theatres; but that such enjoyment shall not be subject to any conditions applicable only to citizens of a particular race or color, or who had been in a previous condition of servitude. In other words, it is the purpose of the law to declare that, in the enjoyment of the accommodations and privileges of inns, public conveyances, theatres, and other places of public amusement, no distinction shall be made between citizens of different race or color, or between those who have, and those who have not, been slaves. Its effect is to declare, that in all inns, public conveyances, and places of amusement, colored citizens, whether formerly slaves or not, and citizens of other races, shall have the same accommodations and privileges in all inns, public conveyances, and places of amusement as are enjoyed by white citizens; and *vice versa*. The second section makes it a penal offence in any person to deny to any citizen of any race or color, regardless of previous servitude, any of the accommodations or privileges mentioned in the first section.

Has Congress constitutional power to make such a law? Of course, no one will contend that the power to pass it was contained in the Constitution before the adoption of the last three amendments. The power is sought, first, in the Fourteenth Amendment, and the views and arguments of distinguished Senators, advanced whilst the law was under consideration, claiming authority to pass it by virtue of that amendment, are the principal arguments adduced in favor of the power. We have carefully considered those arguments, as was due to the eminent ability of those who put them forward, and have felt, in all its force, the weight of authority which always invests a law that Congress deems itself competent to pass. But the responsibility of an independent judgment is now thrown upon this court; and we are bound to exercise it according to the best lights we have.

The 1st section of the 14th Amendment, which is the one relied on, after declaring who shall be citizens of the United States, and of the several States, is prohibitory in its character, and prohibitory upon the States. It declares that "No State shall make or enforce any law which shall abridge the privileges or immunities of citizens of the United States; nor shall any State deprive any person of life, liberty or property without due process of law; nor deny to any person within its jurisdiction the equal protection of the laws." It is state action of a particular character that is prohibited. Individual invasion of individual rights is not the subject-matter of the Amendment. It has a deeper and broader scope. It nullifies and makes void all state legislation, and state action of every kind, which impairs the privileges and immunities of citizens of the United States, or which injures them in life, liberty or property without due process of law, or which denies to any of them the equal protection of the laws. It not only does this, but, in order that the national will, thus declared, may not be a mere *brutum fulmen* [an empty noise or threat], the last section of the Amendment invests Congress with power to enforce it by appropriate legislation. To enforce what? To enforce the prohibition. To adopt appropriate legislation for correcting the effects of such prohibited state laws and state Acts, and thus to render them effectually null, void and innocuous. This is the legislative power conferred upon Congress, and this is the whole of it. It does not invest Congress with power to legislate upon subjects which are within the domain of state legislation; but to provide modes of relief against state legislation or state action, of the kind referred to. It does not authorize Congress to create a code of municipal law for the regulation of private rights; but to provide modes of redress against the operation of state laws, and the action of state officers executive or judicial, when these are subversive of the fundamental rights specified in the Amendment. Positive rights and privileges are undoubtedly secured by the 14th Amendment; but they are secured by way of prohibition against state laws and state proceedings affecting those rights and privileges, and by power given to Congress to legislate for the purpose of carrying such prohibition into effect; and such legislation must, necessarily, be predicated upon such supposed state laws or state proceedings, and be directed to the correction of their operation and effect. . . .

And so in the present case, until some state law has been passed or some state action through its officers or agents has been taken, adverse to the rights of citizens sought to be protected by the 14th Amendment, no legislation of the United States under said Amendment, nor any proceedings under such legislation, can be called into activity; for the prohibitions of the Amendment are against state laws and acts done under state authority. Of course, legislation may and should be provided in advance to meet the exigency when it arises; but it should be adapted to the mischief and wrong which the Amendment was intended to provide against; and that is, state laws, or state action of some kind, adverse to the rights of the citizen secured by the Amendment. Such legislation cannot properly cover the whole domain of rights appertaining to life, liberty and property, defining them and providing for their vindication. That would be to establish a code of municipal law regulative of all private rights between man and man in society. It would be to make Congress take the place of the State Legislatures and to supersede them. It is absurd to affirm that, because the rights of life, liberty and property, which include all civil rights that men have, are, by the Amendment, sought to be protected against invasion on the part of the State without due process of law, Congress may, therefore, provide due process of law for their vindication in every case; and that, because the denial by a State to any persons, of equal protection of the laws, is prohibited by the Amendment, therefore Congress may establish laws for their equal protection. In fine, the legislation which Congress is authorized to adopt in this behalf is not general legislation upon the rights of the citizen, but corrective legislation, that is, such as may be necessary and proper for counteracting such laws as the States may adopt or enforce, and which, by the Amendment, they are prohibited from making or enforcing, or such acts and proceedings as the States may commit or take, and which, by the Amendment, they are prohibited from committing or taking. It is not necessary for us to state, if we could, what legislation would be proper for Congress to adopt. It is sufficient for us to examine whether the law in question is of that character.

An inspection of the law shows that it makes no reference whatever to any supposed or apprehended violation of the 14th Amendment on the part of the States. It is not predicated on any such view. It proceeds *ex directo* to declare that certain acts committed by individuals shall be deemed offenses, and shall be prosecuted and punished by proceedings in the courts of the United States. It does not profess to be corrective of any constitutional wrong committed by the States; it does not make its operation to depend upon any such wrong committed. It applies equally to cases arising in States which have the justest laws respecting the personal rights of citizens, and whose authorities are ever ready to enforce such laws, as to those which arise in States that may have violated the prohibition of the Amendment. In other words, it steps into the domain of local jurisprudence, and lays down rules for the conduct of individuals in society towards each other, and imposes sanctions for the enforcement of those rules, without referring in any manner to any supposed action of the State or its authorities.

If this legislation is appropriate for enforcing the prohibitions of the Amendment, it is difficult to see where it is to stop. Why may not Congress with equal show of authority enact a code of laws for the enforcement and vindication of all rights of life, liberty and property? If it is supposable that the States may deprive persons of life, liberty and property without due process of law, and the Amendment itself does suppose this, why should not Congress proceed at once to prescribe due process of law for the protection of every one of these fundamental rights, in every possible case, as well as to prescribe equal privileges in inns, public conveyances and theaters? The truth is, that the implication of a power to legislate in this manner is based upon the assumption that if the States are forbidden to legislate or act in a particular way on a particular subject, and power is conferred upon Congress to enforce the prohibition, this gives Congress power to legislate generally upon that subject, and not merely power to provide modes of redress against such state legislation or action. The assumption is certainly unsound. It is repugnant to the 10th Amendment of the Constitution, which declares that powers not delegated to the United States by the Constitution, nor prohibited by it to the States, are reserved to the States respectively or to the people. . . .

If the principles of interpretation which we have laid down are correct, as we deem them to be . . . it is clear that the law in question cannot be sustained by any grant of legislative power made to Congress by the Fourteenth Amendment. That amendment prohibits the States from denying to any person the equal protection of the laws, and declares that Congress shall have power to enforce, by appropriate legislation, the provisions of the amendment. The law in question, without any reference to adverse State legislation on the subject, declares that all persons shall be entitled to equal accommodations and privileges of inns, public conveyances, and places of public amusement, and imposes a penalty upon any individual who shall deny to any citizen such equal accommodations and privileges. This is not corrective legislation; it is primary and direct; it takes immediate and absolute possession of the subject of the right of admission to inns, public conveyances, and places of amusement. It supersedes and displaces State legislation on the same subject, or only allows it permissive force. It ignores such legislation, and assumes that the matter is one that belongs to the domain of national regulation. Whether it would not have been a more effective protection of the rights of citizens to have clothed Congress with plenary power over the whole subject, is not now the question. What we have to decide is, whether such plenary power has been conferred upon Congress by the Fourteenth Amendment; and, in our judgment, it has not. . . .

Now, conceding, for the sake of the argument, that the admission to an inn, a public conveyance or a place of public amusement, on equal terms with all other citizens, is the right of every man and all classes of men, is it any more than one of those rights which the States by the 14th Amendment are forbidden to deny any person? And is the Constitution violated until the denial of the right has some state sanction or authority? Can the act of a mere individual, the owner of the inn, the public conveyance or place of amusement, refusing the accommodation, be justly regarded as imposing any badge of slavery or servitude upon the applicant or only as inflicting an ordinary civil injury, properly cognizable by the laws of the State, and presumably subject to redress by those laws until the contrary appears?

After giving to these questions all the consideration which their importance demands, we are forced to the conclusion that such an act of refusal has nothing to do with slavery or involuntary servitude, and that if it is violative of any right of the party, his redress is to be sought under the laws of the State; or if those laws are adverse to his rights and do not protect him, his remedy will be found in the corrective legislation which Congress has adopted, or may adopt, for counteracting the effect of state laws, of state action, prohibited by the 14th Amendment. It would be running the slavery argument into the ground, to make it apply to every act of discrimination which a person may see fit to make as to the guests he will entertain, or as to the people he will take into his coach or cab or car, or admit to his concert or theater, or deal with in other matters of intercourse or business. Inkeepers and public carriers, by the laws of all the States, so far as we are aware, are bound, to the extent of their facilities, to furnish proper accommodations to all unobjectionable persons who in good faith apply for them. If the laws themselves make any unjust discrimination, amenable to the prohibitions of the 14th Amendment, Congress has full power to afford a remedy, under that Amendment and in accordance with it.

When a man has emerged from slavery, and by the aid of beneficent legislation has shaken off the inseparable concomitants of that state, there must be some stage in the progress of his elevation when he takes the rank of a mere citizen, and ceases to be the special favorite of the laws, and when his rights, as a citizen or a man, are to be protected in the ordinary modes by which other men's rights are protected. There were thousands of free colored people in this country before the abolition of slavery, enjoying all the essential rights of life, liberty and property the same as white citizens; yet no one, at that time, thought that it was any invasion of their personal status as freemen because they were not admitted to all the privileges enjoyed by white citizens, or because they were subjected to discriminations in the enjoyment of accommodations in inns, public conveyances and places of amusement. Mere discriminations on account of race or color were not regarded as badges of slavery. If, since that time, the enjoyment of equal rights in all these respects has become established by constitutional enactment, it is not by force of the 13th Amendment, which merely abolishes slavery, but by force of the 14 and 15th Amendments.

On the whole we are of opinion, that no countenance of authority for the passage of the law in question can be found in either the 13th or 14th Amendment of the Constitution; and no other ground of authority for its passage being suggested, it must necessarily be declared void, at least so far as its operation in the several States is concerned.

This conclusion disposes of the cases now under consideration.

Frederick Douglass

CRITICISM OF
CIVIL RIGHTS CASE

I have only a very few words to say to you this evening, and in order that those few words shall be well-chosen, and not liable to be misunderstood, distorted, or misrepresented, I have been at the pains of writing them out in full. It may be, after all, that the hour calls more loudly for silence than for speech. Later on in this discussion, when we shall have the full text of the recent decision of the Supreme Court before us, and the dissenting opinion of Judge Harlan, who must have weighty reasons for separating from all his associates, and incurring thereby, as he must, an amount of criticism from which even the bravest man might shrink, we may be in better frame of mind, better supplied with facts, and better prepared to speak calmly, correctly, and wisely, than now. The temptation at this time, is of course, to speak more from feeling than reason, more from impulse than reflection.

We have been, as a class, grievously wounded, wounded in the house of our friends, and this wound is too deep and too painful for ordinary measured speech.

> When a deed is done for Freedom,
> Through the broad earth's aching breast
> Runs a thrill of joy prophetic,
> Trembling on from east to west.

But when a deed is done from slavery, caste and oppression, and a blow is struck at human progress, whether so intended or not, the heart of our humanity sickens in sorrow and writhes in pain. It makes us feel as if some one were stamping upon the graves of our mothers, or desecrating our sacred temples of worship. Only base men and oppressors can rejoice in a triumph of injustice over the weak and defenceless, for weakness ought itself to protect from assaults of pride, prejudice and power.

"Proceedings of the Civil Rights Mass Meeting . . . (1883)," *Speeches of Hon. Frederick Douglass and Robert G. Ingersoll* (Washington, D.C.: n. p., 1883).

The cause which has brought us here to-night is neither common nor trivial. Few events in our national history have surpassed it in magnitude, importance and significance. It has swept over the land like a moral cyclone, leaving moral desolation in its track.

We feel it, as we felt the furious attempt, years ago, to force the accursed system of slavery upon the soil of Kansas, the enactment of the Fugitive Slave Bill, the repeal of the Missouri Compromise, the Dred Scott decision. I look upon it as one more shocking development of that moral weakness in high places which has attended the conflict between the spirit of liberty and the spirit of slavery from the beginning, and I venture to predict that it will be so regarded by after-coming generations.

Far down the ages, when men shall wish to inform themselves as to the real state of liberty, law, religion and civilization in the United States at this juncture of our history, they will overhaul the proceedings of the Supreme Court, and read the decision declaring the Civil Rights Bill unconstitutional and void. . . .

I am not here, in this presence, to discuss the constitutionality or unconstitutionality of this decision of the Supreme Court. The decision may or may not be constitutional. That is a question for lawyers, and not for laymen, and there are lawyers on this platform as learned, able, and eloquent as any who have appeared in this case before the Supreme Court, or as any in the land. To these I leave the exposition of the Constitution; but I claim the right to remark upon a strange and glaring inconsistency with former decisions, in the action of the court on this Civil Rights Bill. It is a new departure, entirely out of the line of the precedents and decisions of the Supreme Court at other times and in other directions where the rights of colored men were concerned. It has utterly ignored and rejected the force and application of object and intention as a rule of interpretation. It has construed the Constitution in defiant disregard of what was the object and intention of the adoption of the Fourteenth Amendment. It has made no account whatever of the intention and purpose of Congress and the President in putting the Civil Rights Bill upon the Statute Book of the Nation. It has seen fit in this case, affecting a weak and much-persecuted people, to be guided by the narrowest and most restricted rules of legal interpretation. It has viewed both the Constitution and the law with a strict regard to their letter, but without any generous recognition of their broad and liberal spirit. Upon those narrow principles the decision is logical and legal, of course. But what I complain of, and what every lover of liberty in the United States has a right to complain of, is this sudden and causeless reversal of all the great rules of legal interpretation by which this Court was governed in other days, in the construction of the Constitution and of laws respecting colored people.

In the dark day of slavery, this Court, on all occasions, gave the greatest importance to *intention* as a guide to interpretation. The object and *intention* of the law, it was said, must prevail. Everything in favor of slavery and against the Negro was settled by this object and *intention*. The Constitution was construed according to its *intention*. We were over and over again referred to what the framers *meant*, and plain language was sacrificed that the so affirmed *intention* of these framers might be positively asserted. When we said in behalf of the Negro that the Constitution of the United States was intended to establish justice and to secure the blessings of liberty to ourselves and our posterity, we were told that the words said so but that that was obviously not its *intention;* that it was intended to apply only to white people, and that the *intention* must govern.

When we came to that clause of the Constitution which declares that the immigration or importation of such persons as any of the States may see fit to admit shall not be prohibited, and the friends of liberty declared that that provision of the Constitution did not describe the slave-trade, they were told that while its language applied not to slaves, but to persons, still the object and *intention* of that clause of the Constitution was plainly to protect the slave-trade and that that *intention* was the law. When we came to that clause of the Constitution which declares that "No person held to service or labor in one State, under the laws thereof, escaping into another, shall in consequence of any law or regulation therein be discharged from such service or labor, but shall be delivered up on claim of the party to whom such service or labor may be due," we insisted that it neither described nor applied to slaves; that it applied only to persons owing service and labor; that slaves did not and could not owe service and labor; that this clause of the Constitution said nothing of slaves or the masters of slaves; that it was silent as to slave States or free States; that it was simply a provision to enforce a contract; to discharge an obligation between two persons capable of making a contract, and not to force any man into slavery, for the slave could not owe service or make a contract.

We affirmed that it gave no warrant for what was called the "Fugitive Slave Bill," and we contended that that bill was therefore unconstitutional; but our arguments were laughed to scorn by that Court. We were told that the *intention* of the Constitution was to enable masters to recapture their slaves, and that the law of Ninety-three and the Fugitive Slave Law of 1850 were constitutional.

Fellow-citizens! While slavery was the base line of American society, while it ruled the church and the state, while it was the interpreter of our law and the exponent of our religion, it admitted no quibbling, no narrow rules of legal or scriptural interpretations of Bible or Constitution. It sternly demanded its pound of flesh, no matter how much blood was shed in the taking of it. It was enough for it to be able to show the *intention* to get all it asked in the Courts or out of the Courts. But now slavery is abolished. Its reign was long, dark and bloody. Liberty *now,* is the base line of the Republic. Liberty has supplanted slavery, but I fear it has not supplanted the spirit or power of slavery. Where slavery was strong, liberty is now weak.

O for a Supreme Court of the United States which shall be as true to the claims of humanity as the Supreme Court formerly was to the demands of slavery! When that day comes, as come it will, a Civil Rights Bill will not be declared unconstitutional and void, in utter and flagrant disregard of the objects and *intentions* of the National legislature by which it was enacted, and of the rights plainly secured by the Constitution.

This decision of the Supreme Court admits that the Fourteenth Amendment is a prohibition on the States. It admits that a State shall not abridge the privileges or immunities of citizens of the United States, but commits the seeming absurdity of allowing the people of a State to do what it prohibits the State itself from doing. . . .

It is said that this decision will make no difference in the treatment of colored people; that the Civil Rights Bill was a dead letter, and could not be enforced. There is some truth in all this, but it is not the whole truth. That bill, like all advance legislation, was a banner on the outer wall of American liberty, a noble moral standard, uplifted for the education of the American people. There are tongues in trees, books, in the running brooks,—sermons in stones. This law, though dead, did speak. It expressed the sentiment of justice and fair play, common to every honest heart. Its voice was against popular prejudice and meanness. It appealed to all the noble and patriotic instincts of the American people. It told the American people that they were all equal before the law; that they belonged to a common country and were equal citizens. The Supreme Court has hauled down this flag of liberty in open day, and before all the people, and has thereby given joy to the heart of every man in the land who wishes to deny to others what he claims for himself. It is a concession to race pride, selfishness and meanness, and will be received with joy by every upholder of caste in the land, and for this I deplore and denounce that decision.

THE FUTURE
OF THE NEGRO
(1884)

It would require the ken of a statesman and the vision of a prophet combined to tell with certainty what will be the ultimate future of the colored people of the United States, and to neither of these qualifications can I lay claim. We have known the colored man long as a slave, but we have not known him long as a freeman and as an American citizen. What he was as a slave we know; what he will be in his new relation to his fellowmen, time and events will make clear. One thing, however, may safely be laid down as probable, and that is, that the Negro, in one form and complexion or another, may be counted upon as a permanent element of the population of the United States. He is now seven millions, has doubled his number in thirty years, and is increasing more rapidly than the more favored population of the South. The idea of his becoming extinct finds no support in this fact. But will he emigrate? No! Individuals may, but the masses will not. Dust will fly, but the earth will remain. The expense of removal to a foreign land, the difficulty of finding a country where the conditions of existence are more favorable than here, attachment to native land, gradual improvement in moral surroundings, increasing hope of a better future, improvement in character and value by education, impossibility of finding any part of the globe free from the presence of white men,—all conspire to keep the Negro here, and compel him to adjust himself to American civilization.

In the face of history I do not deny that a darker future than I have indicated may await the black man. Contact of weak races with strong has not always been beneficent. The weak have been oppressed, persecuted, driven out, and destroyed. The Hebrews in Egypt, the Moors in Spain, the Caribs in the West Indies, the Picts in Scotland, the Indians and Chinese in our own country, show what may happen to the Negro. But happily he has a moral and political hold upon this country, deep and firm, one which

Frederick Douglass, "The Future of the Negro," *North American Review* (July 1884), pp. 84–86.

in some measure destroys the analogy between him and other weak peoples and classes. His religion and civilization are in harmony with those of the people among whom he lives. He worships with them in a common temple and at a common altar, and to drag him away is to destroy the temple and tear down the altar. Drive out the Negro and you drive out Christ, the Bible, and American liberty with him. The thought of setting apart a State or Territory and confining the Negro within its borders is a delusion. If the North and South could not live separately in peace, and without bloody and barbarous border wars, the white and black cannot. If the Negro could be bottled up, who could or would bottle up the irrepressible white man? What barrier has been strong enough to confine him? Plainly enough, migration is no policy for the Negro. He would invite the fate of the Indian, and be pushed away before the white man's bayonet.

Nor do I think that the Negro will become more distinct as a class. Ignorant, degraded, and repulsive as he was during his two hundred years of slavery, he was sufficiently attractive to make possible an intermediate race of a million, more or less. If this has taken place in the face of those odious barriers, what is likely to occur when the colored man puts away his ignorance and degradation and becomes educated and prosperous? The tendency of the age is unification, not isolation; not to clans and classes, but to human brotherhood. It was once degradation intensified for a Norman to associate with a Saxon; but time and events have swept down the barriers between them, and Norman and Saxon have become Englishmen. The Jew was once despised and hated in Europe, and is so still in some parts of that continent; but he has risen, and is rising to higher consideration, and no man is now degraded by association with him anywhere. In like manner the Negro will rise in social scale. For a time the social and political privileges of the colored people may decrease. This, however, will be apparent rather than real. An abnormal condition, born of war, carried him to an altitude unsuited to his attainments. He could not sustain himself there. He will now rise naturally and gradually, and hold on to what he gets, and will not drop from dizziness. He will gain both by concession and by self-assertion. Shrinking cowardice wins nothing from either meanness or magnanimity. Manly self-assertion and eternal vigilance are essential to Negro liberty, not less than to that of the white man.

Booker T. Washington

ATLANTA EXPOSITION ADDRESS (1895)

One third of the population of the South is of the Negro race. No enter-prise seeking the material, civil, or moral welfare of this section can disre-gard this element of our population and reach the highest success. I but convey to you, Mr. President and Directors, the sentiment of the masses of my race when I say that in no way have the value and manhood of the American Negro been more fittingly and generously recognized than by the managers of this magnificent exposition at every stage of its progress. It is a recognition that will do more to cement the friendship of the two races than any occurrence since the dawn of our freedom.

Not only this, but the opportunity here afforded will awaken among us a new era of industrial progress. Ignorant and inexperienced, it is not strange that in the first years of our new life we began at the top instead of at the bottom; that a seat in Congress or the State Legislature was more sought than real estate or industrial skill; that the political convention or stump-speaking had more attraction than starting a dairy farm or truck garden.

A ship lost at sea for many days suddenly sighted a friendly vessel. From the mast of the unfortunate vessel was seen a signal: "Water, water; we die of thirst!" The answer from the friendly vessel at once came back: "Cast down your bucket where you are." A second time the signal, "Water, water; send us water!" ran up from the distressed vessel, and was an-swered: "Cast down your bucket where you are." And a third and fourth signal for water was answered, "Cast down your bucket where you are." The captain of the distressed vessel, at last heeding the injunction, cast down his bucket, and it came up full of fresh, sparkling water from the mouth of the Amazon River. To those of my race who depend upon bettering their condition in a foreign land, or who underestimate the importance of cultivating friendly relations with the Southern white man who is their next-door neighbor, I would say: "Cast down your bucket

Booker T. Washington, *The Story of My Life and Times* (Naperville, Ill., and Atlanta: n. p., 1900), pp. 165–171.

where you are"—cast it down in making friends, in every manly way, of the people of all races by whom we are surrounded.

Cast it down in agriculture, mechanics, in commerce, in domestic service, and in the professions. And in this connection it is well to bear in mind that whatever other sins the South may be called to bear, when it comes to business, pure and simple, it is in the South that the Negro is given a man's chance in the commercial world, and in nothing is this Exposition more eloquent than in emphasizing this chance. Our greatest danger is that in the great leap from slavery to freedom we may over-look the fact that the masses of us are to live by the productions of our hands, and fail to keep in mind that we shall prosper in proportion as we learn to dignify and glorify common labor, and put brains and skill into the common occupations of life; shall prosper in proportion as we learn to draw the line between the superficial and the substantial, the ornamental gewgaws of life and the useful. No race can prosper till it learns that there is as much dignity in tilling a field as in writing a poem. It is at the bottom of life we must begin, and not at the top. Nor should we permit our grievances to overshadow our opportunities.

To those of the white race who look to the incoming of those of foreign birth and strange tongue and habits for the prosperity of the South, were I permitted, I would repeat what I say to my own race, "Cast down your bucket where you are." Cast it down among the eight million Negroes whose habits you know, whose fidelity and love you have tested in days when to have proved treacherous meant the ruin of your firesides. Cast down your bucket among these people who have without strikes and labor wars tilled your fields, cleared your forests, builded your railroads and cities, brought forth treasures from the bowels of the earth, and helped make possible this magnificent representation of the progress of the South. Casting down your bucket among my people, helping and encouraging them as you are doing on these grounds, and, with education of head, hand, and heart, you will find that they will buy your surplus land, make blossom the waste places in your fields, and run your factories. While doing this, you can be sure in the future, as in the past, that you and your families will be surrounded by the most patient, faithful, law-abiding, and unresentful people that the world has seen. As we have proved our loyalty to you in the past, in nursing your children, watching by the sick bed of your mothers and fathers, and often following them with tear-dimmed eyes to their graves, so in the future, in our humble way, we shall stand by you with a devotion that no foreigner can approach, ready to lay down our lives, if need be, in defense of yours, interlacing our industrial, commercial, civil, and re-ligious life with yours in a way that shall make the interests of both races one. In all things that are purely social we can be as separate as the fingers, yet one as the hand in all things essential to mutual progress.

There is no defense or security for any of us except in the highest intelligence and development of all. If anywhere there are efforts tending to curtail the fullest growth of the Negro, let these efforts be turned into stimulating, encouraging, and making him the most useful and intelligent citizen. Effort or means so invested will pay a thousand per cent interest. These efforts will be twice blessed—"Blessing him that gives and him that takes."

There is no escape through law of man or God from the inevitable:

> The laws of changeless justice bind
> Oppressor with oppressed;
> And close as sin and suffering joined
> We march to fare abreast.

Nearly sixteen millions of hands will aid you in pulling the load upward, or they will pull, against you, the load downward. We shall constitute one third and more of the ignorance and crime of the South, or one third its intelligence and progress; we shall contribute one third to the business and industrial prosperity of the South, or we shall prove a veritable body of death, stagnating, depressing, retarding every effort to advance the body politic.

Gentlemen of the Exposition, as we present to you our humble effort at an exhibition of our progress, you must not expect overmuch. Starting thirty years ago with ownership here and there in a few quilts and pumpkins and chickens (gathered from miscellaneous sources), remember, the path that has led from these to the inventions and production of agricultural implements, buggies, steam engines, newspapers, books, statuary carving, paintings, the management of drugstores and banks, has not been trodden without contact with thorns and thistles. While we take pride in what we exhibit as a result of our independent efforts, we do not for a moment forget that our part in this exhibition would fall far short of your expectations but for the constant help that has come to our educational life, not only from the Southern states, but especially from Northern philanthropists, who have made their gifts a constant stream of blessing and encouragement.

The wisest among my race understand that the agitation of questions of social equality is the extremest folly, and that progress in the enjoyment of all the privileges that will come to us must be the result of severe and constant struggle rather than of artificial forcing. No race that has anything to contribute to the markets of the world is long, in any degree, ostracized. It is important and right that all privileges of the law be ours, but it is vastly more important that we be prepared for the exercise of those privileges. The opportunity to earn a dollar in a factory just now is worth infinitely more than the opportunity to spend a dollar in an opera house.

In conclusion, may I repeat that nothing in thirty years has given us more hope and encouragement, and drawn us so near to you of the white race, as this opportunity offered by the Exposition; and here bending, as it were, over the altar that represents the results of the struggles of your race and mine, both starting practically empty-handed three decades ago, I pledge that, in your effort to work out the great and intricate problem which God has laid at the doors of the South, you shall have at all times the patient, sympathetic help of my race; only let this be constantly in mind, that while, from representations in these buildings of the product of field, of forest, of mine, of factory, letters, and art, much good will come, yet far above and beyond material benefits will be that higher good, that, let us pray God, will come in a blotting out of sectional differences and racial animosities and suspicions, in a determination to administer absolute justice, in a willing obedience among all classes to the mandates of law. This, coupled with our material prosperity, will bring into our beloved South a new heaven and a new earth.

PLESSY v. FERGUSON
163 U.S. 537 (1896)

MR. JUSTICE BROWN, after stating the case, delivered the opinion of the court:

This case turns upon the constitutionality of an act of the General Assembly of the State of Louisiana, passed in 1890, providing for separate railway carriages for the white and colored races. Acts 1890, No. 111, p. 152.

The first section of the statute enacts "that all railway companies carrying passengers in their coaches in this State, shall provide equal but separate accommodations for the white, and colored races, by providing two or more passenger coaches for each passenger train, or by dividing the passenger coaches by a partition so as to secure separate accommodations: *Provided*, That this section shall not be construed to apply to street railroads. No person or persons, shall be admitted to occupy seats in coaches, other than, the ones, assigned, to them on account of the race they belong to."

By the second section it was enacted "that the officers of such passenger trains shall have power and are hereby required to assign each passenger to the coach or compartment used for the race to which such passenger belongs; any passenger insisting on going into a coach or compartment to which by race he does not belong, shall be liable to a fine of twenty-five dollars, or in lieu thereof to imprisonment for a period of not more than twenty days in the parish prison, and any officer of any railroad insisting on assigning a passenger to a coach or compartment other than the one set aside for the race to which said passenger belongs, shall be liable to a fine of twenty-five dollars, or in lieu thereof to imprisonment for a period of not more than twenty days in the parish prison; and should any passenger refuse to occupy the coach or compartment to which he or she is assigned by the officer of such railway, said officer shall have power to refuse to carry such passenger on his train, and for such refusal neither he nor the railway company which he represents shall be liable for damages in any of the courts of this State." ...

The information filed in the criminal District Court charged in substance that Plessy, being a passenger between two stations within the

State of Louisiana, was assigned by officers of the company to the coach used for the race to which he belonged, but he insisted upon going into a coach used by the race to which he did not belong. Neither in the information nor plea was his particular race or color averred.

The petition for the writ of prohibition averred that petitioner was seven eighths Caucasian and one eighth African blood; that the mixture of colored blood was not discernible in him, and that he was entitled to every right, privilege and immunity secured to citizens of the United States of the white race; and that, upon such theory, he took possession of a vacant seat in a coach where passengers of the white race were accommodated, and was ordered by the conductor to vacate said coach and take a seat in another assigned to persons of the colored race, and having refused to comply with such demand he was forcibly ejected with the aid of a police officer, and imprisoned in the parish jail to answer a charge of having violated the above act.

The constitutionality of this act is attacked upon the ground that it conflicts both with the Thirteenth Amendment of the Constitution, abolishing slavery, and the Fourteenth Amendment, which prohibits certain restrictive legislation on the part of the States.

1. That it does not conflict with the Thirteenth Amendment, which abolished slavery and involuntary servitude, except as a punishment for crime, is too clear for argument. . . .

A statute which implies merely a legal distinction between the white and colored races—a distinction which is founded in the color of the two races, and which must always exist so long as white men are distinguished from the other race by color—has no tendency to destroy the legal equality of the two races, or reëstablish a state of involuntary servitude. Indeed, we do not understand that the Thirteenth Amendment is strenuously relied upon by the plaintiff in error in this connection.

2. By the Fourteenth Amendment, all persons born or naturalized in the United States, and subject to the jurisdiction thereof, are made citizens of the United States and of the State wherein they reside; and the States are forbidden from making or enforcing any law which shall abridge the privileges or immunities of citizens of the United States, or shall deprive any person of life, liberty or property without due process of law, or deny to any person within their jurisdiction the equal protection of the laws. . . .

The object of the amendment was undoubtedly to enforce the absolute equality of the two races before the law, but in the nature of things it could not have been intended to abolish distinctions based upon color, or to enforce social, as distinguished from political equality, or a commingling of the two races upon terms unsatisfactory to either. Laws permitting, and even requiring, their separation in places where they are liable to be brought into contact do not necessarily imply the inferiority of either race to the other, and have been generally, if not universally, recognized as within the competency of the state legislatures in the exercise of their police power. The most common instance of this is connected with the establishment of separate schools for white and colored children, which has been held to be a valid exercise of the legislative power even by courts of States where the political rights of the colored race have been longest and most earnestly enforced. . . .

So far, then, as a conflict with the Fourteenth Amendment is concerned, the case reduces itself to the question whether the statute of Louisiana is a reasonable regulation, and with respect to this there must necessarily be a large discretion on the part of the legislature. In determining the question of reasonableness it is at liberty to act with reference to the established usages, customs and traditions of the people, and with a view to the promotion of their comfort, and the preservation of the public peace and good order. Gauged by this standard, we cannot say that a law which authorizes or even requires the separation of the two races in public conveyances is unreasonable, or more obnoxious to the Fourteenth Amendment than the acts of Congress requiring separate schools for colored children in the District of Columbia, the constitutionality of which does not seem to have been questioned, or the corresponding acts of state legislatures.

We consider the underlying fallacy of the plaintiff's argument to consist in the assumption that the enforced separation of the two races stamps the colored race with a badge of inferiority. If this be so, it is not by reason of anything found in the act, but solely because the colored race chooses to put that construction upon it. The argument necessarily assumes that if, as has been more than once the case, and is not unlikely to be so again, the colored race should become the dominant power in the state legislature, and should enact a law in precisely similar terms, it would thereby relegate the white race to an inferior position. We imagine that the white race, at least, would not acquiesce in this assumption. The argument also assumes that social prejudices may be overcome by legislation, and that equal rights cannot be secured to the negro except by an enforced commingling of the two races. We cannot accept this proposition. If the two races are to meet upon terms of social equality, it must be the result of natural affinities, a mutual appreciation of each other's merits and a voluntary consent of individuals. As was said by the Court of Appeals of New York in *People* v. *Gallagher,* 93 N. Y. 438, 448, "this end can neither be accomplished nor promoted by laws which conflict with the general sentiment of the community upon whom they are designed to operate. When the government, therefore, has secured to each of its citizens equal rights before the law and equal opportunities for improvement and progress, it has accomplished the end for which it was organized and performed all of the functions respecting social advantages with which it is endowed." Legislation is powerless to eradicate racial instincts or to abolish distinctions based upon physical differences, and the attempt to do so can only result in accentuating the difficulties of the present situation. If the civil and political rights of both races be equal one cannot be inferior to the other civilly or politically. If one race be inferior to the other socially, the Constitution of the United States cannot put them upon the same plane.

It is true that the question of the proportion of colored blood necessary to constitute a colored person, as distinguished from a white person, is one upon which there is a difference of opinion in the different States, some holding that any visible admixture of black blood stamps the person as belonging to the colored race, (*State* v. *Chavers*, 5 Jones, [N.C.] 1, p. 11); others that it depends upon the preponderance of blood, (*Gray* v. *State*, 4 Ohio, 354; *Monroe* v. *Collins*, 17 Ohio St. 665); and still others that the predominance of white blood must only be in the proportion of three fourths. (*People* v. *Dean*, 14 Michigan, 406; *Jones* v. *Commonwealth*, 80 Virginia, 538.) But these are questions to be determined under the laws of each State and are not properly put in issue in this case. Under the allegations of his petition it may undoubtedly become a question of importance whether, under the laws of Louisiana, the petitioner belongs to the white or colored race.

The judgment of the court below is, therefore,

Affirmed.

MR. JUSTICE HARLAN dissenting. . . .

In respect of civil rights, common to all citizens, the Constitution of the United States does not, I think, permit any public authority to know the race of those entitled to be protected in the enjoyment of such rights. Every true man has pride of race, and under appropriate circumstances when the rights of others, his equals before the law, are not to be affected, it is his privilege to express such pride and to take such action based upon it as to him seems proper. But I deny that any legislative body or judicial tribunal may have regard to the race of citizens when the civil rights of those citizens are involved. Indeed, such legislation, as that here in question, is inconsistent not only with that equality of rights which pertains to citizenship, National and State, but with the personal liberty enjoyed by every one within the United States.

The Thirteenth Amendment does not permit the withholding or the deprivation of any right necessarily inhering in freedom. It not only struck down the institution of slavery as previously existing in the United States, but it prevents the imposition of any burdens or disabilities that constitute badges of slavery or servitude. It decreed universal civil freedom in this country. This court has so adjudged. But that amendment having been found inadequate to the protection of the rights of those who had been in slavery, it was followed by the Fourteenth Amendment, which added greatly to the dignity and glory of American citizenship, and to the security of personal liberty, by declaring that "all persons born or naturalized in the United States, and subject to the jurisdiction thereof, are citizens of the United States and of the State wherein they reside," and that "no State shall make or enforce any law which shall abridge the privileges or immunities of citizens of the United States; nor shall any State deprive any person of life, liberty or property without due process of law, nor deny to any person within its jurisdiction the equal protection of the laws." These two amendments, if enforced according to their true intent and meaning, will protect all the civil rights that pertain to freedom and citizenship. Finally, and to the end that no citizen should be denied, on account of his race, the privilege of participating in the political control of his country, it was declared by the Fifteenth Amendment that "the right of citizens of the United States to vote shall not be denied or abridged by the United States or by any State on account of race, color or previous condition of servitude."

These notable additions to the fundamental law were welcomed by the friends of liberty throughout the world. They removed the race line from our governmental systems. They had, as this court has said, a common purpose, namely, to secure "to a race recently emancipated, a race that through many generations have been held in slavery, all the civil rights that the superior race enjoy." They declared, in legal effect, this court has further said, "that the law in the States shall be the same for the black as for the white; that all persons, whether colored or white, shall stand equal before the laws of the States, and, in regard to the colored race, for whose protection the amendment was primarily designed, that no discrimination shall be made against them by law because of their color." We also said: "The words of the amendment, it is true, are prohibitory, but they contain a necessary implication of a positive immunity, or right, most valuable to the colored race—the right to exemption from unfriendly legislation against them distinctively as colored—exemption from legal discriminations, implying inferiority in civil society, lessening the security of their enjoyment of the rights which others enjoy, and discriminations which are steps towards reducing them to the condition of a subject race." . . .

I am of opinion that the statute of Louisiana is inconsistent with the personal liberty of citizens, white and black, in that State, and hostile to both the spirit and letter of the Constitution of the United States. If laws of like character should be enacted in the several States of the Union, the effect would be in the highest degree mischievous. Slavery, as an institution tolerated by law would, it is true, have disappeared from our country, but there would remain a power in the States, by sinister legislation, to interfere with the full enjoyment of the blessings of freedom; to regulate civil rights, common to all citizens, upon the basis of race; and to place in a condition of legal inferiority a large body of American citizens, now constituting a part of the political community called the People of the United States, for whom, and by whom through representatives, our government is administered. Such a system is inconsistent with the guarantee given by the Constitution to each State of a republican form of government, and may be stricken down by Congressional action, or by the courts in the discharge of their solemn duty to maintain the supreme law of the land, anything in the constitution or laws of any State to the contrary notwithstanding.

For the reasons stated, I am constrained to withhold my assent from the opinion and judgment of the majority.

William Edward Burghardt Du Bois

ON BOOKER T. WASHINGTON

Mr. Washington represents in Negro thought the old attitude of adjustment and submission; but adjustment at such a peculiar time as to make his programme unique. This is an age of unusual economic development, and Mr. Washington's programme naturally takes an economic cast, becoming a gospel of Work and Money to such an extent as apparently almost completely to overshadow the higher aims of life. Moreover, this is an age when the more advanced races are coming in closer contact with the less developed races, and the race-feeling is therefore intensified; and Mr. Washington's programme practically accepts the alleged inferiority of the Negro races. Again, in our own land, the reaction from the sentiment of war time has given impetus to race-prejudice against Negroes, and Mr. Washington withdraws many of the high demands of Negroes as men and American citizens. In other periods of intensified prejudice all the Negro's tendency to self-assertion has been called forth; at this period a policy of submission is advocated. In the history of nearly all other races and peoples the doctrine preached at such crises has been that manly self-respect is worth more than lands and houses, and that a people who voluntarily surrender such respect, or cease striving for it, are not worth civilizing.

In answer to this, it has been claimed that the Negro can survive only through submission. Mr. Washington distinctly asks that black people give up, at least for the present, three things,—

First, political power,

Second, insistence on civil rights,

Third, higher education of Negro youth,—

and concentrate all their energies on industrial education, the accumulation of wealth, and the conciliation of the South. This policy has been courageously and insistently advocated for over fifteen years, and has been triumphant for perhaps ten years. As a result of this tender of the palm-branch, what has been the return? In these years there have occurred:

1. The disfranchisement of the Negro.

2. The legal creation of a distinct status of civil inferiority for the Negro.

3. The steady withdrawal of aid from institutions for the higher training of the Negro.

These movements are not, to be sure, direct results of Mr. Washington's teachings; but his propaganda has, without a shadow of doubt, helped their speedier accomplishment. The question then comes: Is it possible, and probable, that nine millions of men can make effective progress in economic lines if they are deprived of political rights, made a servile caste, and allowed only the most meagre chance for developing their exceptional men? If history and reason give any distinct answer to these questions, it is an emphatic *No*. And Mr. Washington thus faces the triple paradox of his career:

1. He is striving nobly to make Negro artisans business men and property-owners; but it is utterly impossible, under modern competitive methods, for workingmen and property-owners to defend their rights and exist without the right of suffrage.

2. He insists on thrift and self-respect, but at the same time counsels a silent submission to civic inferiority such as is bound to sap the manhood of any race in the long run.

3. He advocates common-school and industrial training, and depreciates institutions of higher learning; but neither the Negro common-schools, nor Tuskegee itself, could remain open a day were it not for teachers trained in Negro colleges, or trained by their graduates.

This triple paradox in Mr. Washington's position is the object of criticism by two classes of colored Americans. One class is spiritually descended from Toussaint the Savior, through Gabriel, Vesey, and Turner, and they represent the attitude of revolt and revenge; they hate the white South blindly and distrust the white race generally, and so far as they agree on definite action, think that the Negro's only hope lies in emigration beyond the borders of the United States. And yet, by the irony of fate, nothing has more effectually made this programme seem hopeless than the recent course of the United States toward weaker and darker peoples in the West Indies, Hawaii, and the Philippines,—for where in the world may we go and be safe from lying and brute force?

The other class of Negroes who cannot agree with Mr. Washington has hitherto said little aloud. They deprecate the sight of scattered counsels, of internal disagreement; and especially they dislike making their just criticism of a useful and earnest man an excuse for a general discharge of venom from small-minded opponents. Nevertheless, the questions involved are so fundamental and serious that it is difficult to see how men like the Grimkes, Kelly Miller, J. W. E. Bowen, and other representatives of this group, can much longer be silent. Such men feel in conscience bound to ask of this nation three things:

1. The right to vote.
2. Civic equality.
3. The education of youth according to ability.

They acknowledge Mr. Washington's invaluable service in counselling patience and courtesy in such demands; they do not ask that ignorant black men vote when ignorant whites are debarred, or that any reasonable restrictions in the suffrage should not be applied; they know that the low social level of the mass of the race is responsible for much discrimination against it, but they also know, and the nation knows, that relentless color-prejudice is more often a cause than a result of the Negro's degradation; they seek the abatement of this relic of barbarism, and not its systematic encouragement and pampering by all agencies of social power from the Associated Press to the Church of Christ. They advocate, with Mr. Washington, a broad system of Negro common schools supplemented by thorough industrial training; but they are surprised that a man of Mr. Washington's insight cannot see that no such educational system ever has rested or can rest on any other basis than that of the well-equipped college and university, and they insist that there is a demand for a few such institutions throughout the South to train the best of the Negro youth as teachers, professional men, and leaders.

This group of men honor Mr. Washington for his attitude of conciliation toward the white South; they accept the "Atlanta Compromise" in its broadest interpretation; they recognize, with him, many signs of promise, many men of high purpose and fair judgment, in this section; they know that no easy task has been laid upon a region already tottering under heavy burdens. But, nevertheless, they insist that the way to truth and right lies in straightforward honesty, not in indiscriminate flattery; in praising those of the South who do well and criticising uncompromisingly those who do ill; in taking advantage of the opportunities at hand and urging their fellows to do the same, but at the same time in remembering that only a firm adherence to their higher ideals and aspirations will ever keep those ideals within the realm of possibility. They do not expect that the free right to vote, to enjoy civic rights, and to be educated, will come in a moment; they do not expect to see the bias and prejudices of years disappear at the blast of a trumpet; but they are absolutely certain that the way for a people to gain their reasonable rights is not by voluntarily throwing them away and insisting that they do not want them; that the way for a people to gain respect is not by continually belittling and ridiculing themselves; that, on the contrary, Negroes must insist continually, in season and out of season, that voting is necessary to modern manhood, that color discrimination is barbarism, and that black boys need education as well as white boys.

In failing thus to state plainly and unequivocally the legitimate demands of their people, even at the cost of opposing an honored leader, the thinking classes of American Negroes would shirk a heavy responsibility, —a responsibility to themselves, a responsibility to the struggling masses, a responsibility to the darker races of men whose future depends so largely on this American experiment, but especially a responsibility to this nation, —this common Fatherland. It is wrong to encourage a man or a people in evil-doing; it is wrong to aid and abet a national crime simply because it is unpopular not to do so. The growing spirit of kindliness and reconciliation between the North and South after the frightful differences of a generation ago ought to be a source of deep congratulation to all, and especially to those whose mistreatment caused the war; but if that reconciliation is to be marked by the industrial slavery and civic death of those same black men, with permanent legislation into a position of inferiority, then those black men, if they are really men, are called upon by every consideration of patriotism and loyalty to oppose such a course by all civilized methods, even though such opposition involves disagreement with Mr. Booker T. Washington. We have no right to sit silently by while the inevitable seeds are sown for a harvest of disaster to our children, black and white.

First, it is the duty of black men to judge the South discriminatingly. The present generation of Southerners are not responsible for the past, and they should not be blindly hated or blamed for it. Furthermore, to no class is the indiscriminate endorsement of the recent course of the South toward Negroes more nauseating than to the best thought of the South. The South is not "solid"; it is a land in the ferment of social change, wherein forces of all kinds are fighting for supremacy; and to praise the ill the South is to-day perpetrating is just as wrong as to condemn the good. Discriminating and broad-minded criticism is what the South needs,— needs it for the sake of her own white sons and daughters, and for the insurance of robust, healthy mental and moral development.

To-day even the attitude of the Southern whites toward the blacks is not, as so many assume, in all cases the same; the ignorant Southerner hates the Negro, the workingmen fear his competition, the money-makers wish to use him as a laborer, some of the educated see a menace in his upward development, while others—usually the sons of the masters—wish to help him to rise. National opinion has enabled this last class to maintain the Negro common schools, and to protect the Negro partially in property, life, and limb. Through the pressure of the money-makers, the

Negro is in danger of being reduced to semi-slavery, especially in the country districts; the workingmen, and those of the educated who fear the Negro, have united to disfranchise him, and some have urged his deportation; while the passions of the ignorant are easily aroused to lynch and abuse any black man. To praise this intricate whirl of thought and prejudice is nonsense; to inveigh indiscriminately against "the South" is unjust; but to use the same breath in praising Governor Aycock, exposing Senator Morgan, arguing with Mr. Thomas Nelson Page, and denouncing Senator Ben Tillman, is not only sane, but the imperative duty of the thinking black men.

It would be unjust to Mr. Washington not to acknowledge that in several instances he has opposed movements in the South which were unjust to the Negro; he sent memorials to the Louisiana and Alabama constitutional conventions, he has spoken against lynching, and in other ways has openly or silently set his influence against sinister schemes and unfortunate happenings. Notwithstanding this, it is equally true to assert that on the whole the distinct impression left by Mr. Washington's propaganda is, first, that the South is justified in its present attitude toward the Negro because of the Negro's degradation; secondly, that the prime cause of the Negro's failure to rise more quickly is his wrong education in the past; and, thirdly, that his future rise depends primarily on his own efforts. Each of these propositions is a dangerous half-truth. The supplementary truths must never be lost sight of: first, slavery and race-prejudice are potent if not sufficient causes of the Negro's position; second, industrial and common-school training were necessarily slow in planting because they had to await the black teachers trained by higher institutions, —it being extremely doubtful if any essentially different development was possible, and certainly a Tuskegee was unthinkable before 1880; and, third, while it is great truth to say that the Negro must strive and strive *mightily* to help himself, it is equally true that unless his striving be not simply seconded, but rather aroused and encouraged, by the initiative of the richer and wiser environing group, he cannot hope for great success.

In his failure to realize and impress this last point, Mr. Washington is especially to be criticised. His doctrine has tended to make the whites, North and South, shift the burden of the Negro problem to the Negro's shoulders and stand aside as critical and rather pessimistic spectators; when in fact the burden belongs to the nation, and the hands of none of us are clean if we bend not our energies to righting these great wrongs.

The South ought to be led, by candid and honest criticism, to assert her better self and do her full duty to the race she has cruelly wronged and is still wronging. The North—her co-partner in guilt—cannot salve her conscience by plastering it with gold. We cannot settle this problem by diplomacy and suaveness, by "policy" alone. If worse come to worst, can the moral fibre of this country survive the slow throttling and murder of nine millions of men?

The black men of America have a duty to perform, a duty stern and delicate,—a forward movement to oppose a part of the work of their greatest leader. So far as Mr. Washington preaches Thrift, Patience, and Industrial Training for the masses, we must hold up his hands and strive with him, rejoicing in his honors and glorying in the strength of this Joshua called of God and of man to lead the headless host. But so far as Mr. Washington apologizes for injustice, North or South, does not rightly value the privilege and duty of voting, belittles the emasculating effects of caste distinctions, and opposes the higher training and ambition of our brighter minds,—so far as he, the South, or the Nation, does this,—we must unceasingly and firmly oppose them. By every civilized and peaceful method we must strive for the rights which the world accords to men, clinging unwaveringly to those great words which the sons of the Fathers would fain forget: "We hold these truths to be self-evident: That all men are created equal; that they are endowed by their Creator with certain unalienable rights; that among these are life, liberty, and the pursuit of happiness."

THE NIAGARA MOVEMENT

DECLARATION OF PRINCIPLES

Progress

The members of the conference, known as the Niagara Movement, assembled in annual meeting in Buffalo, July 11th, 12th and 13th, 1905, congratulate the Negro-Americans on certain undoubted evidences of progress in the last decade, particularly the increase of intelligence, the buying of property, the checking of crime, the uplift in home life, the advance in literature and art, and the demonstration of constructive and executive ability in the conduct of great religious, economic and educational institutions.

Suffrage

At the same time, we believe that this class of American citizens should protest emphatically and continually against the curtailment of their political rights. We believe in manhood suffrage; we believe that no man is so good, intelligent or wealthy as to be entrusted wholly with the welfare of his neighbor.

Civil Liberty

We believe also in protest against the curtailment of our civil rights. All American citizens have the right to equal treatment in places of public entertainment according to their behavior and deserts.

Economic Opportunity

We especially complain against the denial of equal opportunities to us in economic life; in the rural districts of the South this amounts to peonage

"Declaration of Principles of the Niagara Movement" and "Resolutions of the Niagara Movement," brochures in the Schomburg Collection, New York Public Library. Reprinted in Howard Brotz, ed., *Negro Social and Political Thought, 1850–1920* (New York: Basic Books, 1966), pp. 533–539.

and virtual slavery; all over the South it tends to crush labor and small business enterprises; and everywhere American prejudice, helped often by iniquitous laws, is making it more difficult for Negro-Americans to earn a decent living.

Education

Common school education should be free to all American children and compulsory. High school training should be adequately provided for all, and college training should be the monopoly of no class or race in any section of our common country. We believe that, in defense of our own institutions, the United States should aid common school education, particularly in the South, and we especially recommend concerted agitation to this end. We urge an increase in public high school facilities in the South, where the Negro-Americans are almost wholly without such provisions. We favor well-equipped trade and technical schools for the training of artisans, and the need of adequate and liberal endowment for a few institutions of higher education must be patent to sincere well-wishers of the race.

Courts

We demand upright judges in courts, juries selected without discrimination on account of color and the same measure of punishment and the same efforts at reformation for blacks as well as for white offenders. We need orphanages and farm schools for dependent children, juvenile reformatories for delinquents, and the abolition of the dehumanizing convict-lease system.

Public Opinion

We note with alarm the evident retrogression in the land of sound public opinion on the subject of manhood rights, republican government and human brotherhood, and we pray God that this nation will not degenerate into a mob of boasters and oppressors, but rather will return to the faith of the fathers, that all men were created free and equal, with certain unalienable rights.

Health

We plead for health—for an opportunity to live in decent houses and localities, for a chance to rear our children in physical and moral cleanliness.

Employers and Labor Unions

We hold up for public execration the conduct of two opposite classes of men: The practice among employers of importing ignorant Negro-American laborers in emergencies, and then affording them neither protection nor permanent employment; and the practice of labor unions in proscribing and boycotting and oppressing thousands of their fellow-toilers, simply because they are black. These methods have accentuated and will accentuate the war of labor and capital, and they are disgraceful to both sides.

Protest

We refuse to allow the impression to remain that the Negro-American assents to inferiority, is submissive under oppression and apologetic before insults. Through helplessness we may submit, but the voice of protest of ten million Americans must never cease to assail the ears of their fellows, so long as America is unjust.

Color-Line

Any discrimination based simply on race or color is barbarous, we care not how hallowed it be by custom, expediency, or prejudice. Differences made on account of ignorance, immorality, or disease are legitimate methods of fighting evil, and against them we have no word of protest; but discriminations based simply and solely on physical peculiarities, place of birth, color or skin, are relics of that unreasoning savagery of which the world is and ought to be thoroughly ashamed.

"Jim Crow" Cars

We protest against the "Jim Crow" car, since its effect is and must be to make us pay first-class fare for third-class accomodations, render us open to insults and discomfort and to crucify wantonly our manhood, womanhood and self-respect.

Soldiers

We regret that this nation has never seen fit adequately to reward the black soldiers who, in its five wars, have defended their country with their blood, and yet have been systematically denied the promotions which their abilities deserve. And we regard as unjust, the exclusion of black boys from the military and navy training schools.

War Amendments

We urge upon Congress the enactment of appropriate legislation for securing the proper enforcement of those articles of freedom, the thirteenth, fourteenth and fifteenth amendments of the Constitution of the United States.

We repudiate the monstrous doctrine that the oppressor should be the sole authority as to the rights of the oppressed.

Oppression

The Negro race in America stolen, ravished and degraded, struggling up through difficulties and oppression, needs sympathy and receives criticism; needs help, and is given hindrance, needs protection and is given mob-violence, needs justice and is given charity, needs leadership and is given cowardice and apology, needs bread and is given a stone. The nation will never stand justified before God until these things are changed.

The Church

Especially are we surprised and astonished at the recent attitude of the church of Christ—on the increase of a desire to bow to racial prejudice, to narrow the bounds of human brotherhood, and to segregate black men in some outer sanctuary. This is wrong, unchristian and disgraceful to the twentieth century civilization.

Agitation

Of the above grievances we do not hesitate to complain, and to complain loudly and insistently. To ignore, overlook, or apologize for these wrongs is to prove ourselves unworthy of freedom. Persistent manly agitation is the way to liberty, and toward this goal the Niagara Movement has started and asks the co-operation of all men of all races.

Help

At the same time we want to acknowledge with deep thankfulness the help of our fellowmen from the abolitionist down to those who to-day still stand for equal opportunity and who have given and still give of their wealth and of their poverty for our advancement.

Duties

And while we are demanding, and ought to demand, and will continue to demand the rights enumerated above, God forbid that we should ever forget to urge corresponding duties upon our people:

The duty to vote
The duty to respect the rights of others
The duty to work
The duty to obey the laws
The duty to be clean and orderly
The duty to send our children to school
The duty to respect ourselves, even as we respect others

This statement, complaint and prayer we do submit to the American people and Almighty God—*1905.*

RESOLUTIONS OF THE NIAGARA MOVEMENT

The men of the Niagara Movement, coming from the toil of the year's hard work, and pausing a moment from the earning of their daily bread, turn toward the nation and again ask in the name of ten million the privilege of a hearing. In the past year the work of the Negro hater has flourished in the land. Step by step the defenders of the rights of American citizens have retreated. The work of stealing the black man's ballot has progressed and the fifty and more representatives of stolen votes still sit in the nation's capital. Discrimination in travel and public accommodation has so spread that some of our weaker brethren are actually afraid to thunder against color discrimination as such and are simply whispering for ordinary decencies.

Against this the Niagara Movement eternally protests. We will not be satisfied to take one jot or tittle less than our full manhood rights. We claim for ourselves every single right that belongs to a freeborn American, political, civil and social; and until we get these rights we will never cease to protest and assail the ears of America. The battle we wage is not for ourselves alone, but for all true Americans. It is a fight for ideals, lest this, our common fatherland, false to its founding, become in truth the land of the Thief and the home of the Slave—a by-word and a hissing among the nations for its sounding pretensions and pitiful accomplishment.

Never before in the modern age has a great and civilized folk threatened to adopt so cowardly a creed in the treatment of its fellow-citizens, born and bred on its soil. Stripped of verbiage and subterfuge and in its naked nastiness, the new American creed says: fear to let black men even try to rise lest they become the equals of the white. And this is the land that professes to follow Jesus Christ. The blasphemy of such a course is only matched by its cowardice.

In detail our demands are clear and unequivocal.

First. We would vote; with the right to vote goes everything: freedom, manhood, the honor of your wives, the chastity of your daughters, the right to work, and the chance to rise; let no man listen to those who deny this.

We want full manhood suffrage, and we want it now, henceforth and forever.

Second. We want discrimination in public accommodation to cease. Separation in railway and street cars, based simply on race and color, is un-American, undemocratic, and silly. We protest against all such discrimination.

Third. We claim the right of freemen to walk, talk and be with them that wish to be with us. No man has the right to choose another man's friends, and to attempt to do so is an impudent interference with the most fundamental human privilege.

Fourth. We want the laws enforced against rich as well as poor; against Capitalist as well as Laborer; against white as well as black. We are not more lawless than the white race, we are more often arrested, convicted and mobbed. We want justice even for criminals and outlaws. We want the Constitution of the country enforced. We want Congress to take charge of the Congressional elections. We want the Fourteenth Amendment carried out to the letter and every State disfranchised in Congress which attempts to disfranchise its rightful voters. We want the Fifteenth Amendment enforced and no State allowed to base its franchise simply on color.

The failure of the Republican Party in Congress at the session just closed to redeem its pledge of 1904 with reference to suffrage conditions at the South seems a plain, deliberate, and premeditated breach of promise, and stamps that party as guilty of obtaining votes under false pretense.

Fifth. We want our children educated. The school system in the country districts of the South is a disgrace and in few towns and cities are the Negro schools what they ought to be. We want the national government to step in and wipe out illiteracy in the South. Either the United States will destroy ignorance or ignorance will destroy the United States.

And when we call for education, we mean real education. We believe in work. We ourselves are workers, but work is not necessarily education. Education is the development of power and ideal. We want our children trained as intelligent human beings should be, and we will fight for all time against any proposal to educate black boys and girls simply as servants and underlings, or simply for the use of other people. They have a right to know, to think, to aspire.

These are some of the chief things which we want. How shall we get them? By voting where we may vote; by persistent, unceasing agitation; by hammering at the truth; by sacrifice and work.

We do not believe in violence, neither in the despised vio.ence of the raid nor the lauded violence of the soldier, nor the barbarous violence of the mob; but we do believe in John Brown, in that incarnate spirit of justice, that hatred of a lie, that willingness to sacrifice money, reputation, and life itself on the altar of right. And here on the scene of John Brown's martyrdom, we reconsecrate ourselves, our honor, our property to the final emancipation of the race for whose freedom John Brown died—
August 15, 1906.

Marcus Garvey

BLACK SEPARATISM

RACE ASSIMILATION

Some Negro leaders have advanced the belief that in another few years the white people will make up their minds to assimilate their black populations; thereby sinking all racial prejudice in the welcoming of the black race into the social companionship of the white. Such leaders further believe that by the amalgamation of black and white, a new type will spring up, and that type will become the American and West Indian of the future.

This belief is preposterous. I believe that white men should be white, yellow men should be yellow, and black men should be black in the great panorama of races, until each and every race by its own initiative lifts itself up to the common standard of humanity, as to compel the respect and appreciation of all, and so make it possible for each one to stretch out the hand of welcome without being able to be prejudiced against the other because of any inferior and unfortunate condition.

The white man of America will not, to any organized extent, assimilate the Negro, because in so doing, he feels that he will be committing racial suicide. This he is not prepared to do. It is true he illegitimately carries on a system of assimilation; but such assimilation, as practised, is one that he is not prepared to support because he becomes prejudiced against his own offspring, if that offspring is the product of black and white; hence, to the white man the question of racial differences is eternal. So long as Negroes occupy an inferior position among the races and nations of the world, just so long will others be prejudiced against them, because it will be profitable for them to keep up their system of superiority. But when the Negro by his own initiative lifts himself from his low state to the highest human standard he will be in a position to stop begging and praying, and demand a place that no individual, race or nation will be able to deny him.

The Philosophy and Opinions of Marcus Garvey, Amy Jacques-Garvey, ed. (New York: The Universal Publishing House, 1923), pp. 26, 52–3. Reprinted by permission of Amy Jacques-Garvey.

THE TRUE SOLUTION OF THE NEGRO PROBLEM

As far as Negroes are concerned, in America we have the problem of lynching, peonage and dis-franchisement.

In the West Indies, South and Central America we have the problem of peonage, serfdom, industrial and political governmental inequality.

In Africa we have, not only peonage and serfdom, but outright slavery, racial exploitation and alien political monopoly.

We cannot allow a continuation of these crimes against our race. As four hundred million men, women and children, worthy of the existence given us by the Divine Creator, we are determined to solve our own problem, by redeeming our Motherland Africa from the hands of alien exploiters and found there a government, a nation of our own, strong enough to lend protection to the members of our race scattered all over the world, and to compel the respect of the nations and races of the earth.

Do they lynch Englishmen, Frenchmen, Germans or Japanese? No. And Why? Because these people are represented by great governments, mighty nations and empires, strongly organized. Yes, and ever ready to shed the last drop of blood and spend the last penny in the national treasury to protect the honor and integrity of a citizen outraged anywhere.

Until the Negro reaches this point of national independence, all he does as a race will count for naught, because the prejudice that will stand out against him even with his ballot in his hand, with his industrial progress to show, will be of such an overwhelming nature as to perpetuate mob violence and mob rule, from which he will suffer, and which he will not be able to stop with his industrial wealth and with his ballot.

You may argue that he can use his industrial wealth and his ballot to force the government to recognize him, but he must understand that the government is the people. That the majority of the people dictate the policy of governments, and if the majority are against a measure, a thing, or a race, then the government is impotent to protect that measure, thing or race.

If the Negro were to live in this Western Hemisphere for another five hundred years he would still be outnumbered by other races who are prejudiced against him. He cannot resort to the government for protection for government will be in the hands of the majority of the people who are prejudiced against him, hence for the Negro to depend on the ballot and his industrial progress alone, will be hopeless as it does not help him when he is lynched, burned, jim-crowed and segregated. The future of the Negro therefore, outside of Africa, spells ruin and disaster.

BROWN v. BOARD OF EDUCATION
347 U.S. 483 (1954)

MR. CHIEF JUSTICE WARREN delivered the opinion of the Court:

These cases come to us from the States of Kansas, South Carolina, Virginia, and Delaware. They are premised on different facts and different local conditions, but a common legal question justifies their consideration together in this consolidated opinion.

In each of the cases, minors of the Negro race, through their legal representatives, seek the aid of the courts in obtaining admission to the public schools of their community on a nonsegregated basis. In each instance, they had been denied admission to schools attended by white children under laws requiring or permitting segregation according to race. This segregation was alleged to deprive the plaintiffs of the equal protection of the laws under the Fourteenth Amendment. In each of the cases other than the Delaware case, a three-judge federal district court denied relief to the plaintiffs on the so-called "separate but equal" doctrine announced by this Court in *Plessy* v. *Ferguson,* 163 U.S. 537. Under that doctrine, equality of treatment is accorded when the races are provided substantially equal facilities, even though these facilities be separate. In the Delaware case, the Supreme Court of Delaware adhered to that doctrine, but ordered that the plaintiffs be admitted to the white schools because of their superiority to the Negro schools.

The plaintiffs contend that segregated public schools are not "equal" and cannot be made "equal," and that hence they are deprived of the equal protection of the laws. Because of the obvious importance of the question presented, the Court took jurisdiction. Argument was heard in the 1952 Term, and reargument was heard this Term on certain questions propounded by the Court.

Reargument was largely devoted to the circumstances surrounding the adoption of the Fourteenth Amendment in 1868. It covered exhaustively consideration of the Amendment in Congress, ratification by the states, then existing practices in racial segregation, and the views of proponents and opponents of the Amendment. This discussion and our own investigation convince us that, although these sources cast some light, it is not enough to resolve the problem with which we are faced. At best, they are inconclusive. The most avid proponents of the post-War Amendments undoubtedly intended them to remove all legal distinctions among "all persons born or naturalized in the United States." Their opponents, just as certainly, were antagonistic to both the letter and the spirit of the Amendments and wished them to have the most limited effect. What others in Congress and the state legislatures had in mind cannot be determined with any degree of certainty.

An additional reason for the inconclusive nature of the Amendment's history, with respect to segregated schools, is the status of public education at that time. In the South, the movement toward free common schools, supported by general taxation, had not yet taken hold. Education of white children was largely in the hands of private groups. Education of Negroes was almost nonexistent, and practically all of the race were illiterate. In fact, any education of Negroes was forbidden by law in some states. Today, in contrast, many Negroes have achieved outstanding success in the arts and sciences as well as in the business and professional world. It is true that public school education at the time of the Amendment had advanced further in the North, but the effect of the Amendment on Northern States was generally ignored in the congressional debates. Even in the North, the conditions of public education did not approximate those existing today. The curriculum was usually rudimentary; ungraded schools were common in rural areas; the school term was but three months a year in many states; and compulsory school attendance was virtually unknown. As a consequence, it is not surprising that there should be so little in the history of the Fourteenth Amendment relating to its intended effect on public education.

In the first cases in this Court construing the Fourteenth Amendment, decided shortly after its adoption, the Court interpreted it as proscribing all state-imposed discriminations against the Negro race. The doctrine of "separate but equal" did not make its appearance in this Court until 1896 in the case of *Plessy* v. *Ferguson, supra,* involving not education but transportation. American courts have since labored with the doctrine for over half a century. In this Court, there have been six cases involving the "separate but equal" doctrine in the field of public education. In *Cumming* v. *County Board of Education,* 175 U. S. 528, and *Gong Lum* v. *Rice,* 275 U. S. 78, the validity of the doctrine itself was not challenged. In more recent cases, all on the graduate school level, inequality was found in that specific benefits enjoyed by white students were denied to Negro students of the same educational qualifications. *Missouri ex rel. Gaines* v. *Canada,* 305 U. S. 337; *Sipuel* v. *Oklahoma,* 332 U. S. 631; *Sweatt* v. *Painter,* 339 U. S. 629; *McLaurin* v. *Oklahoma State Regents,* 339 U. S. 637. In none of these cases was it necessary to re-examine the doctrine to grant relief to the Negro plaintiff. And in *Sweatt* v. *Painter, supra,* the

Court expressly reserved decision on the question whether *Plessy* v. *Ferguson* should be held inapplicable to public education.

In the instant cases, that question is directly presented. Here, unlike *Sweatt* v. *Painter*, there are findings below that the Negro and white schools involved have been equalized, or are being equalized, with respect to buildings, curricula, qualifications and salaries of teachers, and other "tangible" factors. Our decision, therefore, cannot turn on merely a comparison of these tangible factors in the Negro and white schools involved in each of the cases. We must look instead to the effect of segregation itself on public education.

In approaching this problem, we cannot turn the clock back to 1868 when the Amendment was adopted, or even to 1896 when *Plessy* v. *Ferguson* was written. We must consider public education in the light of its full development and its present place in American life throughout the Nation. Only in this way can it be determined if segregation in public schools deprives these plaintiffs of the equal protection of the laws.

Today, education is perhaps the most important function of state and local governments. Compulsory school attendance laws and the great expenditures for education both demonstrate our recognition of the importance of education to our democratic society. It is required in the performance of our most basic public responsibilities, even service in the armed forces. It is the very foundation of good citizenship. Today it is a principal instrument in awakening the child to cultural values, in preparing him for later professional training, and in helping him to adjust normally to his environment. In these days, it is doubtful that any child may reasonably be expected to succeed in life if he is denied the opportunity of an education. Such an opportunity, where the state has undertaken to provide it, is a right which must be made available to all on equal terms.

We come then to the question presented: Does segregation of children in public schools solely on the basis of race, even though the physical facilities and other "tangible" factors may be equal, deprive the children of the minority group of equal educational opportunities? We believe that it does.

In *Sweatt* v. *Painter, supra,* in finding that a segregated law school for Negroes could not provide them equal educational opportunities, this Court relied in large part on "those qualities which are incapable of objective measurement but which make for greatness in a law school." In *McLaurin* v. *Oklahoma State Regents, supra,* the Court, in requiring that a Negro admitted to a white graduate school be treated like all other students, again resorted to intangible considerations: ". . . his ability to study, to engage in discussions and exchange views with other students, and, in general, to learn his profession." Such considerations apply with added force to children in grade and high schools. To separate them from

others of similar age and qualifications solely because of their race gener-
ates a feeling of inferiority as to their status in the community that may
affect their hearts and minds in a way unlikely ever to be undone. The
effect of this separation on their educational opportunities was well
stated by a finding in the Kansas case by a court which nevertheless felt
compelled to rule against the Negro plaintiffs:

> Segregation of white and colored children in public schools has a det-
> rimental effect upon the colored children. The impact is greater when it
> has the sanction of the law; for the policy of separating the races is usually
> interpreted as denoting the inferiority of the negro group. A sense of
> inferiority affects the motivation of a child to learn. Segregation with the
> sanction of law, therefore, has a tendency to [retard] the educational and
> mental development of negro children and to deprive them of some of
> the benefits they would receive in a racial[ly] integrated school system.

Whatever may have been the extent of psychological knowledge at the
time of *Plessy* v. *Ferguson,* this finding is amply supported by modern
authority. Any language in *Plessy* v. *Ferguson* contrary to this finding is
rejected.

We conclude that in the field of public education the doctrine of
"separate but equal" has no place. Separate educational facilities are inherently unequal. Therefore, we hold that the plaintiffs and others
similarly situated for whom the actions have been brought are, by reason
of the segregation complained of, deprived of the equal protection of the
laws guaranteed by the Fourteenth Amendment. This disposition makes
unnecessary any discussion whether such segregation also violates the Due
Process Clause of the Fourteenth Amendment.

Because these are class actions, because of the wide applicability of
this decision, and because of the great variety of local conditions, the
formulation of decrees in these cases presents problems of considerable
complexity. On reargument, the consideration of appropriate relief was
necessarily subordinated to the primary question—the constitutionality of
segregation in public education. We have now announced that such
segregation is a denial of the equal protection of the laws. In order that
we may have the full assistance of the parties in formulating decrees, the
cases will be restored to the docket, and the parties are requested to present
further argument on Questions 4 and 5 previously propounded by the
Court for the reargument this Term. The Attorney General of the United
States is again invited to participate. The Attorneys General of the states
requiring or permitting segregation in public education will also be permitted to appear as *amici curiae* upon request to do so by September 15,
1954, and submission of briefs by October 1, 1954

It is so ordered.

9
LIBERTY AND EQUALITY

*All of our people have the same goals, the same objective. That objective
is freedom, justice, equality. All of us want recognition and respect as
human beings. We don't want to be integrationists. Nor do we want to be
separationists. We want to be human beings. Integration is only a
method that is used by some groups to obtain freedom, justice, equality
and respect as human beings. Separation is only a method that is used by
other groups to obtain freedom, justice, equality or human dignity.*

MALCOLM X

*We seek the establishment of a democracy of individual participation,
governed by two central aims: that the individual share in those
social decisions determining the quality and direction of his life; that
society be organized to encourage independence in men and provide the
media for their common participation.*

Port Huron Statement

*We must and we shall return to proven ways—not because they are old
but because they are true. We must and we shall set the tides running again
in the cause of freedom.*
    *This party, with its every action, every word, every breath, and
every heartbeat has but a single resolve: Freedom!*

BARRY GOLDWATER

Contemporary America has experienced as much—perhaps, more—
incendiary rhetoric on the subjects of equality and liberty as during any
period in its history. Moreover, differences over these ideas have been
and are being expressed in ways which go far beyond such rhetoric but
are in keeping with its incendiary nature. Whether it takes the form
of turning children away from schools, of burning portions of cities,
or the bombing of banks, violence in the name of ideas or ideals is
not unfamiliar today. How this kind of rhetoric and activity fits within
traditional American political thinking, however, is not so clear.
That it does fit becomes evident if the irony of the modern radical stance
in America is grasped. Essentially, this irony is that the more shocking

304

words and deeds of militant Americans arise from the same roots as the
government that is so often their target. If America is, as some
would claim, in the midst of a crisis, it is one which is characterized by
issues which have long impelled American domestic conflict. The crucial
issues of today fit as readily within the context of American political
thought as those of former days. That the Black Panther Party Platform
concludes by quoting directly from the Declaration of Independence
is NOT surprising, for the words of the Declaration still compel American
political thinking and American political causes.

In the following chapter, there is no attempt to analyze in any
depth the various groups and causes figuring prominently in current
American politics. Rather, an attempt will be made to suggest how such
causes fit into the framework of American political thought as
discussed earlier in this volume. American government has been presented
as the product primarily of principles embodied in the Declaration and
the tensions which have bedeviled it periodically as reflections of
tensions which exist in the same set of principles. It is fundamental in
American life that both libertarian and egalitarian purposes be satisfied,
despite the difficulty, and even impossibility, of ever entirely harmonizing
them. Both of these purposes tend to generate the same revolutionary
fervor evident at the founding, if Americans believe them to be in
jeopardy. It is in this context that the relationship of contemporary
American political causes to traditional American political thought begins
to emerge. First, the causes and their goals are markedly "American" in
that they reflect the same principles which have been at issue since the
founding. Second, the fervor which is characteristic of modern causes
is the same revolutionary fervor which has accompanied American
political movements in the past whenever basic principles were thought
to be endangered or denied. That is, Americans characteristically recall
and respond to their revolutionary origins when defending their
principles and ideals. Finally, the tensions which are the effect
of present-day causes are the same sorts of tensions which have occurred
whenever serious differences in principle have appeared in American
history. When egalitarian demands clash with libertarian beliefs, the
result is invariably a struggle of some proportion. America's problem has
almost always been to harmonize egalitarian demands with libertarian
protections. In this respect, contemporary problems are no exception.

In no single group is the appeal to American principle more clear—
or justified—and the revolutionary fervor more pronounced today than
among black people. While it is difficult to accurately describe "the"
black movement, "the" black leader, or "the" black platform, given the
disparate groups and programs identifiable in the black community, it
is possible to distinguish characteristics common to black political

activity in general. Basically, blacks ask for or demand the equality and
liberty which they recognize as the birthright of Americans. Much can be
made of the differences in the programs or methods employed by men
such as Martin Luther King, Malcolm X, and other black leaders,
but beneath such differences there are impressive similarities.
For example, Dr. King and Malcolm X differed greatly on the tactics that
the black revolution required, but fundamentally their objectives were
the same. King was, from the present perspective, a moderate in that his
use of the tactics of civil disobedience did not imply, in his own mind,
the condoning of violence. More essential in our context is that, while
he identified himself with the oppressed of all nations, he acknowledged
that what he desired for all was owed particularly to Americans. That
is, for King the denial of certain human rights was especially intolerable
in America, founded as it is on the proposition that such rights are
promised at birth.

Oppressed people cannot remain oppressed forever. The yearning for
freedom eventually manifests itself, and that is what has happened to the
American Negro. Something within has reminded him of his birthright
of freedom, and something without has reminded him that it can be gained.[1]

Thus, King regarded human rights as universal but the expression of
them upon which he most depended is typically American.

We will reach the goal of freedom . . . all over the nation, because the
goal of America is freedom. Abused and scorned though we may be, our
destiny is tied up with America's destiny.

If the inexpressible cruelties of slavery could not stop us, the opposition
we now face will surely fail. We will win our freedom because the
sacred heritage of our nation and the eternal will of God are embodied
in our echoing demands.[2]

The doctrines King espoused were no less American than those in the
Declaration.
        Malcolm X, in this sense, shared the same roots as Dr. King.
And his advocacy of black self-determination, black nationalism, and what
later became known as black power was in pursuit of ends similar
to those of King. Freedom and equality were and are the goals of black
militants as much as of black moderates. Malcolm X was as explicit
as King in this respect. Only in his overt militancy did Malcolm depart
from ideas advanced by earlier black leaders.

[1] Martin Luther King, Jr., *Why We Can't Wait* (New York: Signet Books, 1963), p. 87.
[2] *Ibid.*, pp. 92–93.

Any time you know you're within the law, within your legal rights,
within your moral rights, in accord with justice, then die for what you
believe in. But don't die alone. Let your dying be reciprocal. This is what
is meant by equality. What's good for the goose is good for the gander. . . .
We want freedom now, but we're not going to get it saying "We Shall
Overcome." We've got to fight until we overcome. . . . If it's necessary to
form a black nationalist army, we'll form a black nationalist army. It'll be
the ballot or the bullet. It'll be liberty or it'll be death. . . . You let that
white man know, if this is a country of freedom, let it be a country of
freedom; and if it's not a country of freedom, change it.[3]

Such goals explain why it is not surprising that the Black Panthers—
most identified with black militance today—end their party platform with
the Declaration of Independence. Whatever else is said of black politics
today, central to the black cause are principles long engrained in
American life. It is not as aliens to American politics that blacks make
their demands. James Baldwin describes the situation sensitively and
clearly. The American black is incontrovertibly American, and the
questions he poses are American questions.

Despite the terrorization which the Negro in America endured and endures
sporadically until today, despite the cruel and totally inescapable
ambivalence of his status in his country, the battle for his identity has
long ago been won. He is not a visitor to the West but a citizen there, an
American; as American as the Americans who despise him, the Americans
who fear him, the Americans who love him—the Americans who became
less than themselves, or rose to become greater than themselves by virtue of
the fact that the challenge he represented was inescapable.[4]

Other contemporary American causes have different demands but
may be appreciated from the same perspective noted above. In most cases,
to understand their appeals is to understand the traditonal and
revolutionary appeal of American principles. For example, the rhetoric
of women's liberation groups may be shocking to the majority of
present-day Americans, but it is more shocking than new. The
intemperance of some women's rights language cannot mask the fact that
the arguments rely on traditional American ideas. As early as 1837, Harriet
Martineau—the perceptive student of America already mentioned in
a previous chapter—argued that according to the Declaration's principles
women ought to be considered equal in America. Her words are not
foreign to the women's movement today.

[3] Malcolm X, "Ballot or the Bullet," in Herbert J. Storing, *What Country Have I?*
(New York: St. Martin's Press, 1970), p. 155.
[4] James Baldwin, "Stranger in the Village," *ibid.*, p. 223.

One of the fundamental principles announced in the Declaration of
Independence is, that governments derive their just powers from the
consent of the governed. How can the political condition of women be
reconciled with this? . . . The question has been asked, from time
to time, in more countries than one, how obedience to the laws can be
required of women, when no woman has, either actually or virtually, given
any assent to any law. No plausible answer has, as far as I can discover,
been offered; for the good reason, that no plausible answer can be devised.
. . . The principle of the equal rights of both halves of the human race
is all we have to do with here. It is the true democratic principle which can
never be seriously controverted, and only for a short time evaded.[5]

Not long after, in 1848, the First Women's Rights Convention adopted
a set of resolutions intentionally paralleling the Declaration and
stating, in so many words, that females are the equal of males and should
be so treated.[6] Strictly speaking, the analysis of sexual matters included
in much women's liberation literature is beyond the scope of
American politics, yet the demands contained in that literature are
a recognizable part of the American political tradition.

And finally, while there is no single group whose rhetoric seems as
alien to American politics as that of the more agitated of American
young people, there too one may note American roots. The revolutionary
quality of the statements of groups like Students for a Democratic
Society is patterned on what they consider the revolutionary experience
of the American founding. For all their references to systems of
thought not indigenous to America, no symbol is more common to
radical young people than the American Revolution. Thus Tom Hayden
calls for a "New American Revolution," but one patterned upon that
of 1776, both in its style and principles.[7] The use of phrases more
commonly equated with Marxism than American political thought—i.e.,
class struggle, anticolonialist struggle, power to the people, et al.—
by the radical young signifies their disaffection with contemporary
American society and its government, not rejection of American
principles in the abstract. They see themselves as faithful to such
principles in a society in which they have fallen into disuse. Simply, the
revolution of the young radicals arises out of a feeling that America
has been untrue to her own founding. It is because they believe that the
principles of that founding have become moribund that young radicals

[5] Harriet Martineau, *Society in America* (London: Saunders and Otley, 1837), pp. 199 ff.
[6] The First Women's Rights Convention, "Declaration of Sentiments and Resolutions,"
Seneca Falls, New York, July 19–20, 1848, in Leslie B. Tanner, ed., *Voices from
Women's Liberation* (New York: New American Library, 1970), pp. 43–47.
[7] Tom Hayden, *Trial* (New York: Holt, Rinehart and Winston, 1970), Chap. XVI.

choose to advocate revolutionary activity. The S.D.S.'s *Port Huron Statement* of 1962—subsequently discarded by that organization as too moderate in its nonviolent stance—remains an indicator of radical concerns in this regard.

Although mankind desperately needs revolutionary leadership, America rests in national stalemate, its goals ambiguous and tradition-bound instead of informed and clear, its democratic system apathetic and manipulated rather than "of, by, and for the people."[8]

As evidenced by the *Statement,* the S.D.S. commitment is to the things for which America once stood.

The worldwide outbreak of revolution against colonialism and imperialism, the entrenchment of totalitarian states, the menace of war, overpopulation, international disorder, supertechnology—these trends were testing the tenacity of our own commitment to democracy and freedom and our abilities to visualize their application to a world of upheaval.[9]

Paradoxically, then, young radicals join Marxist rhetoric and American principle to advocate the destruction of America for the most American of ends: "to encourage independence in men and provide the media for their common participation."[10] In this respect, the purported socialism of American youth does not mark them as un-American.

    The discovery that contemporary political causes are founded in basic American principles does not ease the problem of satisfying contemporary political demands and relieving dissatisfaction. The claim that a person's desires are in tune with the propositions of the Declaration does not mean that such desires can be easily met. It is possible that a contrary set of desires may be equally in tune with the Declaration. Indeed, the fact that disparate groups can rely on the same set of principles to serve disparate purposes leads to the difficulty of accommodating all the various causes which call for attention today. Antithetical causes, in other words, may use the principles of the Declaration to support antithetical ends. Thus, Senator Goldwater in the 1964 Presidential campaign laid claim to the same ideals as the civil rights groups to whom he was supposedly opposed. Indeed, the principles and intentions Goldwater announced in his acceptance speech at the Republican Convention appear very much in keeping with the rhetoric of civil rights campaigns.

[8] *Port Huron Statement* (Chicago: By Students for a Democratic Society, 1966), pp. 3–4.
[9] *Ibid.*, p. 4.
[10] *Ibid.*, p. 7.

The tide has been running against freedom. Our people have followed
false prophets. We must and we shall return to proven ways—not because
they are old but because they are true. We must and we shall set the
tides running again in the cause of freedom.[11]

Goldwater's position exemplifies once again the tension which is a
principal theme of American political thought. Principled disputes in
America are very often the product of the contradictory directions in
which the basic propositions of American thought lead. A call for
liberty can, and will, be read as a stand against equality, and, contrarily,
a request for equality can, and will, be interpreted as antithetical to
the preservation of liberty.

    These tendencies are very evident today. Such issues as the busing
of school children to achieve racial balance and educational equality
in our schools, what power state legislatures ought to have to determine
the voting districts in their states, and, most obviously, the extent
to which state and federal governing agencies can force compliance with
civil rights legislation all bring up the tensions involved in harmonizing
fundamental American principles. For example, when Senator
Goldwater chose to vote against the Civil Rights Bill of 1964, the
position he took provides a noteworthy expression of the tensions.
While the Senator declared that he was "unalterably opposed to
discrimination," he could not abide features of the Civil Rights Bill
which imposed government regulation of private enterprises in the areas
of public accommodation and employment. For Goldwater, the equal
treatment that government regulation would produce did not offset the
possible damage it might do to individual liberties. In other words,
he held that the egalitarian purposes of the bill had to be measured against
its effects upon "our God-given liberties." [12] Goldwater's decision on the
Civil Rights Bill notwithstanding, his position demonstrates the
difficulty of balancing the demands of liberty and equality. The two
are in continual tension in America and there can be no permanent
resolution short of destroying one of the principles themselves. Using a
word that is in some disfavor today, the best that can be hoped for is
accommodating the two principles in a manner which does not hopelessly
deny either of them. If Senator Goldwater's statement that "extremism
in defense of liberty is no vice" is overdrawn in a democratic regime,
so too would be any effort or demand for equality which employed means
destructive of liberty. It is not fashionable today to speak of

[11] Barry Goldwater, "Acceptance Speech to the Republican National Convention, 1964,"
in James M. Perry, *Barry Goldwater* (Silver Spring, Md.: The National Observer,
1964), p. 140.
[12] Barry Goldwater, "This is Where I Stand," *ibid.*, p. 149.

accommodation or of political prudence. However, these courses seem the only hope that America will not be shattered by the divisive forces inherent in her own principles.

The following selections include examples from a number of the more prominent political movements of the day. Contemporary black political thought is represented by pieces from Martin Luther King ("Letter from Birmingham Jail"), Malcolm X (" The Black Revolution"), and the "Party Platform and Program" of the Black Panther Party. These suggest the wide range of opinions on political action which exist in the black community and also the common foundation from which they all spring. Some of the arguments and demands which exemplify the position of Mexican-Americans are represented by Cesar Chavez's "Letter from Delano." In the realm of women's rights, three selections are offered for comparison, two contemporary and one a good deal older. The contrast between the writing of Harriet Martineau on women's rights in 1837 and contemporary statements of the National Organization of Women (N.O.W.) and the more militant Redstockings is interesting and does not completely obscure their common concerns. A piece from Tom Hayden ("The New American Revolution"), and the S.D.S.'s *Port Huron Statement* stand for today's radical youth and indicate both the revolutionary and traditional qualities of the radical position. Space limitations forbid including a greater sample of the positions of active political groups of the day but these selections, we hope, will give some idea of the quality and tone of their arguments. Finally, and as counterpoint to the selections already mentioned, Senator Goldwater's speech to the Republican Convention of 1964 accepting the Presidential nomination is included.

Martin Luther King, Jr.

LETTER FROM
BIRMINGHAM JAIL

April 16, 1963

My dear fellow clergymen:

While confined here in the Birmingham city jail, I came across your recent statement calling my present activities "unwise and untimely." Seldom do I pause to answer criticism of my work and ideas. If I sought to answer all the criticisms that cross my desk, my secretaries would have little time for anything other than such correspondence in the course of the day, and I would have no time for constructive work. But since I feel that you are men of genuine good will and that your criticisms are sincerely set forth, I want to try to answer your statement in what I hope will be patient and reasonable terms.

I think I should indicate why I am here in Birmingham, since you have been influenced by the view which argues against "outsiders coming in." I have the honor of serving as president of the Southern Christian Leadership Conference, an organization operating in every southern state, with headquarters in Atlanta, Georgia. We have some eighty-five affiliated organizations across the South, and one of them is the Alabama Christian Movement for Human Rights. Frequently we share staff, educational and financial resources with our affiliates. Several months ago the affiliate here in Birmingham asked us to be on call to engage in a nonviolent direct-action program if such were deemed necessary. We readily consented, and when the hour came we lived up to our promise. So I, along with several members of my staff, am here because I was invited here. I am here because I have organizational ties here.

But more basically, I am in Birmingham because injustice is here. Just as the prophets of the eighth century B.C. left their villages and carried their "thus saith the Lord" far beyond the boundaries of their home towns, and just as the Apostle Paul left his village of Tarsus and carried the gospel of Jesus Christ to the far corners of the Greco-Roman world, so am I compelled to carry the gospel of freedom beyond my own home town. Like Paul, I must constantly respond to the Macedonian call for aid.

Moreover, I am cognizant of the interrelatedness of all communities and states. I cannot sit idly by in Atlanta and not be concerned about what happens in Birmingham. Injustice anywhere is a threat to justice everywhere. We are caught in an inescapable network of mutuality, tied in a single garment of destiny. Whatever affects one directly, affects all indirectly. Never again can we afford to live with the narrow, provincial "outside agitator" idea. Anyone who lives inside the United States can never be considered an outsider anywhere within its bounds.

You deplore the demonstrations taking place in Birmingham. But your statement, I am sorry to say, fails to express a similar concern for the conditions that brought about the demonstrations. I am sure that none of you would want to rest content with the superficial kind of social analysis that deals merely with effects and does not grapple with underlying causes. It is unfortunate that demonstrations are taking place in Birmingham, but it is even more unfortunate that the city's white power structure left the Negro community with no alternative.

In any nonviolent campaign there are four basic steps: collection of the facts to determine whether injustices exist; negotiation; self-purification; and direct action. We have gone through all these steps in Birmingham. There can be no gainsaying the fact that racial injustice engulfs this community. Birmingham is probably the most thoroughly segregated city in the United States. Its ugly record of brutality is widely known. Negroes have experienced grossly unjust treatment in the courts. There have been more unsolved bombings of Negro homes and churches in Birmingham than in any other city in the nation. These are the hard, brutal facts of the case. On the basis of these conditions, Negro leaders sought to negotiate with the city fathers. But the latter consistently refused to engage in good-faith negotiation. . . .

You may well ask: "Why direct action? Why sit-ins, marches and so forth? Isn't negotiation a better path?" You are quite right in calling for negotiation. Indeed, this is the very purpose of direct action. Nonviolent direct action seeks to create such a crisis and foster such a tension that a community which has constantly refused to negotiate is forced to confront the issue. It seeks so to dramatize the issue that it can no longer be ignored. My citing the creation of tension as part of the work of the nonviolent-resister may sound rather shocking. But I must confess that I am not afraid of the word "tension." I have earnestly opposed violent tension, but there is a type of constructive, nonviolent tension which is necessary for growth. Just as Socrates felt that it was necessary to create a tension in the mind so that individuals could rise from the bondage of myths and half-truths to the unfettered realm of creative analysis and objective appraisal, so must we see the need for nonviolent gadflies to create the kind of tension in society that will help men rise from the dark depths of prejudice and racism to the majestic heights of understanding and brotherhood.

The purpose of our direct-action program is to create a situation so crisis-packed that it will inevitably open the door to negotiation. I therefore concur with you in your call for negotiation. Too long has our beloved Southland been bogged down in a tragic effort to live in monologue rather than dialogue.

One of the basic points in your statement is that the action that I and my associates have taken in Birmingham is untimely. Some have asked: "Why didn't you give the new city administration time to act?" The only answer that I can give to this query is that the new Birmingham administration must be prodded about as much as the outgoing one, before it will act. We are sadly mistaken if we feel that the election of Albert Boutwell as mayor will bring the millennium to Birmingham. While Mr. Boutwell is a much more gentle person than Mr. Connor, they are both segregationists, dedicated to maintenance of the status quo. I have hope that Mr. Boutwell will be reasonable enough to see the futility of massive resistance to desegregation. But he will not see this without pressure from devotees of civil rights. My friends, I must say to you that we have not made a single gain in civil rights without determined legal and nonviolent pressure. Lamentably, it is an historical fact that privileged groups seldom give up their privileges voluntarily. Individuals may see the moral light and voluntarily give up their unjust posture; but, as Reinhold Niebuhr has reminded us, groups tend to be more immoral than individuals.

We know through painful experience that freedom is never voluntarily given by the oppressor; it must be demanded by the oppressed. Frankly, I have yet to engage in a direct-action campaign that was "well-timed" in the view of those who have not suffered unduly from the disease of segregation. For years now I have heard the word "Wait!" It rings in the ear of every Negro with piercing familiarity. This "Wait" has almost always meant "Never." We must come to see, with one of our distinguished jurists, that "justice too long delayed is justice denied."

We have waited for more than 340 years for our constitutional and God-given rights. The nations of Asia and Africa are moving with jet-like speed toward gaining political independence, but we still creep at horse-and-buggy pace toward gaining a cup of coffee at a lunch counter.

Perhaps it is easy for those who have never felt the stinging darts of segregation to say, "Wait." But when you have seen vicious mobs lynch your mothers and fathers at will and drown your sisters and brothers at whim; when you have seen hate-filled policemen curse, kick and even kill your black brothers and sisters; when you see the vast majority of your twenty million Negro brothers smothering in an airtight cage of poverty in the midst of an affluent society; when you suddenly find your tongue twisted and your speech stammering as you seek to explain to your six-year-old-daughter why she can't go to the public amusement park that has just been advertised on television, and see tears welling up in her eyes when she is told that Funtown is closed to colored children, and see ominous clouds of inferiority beginning to form in her little mental sky, and see her beginning to distort her personality by developing an unconscious bitterness toward white people; when you have to concoct an answer for a five-year-old son who is asking: "Daddy, why do white people treat colored people so mean?"; when you take a cross-county drive and find it necessary to sleep night after night in the uncomfortable corners of your automobile because no motel will accept you; when you are humiliated day in and day out by nagging signs reading "white" and "colored"; when your first name becomes "nigger," your middle name becomes "boy" (however old you are) and your last name becomes "John," and your wife and mother are never given the respected title "Mrs."; when you are harried by day and haunted by night by the fact that you are a Negro, living constantly at tiptoe stance, never quite knowing what to expect next, and are plagued with inner fears and outer resentments; when you are forever fighting a degenerating sense of "nobodiness"—then you will understand why we find it difficult to wait. There comes a time when the cup of endurance runs over, and men are no longer willing to be plunged into the abyss of despair. I hope, sirs, you can understand our legitimate and unavoidable impatience.

You express a great deal of anxiety over our willingness to break laws. This is certainly a legitimate concern. Since we so diligently urge people to obey the Supreme Court's decision of 1954 outlawing segregation in the public schools, at first glance it may seem rather paradoxical for us consciously to break laws. One may well ask: "How can you advocate breaking some laws and obeying others?" The answer lies in the fact that there are two types of laws: just and unjust. I would be the first to advocate obeying just laws. One has not only a legal but a moral responsibility to obey just laws. Conversely, one has a moral responsibility to disobey unjust laws. I would agree with St. Augustine that "an unjust law is no law at all."

Now, what is the difference between the two? How does one determine whether a law is just or unjust? A just law is a man-made code that squares with the moral law or the law of God. An unjust law is a code that is out of harmony with the moral law. To put it in the terms of St. Thomas Aquinas: An unjust law is a human law that is not rooted in eternal law and natural law. Any law that uplifts human personality is just. Any law that degrades human personality is unjust. All segregation statutes are unjust because segregation distorts the soul and damages the personality. It gives the segregator a false sense of superiority and segregated a false sense of inferiority. Segregation, to use the terminology of the Jewish philosopher Martin Buber, substitutes an "I-it" relationship for an "I-thou" relationship and ends up relegating persons to the status of things. Hence segregation is not only politically, economically and sociologically unsound, it is morally wrong and sinful. Paul Tillich has said that sin is separation. Is not segregation an existential expression of man's tragic separation, his awful estrangement, his terrible sinfulness? Thus it is that I can urge men to obey the 1954 decision of the Supreme Court, for it is morally right; and I can urge them to disobey segregation ordinances, for they are morally wrong.

Let us consider a more concrete example of just and unjust laws. An unjust law is a code that a numerical or power majority group compels a minority group to obey but does not make binding on itself. This is *difference* made legal. By the same token, a just law is a code that a majority compels a minority to follow and that it is willing to follow itself. This is *sameness* made legal.

Let me give another explanation. A law is unjust if it is inflicted on a minority that, as a result of being denied the right to vote, had no part in enacting or devising the law. Who can say that the legislature of Alabama which set up that State's segregation laws was democratically elected? Throughout Alabama all sorts of devious methods are used to prevent Negroes from becoming registered voters, and there are some counties in which, even though Negroes constitute a majority of the population, not a single Negro is registered. Can any law enacted under such circumstances be considered democratically structured?

Sometimes a law is just on its face and unjust in its application. For instance, I have been arrested on a charge of parading without a permit. Now, there is nothing wrong in having an ordinance which requires a permit for a parade. But such an ordinance becomes unjust when it is used to maintain segregation and to deny citizens the First-Amendment privilege of peaceful assembly and protest.

I hope you are able to see the distinction I am trying to point out. In no sense do I advocate evading or defying the law, as would the rabid segregationist. That would lead to anarchy. One who breaks an unjust law must do so openly, lovingly, and with a willingness to accept the penalty. I submit that an individual who breaks a law that conscience tells him is unjust, and who willingly accepts the penalty of imprisonment in order to arouse the conscience of the community over its injustice, is in reality expressing the highest respect for law.

Of course, there is nothing new about this kind of civil disobedience. It was evidenced sublimely in the refusal of Shadrach, Meshach and Abednego to obey the laws of Nebuchadnezzar, on the ground that a higher moral law was at stake. It was practiced superbly by the early Christians, who were willing to face hungry lions and the excruciating pain of chopping blocks rather than submit to certain unjust laws of the Roman Empire. To a degree, academic freedom is a reality today because Socrates practiced civil disobedience. In our own nation, the Boston Tea Party represented a massive act of civil disobedience.

We should never forget that everything Adolf Hitler did in Germany was "legal" and everything the Hungarian freedom fighters did in Hungary was "illegal." It was "illegal" to aid and comfort a Jew in Hitler's Germany. Even so, I am sure that, had I lived in Germany at the time, I would have aided and comforted my Jewish brothers. If today I lived in a Communist country where certain principles dear to the Christian faith are suppressed, I would openly advocate disobeying that country's antireligious laws.

I must make two honest confessions to you, my Christian and Jewish brothers. First, I must confess that over the past few years I have been gravely disappointed with the white moderate. I have almost reached the regrettable conclusion that the Negro's great stumbling block in his stride toward freedom is not the White Citizen's Counciler or the Ku Klux Klanner, but the white moderate, who is more devoted to "order" than to justice; who prefers a negative peace which is the absence of tension to a positive peace which is the presence of justice; who constantly says: "I agree with you in the goal you seek, but I cannot agree with your methods of direct action"; who paternalistically believes he can set the timetable for another man's freedom; who lives by a mythical concept of time and who constantly advises the Negro to wait for a "more convenient season." Shallow understanding from people of good will is more frustrating than absolute misunderstanding from people of ill will. Lukewarm acceptance is much more bewildering than outright rejection.

I had hoped that the white moderate would understand that law and order exist for the purpose of establishing justice and that when they fail in this purpose they become the dangerously structured dams that block the flow of social progress. I had hoped that the white moderate would understand that the present tension in the South is a necessary phase of the transition from an obnoxious negative peace, in which the Negro passively accepted his unjust plight, to a substantive and positive peace, in which all men will respect the dignity and worth of human personality. Actually, we who engage in nonviolent direct action are not the creators of tension. We merely bring to the surface the hidden tension that is already alive. We bring it out in the open, where it can be seen and dealt with. Like a boil that can never be cured so long as it is covered up but must be opened with all its ugliness to the natural medicines of air and light, injustice must be exposed, with all the tension its exposure creates, to the light of human conscience and the air of national opinion before it can be cured.

In your statement you assert that our actions, even though peaceful, must be condemned because they precipitate violence. But is this a logical assertion? Isn't this like condemning a robbed man because his possession of money precipitated the evil act of robbery? Isn't this like condemning Socrates because his unswerving commitment to truth and his philosophical inquiries precipitated the act by the misguided populace in which they made him drink hemlock? Isn't this like condemning Jesus because his unique God-consciousness and never-ceasing devotion to God's will precipitated the evil act of crucifixion? We must come to see that, as the federal courts have consistently affirmed, it is wrong to urge an individual to cease his efforts to gain his basic constitutional rights because the quest may precipitate violence. Society must protect the robbed and punish the robber.

I had also hoped that the white moderate would reject the myth concerning time in relation to the struggle for freedom. I have just received a letter from a white brother in Texas. He writes: "All Christians know that the colored people will receive equal rights eventually, but it is possible that you are in too great a religious hurry. It has taken Christianity almost two thousand years to accomplish what it has. The teachings of Christ take time to come to earth." Such an attitude stems from a tragic misconception of time, from the strangely irrational notion that there is something in the very flow of time that will inevitably cure all ills. Actually, time itself is neutral; it can be used either destructively or constructively. More and more I feel that the people of ill will have used time much more effectively than have the people of good will. We will have to repent in this generation not merely for the hateful words and actions of the bad people but for the appalling silence of the good people. Human progress never rolls in on wheels of inevitability; it comes through the tireless efforts of men willing to be co-workers with God, and without this hard work, time itself becomes an ally of the forces of social stagnation. We must use time creatively, in the knowledge that the time is always ripe to do right. Now is the time to make real the promise of democracy and transform our pending national elegy into a creative psalm of brotherhood. Now is the time to lift our national policy from the quicksand of racial injustice to the solid rock of human dignity. . . .

Oppressed people cannot remain oppressed forever. The yearning for freedom eventually manifests itself, and that is what has happened to the American Negro. Something within has reminded him of his birthright of freedom, and something without has reminded him that it can be gained. Consciously or unconsciously, he has been caught up by the *Zeitgeist*, and with his black brothers of Africa and his brown and yellow brothers of Asia, South America and the Caribbean, the United States Negro is moving with a sense of great urgency toward the promised land of racial justice. If one recognizes this vital urge that has engulfed the Negro community, one should readily understand why public demonstrations are taking place. The Negro has many pent-up resentments and latent frustrations, and he must release them. So let him march; let him make prayer pilgrimages to the city hall; let him go on freedom rides— and try to understand why he must do so. If his repressed emotions are not released in nonviolent ways, they will seek expression through violence; this is not a threat but a fact of history. So I have not said to my people: "Get rid of your discontent." Rather, I have tried to say that this normal and healthy discontent can be channeled into the creative outlet of nonviolent direct action. And now this approach is being termed extremist. . . .

I hope the church as a whole will meet the challenge of this decisive hour. But even if the church does not come to the aid of justice, I have no despair about the future. I have no fear about the outcome of our struggle in Birmingham, even if our motives are at present misunderstood. We will reach the goal of freedom in Birmingham and all over the nation, because the goal of America is freedom. Abused and scorned though we may be, our destiny is tied up with America's destiny. Before the pilgrims landed at Plymouth, we were here. Before the pen of Jefferson etched the majestic words of the Declaration of Independence across the pages of history, we were here. For more than two centuries our forebears labored in this country without wages; they made cotton king; they built the homes of their masters while suffering gross injustice and shameful humiliation—and yet out of a bottomless vitality they continued to thrive and develop. If the inexpressible cruelties of slavery could not stop us, the opposition we now face will surely fail. We will win our freedom because the sacred heritage of our nation and the eternal will of God are embodied in our echoing demands. . . .

I wish you had commended the Negro sit-inners and demonstrators of Birmingham for their sublime courage, their willingness to suffer and their amazing discipline in the midst of great provocation. One day the South will recognize its real heroes. They will be the James Merediths, with the noble sense of purpose that enables them to face jeering and hostile mobs, and with the agonizing loneliness that characterizes the life of the pioneer. They will be old, oppressed, battered Negro women, symbolized in a seventy-two-year-old woman in Montgomery, Alabama, who rose up with a sense of dignity and with her people decided not to ride segregated buses, and who responded with ungrammatical profundity to one who inquired about her weariness: "My feets is tired, but my soul is at rest." They will be the young high school and college students, the young ministers of the gospel and a host of their elders, courageously and nonviolently sitting in at lunch counters and willingly going to jail for conscience' sake. One day the South will know that when these disinherited children of God sat down at lunch counters, they were in reality standing up for what is best in the American dream and for the most sacred values in our Judaeo-Christian heritage, thereby bringing our nation back to those great wells of democracy which were dug deep by the founding fathers in their formulation of the Constitution and the Declaration of Independence.

Never before have I written so long a letter. I'm afraid it is much too long to take your precious time. I can assure you that it would have been much shorter if I had been writing from a comfortable desk, but what else can one do when he is alone in a narrow jail cell, other than write long letters, think long thoughts and pray long prayers?

If I have said anything in this letter that overstates the truth and indicates an unreasonable impatience, I beg you to forgive me. If I have said anything that understates the truth and indicates my having a patience that allows me to settle for anything less than brotherhood, I beg God to forgive me.

I hope this letter finds you strong in the faith. I also hope that circumstances will soon make it possible for me to meet each of you, not as an integrationist or a civil-rights leader but as a fellow clergyman and a Christian brother. Let us all hope that the dark clouds of racial prejudice will soon pass away and the deep fog of misunderstanding will be lifted from our fear-drenched communities, and in some not too distant tomorrow the radiant stars of love and brotherhood will shine over our great nation with all their scintillating beauty.

Yours for the cause of Peace and Brotherhood,
Martin Luther King, Jr.

Malcolm X

THE BLACK REVOLUTION

There is no system more corrupt than a system that represents itself as the example of freedom, the example of democracy, and can go all over this earth telling other people how to straighten out their house, when you have citizens of this country who have to use bullets if they want to cast a ballot.

The greatest weapon the colonial powers have used in the past against our people has always been divide-and-conquer. America is a colonial power. She has colonized 22 million Afro-Americans by depriving us of first-class citizenship, by depriving us of civil rights, actually by depriving us of human rights. She has not only deprived us of the right to be a citizen, she has deprived us of the right to be human beings, the right to be recognized and respected as men and women. In this country the black can be fifty years old and he is still a "boy."

I grew up with white people. I was integrated before they even invented the word and I have never met white people yet—if you are around them long enough—who won't refer to you as a "boy" or a "gal," no matter how old you are or what school you came out of, no matter what your intellectual or professional level is. In this society we remain "boys."

So America's strategy is the same strategy as that which was used in the past by the colonial powers: divide and conquer. She plays one Negro leader against the other. She plays one Negro organization against the other. She makes us think we have different objectives, different goals. As soon as one Negro says something, she runs to this Negro and asks him, "What do you think about what he said?" Why, anybody can see through that today—except some of the Negro leaders.

All of our people have the same goals, the same objective. That objective is freedom, justice, equality. All of us want recognition and respect as human beings. We don't want to be integrationists. Nor do we want to be separationists. We want to be human beings. Integration is only a method that is used by some groups to obtain freedom, justice, equality and respect as human beings. Separation is only a method that is used by other groups to obtain freedom, justice, equality or human dignity.

Our people have made the mistake of confusing the methods with the objectives. As long as we agree on objectives, we should never fall out with each other just because we believe in different methods or tactics or strategy to reach a common objective.

We have to keep in mind at all times that we are not fighting for integration, nor are we fighting for separation. We are fighting for recognition as human beings. We are fighting for the right to live as free humans in this society. In fact, we are actually fighting for rights that are even greater than civil rights and that is human rights. . . .

Among the so-called Negroes in this country, as a rule the civil-rights groups, those who believe in civil rights, spend most of their time trying to prove they are Americans. Their thinking is usually domestic, confined to the boundaries of America, and they always look upon themselves as a minority. When they look upon themselves upon the American stage, the American stage is a white stage. So a black man standing on that stage in America automatically is in the minority. He is the under-dog, and in his struggle he always uses an approach that is a begging, hat-in-hand, compromising approach.

Whereas the other segment or section in America, known as the black nationalists, are more interested in human rights than they are in civil rights. And they place more stress on human rights than they do on civil rights. The difference between the thinking and the scope of the Negroes who are involved in the human-rights struggle and those who are involved in the civil-rights struggle is that those so-called Negroes involved in the human-rights struggle don't look upon themselves as Americans.

They look upon themselves as a part of dark mankind. They see the whole struggle not within the confines of the American stage, but they look upon the struggle on the world stage. And, in the world context, they see that the dark man outnumbers the white man. On the world stage the white man is just a microscopic minority.

So in this country you find two different types of Afro-Americans— the type who looks upon himself as a minority and you as the majority, because his scope is limited to the American scene; and then you have the type who looks upon himself as part of the majority and you as part of a microscopic minority. And this one uses a different approach in trying to struggle for his rights. He doesn't beg. He doesn't thank you for what you give him, because you are only giving him what he should have had a hundred years ago. He doesn't think you are doing him any favors.

He doesn't see any progress that he has made since the Civil War. He sees not one iota of progress because, number one, if the Civil War had freed him, he wouldn't need civil-rights legislation today. If the Emancipation Proclamation, issued by that great shining liberal called Lincoln, had freed him, he wouldn't be singing "We Shall Overcome" today. If the amendments to the Constitution had solved his problem, his problem wouldn't still be here today. And if the Supreme Court desegregation decision of 1954 was genuinely and sincerely designed to solve his problem, his problem wouldn't be with us today.

So this kind of black man is thinking. He can see where every maneuver that America has made, supposedly to solve this problem, has been nothing but political trickery and treachery of the worst order. Today he doesn't have any confidence in these so-called liberals. (I know that all that have come in here tonight don't call yourselves liberals. Because that's a nasty name today. It represents hypocrisy.) So these two different types of black people exist in the so-called Negro community and they are beginning to wake up and their awakening is producing a very dangerous situation.

You have whites in the community who express sincerity when they say they want to help. Well, how can they help? How can a white person help the black man solve his problem? Number one, you can't solve it for him. You can help him solve it, but you can't solve it for him today. One of the best ways that you can help him solve it is to let the so-called Negro, who has been involved in the civil-rights struggle, see that the civil-rights struggle must be expanded beyond the level of civil rights to human rights. Once it is expanded beyond the level of civil rights to the level of human rights, it opens the door for all of our brothers and sisters in Africa and Asia, who have their independence, to come to our rescue.

When you go to Washington, D.C., expecting those crooks down there—and that's what they are—to pass some kind of civil-rights legislation to correct a very criminal situation, what you are doing is encouraging the black man, who is the victim, to take his case into the court that's controlled by the criminal that made him the victim. It will never be solved in that way. . . .

The civil-rights struggle involves the black man taking his case to the white man's court. But when he fights it at the human-rights level, it is a different situation. It opens the door to take Uncle Sam to the world court. The black man doesn't have to go to court to be free. Uncle Sam should be taken to court and made to tell why the black man is not free in a so-called free society. Uncle Sam should be taken into the United Nations and charged with violating the UN charter of human rights.

You can forget civil rights. How are you going to get civil rights with men like Eastland and men like Dirksen and men like Johnson? It has to be taken out of their hands and taken into the hands of those whose power and authority exceed theirs. Washington has become too corrupt. Uncle Sam has become bankrupt when it comes to a conscience—it is impossible for Uncle Sam to solve the problem of 22 million black people in this country. It is absolutely impossible to do it in Uncle Sam's courts —whether it is the Supreme Court or any other kind of court that comes under Uncle Sam's jurisdiction.

The only alternative that the black man has in America today is to take it out of Senator Dirksen's and Senator Eastland's and President Johnson's jurisdiction and take it downtown on the East River and place it before that body of men who represent international law, and let them know that the human rights of black people are being violated in a country that professes to be the moral leader of the free world.

Any time you have a filibuster in America, in the Senate, in 1964 over the rights of 22 million black people, over the citizenship of 22 million black people, or that will affect the freedom and justice and equality of 22 million black people, it's time for that government itself to be taken before a world court. How can you condemn South Africa? There are only 11 million of our people in South Africa, there are 22 million of them here. And we are receiving an injustice which is just as criminal as that which is being done to the black people of South Africa.

So today those whites who profess to be liberals—and as far as I am concerned it's just lip-profession—you understand why our people don't have civil rights. You're white. You can go and hang out with another white liberal and see how hypocritical they are. A lot of you sitting right here know that you've seen whites up in a Negro's face with flowery words, and as soon as that Negro walks away you listen to how your white friend talks. We have black people who can pass as white. We know how you talk.

We can see that it is nothing but a governmental conspiracy to continue to deprive the black people in this country of their rights. And the only way we will get these rights restored is by taking it out of Uncle Sam's hands. Take him to court and charge him with genocide, the mass murder of millions of black people in this country—political murder, economic murder, social murder, mental murder. This is the crime that this government has committed, and if you yourself don't do something about it in time, you are going to open the doors for something to be done about it from outside forces.

I read in the paper yesterday where one of the Supreme Court justices, Goldberg, was crying about the violation of human rights of three million Jews in the Soviet Union. Imagine this. I haven't got anything against Jews, but that's their problem. How in the world are you going to cry about problems on the other side of the world when you haven't got the problems straightened out here? How can the plight of three million Jews in Russia be qualified to be taken to the United Nations by a man who is a justice in this Supreme Court, and is supposed to be a liberal, supposed to be a friend of black people, and hasn't opened up his mouth one time about taking the plight of black people down here to the United Nations? ...

If Negroes could vote south of the—yes, if Negroes could vote south of the Canadian border—south South, if Negroes could vote in the southern part of the South, Ellender wouldn't be the head of the Agricultural and Forestry Committee, Richard Russell wouldn't be head of the Armed Services Committee, Robertson of Virginia wouldn't be head of the Banking and Currency Committee. Imagine that, all of the banking and currency of the government is in the hands of a cracker.

In fact, when you see how many of these committee men are from the South, you can see that we have nothing but a cracker government in Washington, D.C. And their head is a cracker president. I said a cracker president. Texas is just as much a cracker state as Mississippi. . . .

The first thing this man did when he came in office was invite all the big Negroes down for coffee. James Farmer was one of the first ones, the head of CORE. I have nothing against him. He's all right—Farmer, that is. But could that same president have invited James Farmer to Texas for coffee? And if James Farmer went to Texas, could he have taken his white wife with him to have coffee with the president? Any time you have a man who can't straighten out Texas, how can he straighten out the country? No, you're barking up the wrong tree.

If Negroes in the South could vote, the Dixiecrats would lose power. When the Dixiecrats lost power, the Democrats would lose power. A Dixiecrat lost is a Democrat lost. Therefore the two of them have to conspire with each other to stay in power. The Northern Dixiecrat puts all the blame on the Southern Dixiecrat. It's a con game, a giant political con game. The job of the Northern Democrat is to make the Negro think that he is our friend. He is always smiling and wagging his tail and telling us how much he can do for us if we vote for him. But at the same time that he's out in front telling us what he's going to do, behind the door he's in cahoots with the Southern Democrat setting up the machinery to make sure he'll never have to keep his promise.

This is the conspiracy that our people have faced in this country for the past hundred years. And today you have a new generation of black people who have come on the scene, who have become disenchanted with the entire system, who have become disillusioned over the system, and who are ready now and willing to do something about it.

So, in my conclusion, in speaking about the black revolution, America today is at a time or in a day or at an hour where she is the first country on this earth that can actually have a bloodless revolution. In the past, revolutions have been bloody. Historically you just don't have a peaceful revolution. Revolutions are bloody, revolutions are violent, revolutions cause bloodshed and death follows in their paths. America is the only country in history in a position to bring about a revolution without violence and bloodshed. But America is not morally equipped to do so.

Why is America in a position to bring about a bloodless revolution? Because the Negro in this country holds the balance of power, and if the Negro in this country were given what the Constitution says he is supposed to have, the added power of the Negro in this country would sweep all of the racists and the segregationists out of office. It would change the entire political structure of the country. It would wipe out the Southern segregationism that now controls America's foreign policy, as well as America's domestic policy.

And the only way without bloodshed that this can be brought about is that the black man has to be given full use of the ballot in every one of the fifty states. But if the black man doesn't get the ballot, then you are going to be faced with another man who forgets the ballot and starts using the bullet.

Revolutions are fought to get control of land, to remove the absentee landlord and gain control of the land and the institutions that flow from that land. The black man has been in a very low condition because he has had no control whatsoever over any land. He has been a beggar economically, a beggar politically, a beggar socially, a beggar even when it comes to trying to get some education. The past type of mentality, that was developed in this colonial system among our people, today is being overcome. And as the young ones come up, they know what they want. And as they listen to your beautiful preaching about democracy and all those other flowery words, they know what they're supposed to have.

So you have a people today who not only know what they want, but also know what they are supposed to have. And they themselves are creating another generation that is coming up that not only will know what it wants and know what it should have, but also will be ready and willing to do whatever is necessary to see that what they should have materializes immediately. Thank you.

PLATFORM, PROGRAM, AND RULES
(1966)

PARTY PLATFORM AND PROGRAM

What We Want
What We Believe

1. *We want freedom. We want power to determine the destiny of our Black Community.*

We believe that black people will not be free until we are able to determine our destiny.

2. *We want full employment for our people.*

We believe that the federal government is responsible and obligated to give every man employment or a guaranteed income. We believe that if the white American businessmen will not give full employment, then the means of production should be taken from the businessmen and placed in the community so that the people of the community can organize and employ all of its people and give a high standard of living.

3. *We want an end to the robbery by the white man of our Black Community.*

We believe that this racist government has robbed us and now we are demanding the overdue debt of forty acres and two mules. Forty acres and two mules was promised 100 years ago as restitution for slave labor and mass murder of black people. We will accept the payment in currency which will be distributed to our many communities. The Germans are now aiding the Jews in Israel for the genocide of the Jewish people. The Germans murdered six million Jews. The American racist has taken part in the slaughter of over fifty million black people; therefore, we feel that this is a modest demand that we make.

4. *We want decent housing, fit for shelter of human beings.*

We believe that if the white landlords will not give decent housing to our black community, then the housing and the land should be made into cooperatives so that our community, with government aid, can build and make decent housing for its people.

5. *We want education for our people that exposes the true nature of this decadent American society. We want education that teaches us our true history and our role in the present-day society.*

We believe in an educational system that will give to our people a knowledge of self. If a man does not have knowledge of himself and his position in society and the world, then he has little chance to relate to anything else.

6. *We want all black men to be exempt from military service.*

We believe that Black people should not be forced to fight in the military service to defend a racist government that does not protect us. We will not fight and kill other people of color in the world who, like black people, are being victimized by the white racist government of America. We will protect ourselves from the force and violence of the racist police and the racist military, by whatever means necessary.

7. *We want an immediate end to* POLICE BRUTALITY *and* MURDER *of black people.*

We believe we can end police brutality in our black community by organizing black self-defense groups that are dedicated to defending our black community from racist police oppression and brutality. The Second Amendment to the Constitution of the United States gives a right to bear arms. We therefore believe that all black people should arm themselves for self-defense.

8. *We want freedom for all black men held in federal, state, county and city prisons and jails.*

We believe that all black people should be released from the many jails and prisons because they have not received a fair and impartial trial.

9. *We want all black people when brought to trial to be tried in court by a jury of their peer group or people from their black communities, as defined by the Constitution of the United States.*

We believe that the courts should follow the United States Constitution so that black people will receive fair trials. The 14th Amendment of the U.S. Constitution gives a man a right to be tried by his peer group. A peer is a person from a similar economic, social, religious, geographical, environmental, historical and racial background. To do this the court will be forced to select a jury from the black community from which the black defendant came. We have been, and are being tried by all-white juries that have no understanding of the "average reasoning man" of the black community.

10. *We want land, bread, housing, education, clothing, justice and peace. And as our major political objective, a United Nations-supervised*

plebiscite to be held throughout the black colony in which only black colonial subjects will be allowed to participate, for the purpose of determining the will of black people as to their national destiny.

When, in the course of human events, it becomes necessary for one people to dissolve the political bands which have connected them with another, and to assume, among the powers of the earth, the separate and equal station to which the laws of nature and nature's God entitle them, a decent respect to the opinions of mankind requires that they should declare the causes which impel them to the separation.

We hold these truths to be self-evident, that all men are created equal; that they are endowed by their Creator with certain unalienable rights; that among these are life, liberty, and the pursuit of happiness. *That, to secure these rights, governments are instituted among men, deriving their just powers from the consent of the governed; that, whenever any form of government becomes destructive of these ends, it is the right of the people to alter or to abolish it, and to institute a new government, laying its foundation on such principles, and organizing its powers in such form, as to them shall seem most likely to effect their safety and happiness.* Prudence, indeed, will dictate that governments long established should not be changed for light and transient causes; and, accordingly, all experience hath shown, that mankind are more disposed to suffer, while evils are sufferable, than to right themselves by abolishing the forms to which they are accustomed. *But, when a long train of abuses and usurpations, pursuing invariably the same object, evinces a design to reduce them under absolute despotism, it is their right, it is their duty, to throw off such government, and to provide new guards for their future security.*

RULES OF THE BLACK PANTHER PARTY

Every member of the BLACK PANTHER PARTY throughout this country of racist America must abide by these rules as functional members of this party. CENTRAL COMMITTEE members, CENTRAL STAFFS, and LOCAL STAFFS, including all captains subordinate to either national, state, and local leadership of the BLACK PANTHER PARTY will enforce these rules. Length of suspension or other disciplinary action necessary for violation of these rules will depend on national decisions by national, state or state area, and local committees and staffs where said rule or rules of the BLACK PANTHER PARTY WERE VIOLATED.

Every member of the party must know these verbatim by heart. And apply them daily. Each member must report any violation of these rules to their leadership or they are counter-revolutionary and are also subjected to suspension by the BLACK PANTHER PARTY.

The rules are:

1. No party member can have narcotics or weed in his possession while doing party work.

2. Any party member found shooting narcotics will be expelled from this party.

3. No party member can be DRUNK while doing daily party work.

4. No party member will violate rules relating to office work, general meetings of the BLACK PANTHER PARTY, and meetings of the BLACK PANTHER PARTY ANYWHERE.

5. No party member will USE, POINT, or FIRE a weapon of any kind unnecessarily or accidentally at anyone.

6. No party member can join any other army force other than the BLACK LIBERATION ARMY.

7. No party member can have a weapon in his possession while DRUNK or loaded off narcotics or weed.

8. No party member will commit any crimes against other party members or BLACK people at all, and cannot steal or take from the people, not even a needle or a piece of thread.

9. When arrested BLACK PANTHER MEMBERS will give only name, address, and will sign nothing. Legal first aid must be understood by all Party members.

10. The Ten-Point Program and platform of the BLACK PANTHER PARTY must be known and understood by each Party member.

11. Party Communications must be National and Local.

12. The 10-10-10 program should be known by all members and also understood by all members.

13. All Finance officers will operate under the jurisdiction of the Ministry of Finance.

14. Each person will submit a report of daily work.

15. Each Sub-Section Leaders, Section Leaders, and Lieutenants, Captains must submit Daily reports of work.

16. All Panthers must learn to operate and service weapons correctly.

17. All Leadership personnel who expel a member must submit this information to the Editor of the Newspaper, so that it will be published in the paper and will be known by all chapters and branches.

18. Political Education Classes are mandatory for general membership.

19. Only office personnel assigned to respective offices each day should be there. All others are to sell papers and do Political work out in the community, including Captains, Section Leaders, etc.

20. COMMUNICATIONS—all chapters must submit weekly reports in writing to the National Headquarters.

21. All Branches must implement First Aid and/or Medical Cadres.

22. All Chapters, Branches, and components of the BLACK PANTHER PARTY must submit a monthly Financial Report to the Ministry of Finance, and also the Central Committee.

23. Everyone in a leadership position must read no less than two hours per day to keep abreast of the changing political situation.

24. No chapter or branch shall accept grants, poverty funds, money or any other aid from any government agency without contacting the National Headquarters.

25. All chapters must adhere to the policy and the ideology laid down by the CENTRAL COMMITTEE of the BLACK PANTHER PARTY.

26. All Branches must submit weekly reports in writing to their respective Chapters.

8 Points of Attention
1. Speak politely.
2. Pay fairly for what you buy.
3. Return everything you borrow.
4. Pay for anything you damage.
5. Do not hit or swear at people.
6. Do not damage property or crops of the poor, oppressed masses.
7. Do not take liberties with women.
8. If we ever have to take captives do not ill-treat them.

3 Main Rules of Discipline
1. Obey orders in all your actions.
2. Do not take a single needle or a piece of thread from the poor and oppressed masses.
3. Turn in everything captured from the attacking enemy.

LETTER FROM DELANO

Good Friday 1969.

E. L. Barr, Jr., President
California Grape and Tree Fruit League
717 Market St.
San Francisco, California

Dear Mr. Barr:

I am sad to hear about your accusations in the press that our union movement and table grape boycott have been successful because we have used violence and terror tactics. If what you say is true, I have been a failure and should withdraw from the struggle; but you are left with the awesome moral responsibility, before God and man, to come forward with whatever information you have so that corrective action can begin at once. If for any reason you fail to come forth to substantiate your charges, then you must be held responsible for committing violence against us, albeit violence of the tongue. I am convinced that you as a human being did not mean what you said but rather acted hastily under pressure from the public relations firm that has been hired to try to counteract the tremendous moral force of our movement. How many times we ourselves have felt the need to lash out in anger and bitterness.

Today on Good Friday 1969 we remember the life and the sacrifice of Martin Luther King, Jr., who gave himself totally to the nonviolent struggle for peace and justice. In his "Letter from Birmingham Jail" Dr. King describes better than I could our hopes for the strike and boycott: "Injustice must be exposed, with all the tension its exposure creates, to the light of human conscience and the air of national opinion before it can be cured." For our part I admit that we have seized upon every tactic and strategy consistent with the morality of our cause to expose that injustice and thus to heighten the sensitivity of the American conscience so that farm workers will have without bloodshed their own union and the dignity of bargaining with their agribusiness employers. By lying about the nature of our movement, Mr. Barr, you are working against nonviolent social change. Unwittingly perhaps, you may unleash that other force which our union by discipline and deed, censure and education has sought to avoid, that panacean shortcut: that senseless violence which honors no color, class or neighborhood.

You must understand—I must make you understand—that our membership and the hopes and aspirations of the hundreds of thousands of the poor and dispossessed that have been raised on our account are, above all, human beings, no better and no worse than any other cross-section of human society; we are not saints because we are poor, but by the same measure neither are we immoral. We are men and women who have suffered and endured much, and not only because of our abject poverty but because we have been kept poor. The colors of our skins, the languages of our cultural and native origins, the lack of formal education, the exclusion from the democratic process, the numbers of our slain in recent wars—all these burdens generation after generation have sought to demoralize us, to break our human spirit. But God knows that we are not beasts of burden, agricultural implements or rented slaves; we are men. And mark this well, Mr. Barr, we are men locked in a death struggle against man's inhumanity to man in the industry that you represent. And this struggle itself gives meaning to our life and ennobles our dying.

As your industry has experienced, our strikers here in Delano and those who represent us throughout the world are well trained for this struggle. They have been under the gun, they have been kicked and beaten and herded by dogs, they have been cursed and ridiculed, they have been stripped and chained and jailed, they have been sprayed with the poisons used in the vineyards; but they have been taught not to lie down and die nor to flee in shame, but to resist with every ounce of human endurance and spirit. To resist not with retaliation in kind but to overcome with love and compassion, with ingenuity and creativity, with hard work and longer hours, with stamina and patient tenacity, with truth and public appeal, with friends and allies, with mobility and discipline, with politics and law, and with prayer and fasting. They were not trained in a month or even a year; after all, this new harvest season will mark our fourth full year of strike and even now we continue to plan and prepare for the years to come. Time accomplishes for the poor what money does for the rich.

This is not to pretend that we have everywhere been successful enough or that we have not made mistakes. And while we do not belittle or underestimate our adversaries—for they are the rich and the powerful and they possess the land—we are not afraid nor do we cringe from the confrontation. We welcome it! We have planned for it. We know that our cause is just, that history is a story of social revolution, and that the poor shall inherit the land.

Once again, I appeal to you as the representative of your industry and as a man. I ask you to recognize and bargain with our union before the economic pressure of the boycott and strike takes an irrevocable toll; but if not, I ask you to at least sit down with us to discuss the safeguards necessary to keep our historical struggle free of violence. I make this appeal because as one of the leaders of our nonviolent movement, I know and accept my responsibility for preventing, if possible, the destruction of human life and property. For these reasons and knowing of Gandhi's admonition that fasting is the last resort in place of the sword, during a most critical time in our movement last February 1968 I undertook a 25-day fast. I repeat to you the principle enunciated to the membership at the start of the fast: if to build our union required the deliberate taking of life, either the life of a grower or his child, or the life of a farm worker or his child, then I choose not to see the union built.

Mr. Barr, let me be painfully honest with you. You must understand these things. We advocate militant nonviolence as our means for social revolution and to achieve justice for our people, but we are not blind or deaf to the desperate and moody winds of human frustration, impatience and rage that blow among us. Gandhi himself admitted that if his only choice were cowardice or violence, he would choose violence. Men are not angels, and time and tide wait for no man. Precisely because of these powerful human emotions, we have tried to involve masses of people in their own struggle. Participation and self-determination remain the best experience of freedom, and free men instinctively prefer democratic change and even protect the rights guaranteed to seek it. Only the enslaved in despair have need of violent overthrow.

This letter does not express all that is in my heart Mr. Barr. But if it says nothing else it says that we do not hate you or rejoice to see your industry destroyed; we hate the agribusiness system that seeks to keep us enslaved, and we shall overcome and change it not by retaliation or bloodshed but by a determined nonviolent struggle carried on by the masses of farm workers who intend to be free and human.

Sincerely yours,
Cesar E. Chavez

United Farm Workers Organizing
    Committee, A.F.L.-C.I.O.
Delano, California

Harriet Martineau

WOMEN'S POLITICAL RIGHTS
(1837)

POLITICAL NON-EXISTENCE OF WOMEN

One of the fundamental principles announced in the Declaration of Independence is, that governments derive their just powers from the consent of the governed. How can the political condition of women be reconciled with this?

Governments in the United States have power to tax women who hold property; to divorce them from their husbands; to fine, imprison, and execute them for certain offences. Whence do these governments derive their powers? They are not "just," as they are not derived from the consent of the women thus governed.

Governments in the United States have power to enslave certain women; and also to punish other women for inhuman treatment of such slaves. Neither of these powers are "just;" not being derived from the consent of the governed.

Governments decree to women in some States half their husband's property; in others one-third. In some, a woman, on her marriage, is made to yield all her property to her husband; in others, to retain a portion, or the whole, in her own hands. Whence do governments derive the unjust power of thus disposing of property without the consent of the governed?

The democratic principle condemns all this as wrong; and requires the equal political representation of all rational beings. Children, idiots, and criminals, during the season of sequestration, are the only fair exceptions.

The case is so plain that I might close it here; but it is interesting to inquire how so obvious a decision has been so evaded as to leave to women no political rights whatever. The question has been asked, from time to time, in more countries than one, how obedience to the laws can be required of women, when no woman has, either actually or virtually, given any assent to any law. No plausible answer has, as far as I can

Harriet Martineau, *Society in America* (London: Saunders and Otley, 1837), Vol. I, pp. 199–207.

discover, been offered; for the good reason, that no plausible answer can be devised. The most principled democratic writers on government have on this subject sunk into fallacies, as disgraceful as any advocate of despotism has adduced. In fact, they have thus sunk from being, for the moment, advocates of despotism. Jefferson in America, and James Mill at home, subside, for the occasion, to the level of the author of the Emperor of Russia's Catechism for the young Poles.

Jefferson says, "Were our State a pure democracy, in which all the inhabitants should meet together to transact all their business, there would yet be excluded from their deliberations,

"1. Infants, until arrived at years of discretion;

"2. Women, who, to prevent depravation of morals, and ambiguity of issue, could not mix promiscuously in the public meetings of men;

"3. Slaves, from whom the unfortunate state of things with us takes away the rights of will and of property."

If the slave disqualification, here assigned, were shifted up under the head of Women, their case would be nearer the truth than as it now stands. Woman's lack of will and of property, is more like the true cause of her exclusion from the representation, than that which is actually set down against her. As if there could be no means of conducting public affairs but by promiscuous meetings! As if there would be more danger in promiscuous meetings for political business than in such meetings for worship, for oratory, for music, for dramatic entertainments,—for any of the thousand transactions of civilized life! The plea is not worth another word.

Mill says, with regard to representation, in his Essay on Government, "One thing is pretty clear; that all those individuals, whose interests are involved in those of other individuals, may be struck off without inconvenience. . . . In this light, women may be regarded, the interest of almost all of whom is involved, either in that of their fathers or in that of their husbands."

The true democratic principle is, that no person's interests can be, or can be ascertained to be, identical with those of any other person. This allows the exclusion of none but incapables.

The word "almost," in Mr. Mill's second sentence, rescues women from the exclusion he proposes. As long as there are women who have neither husbands nor fathers, his proposition remains an absurdity.

The interests of women who have fathers and husbands can never be identical with theirs, while there is a necessity for laws to protect women against their husbands and fathers. This statement is not worth another word.

Some who desire that there should be an equality of property between men and women, oppose representation, on the ground that political duties would be incompatible with the other duties which women have to discharge. The reply to this is, that women are the best judges here. God has given time and power for the discharge of all duties; and, if he had not, it would be for women to decide which they would take, and which they would leave. But their guardians follow the ancient fashion of deciding what is best for their wards. The Emperor of Russia discovers when a coat of arms and title do not agree with a subject prince. The King of France early perceives that the air of Paris does not agree with a free-thinking foreigner. The English Tories feel the hardship that it would be to impose the franchise on every artizan, busy as he is in getting his bread. The Georgian planter perceives the hardship that freedom would be to his slaves. And the best friends of half the human race peremptorily decide for them as to their rights, their duties, their feelings, their powers. In all these cases, the persons thus cared for feel that the abstract decision rests with themselves; that, though they may be compelled to submit, they need not acquiesce.

It is pleaded that half of the human race does acquiesce in the decision of the other half, as to their rights and duties. And some instances, not only of submission, but of acquiescence, there are. Forty years ago, the women of New Jersey went to the poll, and voted, at state elections. The general term, "inhabitants," stood unqualified;—as it will again, when the true democratic principle comes to be fully understood. A motion was made to correct the inadvertence; and it was done, as a matter of course; without any appeal, as far as I could learn, from the persons about to be injured. Such acquiescence proves nothing but the degradation of the injured party. It inspires the same emotions of pity as the supplication of the freed slave who kneels to his master to restore him to slavery, that he may have his animal wants supplied, without being troubled with human rights and duties. Acquiescence like this is an argument which cuts the wrong way for those who use it.

But this acquiescence is only partial; and, to give any semblance of strength to the plea, the acquiescence must be complete. I, for one, do not acquiesce. I declare that whatever obedience I yield to the laws of the society in which I live is a matter between, not the community and myself, but my judgment and my will. Any punishment inflicted on me for the breach of the laws, I should regard as so much gratuitous injury; for to those laws I have never, actually or virtually, assented. I know that there are women in England who agree with me in this—I know that there are women in America who agree with me in this. The plea of acquiescence is invalidated by us.

It is pleaded that, by enjoying the protection of some laws, women give their assent to all. This needs but a brief answer. Any protection thus conferred is, under woman's circumstances, a boon bestowed at the pleasure of those in whose power she is. A boon of any sort is no compensation for the privation of something else; nor can the enjoyment of it bind to the performance of anything to which it bears no relation. Because I, by favour, may procure the imprisonment of the thief who robs my house, am I, unrepresented, therefore bound not to smuggle French ribbons? The obligation not to smuggle has a widely different derivation.

I cannot enter upon the commonest order of pleas of all;—those which relate to the virtual influence of woman; her swaying the judgment and will of man through the heart; and so forth. One might as well try to dissect the morning mist. I knew a gentleman in America who told me how much rather he had be a woman than the man he is;—a professional man, a father, a citizen. He would give up all this for a woman's influence. I thought he was mated too soon. He should have married a lady, also of my acquaintance, who would not at all object to being a slave, if ever the blacks should have the upper hand; "it is so right that the one race should be subservient to the other!" Or rather,—I thought it a pity that the one could not be a woman, and the other a slave; so that an injured individual of each class might be exalted into their places, to fulfill and enjoy the duties and privileges which they despise, and, in despising, disgrace.

The truth is, that while there is much said about "the sphere of woman," two widely different notions are entertained of what is meant by the phrase. The narrow, and, to the ruling party, the more convenient notion is that sphere appointed by men, and bounded by their ideas of propriety;—a notion from which any and every woman may fairly dissent. The broad and true conception is of the sphere appointed by God, and bounded by the powers which he has bestowed. This commands the assent of man and woman; and only the question of powers remains to be proved.

That woman has power to represent her own interests, no one can deny till she has been tried. The modes need not be discussed here: they must vary with circumstances. The fearful and absurd images which are perpetually called up to perplex the question,—images of women on woolsacks in England, and under canopies in America, have nothing to do with the matter. The principle being once established, the methods will follow, easily, naturally, and under a remarkable transmutation of the ludicrous into the sublime. The kings of Europe would have laughed mightily, two centuries ago, at the idea of a commoner, without robes, crown, or sceptre, stepping into the throne of a strong nation. Yet who dared to laugh when Washington's super-royal voice greeted the New World from the presidential chair, and the old world stood still to catch the echo?

The principle of the equal rights of both halves of the human race is all we have to do with here. It is the true democratic principle which can never be seriously controverted, and only for a short time evaded. Governments can derive their just powers only from the consent of the governed.

National Organization for Women (N.O.W.)

BILL OF RIGHTS (1967)

WE DEMAND:

I. That the U.S. Congress immediately pass the Equal Rights Amendment to the Constitution to provide that "Equality of rights under the law shall not be denied or abridged by the United States or by any State on account of sex," and that such then be immediately ratified by the several States.

II. That equal employment opportunity be guaranteed to all women, as well as men, by insisting that the Equal Employment Opportunity Commission enforces the prohibitions against racial discrimination.

III. That women be protected by law to ensure their rights to return to their jobs within a reasonable time after childbirth without loss of seniority or other accrued benefits, and be paid maternity leave as a form of social security and/or employee benefit.

IV. Immediate revision of tax laws to permit the deduction of home and child-care expenses for working parents.

V. That child-care facilities be established by law on the same basis as parks, libraries, and public schools, adequate to the needs of children from the pre-school years through adolescence, as a community resource to be used by all citizens from all income levels.

VI. That the right of women to be educated to their full potential equally with men be secured by Federal and State legislation, eliminating all discrimination and segregation by sex, written and unwritten, at all levels of education, including colleges, graduate and professional schools, loans and fellowships, and Federal and State training programs such as the Job Corps.

VII. The right of women in poverty to secure job training, housing, and family allowances on equal terms with men, but without prejudice to a parent's right to remain at home to care for his or her children; revision of welfare legislation and poverty programs which deny women dignity, privacy, and self-respect.

VIII. The right of women to control their own reproductive lives by removing from the penal code laws limiting access to contraceptive information and devices, and by repealing penal laws governing abortion.

REDSTOCKINGS MANIFESTO
(1969)

I. After centuries of individual and preliminary political struggle, women are united to achieve their final liberation from male supremacy. Redstockings is dedicated to building this unity and winning our freedom.

II. Women are an oppressed class. Our oppression is total, affecting every facet of our lives. We are exploited as sex objects, breeders, domestic servants, and cheap labor. We are considered inferior beings, whose only purpose is to enhance men's lives. Our humanity is denied. Our prescribed behavior is enforced by the threat of physical violence.

Because we have lived so intimately with our oppressors, in isolation from each other, we have been kept from seeing our personal suffering as a political condition. This creates the illusion that a woman's relationship with her man is a matter of interplay between two unique personalities, and can be worked out individually. In reality, every such relationship is a *class* relationship, and the conflicts between individual men and women are *political* conflicts that can only be solved collectively.

III. We identify the agents of our oppression as men. Male supremacy is the oldest, most basic form of domination. All other forms of exploitation and oppression (racism, capitalism, imperialism, etc.) are extensions of male supremacy: men dominate women, a few men dominate the rest. All power structures throughout history have been male-dominated and male-oriented. Men have controlled all political, economic and cultural institutions and backed up this control with physical force. They have used their power to keep women in an inferior position. *All men* receive economic, sexual, and psychological benefits from male supremacy. *All men* have oppressed women.

IV. Attempts have been made to shift the burden of responsibility from men to institutions or to women themselves. We condemn these arguments as evasions. Institutions alone do not oppress; they are merely tools of the oppressor. To blame institutions implies that men and women are equally victimized, obscures the fact that men benefit from the subordination of women, and gives men the excuse that they are forced to be

WOMEN'S HISTORY RESEARCH CENTER, INC., 2325 Oak Street, Berkeley, Calif. 94708.

oppressors. On the contrary, any man is free to renounce his superior position provided that he is willing to be treated like a woman by other men.

We also reject the idea that women consent to or are to blame for their own oppression. Women's submission is not the result of brainwashing, stupidity, or mental illness but of continual, daily pressure from men. We do not need to change ourselves, but to change men.

The most slanderous evasion of all is that women can oppress men. The basis for this illusion is the isolation of individual relationships from their political context and the tendency of men to see any legitimate challenge to their privileges as persecution.

V. We regard our personal experience, and our feelings about that experience, as the basis for an analysis of our common situation. We cannot rely on existing ideologies as they are all products of male supremacist culture. We question every generalization and accept none that are not confirmed by our experience.

Our chief task at present is to develop female class consciousness through sharing experience and publicly exposing the sexist foundation of all our institutions. Consciousness-raising is not "therapy," which implies the existence of individual solutions and falsely assumes that the male-female relationship is purely personal, but the only method by which we can ensure that our program for liberation is based on the concrete realities of our lives.

The first requirement for raising class consciousness is honesty, in private and in public, with ourselves and other women.

VI. We identify with all women. We define our best interest as that of the poorest, most brutally exploited woman.

We repudiate all economic, racial, education or status privileges that divide us from other women. We are determined to recognize and eliminate any prejudices we may hold against other women.

We are committed to achieving internal democracy. We will do whatever is necessary to ensure that every woman in our movement has an equal chance to participate, assume responsibility, and develop her political potential.

VII. We call on all our sisters to unite with us in struggle.

We call on all men to give up their male privileges and support women's liberation in the interest of our humanity and their own.

In fighting for our liberation we will always take the side of women against their oppressors. We will not ask what is "revolutionary" or "reformist," only what is good for women.

The time for individual skirmishes has passed. This time we are going all the way.

July 7, 1969

Students for a Democratic Society (S.D.S.)

PORT HURON STATEMENT (1962)

INTRODUCTION: AGENDA FOR A GENERATION

We are people of this generation, bred in at least modest comfort, housed now in universities, looking uncomfortably to the world we inherit.

When we were kids the United States was the wealthiest and strongest country in the world; the only one with the atom bomb, the least scarred by modern war, an initiator of the United Nations that we thought would distribute Western influence throughout the world. Freedom and equality for each individual, government of, by, and for the people—these American values we found good, principles by which we could live as men. Many of us began maturing in complacency.

As we grew, however, our comfort was penetrated by events too troubling to dismiss. First, the permeating and victimizing fact of human degradation, symbolized by the Southern struggle against racial bigotry, compelled most of us from silence to activism. Second, the enclosing fact of the Cold War, symbolized by the presence of the Bomb, brought awareness that we ourselves, and our friends, and millions of abstract "others" we knew more directly because of our common peril, might die at any time. We might deliberately ignore, or avoid, or fail to feel all other human problems, but not these two, for these were too immediate and crushing in their impact, too challenging in the demand that we as individuals take the responsibility for encounter and resolution.

While these and other problems either directly oppressed us or rankled our consciences and became our own subjective concerns, we began to see complicated and disturbing paradoxes in our surrounding America. The declaration "all men are created equal . . ." rang hollow before the facts of Negro life in the South and the big cities of the North. The proclaimed peaceful intentions of the United States contradicted its economic and military investments in the Cold War status quo.

Although S.D.S. no longer distributes the *Port Huron Statement*, it remains one of the better pronouncements of New Left democratic thinking.

We witnessed, and continue to witness, other paradoxes. With nuclear energy whole cities can easily be powered, yet the dominant nation-states seem more likely to unleash destruction greater than that incurred in all wars of human history. Although our own technology is destroying old and creating new forms of social organization, men still tolerate meaningless work and idleness. While two-thirds of mankind suffers undernourishment, our own upper classes revel amidst superfluous abundance. Although world population is expected to double in forty years, the nations still tolerate anarchy as a major principle of international conduct and uncontrolled exploitation governs the sapping of the earth's physical resources. Although mankind desperately needs revolutionary leadership, America rests in national stalemate, its goals ambiguous and tradition-bound instead of informed and clear, its democratic system apathetic and manipulated rather than "of, by, and for the people."

Not only did tarnish appear on our image of American virtue, not only did disillusion occur when the hypocrisy of American ideals was discovered, but we began to sense that what we had originally seen as the American Golden Age was actually the decline of an era. The world-wide outbreak of revolution against colonialism and imperialism, the entrenchment of totalitarian states, the menace of war, overpopulation, international disorder, supertechnology—these trends were testing the tenacity of our own commitment to democracy and freedom and our abilities to visualize their application to a world in upheaval.

Our work is guided by the sense that we may be the last generation in the experiment with living. But we are a minority—the vast majority of our people regard the temporary equilibriums of our society and world as eternally-functional parts. In this is perhaps the outstanding paradox: we ourselves are imbued with urgency, yet the message of our society is that there is no viable alternative to the present. Beneath the reassuring tones of the politicians, beneath the common opinion that America will "muddle through," beneath the stagnation of those who have closed their minds to the future, is the pervading feeling that there simply are no alternatives, that our times have witnessed the exhaustion not only of Utopias, but of any new departures as well. Feeling the press of complexity upon the emptiness of life, people are fearful of the thought that at any moment things might be thrust out of control. They fear change itself, since change might smash whatever invisible framework seems to hold back chaos for them now. For most Americans, all crusades are suspect, threatening. The fact that each individual sees apathy in his fellows perpetuates the common reluctance to organize for change. The dominant institutions are complex enough to blunt the minds of their potential critics, and entrenched enough to swiftly dissipate or entirely repel the energies of protest and reform, thus limiting human expectancies. Then, too, we are a materially improved society, and by our own improvements we seem to have weakened the case for further change.

Some would have us believe that Americans feel contentment amidst prosperity—but might it not be better be called a glaze above deeply-felt anxieties about their role in the new world? And if these anxieties produce a developed indifference to human affairs, do they not as well produce a yearning to believe there *is* an alternative to the present, that something *can* be done to change circumstances in the school, the workplaces, the bureaucracies, the government? It is to this latter yearning, at once the spark and engine of change, that we direct our present appeal. The search for truly democratic alternatives to the present, and a commitment to social experimentation with them, is a worthy and fulfilling human enterprise, one which moves us and, we hope, others today. On such a basis do we offer this document of our convictions and analysis: as an effort in understanding and changing the conditions of humanity in the late twentieth century, an effort rooted in the ancient, still unfulfilled conception of man attaining determining influence over his circumstances of life.

VALUES

Making values explicit—an initial task in establishing alternatives—is an activity that has been devalued and corrupted. The conventional moral terms of the age, the politician moralities—"free world," "people's democracies"—reflect realities poorly, if at all, and seem to function more as ruling myths than as descriptive principles. But neither has our experience in the universities brought us moral enlightenment. Our professors and administrators sacrifice controversy to public relations; their curriculums change more slowly than the living events of the world; their skills and silence are purchased by investors in the arms race; passion is called unscholastic. The questions we might want raised—what is really important? can we live in a different and better way? if we wanted to change society, how would we do it?—are not thought to be questions of a "fruitful, empirical nature," and thus are brushed aside.

Unlike youth in other countries we are used to moral leadership being exercised and moral dimensions being clarified by our elders. But today, for us, not even the liberal and socialist preachments of the past seem adequate to the forms of the present. Consider the old slogans: Capitalism Cannot Reform Itself, United Front Against Fascism, General Strike, All Out on May Day. Or, more recently, No Cooperation with Commies and Fellow Travellers, Ideologies are Exhausted, Bipartisanship, No Utopias. These are incomplete, and there are few new prophets. It has been said that our liberal and socialist predecessors were plagued by vision without program, while our own generation is plagued by pro-

gram without vision. All around us there is astute grasp of method, tech-
nique—the committee, the ad hoc group, the lobbyist, the hard and soft
sell, the make, the projected image—but, if pressed critically, such expertise
is incompetent to explain its implicit ideals. It is highly fashionable to
identify oneself by old categories, or by naming a respected political
figure, or by explaining "how we would vote" on various issues.

Theoretic chaos has replaced the idealistic thinking of old—and,
unable to reconstitute theoretic order, men have condemned idealism
itself. Doubt has replaced hopefulness—and men act out a defeatism that
is labelled realistic. The decline of utopia and hope is in fact one of the
defining features of social life today. The reasons are various: the dreams
of the older left were perverted by Stalinism and never recreated; the
congressional stalemate makes men narrow their view of the possible;
the specialization of human activity leaves little room for sweeping
thought; the horrors of the twentieth century, symbolized in the gas-ovens
and concentration camps and atom bombs, have blasted hopefulness. To
be idealistic is to be considered apocalyptic, deluded. To have no serious
aspirations, on the contrary, is to be "toughminded."

In suggesting social goals and values, therefore, we are aware of
entering a sphere of some disrepute. Perhaps matured by the past, we
have no sure formulas, no closed theories—but that does not mean
values are beyond discussion and tentative determination. A first task of
any social movement is to convince people that the search for orienting
theories and the creation of human values is complex but worthwhile.
We are aware that to avoid platitudes we must analyze the concrete conditions of social order. But to direct such an analysis we must use the
guideposts of basic principles. Our own social values involve conceptions
of human beings, human relationships, and social systems.

We regard *men* as infinitely precious and possessed of unfulfilled
capacities for reason, freedom, and love. In affirming these principles
we are aware of countering perhaps the dominant conceptions of man
in the twentieth century: that he is a thing to be manipulated, and that
he is inherently incapable of directing his own affairs. We oppose the
depersonalization that reduces human beings to the status of things—if
anything, the brutalities of the twentieth century teach that means and
ends are intimately related, that vague appeals to "posterity" cannot justify the mutilations of the present. We oppose, too, the doctrine of
human incompetence because it rests essentially on the modern fact that
men have been "competently" manipulated into incompetence—we see
little reason why men cannot meet with increasing skill the complexities
and responsibilities of their situation, if society is organized not for
minority, but for majority, participation in decision-making.

Men have unrealized potential for self-cultivation, self-direction, self-understanding, and creativity. It is this potential that we regard as crucial and to which we appeal, not to the human potentiality for violence, unreason, and submission to authority. The goal of man and society should be human independence: a concern not with image of popularity but with finding a meaning in life that is personally authentic; a quality of mind not compulsively driven by a sense of powerlessness, nor one which unthinkingly adopts status values, nor one which represses all threats to its habits, but one which has full, spontaneous access to present and past experiences, one which easily unites the fragmented parts of personal history, one which openly faces problems which are troubling and unresolved; one with an intuitive awareness of possibilities, an active sense of curiosity, an ability and willingness to learn.

This kind of independence does not mean egotistic individualism—the object is not to have one's way so much as it is to have a way that is one's own. Nor do we deify man—we merely have faith in his potential.

Human relationships should involve fraternity and honesty. Human interdependence is contemporary fact; human brotherhood must be willed, however, as a condition of future survival and as the most appropriate form of social relations. Personal links between man and man are needed, especially to go beyond the partial and fragmentary bonds of function that bind men only as worker to worker, employer to employee, teacher to student, American to Russian.

Loneliness, estrangement, isolation describe the vast distance between man and man today. These dominant tendencies cannot be overcome by better personnel management, nor by improved gadgets, but only when a love of man overcomes the idolatrous worship of things by man. As the individualism we affirm is not egoism, the selflessness we affirm is not self-elimination. On the contrary, we believe in generosity of a kind that imprints one's unique individual qualities in the relation to other men, and to all human activity. Further, to dislike isolation is not to favor the abolition of privacy; the latter differs from isolation in that it occurs or is abolished according to individual will.

We would replace power rooted in possession, privileged, or circumstance by power and uniqueness rooted in love, reflectiveness, reason, and creativity. As a *social system* we seek the establishment of a democracy of individual participation, governed by two central aims: that the individual share in those social decisions determining the quality and direction of his life; that society be organized to encourage independence in men and provide the media for their common participation.

In a participatory democracy, the political life would be based in several root principles:

that decision-making of basic social consequence be carried on by public groupings;

that politics be seen positively, as the art of collectively creating an acceptable pattern of social relations;

that politics has the function of bringing people out of isolation and into community, thus being a necessary, though not sufficient, means of finding meaning in personal life;

that the political order should serve to clarify problems in a way instrumental to their solution; it should provide outlets for the expression of personal grievance and aspiration; opposing views should be organized so as to illuminate choices and facilitate the attainment of goals; channels should be commonly available to relate men to knowledge and to power so that private problems—from bad recreation facilities to personal alienation—are formulated as general issues.

The economic sphere would have as its basis the principles:

that work should involve incentives worthier than money or survival. It should be educative, not stultifying; creative, not mechanical; self-directed, not manipulated, encouraging independence, a respect for others, a sense of dignity and a willingness to accept social responsibility, since it is this experience that has crucial influence on habits, perceptions and individual ethics;

that the economic experience is so personally decisive that the individual must share in its full determination;

that the economy itself is of such social importance that its major resources and means of production should be open to democratic participation and subject to democratic social regulation.

Like the political and economic ones, major social institutions—cultural, educational, rehabilitative, and others—should be generally organized with the well-being and dignity of man as the essential measure of success.

In social change or interchange, we find violence to be abhorrent because it requires generally the transformation of the target, be it a human being or a community of people, into a depersonalized object of hate. It is imperative that the means of violence be abolished and the institutions—local, national, international—that encourage nonviolence as a condition of conflict be developed.

These are our central values, in skeletal form. It remains vital to understand their denial or attainment in the context of the modern world.

Tom Hayden

THE NEW AMERICAN REVOLUTION

We for ten years incessantly and ineffectually besieged the throne as supplicants; we reasoned, we remonstrated with Parliament in the most mild and decent language. . . .

—THE CONTINENTAL CONGRESS, "The Declaration of
the Causes and Necessity of Taking Up Arms"
(July 1775)

I feel that I am a citizen of the American dream, and that the revolutionary struggle of which I am a part is a struggle against the American nightmare. . . .

—ELDRIDGE CLEAVER

In the sixties we made our way to the modern throne through trails of spilled blood. Now the Nixon administration is bringing all this experience to a grim climax. The present government has dashed all liberal dreams of the war being "phased out" from above, and instead has provoked a wider war which could well escalate into nuclear attacks on Vietnam and China. The same government has designed a war against black liberation at home through military attacks on the Panthers and "benign neglect" for black people in general. Incendiary propaganda, conspiracy indictments, and killings in Berkeley, Santa Barbara, and Kent State have been the main official reaction to alienated white youth.

We live in a constitutional crisis. The ruling powers have usurped power not only from the people but from their own Senators and Congressmen, to a point where only the President and his military-industrial advisory board know where the next war will begin. Nixon is even said to have requested a Rand Corporation study of the means to declare martial law and suspend the 1972 elections.

We must react immediately to this crisis, if only to delay the escalation and expose it further to the American people. The unprecedented student strike beginning in New Haven is likely to continue and widen

by fall. A revolutionary Continental Congress this summer and the projected September demonstration at the United Nations will mobilize
people here and abroad against the menace our government has become.

But the crisis will not be solved by the election of a few more
"liberals," nor by campaigns, even strikes, against a particular policy. The
political history of the 1960s is one chapter after another of frustrated reform efforts. But in our failures to make the system work these last ten
years, we have learned a most important lesson: *that ordinary people can
and do make history*. Outpourings of disruptive energy have caused these
reform campaigns—the sit-ins leading to the Voting Rights Law, the
resistance leading to the McCarthy campaign, the trashing of ROTC buildings leading to the university "reconstitution" movement just this Spring.
And the same disruptive energy has continued to mount despite all efforts
to "contain" it within reformism. Taking this observation as a starting
point and looking ahead into the seventies, we should look for a revolutionary strategy in the location and direction of this popular energy.
The process of revolution takes shape in the way people are moving
against the structures oppressing them.

First, we need no longer believe that the protest of the sixties involved only a marginal lunatic fringe. There is no new silent majority
maturing to replace the old. In the black community, according to *Time*,
over half the people are positively oriented toward the Panthers (and
much larger numbers of the young than the old). Among whites, where
the "lunatic fringe" analysis is more popular, radicalism also shows
strength—even in the polls of the Establishment. One of the best known
polls, conducted by *Fortune* in 1968, showed 750,000 students who "should
know better" identifying with the New Left, while another two or three
million constituted a supportive base. "This particular younger generation is by all odds the most interesting to come along in U.S. history,"
Fortune concedes, ". . . it will shortly preside over the revolutionary
changes that await us." Now that millions of students across America are
shutting down their schools in protest against the war and repression,
can we any longer doubt our vast potential numbers?

Nor can we believe any longer that we are simply going through
a "generation gap." That shallow theory locates the source of social conflict in failures of communication. Ever since the beginnings of protest
ten years ago we have been told that radicalism is a part of the cycle of
history, that today's radical undergraduate becomes a mellow liberal at
thirty and a responsible citizen at forty. But after a decade this gap seems
as wide as the one between Earth and Mars.

The phrase "generation gap" is a euphemism for the new location
of class struggle. We are not a lunatic fringe; we are a New People
rising from the ruins of the American empire. Not surprisingly, journals

like *Fortune* and *Time* have difficulty coming to this conclusion because that would destroy their game; they would then have to point to themselves, to their system of international capitalism, to find the causes of the revolt.

Modern American capitalism is dooming itself in the very process of its own development. Its current form arose out of the Great Depression and World War II when private enterprise, the State, and the military merged in a centralized structure of power with the world's most advanced level of technology. The result was a total breakdown of traditional images and values, a rupture of the material base of society away from its cultural superstructure, and a permanent breakdown of control over the young.

Private property and puritan morality, while still endorsed by dinosaurs like the Nixon family, became obsolete concepts in this new situation. Enterprising entrepreneurs were replaced by conforming organization men. For the first time in history, most people felt insured against hunger and were able to imagine a less competitive life, a life beyond scarcity.

Militarism and racism, too, suddenly became obsolete values in the postwar world. Warned by successive Presidents that the arms race was ultimately irrational and that white racism was unallowable in the new world of nations, we watched while the government permitted these problems to become more dangerous with each year.

The chief contradiction in America is between a moribund, decadent system and all those people with a stake in the future. Just at the moment when the system seems most exhausted in its potential to solve the problems it has created, it gives birth to a permanently restless generation with the freedom to be idealistic.

It is not simply "internal" changes in American capitalism that bring on the crisis, however. For those changes are largely designed to cope with the worldwide revolutionary process unleashed in the postwar period. As the chief pillar of the free world, the United States is being assaulted on all sides by anti-colonial and socialist revolution. As the vanguard of counterrevolution, the United States is forced to invest ever greater sums in "defense," to neglect even the most modest domestic needs, and to become barbaric in its violence. The image of idealism has passed from the American government (which in World War II could wear an anti-fascist face, and as late as 1960 could announce a "peace corps") to the rebels of the world, including the blacks at home. This revolutionary upsurge opens the eyes of Americans daily, not only to the role of our government but to the idealism and optimism of people rising from their knees the world over. The world has changed from a one-dimensional "American Century" (1945) to a two-dimensional world of empire and revolution. Everyone is confronted with the message: you are either part of the problem or part of the solution.

Virtually every young person in America feels this situation in some way. They know, first, that the United States has the technical ability to create economic security and a better life for everyone in the world and, second, that a new world is taking shape in which the competition, racism, and corruption of the generation now in power will have no place.

That is why the rise of an American student movement in the last decade is a revolutionary, not a routine, event. In fact, during its rise to empire the United States was never plagued by "student unrest" on the scale now being experienced. To find any parallels one would have to look at other countries where student movements have been indicators of fundamental change. Instead of seeing the American youth revolt as a "last gasp" by romantic diehards, as social scientists and journalists often did in the sixties, it would be better understood as the harbinger of a great change. The breakdown of the social order is first and always felt by the young, the students, the people who must plan for the future.

With the passage of time, with the further delay of the American important than "economic class" in analyzing the American struggle. A generation ago it was the industrial working class that felt the shock of industrial change most severely. But since the war, young people of all classes have been the chief victims bearing the burden of the expanding empire. Most young people are in school or in the army or are unemployed. They are tied as technicians, propagandists, service or manual workers to an imperialism that destroys their values and taxes and drafts them for impossible wars. When we see that the youth revolt is international, occurring around the same issues in West Germany, Italy, France, and all the "advanced countries" linked to the United States, we see that the crisis truly is one of a decaying global imperialism.

With the passage of time, with the further decay of the American empire, the discontent now felt most by youth will spread with them wherever they go to work or live. In the long run, then, the alienation of youth may become an alienation of *the whole people.* In a period of collapsing empire, those with a solid stake in the status quo gradually become fewer and fewer. In the Panthers' phrase, the ultimate struggle becomes one "between the people and the pigs."

Barry M. Goldwater

THE TIDE AGAINST FREEDOM

From this moment, united and determined, we will go forward together—dedicated to the ultimate and undeniable greatness of the whole man.

Together, we will win.

I accept your nomination with a deep sense of humility. I accept the responsibility that goes with it. I seek your continued help and guidance.

Our cause is too great for any man to feel worthy of it.

Our task would be too great for any man, did he not have with him the hearts and hands of this great Republican Party.

I promise you that every fiber of my being is consecrated to our cause—that nothing shall be lacking from the struggle that can be brought to it by enthusiasm and devotion—and hard work!

In this world, no person—no party—can guarantee anything. What we can do, and what we shall do, is to deserve victory.

The good Lord raised up this mighty republic to be a home for the brave and to flourish as the land of the free—not to stagnate in the swampland of collectivism—not to cringe before the bullying of communism.

The tide has been running against freedom. Our people have followed false prophets. We must and we shall return to proven ways—not because they are old but because they are true. We must and we shall set the tides running again in the cause of freedom.

This party, with its every action, every word, every breath, and every heartbeat has but a single resolve: Freedom!

Freedom—made orderly for this nation by our Constitutional Government.

Freedom—under a government limited by the laws of nature and of nature's God.

Freedom—balanced so that order, lacking liberty, will not become a slavery of the prison cell; balanced so that liberty, lacking order, will not become the license of the mob and the jungle.

New York Times, July 17, 1964. Reprinted by permission of Senator Barry Goldwater.

We Americans understand freedom. We have earned it, lived for it, and died for it.

This nation and its people are freedom's model in a searching world. We can be freedom's missionaries in a doubting world. But first we must renew freedom's vision in our own hearts and in our own homes.

During four futile years, the Administration which we shall replace has distorted and lost that vision.

It has talked and talked and talked the words of freedom. But it has failed and failed and failed in the works of freedom.

Failures cement the wall of shame in Berlin. Failures blot the sands of shame at the Bay of Pigs. Failures mark the slow death of freedom in Laos. Failures infest the jungles of Vietnam. Failures haunt the houses of our once great alliances, and undermine the greatest bulwark ever erected by free nations: The NATO community.

Failures proclaim lost leadership, obscure purpose, weakening will, and the risk of inciting our sworn enemies to new aggressions and new excesses.

Because of this Administration, we are a world divided; we are a nation becalmed.

We have lost the brisk pace of diversity and the genius of individual creativity. We are plodding at a pace set by centralized planning, red tape, rules without responsibility, and regimentation without recourse.

Rather than useful jobs, our people have been offered bureaucratic make-work. Rather than moral leadership they have been given bread and circuses, spectacle, and even scandal.

There is violence in our streets, corruption in our highest offices, aimlessness among our youth, anxiety among our elders. There is virtual despair among the many who look beyond material success for the inner meaning of their lives.

Where examples of morality should be set, the opposite is seen. Small men, seeking great wealth or power, have too often and too long turned even the highest levels of public service into mere personal opportunity.

Simple Honesty in Government

Certainly, simple honesty is not too much to demand of men in government. We find it in most. Republicans demand it from everyone— no matter how exalted or protected his position.

The growing menace to personal safety, to life, limb, and property, in homes, churches, playgrounds, and places of business, particularly in our great cities, is the mounting concern of every thoughtful citizen. Security from domestic violence, no less than from foreign aggression, is the most elementary and fundamental purpose of any government.

A government that cannot fulfill this purpose is one that cannot long command the loyalty of its citizens. History demonstrates that nothing prepares the way for tyranny more than the failure of public officials to keep the streets safe from bullies and marauders.

We Republicans see all this as more, much more, than the result of mere political differences, or mere political mistakes. We see this as the result of a fundamentally and absolutely wrong view of man, his nature, and his destiny.

Those who seek to live your lives for you, to take your liberties in return for relieving you of your responsibilities—those who elevate the state and downgrade the citizen—must see ultimately a world in which earthly power can be substituted for divine will. This nation was founded upon the rejection of that notion and upon the acceptance of God as the author of freedom.

Those who seek absolute power, even though they seek it to do what they regard as good, are simply demanding the right to enforce their version of heaven on earth. They are the very ones who always create the most hellish tyrannies.

Absolute power does corrupt. And those who seek it must be suspect and must be opposed.

Their mistaken course stems from false notions of equality.

Equality, rightly understood, as our founding fathers understood it, leads to liberty and to the emancipation of creative differences.

Wrongly understood, as it has been so tragically in our time, it leads first to conformity and then to despotism.

It is the cause of Republicanism to resist concentrations of power, private or public, which enforce such conformity and inflict such despotism.

It is the cause of Republicanism to insure that power remains in the hands of the people. And, so help us God, that is exactly what a Republican President will do—with the help of a Republican Congress.

It is the cause of Republicanism to restore a clear understanding of the tyranny of man over man in the world at large. It is our cause to dispel the foggy thinking which avoids hard decisions in the delusion that a world of conflict will mysteriously resolve itself into a world of harmony—if we just don't rock the boat or irritate the forces of aggression. . . .

This nation, whose creative people have enhanced this entire span of history, should again thrive upon the greatness of all those things which we—as individual citizens—can and should do.

During Republican years this again will be a nation of men and women, of families proud of their roles, jealous of their responsibilities, unlimited in their aspirations—a nation where all who can will be self-reliant.

We Republicans see in our Constitutional form of government the great framework which assures the orderly but dynamic fulfillment of the whole man, and we see the whole man as the great reason for instituting orderly government in the first place.

We see, in private property and an economy based upon and fostering private property, the one way to make government a durable ally of the whole man, rather than his determined enemy. We see, in the sanctity of private property, the only durable foundation for Constitutional government in a free society.

And beyond that, we see and cherish diversity of ways, diversity of thoughts, of motives and accomplishments. We do not seek to live anyone's life for him—we seek only to secure his rights, guarantee him opportunity to strive, with government performing only those needed and Constitutionally sanctioned tasks which cannot otherwise be performed.

We Republicans seek a government that attends to its inherent responsibilities of maintaining a stable monetary and fiscal climate—encouraging a free and competitive economy, and enforcing law and order.

Creative Difference

Thus do we seek inventiveness, diversity, and creative difference within a stable order. For we Republicans define government's role, where needed, at many, many levels, preferably through the one closest to the people involved.

Our towns and our cities, then our counties, then our state, then our regional compacts—and only then the national government! That is the ladder of liberty built by decentralized power. On it, also, we must have balance between the branches of government at every level.

Balance, diversity, creative differences—these are the elements of the Republican equation. Republicans agree on these elements and they agree heartily to disagree on many, many of their applications. But we have never disagreed on the basic fundamental issues of why you and I are Republicans.

This is, this Republican Party, a party for free men—not for blind followers and not for conformists.

In 1858, Lincoln said of the Republican Party—and I quote him because he probably could have said it in the last week or so—that it was composed of "strange, discordant, and even hostile elements." Yet all of the elements agreed on one paramount objective—to arrest the progress of slavery and place it in the course of ultimate extinction.

Today as then, but more urgently and more broadly than then, the task of preserving and enlarging freedom at home, and of safeguarding it from the forces of tyranny abroad, is great enough to challenge all our resources and to require all our strength.

Any who join us in all sincerity, we welcome. Those who do not care for our cause we do not expect to enter our ranks in any case.

And let our Republicanism, so focused and so dedicated, not be made fuzzy and futile by unthinking and stupid labels. I would remind you that extremism in the defense of liberty is no vice. And let me remind you also that moderation in the pursuit of justice is no virtue.

The beauty of the very system we Republicans are pledged to restore and revitalize, the beauty of this Federal system of ours, is in its reconciliation of diversity with unity. We must not see malice in honest differences of opinion, no matter how great, so long as they are not inconsistent with the pledges we have given to each other in and through our Constitution.

Our Republican cause is not to level out the world or make its people conform in computer-regimented sameness.

Our Republican cause is to free our people and light the way for liberty throughout the world.

Ours is a very human cause for very humane goals.

This party, its good people, and its unquenchable devotion to freedom will not fulfill the purposes of the campaign—which we launch here and now—until our cause has won the day, inspired the world, and shown the way to a tomorrow worthy of all our yesteryears.

I accept your nomination with humbleness, with pride, and you and I are going to fight for the goodness of our land.